Journey  With Me

Redemptive Threads
Woven Through
the Bible

W. RANDALL LOLLEY

© 2015
Published in the United States by Nurturing Faith Inc., Macon GA,
www.nurturingfaith.net.

Library of Congress Cataloging-in-Publication Data is available.

ISBN 978-1-938514-86-9

Interior and cover design by Amy C. Cook

CONTENTS

ACKNOWLEDGMENTS vi

FOREWORD by John D. Pierce vii

FOREWORD by Larry Hovis...ix

PREFACE by W. Randall Lolley...................................xi

INTRODUCTION: The Primacy of Scripture............................. 1

GENESIS: In the beginning—God 7

EXODUS: Let my people go...................................... 13

LEVITICUS: Halt in the name of the law............................ 19

NUMBERS: You've gotta have heart.................................. 25

DEUTERONOMY: The second time around.......................... 31

JOSHUA: Surgery, not murder 37

JUDGES: A not-so-new morality................................... 41

RUTH: Overcoming prejudice and poverty.......................... 47

1 AND 2 SAMUEL: Renewal through disaster.......................... 53

1 AND 2 KINGS: The sound of silence 59

1 AND 2 CHRONICLES: Back to basics 65

EZRA: Old clay—new pot.. 71

NEHEMIAH: Winning a war of nerves.............................. 77

ESTHER: For such a time as this............................. 83

Job: Declaration of dependence 89

Psalms: Thou hast made him 95

Proverbs: Melting ore into small coins 101

Ecclesiastes: Living by a squint or a vision 107

Song of Solomon: The greatest of these is love 113

Isaiah: I saw the Lord 119

Jeremiah: Cutting a covenant where it counts 125

Lamentations: Strong men do cry 131

Ezekiel: Knocked down but not out 137

Daniel: Man's dark—God's light 143

Hosea: Recovering a false start 149

Joel: The day of the Lord 153

Amos: Privilege means responsibility 159

Obadiah: Evil is a boomerang 165

Jonah: Beware, even prophetic exclusiveness 171

Micah: Remember the grassroots 177

Nahum: The wrath of God's love 183

Habakkuk: What if the bad guys win? 189

Zephaniah: Love is blue—and golden 195

Haggai: Word to flesh to word 199

Zechariah: An unquenchable hope 205

Malachi: Externals without internals 209

Matthew: Something more than Caesar's taxes 215

MARK: Something more than running away...... 221

LUKE: Something more than a fine medical practice...... 227

JOHN: Something more than fishing...... 233

ACTS: They too were human 239

ROMANS: Keep the faith 245

1 AND 2 CORINTHIANS: Together but not alike 251

GALATIANS: Passion and principle 257

EPHESIANS: Building bridges, smashing walls 263

PHILIPPIANS: Count it all joy 269

COLOSSIANS: A crown and a head for it 275

1 AND 2 THESSALONIANS: When gratitude shows 281

1 AND 2 TIMOTHY: Hooray for the homesteader 287

TITUS: Out in the weather together 293

PHILEMON: Born bound—reborn free 297

HEBREWS: This way to God 303

JAMES: Let's be practical 309

1 AND 2 PETER: A lamp in a dark place 315

1, 2, 3 JOHN: Love that will not let us go 321

JUDE: Clouds without water 327

REVELATION: Alpha and omega 333

EDITOR'S NOTE: As indicated in the Introduction, this book is a compilation of sermons intended for a specific setting in a specific time. Therefore, references are made to persons and events familiar to listeners at that time, and there is a lack of footnoting of sources since there was no expectation of the sermons being published two decades later.

ACKNOWLEDGMENTS

This collection of sermons is a generous gift from Randall and Lou Lolley, and a collaborative effort between Baptists Today/Nurturing Faith and the Cooperative Baptist Fellowship of North Carolina.

Royalties from all sales will benefit the Lolley Fund for Theological Education, an initiative of the Cooperative Baptist Fellowship of North Carolina Endowment Trust.

Publication and promotion of the book are made possible by gifts from the following sponsors:

Mary-Stuart Alderman
Thomas R. and Blanche S. Allen
Anonymous
Libby Austell
Max and Doris Baldwin
Laura Lomax and Phil Barbee
Charles D. Barham, Jr.
Hoyt and Mary Beard
Michael C. Blackwell
Lydia Brendle
Caralie Nelson Brown
Nancy Byard
Chris and Sandra Canipe
Tony and Susan Cartledge
Dr. and Mrs. John Chandler
Peggy W. Chestnutt
Jim and Margaret Clary
Kenneth M. Coleman
Betty and Austin Connors
Hillus and Peggy Conrad
Robert F. Crumpler
Donald E. Cunningham
Nancy Curtis
Bob and Carrie Dale
Willard Dean
Frances Y. Dunn
Dr. Robert J. Echerd
The Everette Miller
   Friendship Class of
   First Baptist Church, Raleigh
John and Hazel Fisher
Dr. John C. French
Jack and Barbara Glasgow
James Ed and Cassie Glover
Dr. Don Gordon
Roper Halverson

Rev. E. Arnett Harris
   and Mary Nell Harris
Teliea and Jack Harwell
Jeff and Cecelia Hensley
Diane Eubanks Hill
Richard and Patricia Hipps
John E. Hobson
Sue Holding
Charlotte and Alex Holmes
Rev. Billy and Mrs. Teresa Honeycutt
Don and Jo Ann Horton
Larry and Kim Hovis
Beverly Isley-Landreth
H. Michael and Brenda J. Johnson
   (in memory of
   Mrs. Thelma A. Witherspoon)
Max and Elizabeth Johnson
Fred L. Kelly
William and Jane Kibler
Robert C. Kluttz
   and Joyce W. Kluttz
Diffee and Pat Lambert
Gomer R. Lesch
David and Barbara Matthews
Amy R. McClure
Charles McDowell, III
Dr. Albert L. Meiburg
Agnes and David Moore
Christina and Joseph Moore
Ann White Morton
Jane D. Naish
Clinton and Betsy Neal
Lucian and Robie Neal
Joe and Gretchen Overby
Tom Parrish
Anne Parker Phillips

Steve and Catherine Pressley
Michael and Bobbie Queen
Billie Reeves
Edith D. Rich (in memory
   of Thomas L. Rich, Jr.)
Carolyn E. Ripley
Nancy Robinson
Paul Rogers
Bill and Betty Scales
Dr. William W. Sessoms
Dr. Bob D. Shepherd
Alan and Jenny Sherouse
Jolene and Grady Simmons
Roy and Charlotte Cook Smith
Jimmy L. Taylor
Mr. Dewey E. Teal
   and Dr. Ramona P. Teal
Dr. and Mrs. James R. Thomason
David Vess
Kathy Vestal
Laura Anne Vick
Martha and Pebble Wall
Carey B. Washburn
James and Diane Watkins
Jane Bell Weathers
Dr. and Mrs. Mark T. White
Rev. Mari Wiles
Walter Raphael
   and Florence Gray Wiley
Louie (Juanita) Wilkinson
Charlotte and Claude Williams
Frank Wilson
Bonnie C. Wright
Joe and Corinne Yelton
Phil and Sue Young

FOREWORD

It was seminary convocation in the fall of 1978, and as a new student I was a real sucker. We had gathered in the stately Olin T. Binkley Chapel amid the magnolias on the old Wake Forest campus.

President Randall Lolley took to the pulpit to welcome us and to get us started on our journey of theological education. He began in a self-deprecating manner, assuring us he was just a good ol' boy from L.A. (Lower Alabama).

Then he delivered a powerful message of faith, hope, and love that was theologically brilliant and deeply motivating. By the time he finished, I'd made a mental note to myself: Never fall for that good ol' boy notion again.

In my experience there has never been a campus setting where the institution's president was more beloved than in the glory years of Southeastern Baptist Theological Seminary when Randall Lolley led the way. And he continued to shape many of us long after he handed us our diplomas.

We heard him speak prophetically and watched him act courageously when the rise of fundamentalism threatened his job as well as our theological home and denominational identity. He was never for sale.

The essence of the Christian faith and the Baptist identity that he and others at Old Southeastern had taught us was more than book learning. Dr. Lolley lived out before us a faith that was consistently sacrificial, inclusive, and hopeful even amid trials.

In 2011, the Board of Directors of *Baptists Today* news journal presented its annual Judson-Rice Award to Dr. Lolley for his remarkable impact on congregations and those who lead them. Director Mike Queen, my seminary classmate who served as pastor of the First Baptist Church of Wilmington, North Carolina, paid tribute.

Mike spoke of the impact Dr. Lolley had made on his life after he left a family business to attend seminary as well as in the years that followed. Then Mike asked all of those in attendance who had attended Southeastern Seminary during the Lolley years to stand.

We did—and there were many of us gathered that evening at the First Baptist Church of Raleigh. In the midst of the continuing applause, Mike smiled and said to Randall: "We are your fault."

Dr. Lolley quickly responded: "I accept responsibility."

Former students, parishioners, friends, and colleagues—now spread far and wide—are better Christians and better Baptists because of Randall Lolley. May his inspired words that flow from this book continue to shape us and many others.

John D. Pierce, Executive Editor/Publisher
Baptists Today/Nurturing Faith Publishing

FOREWORD

I first met Randall Lolley in late August 1984. I was an entering Master of Divinity student at Southeastern Baptist Theological Seminary in Wake Forest, North Carolina. In the opening convocation service, held in Owen T. Binkley Chapel, Dr. Lolley preached the convocation sermon. Its title: "Last at the Cross, First at the Tomb." It was perhaps the most moving sermon I had ever heard in my life and made a strong case for women as proclaimers of the gospel of Jesus Christ.

This experience was only the first of many in which I heard Randall Lolley preach the gospel with eloquence, creativity, conviction, passion, and biblical fidelity. My own life, ministry, and spiritual journey have continued to be nurtured by Randall Lolley in the three decades since.

Randall is a wordsmith. He uses words the way an artist uses color—but not just any words . . . gospel words . . . Word of God words. His preaching enables listeners to hear with new ears and see with new eyes. He has an uncanny ability to articulate what we average disciples and preachers think and feel but can't seem to put into words. He speaks what we would speak if we could.

As important as words are to Randall's ministry, they would be less powerful without a life to back them up. Throughout his life Randall has "walked the talk." From his courageous witness to truth and freedom at Southeastern, to his exemplary pastorates at several leading North Carolina churches (including the First Baptist churches of Winston-Salem, Raleigh, and Greensboro), to his leadership in Cooperative Baptist Fellowship (both nationally and in North Carolina), Randall Lolley has served as a vivid example of the best of what "free and faithful Baptists" have to offer to the world.

When he was moderator of Cooperative Baptist Fellowship of North Carolina in its early days, Randall was famous for saying, "There is a Christian way to be human, a Baptist way to be Christian, a CBF way to be Baptist, and a North Carolina way to be CBF." I would add: There is a Randall Lolley way of following Jesus, and all of us who know him, personally or through his preaching, are blessed to learn of the Savior through his life and words.

Larry Hovis, Executive Coordinator
Cooperative Baptist Fellowship of North Carolina

PREFACE

Journey with me . . .

I undertook this preaching journey through the Bible from January 8, 1995 to September 29, 1996. It was a "preach/teach" series that climaxed my pastoral career as well as my seven years at the First Baptist Church of Greensboro, North Carolina.

The purpose of these sermons was to review the entire biblical landscape, and to discern once more the interconnectedness and interrelatedness of the Holy Scriptures.

Hopefully, the redemptive threads woven from Genesis to Revelation have come to light in these sermons. Perhaps, also, Bible study teachers and other lay leaders will find them a ready reference through the years.

The sermons have been printed as they were preached over a period of one and a half years. I acknowledge a large debt to Jo Covert, my able administrative assistant, for her help in producing the manuscripts from my handwritten notes.

Journey on . . .

On a wintry-springy, sunny-damp, cold-warm day (Tax Day, April 15, 2015), Charles (Chuck) Rice and his wife, Leslie—two of our finest friends over the years—came to have lunch with Lou and me where we live at the Cypress of Raleigh.

There and then Chuck dropped the idea of this book on me. Since Chuck had built our house in Raleigh, and it had not fallen in, I thought the idea of this series of sermons might have oxygen in it to help some student, pastor, counselor, or teacher seeking to see the Holy Bible as a whole story.

Thus the title: *Journey with Me.*

One will discover that these messages, sermonic in form, have both a preaching and teaching component. I want to inspire and instruct my readers.

I am grateful to Chuck Rice, Johnny Pierce, Larry Hovis, and many others who have inspired the thoughts contained in this book. The goals of the entire project are to inspire ministers, especially young ministers, and to build the foundation that will provide scholarships for them to receive their education.

W. Randall Lolley

INTRODUCTION

The Primacy of Scripture
Psalm 19:7-11, 2 Timothy 3:16

Except for sin, allegiance to the Scriptures is about the only thing Baptists have in common. Baptists around the world differ almost as much as they are similar. We differ in our worship styles, in our hymn books and hymns, in the doctrines we espouse, in the way we do just about everything.

But on one thing we are gladly, and a bit glibly, agreed: We are "people of the Book." Our preachers even buy their Bibles for their floppiness, so that when they hold them in their hands, they give the impression that they really are preaching the Word.

Now when we say we are people of the Book, what do we mean by that? Well, it depends. It depends on who says it, and it depends upon why who says it says it.

Surely we do not mean by being people of the Book what one church marquee I read recently suggested. That marquee read, "The Bible is God in print." No, that is paper papacy.

In our best moments when we say that we are people of the Book, we are not saying that we are people of the print in the Book. Rather, what we mean is that we are people of the Word in the Book. The Word alive! The Word of the Lord!

We hold no allegiance, then, to mere print on paper pages. Those are just words for us trapped in their cold, impersonal incapacity to give us their message.

Our allegiance is beyond the print. Our allegiance is to the Word: the living spirit that speaks to us through, and over, and under, and around, and above, and below, and between the words that are in the Bible.

We are people, then, of the Word behind the words, in the Word, through the words. Our loyalty lies beyond the words about the Word. Our loyalty lies with the the Word.

With such a primary, foundational allegiance like that we ought to agree both on what the Bible says and on what the Bible means by what it says, shouldn't we? The fact is, we Baptists agree on neither.

The way Baptists read the Bible raises lots of questions. Is the Bible democratic or republican or independent or even interested in government very much at all?

Does the Bible teach capitalism, socialism, or communism, or any other "ism" that one might espouse or loathe? Is it on the side of the owners, the workers, the managers? Does its teaching about prayer extend to touchdowns and home runs and basketball goals? Does it encourage a reader to fly into the teeth of physical laws by which this moral universe is governed?

The Bible is Earth's number-one best seller—still is. Around the world the Bible is the best seller year in, year out—not really a book at all. The binders have done us a disservice. What we hold in our hand when we hold a Bible is not a book as much as it is a library written by many different persons over many hundreds, if not thousands, of years. It is a swirling composite of tremendous and frequently obscure messages—a virtual literary stew of poetry and prose, law and music, history and apocalyptic.

But for us, the people of the Book, the Bible is a word about us—about our lives, about the way you and I engage God, about our believing and unbelieving, our innocence and our guilt, our crusaders and our crooks, our hope and our despair. In short, the Bible is about us. It was written for us by persons very much like us. But preeminently, beyond all that, the Bible is about God. It is about God, who is easier to believe about than to believe in.

We Baptists use many words to describe the Word. Over the months and over the years Baptists have had lots of problems about the Bible. Some have even called ours a battle for the Bible. Not really: the Bible has never really been battled over among Baptists. Interpretations have, opinions have, words to describe it have flown between us and caused a lot of pain among us, but basically, foundationally, and fundamentally Baptists believe the Bible. There is simply no other place where we can go to hear God speak.

I determined a long time ago that the best way to describe the Bible is to let the Bible describe itself, and then use those very words in talking about it in our witness to others. Let me illustrate the Bible's own glossary regarding itself.

The Old Testament is the only Bible the New Testament Christians had—the only Bible Jesus knew—and the only Bible that Paul and Peter and James and John knew was the Old Testament because they actually produced the New Testament during their lifetime.

The Old Testament is replete with references to the Word of the Lord. The Psalms, for example, are a treasury, a glossary, celebrating God's powerful Word. In just three verses in the 19th Psalm there are seven words the Psalmist uses to describe the Word of God for him. Listen to verses 7-9: The Word of the Lord is *perfect*. That means it does exactly what it has been designed to do without exception. It is perfect.

The Word of the Lord is *sure*, certain, dependable, reliable. The Word of the Lord is *right*—not wrong, not maybe, not erroneous by design. The Word of the Lord is not polluted, not poisoned, not impure. The Word of the Lord is *clean*—more than the absence of dirt, but the positive presence of cleanliness and substance. The Word of the Lord is *truth*—not half-truth, untruth, or anti-truth. The Word of the Lord is *righteous*. God's kind of rightness is demonstrated, illustrated, and proclaimed from this Word. What a glossary!

But add to that the Bible's clearest, cleanest, noblest, most climactic word about itself. That word is found in 2 Tim. 3:16. Paul was trying to help Timothy, who was a Gentile more than a Jew in his rearing, to understand something of the significance of what he held in his hands when he held a scroll of scripture. Paul was trying to train young Timothy in the very rudiments of his mission and of his ministry as a servant of God. Paul said to Timothy, "All Scripture, the entire Old Testament that you know, is inspired by God."

The word Paul uses is *theopneustis-theos*, "God," and *pneustis*, meaning "to breathe." Put the word together and Paul is saying "Timothy, Scripture is God-breathed; it is inspired by the very Spirit, the very breath, the very wind of the Lord." That is to say, "Timothy, and Christians in Greensboro, take note: the same Holy Spirit who indwelt the persons, who wrote the Scriptures, now indwells the words of Scripture that they wrote so as to indwell you, the reader, you, the interpreter, when you humbly search the Bible for a word from the Lord."

The entire matrix of origination, transmission, translation, canonization, interpretation, and proclamation of the Scriptures is caught up in that amazing word: that all Scripture is *inspired*, God-breathed by the Lord.

The primacy of Scripture, we are all for it. But what exactly does it mean? How do we read the Bible? How do we live the Bible? What difference does the Bible make in our lives? Does the Bible really underpin the following happening in the Georgia town of Euharlee?

I have never been to Euharlee, Georgia, and probably never will go. Not too long ago *Time* magazine related an actual happening that occurred in Euharlee, Georgia.

Reverend George Miller stood up to preach. Beside him was a box. He quoted Mark 16:16, KJV: "They shall take up serpents, and if they drink any deadly thing, it shall not hurt them." Rev. Miller plunged his hand into the box and brought out two giant rattlesnakes.

Presently, also, he brought out a salvation cocktail, as he called it, and called on one of the worshipers, saying, "Brother Davis, do you believe in the power of the Lord enough to drink what is in this bottle?"

Ernest Davis, a 34-year-old farmer, father of five, grabbed the glass, took several gulps, and four days later was dead of strychnine poisoning. A charge of manslaughter was brought against the preacher, but the charge was thrown out of court on the grounds that there is really no law in Georgia to prevent an individual from carrying poison. It was established in testimony, in court, that Rev. Miller told Ernest Davis: "I warn you, do not take this unless the Lord leads you to do it."

When the charge was dismissed, Rev. Miller clapped his hands, shouted that he would lead a big Holy Ghost celebration at his church the very next Saturday night, and he told the people, right there, in advance to be ready: He would handle snakes and drink poison himself.

Primacy of Scripture: What exactly does it mean for us? Does the Bible being so powerful, potent, and primary in our lives mean that we have to read it exactly like that? How do you read the Bible? How do you live out the Bible?

On her deathbed Gertrude Stein asked, "What is the answer?" But a few moments later, just before she died, she asked, "What is the question?" She affords a clue for the primacy of Scripture in practice. We had best not rely on the Bible just for the answers it gives, and it does give a lot of good answers. We must rely on the Bible, also, for the questions it asks. So many of our questions are here today and gone tomorrow. So many of the questions we are asking in January 1995 are not the questions we asked in 1985 or will ask in 2005.

The questions the Bible asks endure. They are ultimate. They are life-and-death questions for all the ages. Listen: "What has a man profited if he gains the whole world and loses his own soul?" That is a Bible question. Listen: "Am I my brother's keeper?" "If God is for us, who can be against us?" "What is truth?" "If a man dies, will he live again?" "What must we do to inherit eternal life?" Look and listen. You will hear these Bible questions becoming your ultimate questions. That is why Scripture is so primary for us.

There are some who advise that we ought to read the Bible just as literature—just as we read any other book. It has good stories. It has good history. Simply read it like we read anything else. The trouble with that counsel is the Bible is not like anything else. There is no other book God-breathed, no other library God-breathed in the same sense as the Scriptures. To read the Bible as mere literature is like reading *Moby Dick* as a manual for whaling or the Gettysburg Address for its punctuation.

Consider this: If I look *at* the window in the room where I study, I see on that window fly specks, handprints, dust, even the crack where someone hit it, apparently, with a rock. It if I look *through* even that soiled window pane, I see the gorgeous world outside. Something like this is the difference between those who look at the Bible and see it as a nice, neat, little book and those who look through the Bible into the unfathomable depths of humankind's nature and God's great grace adventure.

You remember once a lawyer came to Jesus asking, "What must I do to inherit eternal life?" You remember that Jesus referred that lawyer to the Scriptures. He said, "What is written?" Then Jesus added in Luke 10:25 a very interesting question. He said, "How do you read it?" Now the usual rabbinic formula for introducing a scriptural quote was, "What do you read?" But here Jesus gave a dramatic new twist to the question. He asked, "How do you read it?"

Jesus Christ saw that the *how* is as important as the *what* when it comes to reading the Bible. So he questions his questioner, not only about the content of his Scripture reading, but also about the impact of that word on his life. That is you see, after all, in the final analysis, the test of the primacy of Scripture for us. If the Bible does not make any difference in our lives once we have read it, then it doesn't have primacy, doesn't have ultimacy, doesn't have potency, doesn't have inspiration, doesn't have revelation— not for us.

In order to be primary for us, the Bible must make a difference when we read it. So the question comes as we launch this series of surveying the entire Scriptures from Genesis to Revelation: What difference do these Scriptures make in who we are and the way we behave once we have read them?

In one man's life the Scriptures made a dangerous and a daring difference. His name was William Tyndale. He belonged to the age of the Renaissance and the Protestant Reformation. During his lifetime the church, the state, and the culture were all in ferment.

The times when Tyndale lived were marked by Erasmus, Luther, Cromwell, and Henry VIII. But the biggest bombshell of all came not from England in Tyndale's lifetime, but from Germany. In Germany, Gutenberg set up the first movable-type printing press and produced the first book printed in Europe, the Gutenberg Bible. He printed it 28 years before William Tyndale was born.

William Tyndale went to Oxford and then to Cambridge and became a very well-educated man. He was ordained a priest in the Roman Catholic Church. He early developed two passions.

First, he wanted to embrace the reforming opinions of Luther, Calvin, Zwingli, and other protesters who were perceived by the authorities as being heretical. Tyndale dared to be heretical because he believed what the Protestants were believing.

Second, he wanted to provide with all his soul a translation of the Bible into the common tongue of the English-speaking people. The Bible had never been translated into English. He was driven by a desire to provide an English translation from the Hebrew, the Greek, and other cognate languages so that, as he put it, the boy who drives the plow could know the Scriptures as well as the man who preaches the sermon. He set upon this, his life's dream.

William Tyndale first went to London and then to Hamburg and Wittenburg and Cologne and Worms. Then finally at Antwerp in Belgium he finished his task. William Tyndale translated the New Testament from the tongues that no one in England could read—except just a very, very special few people—into an English New Testament. It was first printed by Gutenberg's printing press technique in the year 1526. It was the only English Bible ever published up until that time.

Christianity was more than 1,500 years old before an English-speaking/reading person could take this library in his or her own hand and read it in his or her own tongue. Tyndale wanted to translate the Old Testament as well. He turned to the task. He completed part of the Old Testament translation, but he was delivered—betrayed, actually—into the hands of the authorities, both sacred and secular, who considered his work a heresy. He never finished translating the Old Testament.

He was in prison for a year and a half near Brussels, and he finally came to trial. He knew that his fate was already sealed. William Tyndale acted as his own lawyer. In his defense, during his trial he maintained that the Christian conscience was free in Christ Jesus; that faith alone justifies a person before God; and that the common people deserved to have a Bible they could read in their own language. He was condemned a heretic. On the morning of October 6, 1536, just a little more than 458 years ago, William Tyndale was strangled until he died, and then his body was burned. His last words before his death were: "Lord, open the king of England's eyes."

The deed was done. The costly biblical ethic of salt and light had won its way. But Tyndale's English Bible was loose in the world. Today, you and I safely and freely can open it and read it. Never again will the Scriptures be locked into Latin and Hebrew and Greek. Now it is available to the English-speaking/reading people around the world.

The Bible: How do you read it? Read it with me this year and a half or so ahead as we journey through its pages. But read it remembering that one man found it so primary that he gave his life that we might have it in our own tongue. For Tyndale, Scripture made a difference! Amen.

January 8, 1995

GENESIS

In the beginning—God
Genesis 1:1, 26-28; 2:15; 3:9-11, 22-24; 4:8; 6:5-8; 12:1-5

"Bereshit bara elohim et hashamayim ve'et ha'aretz." . . . With these majestic words our Bible begins. It certainly starts at the right place with an Everest affirmation: "In the beginning God created the heavens and the earth."

We know by now that the Bible is really more than a book. It is a library of books—a compilation of 66 of them. The first book in this collection of books is titled Genesis. The name means "coming into being." Its concern in all 50 chapters is births, beginnings, start-ups.

The Hebrews have a habit of using the very first word in a document as the title for that document. The first word in the first scroll of our Bible is *Bereshit*, which means "in the beginning," so that is what the Hebrews, until this day, call the first book in their Bible and our Bible, because we share the Old Testament together.

What about the author of Genesis? By ancient tradition, the first five books of our Bible—the Pentateuch (five books); the Torah (the law)—were written by Israel's law-giver, the spiritual hero of the Hebrew people who rescued them from slavery in Egypt at the exodus.

Moses may well have written huge portions of the Pentateuch, but there is evidence that these earliest books of our Bible are not the single work of any one person. They are rather the combined, inspired, revealed historical reminiscences of many persons. These 50 chapters in Genesis are accounts of creation and the stories of Noah, Abraham, Isaac, Jacob, and Joseph. They are precious both to Jews and to Christians.

We may not know the author exactly, but we do know the authority and the authenticity of these texts. The worshiping Jewish and Christian communities, through all of these thousands of years since these documents have existed, have hung their hearts and their hopes on this Word of the Lord.

What is the subject matter of the book of Genesis? It is complex, but if you read all 50 chapters and then back away and ask, "What is God saying to us in these texts?" I think it comes down to three basic themes.

First, *generation*: God in these texts tells us about creation of everything. Second, *degeneration*: God in these texts tells us about the start-up of evil and how everything that was good at creation got off track, cosmically. And third, *regeneration*: Given creation and degeneration, then comes salvation, restoration, redemption. The process begins in these texts. So generation, degeneration, regeneration: those are the themes threading through these entire 50 chapters.

When we let Genesis be Genesis, we find it to be a profound, religious record of beginnings. It is faith's story of start-ups—how everything began. Its value is not to be realized by trying to transform its chapters into a textbook on any subject—science or history.

These chapters are to science and history what spirit is to nature. Spirit is super nature, supra-natural—that is beyond the natural. Thus, Genesis is supra-historical. It is supra-scientific—before history, above history, beyond history and science. Its realities are subject to affirmation by categories of faith and trust rather than by categories of investigation and experimentation.

Genesis has its strong word, both for the chapel and for the laboratory, but it has its strongest word in the humble heart of a worshiping believer. That is where Genesis really speaks. The genius of this writing, furthermore, is that it does not try to inject science into the story. Thank God, because if the Genesis writers did try to do that, then we really would have a problem.

Since Copernicus we have known that the "science" of the old Hebrews was upside down. It was "geocentric," not "heliocentric." It was an earth system science, not a solar system science. Their universe was perceived to be three-storied: We lived in the middle, with the heavens above us and the underworld beneath us. That was the way it was. It was completely a closed system as they understood it. The earth was the very center and core of everything else.

The Hebrews knew nothing of the rotations of the earth that produced day and night or the revolutions of the earth from which we derive our seasons. For them, light traveled no faster than sound and mass had very little to do with energy. They were unaware that the sun's rays were thermonuclear, caused by hydrogen fusion; but they did know, like faith always knows, that in the beginning of everything that is, there was God!

Fortunately, therefore, they did not tell us how creation began scientifically. Why do we suppose that we might inject our modern science into these texts and find them satisfying for us? That is not their purpose at all. No, my people, the permanent values of Genesis lie beyond these values of the laboratory. They are values of the heart more than values of the head.

What are the abiding values of Genesis? The book of Genesis provides faith, its foundational truths, for every sphere of human experience. For example, theology starts here: the study of God. Cosmology starts here: the study of the world. Anthropology starts here: the study of humankind. Sociology starts here: the study of human relationships. Ethnology starts here: the study of faith, race, and culture. And soteriology starts here: the study of salvation.

Genesis speaks in terms of revelations made to man, and not in terms of discoveries made by man. Whoever wrote the book of Genesis was not there, present and active, when that history was unfolding—when any of that happened. The writer lived years later and was speaking about that which God had revealed as happening beforehand. These chapters provide their readers with a profound, religious explanation of things supra-naturally, supra-historically, supra-scientifically. Their declarations meet us at the point where our investigation starts.

Investigation is a perfectly normal, needed, necessary exercise of our human minds, and Genesis provides the starting places for investigation, not the ending places. Therefore, to possess the book of Genesis is not to be acquainted with the final truths on any subject. But to possess the book of Genesis is to have in hand the starting truths for many subjects.

Here we have the initial word that no subsequent discovery contradicts, and without which all later investigations can be misconstrued. And what is that initial word? What is the heart of the matter?

Very simply, very profoundly, this is the message of Genesis: four words, "In the beginning—God!" In declaring that foundational word, Genesis has done its job.

Where did Cain get a wife? What happened to Enoch? Who wrestled with Jacob: an angel or a human? Those are good questions, proper questions, but Genesis does not address them. Genesis wants us to know that whenever, wherever, and however these things came to be, God was already there.

Genesis introduces us to some stories: stories of Adam and Eve, Cain and Able, Noah and Abraham, Isaac and Jacob, Rebekah and Rachel, Esau and Joseph. These people and their stories are the stories through which God's beginnings are made known to us.

To ignore them, to deny their stories and the foundational truths they hold, is to cut ourselves loose on a sea of chance. It compels us, if we choose to cut ourselves loose from it, to find some other starting place for our explorations, investigations, and faith principles.

It means that we must embrace an entirely new set of initial truths. This can be done. There are people who are going into the 21st century with a set of different initial truths, but I think there is a hazard to it. The abiding value of Genesis is that it gives us a lively option. We can believe this way. These initial truths can provide for us, and all who have faith in them, a starting place—the best possible starting place for understanding everything else, and everyone else.

Make no mistake about it: Genesis intends, in my judgment, to be dogmatic at one crucial, critical, uncompromising point, and that point is this: "In the beginning God!" When this whole thing started, God was there; not merely as a spectator, but as creator, starter, causer. Genesis proclaims, Genesis trumpets this special religious explanation for beginnings. When the sun was spoken into being and the first day dawned and history began, God was there. God was already there, active, involved, causing it

What then is the message of Genesis for us? I think this is the message: There is one unswerving, uncompromising, essential, ultimate truth in these chapters. All is connected in creation. God is connected to humankind. Humankind is connected to the world in ways in which we must take account.

We must be sensitive to God, humans, and the world for we are all tied together. We are out in the weather together, and if we ignore or deny that incontrovertible fact, ours is the lot of all those east of Eden. We, too, are guilty of the original sin: to rebel against our Creator God and try to run this world ourselves.

In this world that God has made, the meaning of life is much more important than the mere mechanics of it. The "why" of things can never be answered merely with a pair of pliers. Hear Genesis! In this moral universe, God creates and we mortals manufacture. What man manufactures from what God creates must be informed and disciplined by faith, or else it is an unsavory brew that humankind cooks up in the kitchen. Ask Adam, ask Eve, ask Cain and Jacob, ask Esau and Joseph if they got away with trying to run away from the presence of the Creator God.

We can breathe, you and I, throughout this year. We can function, if we are fortunate, biologically throughout this year. But Genesis says that if we live, really live, throughout the new year it will be because of the difference faith makes in our lives. We really live when we come to realize the relationship between the God who creates, humankind who results from that creation, and the interplay between God the Creator and humankind, the creatures, and everything else in this wonderful world. To know and to obey God is to live! It is to be connected with the eternal. Not to know God, to rebel against God is to die!

Nothing in this whole world is more important than that we know God. This is what Genesis is saying. Nothing is more damnable, deadly, and eternally destructive than that we rebel against God. This is what Genesis is saying. We desperately need Genesis to remind us that there is order and system and continuity between the divine and the human, the inevitable partners in these lives we now live.

In his widely read book, *The Future Has Already Begun*, Robert Jungk refers to a lecture by an eminent space-age physician. He makes the point that, measured by the task he faces in space travel, man is from a biological point of view a misconstruction. That is to say that these bodies given to us by our Creator God, with their sensitive circulatory systems and even more sensitive nervous systems, are really no longer equal to the possibilities opened up by our new technologies.

This means that the contributions God has made to us by putting us forth in these kinds of physical forms—these bodies—have been disposed of now and outdistanced by the contribution man has made to us by the creation of all this machinery that will get us from the earth to the other planets in our solar system. Thus the 1990s dawn, according to Robert Jungk, with the divine partner in our lives being pushed away from the center, and the human partner in our lives is jockeying feverishly for prime position.

Biometrics is our new science. Genetic engineering is our new tinker toy, and the goal is to breed a new human, a bi-pod for the space age who can use effectively the information highway. And this new man is convinced that he really can be lord over everything.

Robert Jungk wants us to listen as the new man talks to us: "I have spun a sky full of hardware, and can now see and hear things instantly which happen anywhere on this earth. I can produce rain artificially; grow crops through agri-engineering; I can travel faster than sound; and I can transplant effectively every major body organ. I can make clothing out of coal, change the course of rivers, and transform landscapes into my own devising. I can produce life-forms in a test tube. Give me time, and I can make myself immortal."

Let Genesis say, "In the beginning—God." New man will have nothing of it. New man says, "No, in the beginning—me." So, stand back human race while new man, humanoid, turns the 21st century upside down.

If that is the scenario, Genesis would tell us all today that there is sand in that soup. New man is not content that he has made so much. He is to be complimented on that. New man must be told that he is still creature. He proceeds on a false assumption. He cannot appoint himself general manager of the universe. God, the divine partner in life, cannot be chased off the chart.

New man, the 1990s humanoid, may stand alone on the captain's bridge as this earth's ship lurches through the cosmic cold into the 21st century. But new man is going, increasingly, to discover that there are wild winds blowing. Those wild winds blow now in Chechnya, Bosnia, Somalia, Rwanda, and Haiti. God only knows where they will blow this time next month or next year.

It would seem to be such a fine thing that now we are so completely in control of things on this earth. But look, listen, take stock, make inventory: the captain, new man, 21st century humankind, paces the deck anxiously. Why is he so nervous? Why should he not be what he says—in control? Doesn't all this heady power cheer us all, make our world a virtual utopia? No, because there is no one left for new man to rely upon now. He cannot trust anyone or anything beyond himself. He has to control everyone and everything, everywhere his way. Not one moment can he let down to live by faith in another.

That is what Abraham and Isaac and Jacob and Joseph had to learn the hard way to do. The old-fashioned hard way, humankind had to learn to trust their Creator God. They had to learn how to be creatures, not creators.

Genesis is the record of stumbling and falling and getting back up, and lurching and lunging and eventually making a little bit of progress in the direction of trusting the God of us all.

It is no wonder that the men and the women of the 21st century and beyond will come to middle age burned up, drugged out, and less than half-human if they do not learn the lesson of Genesis. This dazzling merry-go-round is too much for us. Humankind was not made for this. As our own god, you and I are a misconstruction.

We were made for creatureliness and obedience and trust of our Creator God. We were made for sonship and daughterhood. The Genesis trumpet sounds: "In the beginning—God." If you start there, everything else is an adventure of faith and discovery. If you start anywhere else, everything else is a journey into doom! Amen.

January 15, 1995

EXODUS

Let my people go

Exodus 1:7-8, 11-12; 3:1-2, 7-8, 13-14; 5:1; 13:18-22; 20:1-4, 7-8, 12-17; 40:38

Today we take the second step in our journey through the Bible. We will soon discover that the book of Exodus is a sequel to the book of Genesis. In Genesis, God creates a physical universe. In Exodus, God creates a moral universe. In Genesis, we have God's promise. In Exodus, we have God's procedure. God's promise of redemption focuses on Abraham, Isaac, Jacob, and Joseph. God's procedure of redemption focuses on Moses, Aaron, Joshua, and Caleb. In Genesis, God calls us to believe. In Exodus, God calls us to behave.

Listen to two texts in these first two books of our Bible that are absolutely worlds apart. First, Gen. 6:5-6: "The Lord saw that the wickedness of man was great in the earth, and that every imagination of the thoughts of his heart was only evil continuously. And the Lord was sorry that he had ever made man on the earth, and it grieved him to his heart." That text in Genesis points toward sinners in the hands of an angry God.

Now hear this from Exod. 2:24 and 3:7-8: "God heard the people's groaning and God remembered his covenant with Abraham, Isaac, and Jacob. . . . Then the Lord said, 'I have seen the affliction of my people who are in Egypt. . . . I know their suffering, and I have come down to deliver them.'" That text from Exodus points toward sinners in the hands of a loving God.

Between these two texts, God has not changed. What has changed is the way humans apprehend God. Between the end of Genesis and the start of Exodus, there is a large chronological gap—about 300-400 years—a period of time between these two manuscripts longer than the history of our country. Thus, to bridge this gap, Exodus begins with a long list of names; names of the families who, along with Jacob and his sons, came to Egypt in the time of Joseph.

The first word in Exodus in the Hebrew manuscript is *ve-elleh shemoth*. Translated, that means "Now these are the names."

Jews today, following their custom of naming a scroll for the first word in it, call the scroll *shemoth* (the names). What is Exodus for us is *shemoth* for the Jews in the Bible we both share. Exodus in our language means "going out." It is a good name, as good as any, for these 40 chapters, because essentially this entire second book of our Bible deals with a journey, a trip, an exodus of the Hebrews from Egypt to Sinai.

In the shortest possible scope, Exodus treats three themes: repression, redemption, and revelation.

Repression: The first 13 chapters relate the changes of policy in Egypt, the call of Moses, and his contests with the Egyptian pharaoh for the release of the slave-people Israel.

Redemption: The middle seven chapters of Exodus describe the journey itself: the journey of escape, the journey of deliverance, the journey of safety out of Egypt, across the sea of water and mud, through the wilderness, down to Sinai.

Revelation: The final 20 chapters of Exodus contain the covenant God made with the people at Sinai and the commandments that flowed from that covenant, and relate to the tent/tabernacle that the people were instructed to build in the wilderness. Thus, repression and redemption and revelation come together in focus in this second ancient manuscript, the Word of God.

This sketch helps us to understand the message of Exodus. What is that message? In these 40 chapters, if we will watch carefully and prayerfully, God will show us how an instrument is formed, forged; an instrument of deliverance, of redemption, of salvation, throughout all the rest of history.

So let us stop, look, and listen. First, God's instrument was a man, a person: Moses. His mission is all wrapped up in the mystery of his call from a bush ablaze and the equally fiery introduction to a God who thunders, "Tell them I am that I am sends you."

Second, God's instrument, if we will watch carefully, becomes a people, a group; the rag-tag bunch of slave people—the Hebrews in Egypt's delta land of Goshen. God enters into their very blood, sweat, and tears to deliver them. God creates no pets of providence in the process, but God creates a people of God's own choosing with a flaming mandate: "Let my people go!"

Third, God's instrument becomes a covenant, an agreement, struck like flint sparks off the smoking mountain at Horeb, at Sinai. Here God manifests divinity in the rule of law. From amidst the smoke of holy Sinai come 10 mandates for humankind, mandates that become the rules of conduct for the holy people with whom the holy God has cut an everlasting covenant.

Finally, God's instrument in Exodus becomes a tent, a tabernacle, a dwelling place, where God may actually abide in the midst of these special people. Thus, slowly, painstakingly, in these 40 chapters God unveils the truth about divinity to a group of people just like us: a group of covenant people—chosen people.

All this drama begins in the very first chapter of the book of Exodus. Scarcely has the story begun when Egypt changes administrations. In my lifetime I have seen three administrative changes in Egypt, and so have you. Here is a change of administration in Exodus 1:8: "There arose a new king over Egypt who did not know Joseph."

For 150 years the Hyksos kings of Egypt had been friendly to the Hebrews. There was just one problem: The Hyksos kings who ruled Egypt for that century and a half were not really Egyptians at all. They were Asians. They had conquered Egypt in the north and were kindly toward Joseph's kinsmen, to whom they were bound both by language and culture.

All the while, though—up river at Thebes, Luxor—native Egyptians amassed power and hacked away at the control of these non-Egyptian rulers in the north. Finally, in 1570 B.C. Ahmose, the first king in Egypt's 18th dynasty, consolidated his power, marched on Memphis, conquered the delta, and made himself pharaoh over all of Egypt.

Ahmose I may well have been the new king over Egypt who knew not Joseph. Being native Egyptian, he would look with grave suspicion upon those Hebrews who had very fine, friendly relationships with the former Hyksos rulers. So the Israelites soon came to be seen, in Ahmose's opinion, as enemies in the camp. The lot of the Hebrews went from bad to worse, and from worse to terrible.

What Ahmose began, Ramses II continued. Listen to Exod. 1:12: "And the Egyptians were in dread of the people of Israel. So they made them serve with rigor, and made their lives bitter with hard labor."

Mr. Nassar, Mr. Sadat, and Mr. Mubarak are not the only hard men to sit on the hard throne of Egypt. Ramses settled on genocide as his ultimate solution. He ordered all baby boys born to Jewish parents to be killed. But one child escaped Ramses' net, only to end up on Ramses' lap. That child's name was *Mosheh*. We call him Moses.

Ramses was no more successful than Hitler in his efforts to wipe out the sons and daughters of Abraham, Isaac, and Jacob. Albeit Ramses' holocaust was separated from Hitler's by 3200 years, his holocaust was just as fierce and bloody as Hitler's. He tried to destroy the Jews.

Moses was born to Hebrew slave parents just as the noose of oppression began to tighten around his countrymen's neck. Much like a cat, Moses seemed destined to live nine lives. Plucked out of the river in his boat of reeds by one of Ramses' 50 daughters, Moses grew up the child of two mothers: a queen mother and his own slave mother.

Moses was destined ever to stand in two camps: Egypt's court and Israel's slave quarters. As Moses grew, he listened with one ear to the learning and lore of Egypt—groomed to be a prince. With the other ear, he listened to the learning and the lore of Israel—groomed to be a prophet.

Young Moses grew in two opposite directions. Often he and his nurse—mother—watched as half-naked Hebrews toiled under the scorching sun, hewing great stones, hauling great timbers, excavating the burning sands. They were the nameless, faceless, wageless, half-starved nobodies, scourged nightly to their slave quarters.

Here young Moses learned that every stone in Ramses' splendid cities was cemented in Hebrew blood. I can imagine that it hit him hard that day when his nurse—mother—gripped his arm and with flashing eyes and quivering lips said to Moses, scarcely out of his teens:

Listen to me Moses, listen to me, my son, declare by the God of your fathers that I speak the truth, those slaves yonder you look upon are your people. You are not Egyptian, you are not just my charge, you are my child. I am not just your nurse, I am your mother. Not in the palace of Ramses, but in the hovels of yonder slaves is your home. Moses, you are Jewish. You are my son.

With the blood of his people surging in his veins, and the mystical call of the faith of his mother throbbing in his heart, young Moses came to nourish a secret, but imperishable hope: "One day, I will set these people free."

But the hunger was too hot. Not many days passed, and he saw an Egyptian slave master mercilessly whipping a Hebrew slave. With one terrible blow, Moses killed the Egyptian and tried to bury his body in the sand, but too many people saw it. He was guilty!

To escape the judgment of Ramses, Moses fled across the trackless desert, along the rim of the Red Sea to the land of Midian. From that moment on like a Spielberg movie, Exodus records scene after scene of high drama unfolding. Moses, disciplined by the desert, is confronted by God in a bush that burns without burning up. Excuses are followed by commitments to set those people free. Awesome struggles ensue with the Egyptian government. God intervenes with a calamitous series of events on behalf of the Hebrews.

Finally, there is that daring exodus out of Egypt: through the water and the mud, under the sun, over the sand, through the desert to Sinai, where Moses had previously tended the sheep of his father-in-law. Then there is rendezvous: the confrontation with Yahweh, the lawgiver, the covenant-maker God. There follow Ten Commandments and the tent/tabernacle with God's tracks among the people in the wilderness.

Through it all a band of slaves—ignorant, ignoble, nobodies—are painstakingly forged by the grace of God into an instrument of deliverance. These Hebrews—stumbling, mumbling, bumbling Hebrews—become God's people.

But, you say, all this happened so long ago, so far away. That was in Egypt. This is not B.C.; this is A.D. and a long time later. What exactly does Exodus mean for us? I am glad that you asked that, because if any message in the Bible is meant for us, it must be this message.

Here is the Exodus truth: from the infancy of the human race, God has watched over humankind with yearning love. The Old Testament calls it *hessed*—loving kindness. The New Testament calls it *agape*—love. But God's one desire in loving is to impart quality through covenant into these lives of ours; to make folks like us God's people. That is what God has purposed from the beginning. That is the Exodus message—the Exodus revelation.

In that covenant at Sinai, in those Ten Commandments that flow white hot from "moral mountain," God has not laid down some arbitrary prohibitions just to mess up the lives we want to live. No, these mandates rather are God's way of communicating the moral structure of everything else God made in Genesis.

If humankind is made like this, and the universe is made like this, then these mandates tell us how to behave so as to have real fulfillment and freedom in our lives. Thus, in light of the way we are made and our world is made, we had best realize that we cannot disregard these regulations—not and enjoy health and wholeness and fulfillment while living in God's kind of world. Here is the bottom line of it: God's world is not a good world for God's people to be bad in.

Listen then to these mandates to humankind, to you and to me here now as surely as there then. It was 1250 B.C. when God first said this. Yet, listen to the news:

1. Above all else, love God alone.
2. Bow down to neither wood, paper, nor stone.
3. God's name refuse to take in vain.
4. The Sabbath rest with care maintain.
5. Respect your parents all your days.
6. Hold sacred human life always.
7. Be loyal to your chosen mate.
8. Steal nothing, neither small nor great.
9. Report with truth your neighbor's deed.
10. Rid your mind of selfish greed.

There they are: 10 living laws—rules for life written in shorthand. Here is our road map toward being human. But that is precisely our problem nowadays. We are traveling by other maps, and we are increasingly becoming less and less and less human.

For too many nowadays God has no voice. If a partner at all, God is a silent partner with nothing much relevant to say. But God has already said it. God has said it 10 times in the dawn of history: "Live like this, and there is deliverance. Live any other way, and there is slavery."

You are I are born for an exodus—an exodus from our self-centered enslavements into the wonderful, rarefied liberty of God's promises through Jesus Christ.

Here is our problem, however: In our world today we perceive God as one who stays out of sight, up a holy mountain, and shouts occasionally from somewhere on the other side of the sky some meager word of instruction while we, children, playing out here in the real world join up into gangs and drug ourselves silly and mess up our lives and dig too many early graves. God is not with us.

That is not so, my friends. The Exodus word contradicts our perception. Our God is a God who acts. Ours is a Lord who takes children by the hand and leads them on their spiritual journeys. Every one of us is born for exodus. It is just like God to come out from behind the nearest cloud into the rough and tumble where we live and show us how to live in our kind of world.

That is exactly what God is doing here at this time. The trouble is not with God's voice; the trouble is with our ears. The trouble is not with God's hope; the trouble is in our heart.

"Let my people go!" That is God's message in Exodus. "Let my people go!" That is God's message today to all those enslaving persons and passions and things in this drug-crazed, terrorist-threatened, crime-infested, stainless-steel, push-button world we live in.

You and I were born for exodus from everything that would enslave us unto the liberty that the Lord Jesus Christ alone can provide. Amen.

January 29, 1995

LEVITICUS

Halt in the name of the law
Leviticus 1:1-2, 5:10-13, 10:8-11, 16:29-34, 19:1-2, 27:34

J acob had 12 sons. One of them was named Levi. In the economy of "holy history," Levi and his tribe would become the tribe of priests in Israel. They received no land as their inheritance. Instead they were bequeathed an awesome duty: to stand in the terrible gap between God and humans, mediating the affairs of earth with one hand and the affairs of heaven with the other.

The third book in our Bible, Leviticus, is actually a handbook for these priests, the Levites. It is their pastor's manual.

The book is virtually one long, 27-chapter, priestly document given over to ritualistic detail. One of the reasons it is hard for us to understand and appreciate is because we are not priests by our calling. Thus, the casual reader may conclude that Leviticus is really dull reading—a sort of verbal desert with not many an oasis in view.

Our word Leviticus is the Latin equivalent of the Septuagint title of this book, *Levitikon*: it means "the priest's book." The first Hebrew word in the scroll of Leviticus is *vayikra*—"and he called." What is Leviticus for us is *vayikrah* for the Jews, in this Bible we both share.

The book of Exodus ends with a cloud covering the newly constructed tent of meeting—that is the tabernacle—in the wilderness of Sinai.

The book of Leviticus begins with God speaking to Moses out of that cloud hovering over that tent of meeting, the tabernacle in Sinai. The entire 27 chapters of Leviticus really are a parenthesis between two verses: the first verse and the last verse. First, Lev. 1:1: "The Lord called Moses and spoke to him from the tent of meeting." Then Lev. 27:34: "These are the commandments which the Lord commanded unto Moses for the people of Israel on Mount Sinai."

Every page in between these two verses has something to say about worship: why to worship, how to worship, when to worship.

If in Genesis God created man and in Exodus God created morals, then in Leviticus God created mystery. The crux of that mystery is this: How can holy God and unholy humans separated by sin be brought back together again? If that is important in your mind, then Leviticus is important in your reading.

Leviticus is a book as bloody as an Alabama hog-killing. Almost every page of it reeks with the slaughter of sacrifices. All that blood, all those animals killed, certify that in the painful process of redemption innocence always points the way to holiness.

One useful experiment in reading the book of Leviticus is to mark every place in these 27 chapters where the word "holy" occurs. If you will read them with care and mark that word, you will find it appearing 153 times.

The holiness of God: it flashes like a blue light over the landscape of Leviticus. One listens and one hears on every page the shout, "Halt, unholy people, in the name of the Law!"

The ultimate question that Leviticus attempts to answer is this: "How can unholy persons approach such a holy God?"

In the dawn of history Leviticus had an answer: the word *pontifex*, which means "bridge." A priest is a bridge. A priest is a *pontifex* connecting two parties: God/man. They approach each other through the intricate network of priests, and the offerings, the feasts, the sacrifices outlined in these pages of Leviticus. All these had to suffice until the fullness of time when Jesus Christ—Messiah, the perfect priest—would arrive.

The great word of Leviticus is that word from chapter 19, verse 2: "You shall be holy for I, the Lord your God, am holy." That is our homework. That is our assignment. That is the word Leviticus places before us today.

The ever-glowing, white-hot possibility is that there is a way for us, unholy though we are, to reconnect with a holy God. Sinners can approach God. Sinners can be forgiven. Holiness can happen on the human side as well as on the divine side. God has made a bridge. Something/someone stands in that horrible gap. There is a span over all the troubled waters of our alienation.

Here in the dawn of holy history, thousands of years before Jesus, we are being taught in Leviticus that God's great heart compels God to make a way back home for the wayward sons and daughters of men. It is a bloody journey, strewn every step of the way with the carcasses of untold innocent sacrifices, but it is a way home for sinners. That is the message of Leviticus.

The living message of Leviticus is as critical today in our concrete and asphalt wilderness as it was then in Kadesh-Barnea and the wilderness of Sinai a long time ago.

This book speaks its strong word about two themes: our sin and our salvation. Its basic declaration is that our sin is our unholiness—our unlikeness to God, our distance from God, our failure to bear the image of God and to enjoy God's presence forever. Law is broken. Love is betrayed by our evil.

That is why the book of Leviticus is such terrible reading. It refuses to let us take lightly the effects of our sin. Leviticus takes us kicking and screaming back to the scenes of our crimes against God's great love.

It is therefore a tragic document, full of blood and smoke and fire and the sizzle of searing flesh. You do not read Leviticus without feeling deeply that its telling blows leave you awe-struck. We learn that our sin spites God in the face; that our sin wounds a holy God in the heart. Redemption, salvation, our very personal exodus from evil is an infinite and unfathomable mystery in which the taking of guiltless life and the shedding of innocent blood are the only equivalent symbols.

So let's take off our shoes. Let's bow down our hearts. Let's tread softly and stand for a moment together with a chapter out of Leviticus on very holy ground. The chapter is Leviticus 16—the book's mountaintop revelation. When you and I come on our own exodus to Leviticus 16, we are standing in the white, windy glory of Yom Kippur.

We English speakers call it "The Day of Atonement." Even until this very day it is the holiest day of the Jewish religious year—"The Day of at-one-ment." Atonement: the one day of the year in which provision is made for dealing with the people's sins. Here in Leviticus 16 is the Good Friday of the Old Testament.

So stop! Look! Listen! Focus for a moment on this awesome chapter. Set the scene in your mind: It is the tenth day of the seventh month. All the people of God assembled have fasted for seven days preparing themselves for this day of days.

Aaron, the high priest, has lived for that week apart from all the rest of the people—detached, alone. There he has read and re-read the scroll of God's ordinances regarding this Day of Atonement. The night before this awesome morning, he has not slept a wink.

Then suddenly, from out of nowhere, Aaron appears at the door of the tent of meeting. The people of God are assembled as far as he can see all around. The priests' ornate garments are all gone. He wears pure linen—a linen cloak, linen britches, a linen belt, a linen turban. These are the holy garments.

His body has been washed and rewashed seven times with "holy water." He reeks with the aroma of anointing oil. By his side stand an unblemished young bullock and two young goats.

Quick as a flash he sets fire to an urn of incense: smoke fills the place just like a magic show. Almost in the same motion, with one stroke of a well-placed knife blade, Aaron slashes the throat of the young bullock beside him. Rich, red blood from that guiltless, innocent animal flows free. Some of it is caught by the priest on the two fingers of his right hand and daubed on the high mercy seat there in the tent of meeting—the tabernacle in the wilderness.

Other swift thrusts of the knife blade and he lays the carcass of that young bullock, still quivering with life that is leaving it, wide open in place before the altar. Now his hands are bloody all the way up to the elbows, and the priest reaches down into the warm blood and flesh of that slain animal and takes out the kidneys and the fat and places the body in the fire that burns briskly through the smoke on the altar.

The sight of that blood, the smell of that burning flesh punctuate the incantations of the priest, and the ritual moves on.

Now the two goats are brought to Aaron. They are two perfectly formed and immaculately groomed goats—standing trembling before the priest. Lots are drawn from an urn nearby. The lots determine the fate of those two animals.

One goat is selected as an offering, a sin offering for the people. Quick as a wink the goat is sacrificed just like the bullock was—a weird, bloody process repeated. The innocent animal, dying in its own blood, is sacrificed on behalf of the people.

The other goat is kept alive. At the prescribed moment in the ritual, the priest places both his hands on the head of that live goat and confesses the sins of the people. Then that goat, with the people's sins heaped upon it, is driven away into the wilderness. It is the scapegoat.

As the scapegoat lunges through the barren wastes out of sight, the people breath deeply—assured that their sins all go with that goat. The jubilee trumpet sounds, and the people burst out into rejoicing, and the sons and daughters of Israel have celebrated another Yom Kippur—their day of atonement—moving, mysterious, magnificent, majestic.

For more than 12 long centuries this was the prevailing pattern of sacrifice among the people of God. Guiltless animals died. Innocent animals died. The people were delivered from their sins by life given up on their behalf.

These people of God could see and smell and taste and touch and hear their salvation; and they came away from that observance every time aware that something about their sins was costly. Something had to die in order for them to be delivered.

Such bloody religious business is objectionable to some in our time. After all, the depictions of Leviticus are primitive. They are almost pagan. Surely some of you in this room and many across this land are apt to say there should be some tamer symbol of the ultimate activity of salvation than this. It is too bloody! It is too distant! It is too gory!

Surely there is a nicer, neater way to be saved than that. But think like that and you miss the point of Leviticus. The point of Leviticus is this: Our sins are serious business, and in this moral universe our evil touches the very heart of God with wounding. Leviticus refuses to let us take our sin lightly.

This bloody book bids us to halt in the name of the law—the law of sin and death, the law of sacrifice and life. Both are at work in us, and both are at work in our world.

But you are apt to say Leviticus was crafted so long ago, and you are right. So how do we translate these 27 chapters? How do we update these 27 chapters? How do we deliver their message to the address where we live?

The fact is, there is a thread: It is a blood-red thread connecting this document with us today. In time, you see, something really did happen to Israel's splendid levitical sacrificial system.

A young man from Nazareth—named Jesus—visited the synagogues and temple. He went to Yom Kippur in his time. He watched it all transpire when he was young. He came to believe that the whole bloody business had boiled down to just a form, a ritualistic detail without heart in it. So that young man from Nazareth watched his countrymen go through the motions, the very motions that created the mystery from the beginning in Leviticus. Jesus Christ concluded that the mystery was now gone. The awe was missing. The people approached this Day of Atonement, when their sins were forgiven, with a lick and a promise and a rushed-up prayer. They did not take it to heart.

So young Jesus put on riding boots and raced rough-shod over this entire levitical system. He challenged its hypocrisy. He shocked its priests. He upset the sale of their sacrificial paraphernalia. He cut off their profits and slapped the dead carcass of his countrymen's religion.

They did a very natural thing: they reacted violently. In time this young man from Nazareth became just another sacrifice in the system. They arrested young Jesus, tried him, condemned him, and labeled him an outlaw. They drove great stakes through his hands and feet and lashed him to a cross. They put a crown of thorns on his head and left him to die in the scorching sun between two robbers on a hillside outside their holiest city.

In their heart of hearts they honestly thought they had done holy God a service by disposing of this unholy young man from Nazareth.

See that writhing, twisting, dying human form on Golgotha, and you see the fulfillment of everything Leviticus is trying to say. Here is a man instead of an animal in the gap. Here is a new priest—a new *pontifex*—a new bridge from God's purity to our sin.

Here on this cross, as there in the Sinai tabernacle, holy God and unholy man rendezvous. Wayward children begin the journey home. Yom Kippur came to climax the Friday that split history in two.

Three days after the New Testament's Good Friday, Jesus' grave was found to be empty. He was loose; he was free; he was alive again—this Christ, a dead sacrifice that had come back to life. That was new! That was different! Leviticus never did it that way. Yet, Jesus did!

Paul, struggling with the meaning of all this, wrote about it beautifully, powerfully, succinctly in Rom. 12:1: "I appeal to you . . . by the mercies of God that you present yourselves a living sacrifice, holy, acceptable to God which is your reasonable service." That is the connection. That is the direct line between Leviticus and where we are today. One living sacrifice calls for another.

Paul was reared right in the middle of the levitical system. He knew this pastor's manual from cover to cover. He was groomed to be a rabbi carrying out this ritual. He knew about the animals, the pigeons, the doves, slain, and all the innocent blood flowing around the altars in Israel.

Remember that and now listen to what he said: "You—the new Israel—are to offer your very selves a living sacrifice." Do you see it? The sacrifice, with its throat cut on the altars of Leviticus with death in it, has now been replaced by a sacrifice that lives.

For Leviticus the live sacrifice dies! For Romans the dead sacrifice lives! It is a new mystery, a living sacrifice! But it resides at the very heart of Christian faith. That is what you and I become when you and I dare to take upon ourselves the name Christian. We are sacrifices unto God, alive in Christ, who walk away from the altar.

The journey from Sinai to Golgotha—from Moses to Jesus—from Kadesh to Greensboro marks the journey from a dead sacrifice to a live one. That difference is as deep as life.

Thank God for that difference and for the unspeakable gift, Jesus, fulfilling all of Leviticus and standing in the awesome gap between a holy God and our unholiness. Amen.

February 12, 1995

NUMBERS

You've gotta have heart
Numbers 1:1-3, 46; 6:22-27; 13:1-2, 25-33; 14:1-4; 21:6-9

The fourth book in our Bible just may have the most bland title in all the biblical library. It is called simply Numbers—like in arithmetic, like in mathematics. This book includes the results of two census takings of the fighting men in the 12 tribes of the fledgling nation Israel. So those translators gave the book the title *Arithmoi*. Our English title is simply the translation of that word *Arithmoi*: Numbers.

The Jews, according to their custom of taking the title from the first line in a scroll, found in the first line in this fourth scroll their title: it is *Bemidbar*. Translated, that means "in the wilderness."

So, what is Numbers for us is wilderness for the Jews in this scroll of the Bible we share together. While we focus on the census in our title, our Jewish friends focus on the setting in their title.

The book of Numbers continues the flow of "holy history" that we have begun in Genesis and Exodus. Let us review. Exodus closes with these words: "And in the first month in the second year, on the first day of the month the tabernacle (tent of meeting) was erected in the wilderness."

Numbers 1:1 begins like this: "The Lord spoke to Moses in the wilderness of Sinai, in the tent of meeting, on the first day of the second month, in the second year after they had come out of the land of Egypt."

Thus, according to this chronicle, only one month/30 days have transpired between the events with which Exodus closes and the events with which Numbers opens.

In Numbers, from the first chapter to the last, there is an interval of 40 years—four decades—all that while all those people occupy the wilderness of Sinai, on the margin of Canaan, their ancestral land of promise. These 40 years are known by students of scripture as the 40 years of wilderness wandering.

One helpful way for you and me to read Numbers is to mark every time in our translation where the word "service" occurs. You will find service 40 times in these 36 chapters. A reader gets the decided impression that God is here forging a tool, a redemptive tool, for a redemptive service. This wilderness is God's forge for that tool.

Let's set again the situation: In Genesis, God created man. In Exodus, God created morals. In Leviticus, God created mystery. In Numbers, God created management.

Yes, old-fashioned, down-to-earth administration. Moses tries desperately during these chapters in Numbers to organize and manage these people Israel by becoming their spiritual leader and cheerleader.

The people kept their heads, but the people lost their hearts at Kadesh; and there settled over Israel a 40-year paralysis of doubt.

Have you ever been cast into a paralysis of doubt for 40 minutes? 40 days? 40 weeks? Then you can identify just in part, I guess, with these people Israel who were cast into doubt for 40 years. That, generally, is perceived to be a generation—a lifetime.

So, what the Bible is trying to tell us is that here is an entire country, an entire civilization, who for their entire lifetime had all the reasons in the world to be people of faith, but flunked the chance to do it.

Since once every 10 years in our country we take a census, perhaps we ought to stop in passing and look at these two census' head counts from which our book, Numbers, gets its name.

The first census is recorded in chapter 1 as the book begins. The second census is recorded in chapter 26, 40 years later as the book concludes. It seems as if the writer is saying, "These are the people who had their chance and muffed it."

Only the adult males—that is, the men who were able for war—were counted. The total in the first census was 603,550. The total in the second census was 601,730. Those who worry about churches getting smaller rather than larger can take a look at Numbers and get at least some satisfaction out of the fact that in the very beginning God dealt with "ensmallment" rather than with enlargement.

Some tribes gained during those 40 years: Judah, Isaachar, Zebulon, Manasseh, Benjamin, Dan, and Asher became larger. Some tribes decreased during the 40 years: Reuben, Gad, Ephraim, Naphtali, and Simeon—his tribe lost three-fifths of its adult males.

The tribe of Levi was not numbered with those "able for war." You remember that the levitical people were to be priests and not warriors. Theirs was the smallest tribe of all, but they added 1,000 priests during the 40 years of wandering.

Now, if you add these numbers of adult males over 20 to the women, the children, and the camp followers, you are going to begin to see that there were more than a million and a quarter people wandering around in the Sinai peninsula for their entire lifetime.

Some people, seeing that, find these numbers implausible. They suspect either the accuracy of the count, or conclude that this census really did not just include all the men over 20. For me, however, these numbers make sense. After all, this was the nomadic era of human history, and it was not at all unusual for vast hoards of humankind to migrate from one place to another at the slightest provocation.

What is more, if we have trouble with these numbers, then let us consider some numbers we can understand better. For example, some years ago the Nigerian government decided that many foreigners were holding jobs in Nigeria, and thus putting the squeeze on the Nigerian economy and the value of the Nigerian currency.

They determined that all non-Nigerians had to be deported to their homes. This hit, especially hard, multiplied thousands of citizens of Ghana, who lived and worked two countries away from Nigeria.

But the decision was made, and the Ghanians had to go home. They argued about it, but they had to do it. So, you remember just a very few years ago, these multiplied thousands, going by transport, car, bus, plane, train, animal cart, bicycle, motorcycle, anything with wheels, went back home to Ghana. Other multiplied thousands, old and young, trudged through Benin and Togo, back to their homes on foot. Still others went by flimsy boat and sturdy crafts, over the Gulf of Guinea, back to Ghana.

More than a million of them migrated in our lifetime, about the same number as the scriptures say wandered around Sinai for those four decades. And if that is not enough, remember just last year the faces of the Rwandaians—almost a million—leaving their country after the scourge of war and famine.

Suffice it to say that there were substantial numbers of these people for Moses to manage in the wilderness of Sinai. Now, his task would have been bad enough, almost impossible, if things had gone well. But things did not go well. In fact, they went from bad to worse, to terrible, to disastrous.

They had been gone from Sinai for only a week when discontent began to fall over the entire ranks of Israel. Listen as these people not a week in the wilderness shout their complaints on the early pages of Numbers: "O, that we had meat to eat! We remember the fish that we ate in Egypt for nothing, the cucumbers, the melons, the leeks, the onions, and the garlic. But now our strength is all dried up, and there is nothing at all left but this manna to look at" (11:4-6).

Now, we should not be surprised at that. It sounds like an article right off the front page of our morning newspaper. The process of organizing a disorganized people into a new country with a national consciousness and a useful, focused purpose is never an easy task.

Ask Moses of Israel 3,000 years ago, or ask Mr. Rabin of Israel this very morning. Ask King Hussein in Jordan, or Mr. Arafat of the Palestinians. Ask Mr. Yeltsin in Russia, or Mr. Arristede in Haiti, or Mr. Mandela in South Africa, or Mr. Major in Britain, or Mr. Bruton in Ireland. Inquire of Ms. Ghandi how tough it was in India, or Mrs. Aquino how tough it was in the Philippines.

There is an incredible task awaiting anyone who tries anywhere, anytime to forge a nation. Moses in the wilderness of Sinai is trying to forge a nation, a special nation; a nation with a mission to the world—a redemptive mission.

But Moses found out something there that I think is a fact of history. He found that there is a certain subtle satisfaction in slavery, and a certain strange comfort level in colonialism that people miss when they emerge into the larger freedoms that abolish these previous systems.

Remember that these Hebrews had been slaves all of their lives in Egypt's land of Goshen. They, like the Palestinians today, had never known a day when they had a country to call their own. They got up every morning knowing what they had to do. The taskmasters awaited them. Their tasks were appointed. Their work was lined out. Others did their thinking for them.

Now, in their escape from Egypt, they naturally thought that they had escaped everything else. But they found freedom without finding responsibility or appreciation or understanding or focus or energy for freedom. So, at Sinai, these rag-tag ragamuffins learned that real freedom always means bondage to the right things, and they bonded to the wrong things in Sinai.

It was irksome to them, as it is irksome to us. Facing freedom, they actually looked longingly back toward bondage. "Oh, that we had never left Egypt, they moaned." They saw freedom through their rear-view mirrors instead of through their windshield. The road behind looked better to them than the road ahead. They were courting disaster at Kadesh, and the disaster came!

Now, set this situation in your mind. In Numbers 13, Israel developed its first secret service. Twelve spies were chosen—one man from each tribe. They were sent to spy out the region of Canaan, west of the River Jordan. Their report would become the basis for the plan of attack—the strategy to invade.

In time, the 12 returned to Kadesh where Moses had set up a temporary command post. Ten of the spies brought a devastating, negative, majority report. They felt that the Canaanite cities were impregnable. They predicted disaster for any attempt to march on that land.

Only two of those spies, Joshua and Caleb, brought a minority report. They favored an immediate assault, and reminded the people to remember God's promises. They were booed down, and were threatened with stoning.

The 10 spies said what the people wanted to hear: "We saw giants in the land; and we seemed to ourselves as grasshoppers." The lights went out in a million lives at Kadesh-Barnea, and the people wandered in the wilderness for 40 years.

It is right here that the book of Numbers drives home two modern-day truths that I want us to listen to.

In matters of the spirit the majority is always the majority, but it is as often wrong as it is right. Ten to two is an overwhelming majority, but it proved overwhelmingly wrong. Reason chased faith from the field, and left the decision to wait fatally flawed.

At Kadesh, we may be standing very near the place where the people of God took their first vote. The majority were as wrong there in the wilderness about Canaan as they were centuries later in the courtyard of Pilate about Jesus. They refused God's promise; and by choosing Kadesh over Canaan, they refused the chance to be in the purpose of God exactly like that choice they made later in choosing Barabbas over Jesus.

Here is the peril, always the peril, of pinning matters of the spirit onto public opinion polls. This talk-show morality abroad in the land today based on how many people do it, how many people find it satisfying, how many people feel good about it, is the most terribly demonic moral force loose in this country. The majority is always the majority, but as often as not in matters of the spirit the majority is wrong.

Faith and conscience must frequently follow the road less traveled, and free spirits following God must never forget that. Hopefully, Numbers will help us to learn that lesson.

Another lesson is this. The people of God are always accepting for themselves operational images. Listen to Num. 13:33: "We seemed to ourselves like grasshoppers." No wonder they wandered in the wilderness. They had left a million heads, but they lost a million hearts. To be the people of God, you've gotta have heart!

When God's people lose their proper vision of God, they lose their proper vision of themselves. Their operational images, the forces, the energies that fuel their lives get all out of focus. They forget who they are and, worse still, they forget whose they are.

But God is never defeated by the failure of human instruments. Numbers is the story of a failing people under the mastery of a succeeding God.

God's people, with their grasshopper complex, postponed God's purpose at Kadesh, but they could never finally confound it or prevent it.

In our hometown we are exactly where they were here. Today is the first day of the rest of our lives too. We can take the energy of our lives and decide where we are going to spend it, right now. We can grasp our one fistful of sand left in the hourglass of our days and decide where we are going to pile that sand, right here.

James Russell Lowell said it for us as he did for all of those before us: "Once to every man and nation comes the moment to decide."

What we do in our crises spiritually depends on whether we see our difficulties in the light of God, or whether we see God in the light of our difficulties.

At Kadesh they saw Canaan looming larger than they saw God. They waited. Most of them died in the wilderness. They never claimed their land of promise.

This was Israel's challenge at Kadesh. It is our challenge where we live. Today is the day to decide things spiritually. There are some in this very room sitting in these very pews who have determined one of these days to get your life lined up with the purpose of God—planning to do it one time or another; planning to become a part of a church family, like this family, one time or another.

Numbers shouts with a megaphone to you: "Today is the time to decide, no matter what others are deciding around you. It is the time to decide the purpose of God for your life." We do not have 40 years.

Remember Alice in Wonderland? The White Queen had issued an edict. In her kingdom there would be jam and bread yesterday, and there would be jam and bread tomorrow, but there would be no jam and bread today. So, the children in the White Queen's kingdom never enjoyed jam and bread.

I think that is the way the devil works with all of us. There will be this tomorrow, there will be this yesterday, but if you crash through and make the "this" God has got for you to happen in your heart, it will have to be today.

Have you ever noted what Jesus' first public word was in the Gospel of Luke? Here it is: "Today this scripture is fulfilled in your hearing" (Luke 4:21). That is the Lord's first public word of ministry—*today*.

It is no accident that Luke records that as our Lord's first word. That would have kept the Hebrews from disaster at Kadesh. They could have claimed the promise of God—*today*. We can claim the promises of God—*today*. Amen.

February 26, 1995

DEUTERONOMY

The second time around
Deuteronomy 1:1; 5:1-5; 6:4-9; 7:7-8; 10:12-13; 30:6; 34:5-6, 9

E*lle ha-debarim*—"These are the words." Thus begins the fifth book in our Bible. What we call Deuteronomy, our Jewish friends call *'elle ha-debarim*—"these are the words."

Why do we call our book Deuteronomy? It is because the translators of the Septuagint were impressed that these 34 chapters were the law the second time around. So they named it *Deutero* (second) *Nomos* (law)—"a second law."

Thus the first four books in the Bible's law library—Genesis, Exodus, Leviticus, and Numbers—are Torah, Volume I. Deuteronomy is Torah, Volume II.

The book of Deuteronomy does not add anything to our flow of holy history, that flow which we began in our journey through the Bible with Genesis and Exodus. Instead, Deuteronomy constitutes a sort of chronological leap.

To set the table for Deuteronomy, we are catapulted forward into the middle of 2 Kings—seven Old Testament books down the way on our journey.

Listen: "And Hilkiah, the high priest said, 'I have found the book of the law in the house of the Lord'" (2 Kgs. 22:8). Now, most students of scripture agree that the book Hilkiah found in the temple was our book of Deuteronomy. He had found this scroll of the Torah written much earlier but somehow lost.

This lost second law came at a very critical time for Judah. It was 621 B.C., and the people's religious fortunes were at a low ebb.

Evil Manassah and his son, Amon, had just completed a 50-year-long despotic administration. They were puppets of Assyria. Assyrians did not like Jews then anymore than Iraqis like Kurds now. The sword had fallen on the necks of many a holy man in Judah.

Then Josiah ascended to the throne. He was eight years old when he was crowned king about 640 B.C. For 31 years this impressionable boy-king ruled in Judah.

Hilkiah's discovery of the ancient scroll, our book of Deuteronomy, made a profound impact upon the people and on the king. It led to widespread reform, renewal, and revival.

Although there was backsliding after Josiah's death at age 39, the Hebrews had renewed their faith. They had gotten some moral backbone into their spirits, and they were ready for the challenge of the Babylonian exile that came only 35 years later in 586 B.C.

Deuteronomy's original work was done. It was the work to trigger revival, renewal, reform, and a return to the religious roots of the nation 600 years before Jesus was born. Like old Deuteronomy, that venerable cat in the Broadway musical hit *Cats*, our book of Deuteronomy has lived several lives.

Deuteronomy is a well-organized book. It is a summary of the entire Torah—the law of Moses. These 34 chapters consist of six separate divisions. These six discourses fall into three groups. The first two are retrospective: they ask us to look back at the law. The second two are introspective: they ask us to look inside at the law. The third two are prospective: they ask us to look ahead at the horizons of the law.

As the scroll of Deuteronomy summarizes the Torah, so the man, Moses, personalizes the progressive dealings of God with these people and with us.

Do you want a human commentary on the text of Deuteronomy? Then, here it is in the Old Testament, Deut. 34:10: "And there has not arisen a prophet since in Israel like Moses, whom the Lord knew face to face." In the New Testament it is in John's prologue of his gospel, in chapter 1, verse 17: "For the law was given through Moses, but grace and truth came through Jesus Christ."

Moses is as much an incarnation of the first five books of our Old Testament as Jesus is an incarnation of the first four books of our New Testament.

Let's review. While still an infant, Moses' life was risked to the Nile River as an act of faith to save him by his mother. The pharaoh's policy of genocide was aborted. Moses' cradle of reeds was pulled out by a relative of Ramses. He was reared in the court of Egypt while being nursed by his own slave mother. His earliest insight into the purpose of God for these people and for him came through those stories that his slave mother told him when she sang him off to sleep.

Educated among Israel's royalty, young Moses soon saw that the forms of pharaoh's religion had to be purified by the substance of Abraham's faith.

Then, for years on the back side of the desert in Midian, Moses experienced the presence of the God of his fathers in the sights and sounds of the barren wastes, in mountains and plains, calms and storms, stars and stones.

At last, from the midst of a solitary scrub bush afire with a glory he had never seen before, Moses learned God's name: "I am that I am," God said. There, too, he received his commission: Moses was to set these slave people free!

Back in Egypt, sparring with the power structure, he learned that God's glory is not alone God's power, but also God's goodness.

Force and ethics: these are the twin ways of the Lord that combined to bring about the showdown and the release.

There followed another 40 years of wilderness wandering. During this time Moses was the leader of a freshly-freed slave people, struggling to become a nation—a holy nation, a redemptive nation, a people who knew God's name.

Finally, out of the interface between the people he knew and the God he knew, Moses delivered these six discourses that we call the second law, Deuteronomy. These discourses repeat all of the former facts of the law in Genesis, Exodus, Leviticus, and Numbers. They really are the Torah a second time around.

Yet, through them runs a new thread. They sound a new note. It is the note of love. Do not think this to be mere imagination. The word love appears only one time in the entire book of Exodus (15:13): "You have led this people in your steadfast love."

The word love appears only one time in the entire book of Leviticus (19:18): "You must love your neighbor as yourself."

The word love is a lonely stranger in the first four books of the law, but not so in Deuteronomy. Here the landscape has changed. Read these 34 chapters, underscore every time you see the word love, and you will be amazed. You will find it 22 times in Deuteronomy.

This scroll virtually screams out one overwhelming conviction. The conviction is this: God is law, and love is the way God rules us. God is love, and law is the way God loves us. God's laws are expressions of God's love, and our obedience to God's laws express our love for God.

Deuteronomy takes us near to the heart of a throbbing New Testament revelation. That revelation is this: the real cure for our sins is not punishment, but forgiveness. God longs far more to forgive our sins than to punish them. Punishment is the effect of law on sin. Forgiveness is the effect of love on sin. The real evidence of forgiveness is our obedience in love to law.

Mark again this Deuteronomic affirmation: God's laws are expressions of God's love.

To make a human being and put that human being down in this moral universe without some rules, some parameters for being human, would be a guarantee to destroy that human being because we humans are finite. We are creatures. We are made for homage. We must have direction. Without parameters, we perish.

God loves us enough to show us through laws how we are to live in God's kind of world. That is what Deuteronomy is telling us.

Our obedience to God's law is our expression for God's love. Not duty, not fear, not guilt, not gain, nothing but love ought to motivate you and me as we subject our lives to God's law. We are forever rebels until we love God enough to lay down our arms.

God's law, like God's love, is both stern and tender. It will not let us go. In God's kind of world our behavior and God's laws are meant to coincide. When they do, there is blessing. When they do not, there is curse.

All is love! All is law! But love cannot be commanded. You cannot command one to love one. Obedience cannot be guaranteed. That is the glory and that is the agony of our fifth book, Deuteronomy.

It required the person of Jesus Christ, his life of obedience, his death at Golgotha to fulfill and perfect this appeal. This law, the second time around, is doing what Paul told us the law always did: It is a "*paidagogos*," a schoolmaster, turning us over to Christ.

What exactly, then, is the message of Deuteronomy when it is delivered to our address today? The message of it, though a bit complex to be honest, boils down to one sentence. The entire message of the law, the second time around, is summarized in 6:4-5: "Hear, O Israel, the Lord our God is one Lord; and you shall love the Lord your God with all your heart, and with all your soul, and with all your might."

Our Jewish friends call that the *Shema* because the first word in it is "hear"— *Shema*. It is as pertinent in the wilderness of our county right now as it ever was in the wilderness of Kadesh-Barnea a long time ago. "Hear, O Greensboro, the Lord our God is one Lord; and you shall love the Lord your God with all your heart, and with all your soul, and with all your might!"

That is how Jesus summarized the entire law and the prophets when they asked him later to tell them in a sentence what it said. Jesus also helped us to understand the gist of the Deuteronomic revelation. He did it for us in the Sermon on the Mountain, Matt. 6:24: "No man can serve two lords, two masters, for either he will hate the one and love the other, or he will be devoted to the one and despise the other. You cannot serve God and any other lord."

Here our Lord Jesus Christ probes to the very heart of our current incompatibility. He underscores for us in this computer age one screaming mathematical contradiction. When it comes to the matter of finding for our lives a redeeming mastery, a cohesive mastery, here is the rule: "One plus one equals zero." That is not mathematically correct, but it is spiritually, deuteronomically, and gospel correct.

"One plus one equals zero." To have two masteries is really to have no mastery at all. To be ruled by two sets of competing values and loyalties is to be ruled, finally, by no value or loyalty at all.

In his application of this Deuteronomic truth, Jesus Christ staked down some rules that apply right here, right now.

Rule one: It is impossible for you to have no master at all. Suppose some one of you says, "I am free. I will live my life any way I want." You are right. You are free. But you are free only to choose a master. You are not so created that you are free to live without any mastery at all. Not one of us can live without a first love—a supreme loyalty—a lord, if you will.

Here, our modern science helps us. We have learned that everything from an atom to a star in this world God has made—the smallest thing to the largest thing—all have to have a center, a core, a nucleus, around which everything revolves. Our most violent reactions in the physical world are caused by matter seeking other centers, other cores, other focal points. That is what happens in the splitting of an atom, and that is what happens in the exploding of a star. Ask the *Endeavor* astronauts, when they get home in a few days, what they see happening out there when matter refuses to live without a mastery, an organizing central core.

You and I are like that. We must be centered in something or someone; else, all sanity is lost. Our freedom, our sanity stem from our obedience to a worthy mastery.

Security, adventure, mastery, recognition, and belonging: these are the ingredients for being human. We are made for a mastery; a mastery is a must.

Rule two: It is impossible to have two masters. Personality is made for homage and also for wholeness; homage that divides us destroys us. The goal in mastery is unity, health, wholeness, cohesion—or else life is destroyed. It blows apart. It comes loose at the seams.

Jesus has made a comment on our lives as they are when he said: "You cannot serve two masters." That is to say that you cannot walk east and west at the same time. It is impossible.

It is a quiet statement of fact that a man may divide his time, his talent, his treasure, his energy, even his mind, but no one who is human can divide his soul. That is the point of this ancient Shema. "You shall love the Lord your God with all your heart, and all your soul, and all your might."

Do you remember John Bunyan's famous "Mr. Facing—Both Ways"? He is one of the most tragic persons in all of literature. In him, good and evil are not struggling in mortal combat. They are rather embracing each other and walking feebly together nowhere. He was a Mr. Anything who cheated himself into becoming a Mr. Nothing. Like the spent shell of a circada plucked from the trunk of a tree, he was a body without an insides to it.

When Jesus said, "You cannot serve two masters," he was telling us exactly how it is. You and I can spend the only life we will ever live battering up against that reality only to discover too little, too late that it is inviolate.

It is true, Deuteronomy tells us, that in the dawn of history we cannot live without a master; we cannot have two masters.

And rule three: It is absolutely imperative that we have one master. The kind and quality of this master is all-important to us.

Carl Jung is an internationally known psychiatrist. He is not particularly religious, but he is professional. Everyone who knows him respects him. Here is something he has said: "During the past 30 years, people from all over the world have consulted me. Among all my patients there has not been one whose problem in the final resort was not that of finding a faith outlook on life (a mastery, if you will). It is safe to say that every one of my patients fell ill because they had lost that which vital religion gives, and none of them has ever really been healed who did not regain this faith outlook."

The riddle of our lives, during this bottleneck of the 20th century, is how do we find wholeness. The mastery of the Lord Jesus Christ, Deuteronomy tells us and Jesus tells us, is the resolution of that riddle. Augustine said it: "Thou hast made us for thyself, O Lord, and our hearts are restless until they rest in thee."

A thousand things we may do today are here today and gone tomorrow. But this one thing we can do, and it will last: You and I can submit to the Lordship of Jesus and love God with all our heart and soul and mind and strength, and we will find wholeness bound by our obedience to the Lord Jesus Christ.

That law becomes our first love, and Jesus' love becomes the first law of our lives. Amen.

March 12, 1995

JOSHUA

Surgery, not murder
Joshua 1:1-2, 10-11; 2:1, 23-24; 5:1; 10:40-42; 13:1, 7; 24:14-15, 29

The sixth book of our Bible bears the name of the citizen-soldier whose exploits punctuate every page of it. His name was Joshua—the same name in the Old Testament as Jesus is in the New Testament. The name means "deliverer." And deliverance is indeed the theme of these 24 chapters that describe a highly compacted account of the invasion of Canaan, Israel's land of promise.

The Torah, that is the Law, closes with Deuteronomy, but not the flow of holy history. Historically, Joshua moves that flow forward about five decades.

In these chapters Joshua, Israel's military leader, continues and completes what Moses, Israel's religious leader, began. This is a book about possession according to promise. It falls into three sections: invasion, conquest, and partition. It is a violent book full of wars and filled with blood. Thousands die on its pages.

One thing for sure, in order to fashion Israel as the instrument of redemption for this whole world, God's people are accomplishing in these texts some awesome and unusual acts of moral surgery. Yet, that is the understanding of God celebrated here 1,000 years before Christ. Were these wars surgery, or were these wars murder?

Consider this: On one street in Greensboro a man slashes an abdomen open to remove a life-threatening tumor. The patient dies. We call that surgery. On another street in Greensboro a man slashes open an abdomen out of a fit of rage. The victim dies. We call that murder.

These wars of possession were terrible surgery, but they were surgery, according to the Bible. For here, moral tumors were being cut out of history so that the healthy part might survive. A cancer half-treated is one not treated at all. So these Hebrews, like some terrible moral huntsmen, possessed their land of promise on their way to becoming God's instruments of redemption.

In Joshua the surgery hurts to heal, to redeem, and ultimately to make healthy all the nations of the earth. And the chief surgeon, Joshua, stays scrubbed and ready as he sets up field hospitals from Dan to Beersheba. Look at him. There Joshua stands, a combination of our Washington, Lee, Grant, McArthur, Eisenhower, Schwarzkopf, and Powell—all wrapped into one person.

Remember that he, too, was born of slave parents in Egypt. He was perhaps not even a teenager at the time of the Exodus. Still a youth when he and Caleb alone of the

12 spies were sent to spy out Jericho, they brought that report: "Let's go do it now." He had been Moses' military leader during 30 years of aimless wandering in the wilderness. Now, as commander-in-chief of Israel's fledgling armies, at Moses' death Joshua faced a chance to do what he advised 40 years before. And remarkably, he did it. Canaan was possessed by the people, Israel.

Joshua holds a megaphone to his mouth and shouts to us. Here is his message: "Our faith is our acceptance of Yahweh's standard of holiness—the God of Israel, the God of Jesus, the God of us all."

Now what does that mean? Let's stop and look and listen for a moment, especially there in the twilight of Joshua's career. On the last page of the last chapter of the book that bears his name, he is speaking to his countrymen not long before his death.

Let's listen in to Joshua 24:15: "And if you are unwilling to serve the Lord, choose this day whom you will serve, whether the gods your fathers served in the region beyond the river or the gods of the Amorites in whose land you now dwell; but as for me and my house we will serve the Lord."

Get the picture: Here were a people who in a brief span of time had undergone a profound transition. They had left Egypt; traversed the Sinai; crossed the Jordan; conquered Jericho, Ai, and Gibeon; divided the territory; forged a loose coalition of the tribes; and begun to settle down into a totally new lifestyle in Canaan.

They possessed their promised land, but alas their promised land possessed them as well. In less than half a century during Joshua's lifetime, these people Israel passed through the first fundamental change that has marked the developing history of all humankind.

Here in Canaan these food gatherers became food growers. These slaves, who had never been free to govern themselves, would struggle along learning what it meant to do that. These wandering herdsmen would become farmers and vineyard keepers. These acquainted with the wilderness would now learn the ways of the fertile countryside. These nomads who had relied on their flocks would now settle down and rely on their crops. These who had been guided by a religious leader, Moses, would now know the excitement of being led by a military leader, Joshua. These who had never had a king but Yahweh would soon be gripped by a new nationalism that demanded another kind of king—one like Saul.

In the twilight of his days Joshua, the old warrior, saw the most far-reaching impact of all from Canaan. Canaan had impacted Israel's heart.

Hear Joshua pleading with his people: "Choose this day whom you will serve." You see, the people thought they had to get some new gods to match their new situation. Here is faith asking an ageless question: Is my old God sufficient for my new lifestyle? Can Yahweh grow corn? Can God lead armies as well as flocks? Can God speak here on the farm and in the vineyard, as well as there in the desert?

Many in Israel were honestly afraid that Yahweh could not do that. So they began to worship deities dictated by their new circumstance. Alongside Yahweh, these people began to worship the gods of Canaan.

What exactly were these gods of Canaan? They were projections of the Canaanite culture; that is all they were. Canaan, you see, was an agricultural civilization, an agrarian economy. They lived off the land. Thus, their gods were projections of their culture and their economy.

They were gods of fertility, life, and growth. The Baal and Ashtoreth—male and female—were agricultural deities. These gods could be enlisted to inject fertility into man and beast and seed and soil. They were gods that could be manipulated and controlled in the best interest of the people who worshiped them.

So Israel proved immensely human. They dared not run the risk of missing out on the benefits of these gods also. So they set up their idols—Baal and Ashtoreth—and they began to worship these gods made in the image of the people and the culture of Canaan.

Later, Israel's psalmist would sing: "This is the day the Lord has made." But for now, in Canaan, God's people sang: "This is the Lord the day has made."

It took these old Hebrews six long centuries after Joshua—years of frustration and conquest and prophetic preaching, even an exile—to teach them that whoever you are and wherever you are, there is but one God, and Yahweh is God's name.

But that was so long ago, back there, back then. What does all this mean for us here now? Well, it does apply. For you see, something has happened to us very much like that which happened to them. These Hebrews made one superlative bequest to us Christians. That was their exalted, prophetic, monotheistic concept of God—transmitted through Abraham, Isaac, Jacob, Moses, Joshua, Isaiah, Jeremiah, Hosea, Amos, and countless others. For 1,600 years their concept prevailed in our Christianity.

Then, a little more than 200 years ago, in northwestern Europe, with England leading the way, something began to happen. Our civilization began to experience the first tremor of the industrial revolution. A new age dawned for us just as it had dawned for them in ancient Israel. A race of people, who had been food growers for all these centuries, now became machine makers. Agriculture gave way to industry.

The Christian church was plunged, kicking and screaming, into an entirely new world—an asphalt, concrete, stainless steel wilderness where science was king and technology was prime minister.

Over here, across our Jordan, across our oceans in our new land, a new day has dawned. Farms have been replaced by factories. Food growing has given way to tool making. Rural life has been swallowed up in urban life. Agriculture has given way to industry. Until now, we have made machines like men; and we have made men like machines.

We, like Joshua's ancient Israel, have found that our entire way of life has changed. The landscape is different. And we, like they, have begun to ask, "Is our old God sufficient for our new situation?"

In an age when force and speed and finance and information are reverenced by so very many, is there any wonder that the idea of the sovereign God and Father of the Lord Jesus Christ has lost some luster? After all, what would Jesus know about cyberspace and computers, about space shuttles and information highways?

So, what have we done? Exactly what Joshua's Israel did. To our peril, we have begun to appropriate for ourselves new gods dictated by our new lifestyles.

What is more, these gods, like the gods of Canaan, are but projections of our own culture—the sum total of our own selfish interests enlarged into divine proportions and projected onto a cosmic screen.

In the midst of all our tool-making nowadays, we have fallen into a basic confusion. The scriptures say: "We belong to God." But we moderns read that to mean: "God belongs to us." Worship starts with us, not with God—with the creature, not the Creator.

So, we busy ourselves making for ourselves gods bearing our image—completely manageable, neatly packageable, and efficiently marketable. *This is the Lord the day has made.*

The tragedy of modem man's 1990 model "god" is this: he cannot save us from ourselves because we ourselves have made him. The mark of our manufacturer is upon him. He bears our patent, our copyright. He is "user friendly."

He is a "god" without judgment, who brings people without sin into a kingdom without requirement, under the administration of a Christ without a cross.

Our "gods" do not show us anything about ourselves because we have made them just like us. We want them to please us and to make us feel good, and they do. But best of all, these gods we have made will shut one eye and approve us just any old way.

So, the ringing mandate of Joshua comes home to us here: "Choose this day whom you will serve, but as for me and my house we will serve the Lord."

Paul Scherer has summed up what Joshua meant: "Genuine worship happens when we bring the gods we have made to confront the God who has made us."

So the issue this morning across our Jordan is exactly the same as the issue in those days across Joshua's Jordan: the people of God or the gods of the people?

See the contemporary model man. He can penetrate the jungles like an elephant, encompass the desert like a lizard, fly through the air like an eagle, and traverse the waters faster than a fish. He can even make tracks on the moon like a cosmic citizen, and live on a space platform out there in the cosmic cold.

Modem man can do just about everything except live on this earth like a man as he was intended to live. At every turn he destroys himself and his fellows with his egocentricity.

We moderns, like those ancients, were made for homage. We were made for mastery by the Creator who made us. Which will our master be: the gods we have made or the God who has made us?

Joshua called Israel to that choice. And Joshua calls you and me to that choice too. Amen.

March 19, 1995

JUDGES

A not-so-new morality
Judges 1:1; 2:10-13, 16-17; 21:25

When I say Judges, what comes to your mind? Who comes to your mind? Some of you think of Judge Lance Ito and the O. J. Simpson trial. He is in the news a lot nowadays. Others of you when you hear the word Judges think about courtrooms, juries, trials, witnesses, verdicts, and sentences. That is alright because judges do mean that to us.

But when we use the word Judges as applied to the title of the seventh book in our Bible, the word means something else entirely. There the judges were warriors, priests, rulers, or deliverers who led Israel between the death of Joshua and the career of Saul. They were civil, religious, and military chieftains in command of Israel's separated and scattered tribes. In peacetimes they settled disputes between the people, and in times of war they led their tribes against their enemies.

We can picture Judges a lot like the American frontier in the days when Native Americans, the Indians, occupied those territories—vast areas of land peopled by tribes here and tribes there, disconnected, disjointed, confederated at best, each one with a chieftain. That is how it was in this particular period of the history of Israel.

These 21 chapters chronicle Israel's dark ages. These are the years when that fledgling nation went into a tunnel. The people of God were in their land of promise, but there was little promise in them. They had wandered long enough in the physical wilderness at Kadesh. Now they would wander three times as long in the spiritual wilderness of Canaan.

The unknown author of Judges is really an editor. He collects records produced by each of the tribes in their territories, and he then weaves them together into the scroll that we call Judges. The story is rough-and-tumble. Morally, it is strictly downhill. The people of God are on a slippery slope, careening spiritually out of control.

They are not much better off politically or economically or militarily than they are spiritually. You see, these Hebrews entered Canaan at the dividing line between the Bronze Age and the Iron Age. While everyone else had iron, these former slaves from Egypt only had bronze.

What they could do by sheer numbers and energy they did. But anyone fighting iron with bronze soon reaches a limit to conquest.

Israel in Canaan quickly found this out the hard way. For example, in Judges, chapter 1, there are five specific places where we are told that five of the tribes failed to take impregnable cities in their territories:

- The tribe of Benjamin did not take Jerusalem.
- The tribe of Manasseh did not take Bethshean.
- The tribe of Ephraim did not take Gezer.
- The tribe of Zebulon did not take Kitron.
- The tribe of Asher did not take Zidon.

So, clinging precariously to the highlands, disunited internally, technologically backward, the Israelites hung on for dear life. Fortunately, they did not have to face any great empires. Egypt, to the south, had just as well been on another planet. They had their hands full internally. To the east, Assyria was rattling sabers, but was not yet a world power.

In this gap of history, between Egypt's agony and Assyria's coming glory, it took all the Hebrews could do to fight off those petty tribes on their western half of the Fertile Crescent. This was the shape of the Mideast conflict 3,000 years ago.

Occasionally, one of the 12 tribes would gain some measure of freedom. Whenever that happened, it was through the activity of one of these judges.

Twelve such judges ruled over the tribes of Israel between the conquest of Canaan and the establishment of the monarchy under Saul. It might appear, on first reading, that each of the judges held sway over all of Israel, and that the period of the judges followed one after the other consecutively, but that was not the case.

Read these 21 chapters carefully, and you note that no one judge ever ruled all 12 tribes. At best each one ruled a tribe or two, and they did not rule consecutively. While one judge was doing this or that somewhere in the land of Canaan, another judge was doing similarly someplace else.

So, the period of the judges put together was about 125-150 years—at best a century and a half—not the total of years that you get if you add up all of the judges' periods of leadership. If you add them all up, they total 410 years for these 12 judges.

Joshua died around 1150 B.C. Saul became king of Israel about 1028 B.C. So, here in this time warp—this gap—was the period of the judges. These were the years when the lights went out all over Israel.

The book of Judges has three parts to it: (1) an introduction, chapters 1 and 2; (2) a center section with the careers of the judges and their exploits outlined, chapters 3-16; and (3) an appendix, chapters 17-21.

In the midsection, chapters 3-16, five minor judges are mentioned, along with seven major ones. Some of the minor judges are introduced in just one sentence or one paragraph. These are the judges whose names are Shamgar, Tola, Jair, Ibzan, Elon, and Abdon. But the exploits of seven leaders are told in more elaborate detail. These judges are named Othniel, Ehud, Deborah, Gideon, Abimelech, Jephthah, and probably the best-known one of all to us, Samson.

The midsection of the book of Judges has seven cycles in it. Each cycle follows the same course. In fact, there is just one refrain in the entire book of Judges, and that refrain is played 12 times. Every judge has the same song surrounding him or her.

Hear the sad music as it surrounds the first judge, Othniel, who is introduced in chapter 3: "And the people of Israel did evil and served Baal and Ashtoreth" (v. 7). "And the Lord sold them into the hand of the King of Mesopotamia, and the people of Israel served him eight years" (v. 8). "But when the people of Israel cried to the Lord, the Lord raised up a deliverer, Othniel, the son of Kenaz, Caleb's younger brother" (v. 9).

Over and over and over, 12 times, this is the sad song heard on the pages of Judges.

There are always the same three stanzas to it: (1) The people sin by serving other gods. (2) The people are punished by being turned over to foreign powers. (3) The people repent, and a judge is sent by God to deliver them.

Sin, punishment, deliverance: that is the music of the night played again and again throughout these dark chapters. It is a song about a not-so-new morality.

What we have here in Judges are some pages snatched right out of a people's spiritual autobiography. It is a checkered set of pages. Let us look at them:

- Page One: Religious Apostasy—The people of God worship the gods of the people.

- Page Two: Political Disorganization—Civil strife gives the whole land a fever.

- Page Three: Social Chaos—The social structures come apart at the seams, and the society goes into a delirious dance of death.

- Page Four: The Return of Faith—People come back to their senses, and the people come back to their God.

Repentance, faith, deliverance: that which was gone with the wind is built back again 12 times in these pages. In this scroll of Judges punishment is severe, but punishment is remedial.

Look at the book of Judges and note how God fitted the tools to the task—12 tools—12 leaders—12 judges at a particular time when the task demanded a particular kind of leadership.

There was Shamgar, that rough, tumble, rugged hill country hero who accomplished a one-man revolution.

There was Deborah, a woman of ice and fire.

There was Barak, a strategist and a fighter.

There was Gideon, who found that courage really is fear that has said its prayers.

There was Jephthah, a man with both iron and sand in his soul.

And there was Samson, a rugged folk hero, a nazarite, who struggled more with Delilah than he did with the Philistines. He found it harder to deliver himself up to God than to deliver his people from their enemies.

So, the truth dawns on the pages of Judges. God was abroad in the land during Israel's dark ages allowing those people to become their own executioners, selecting deliverers from such strange places, and showing then as now that the culture cannot produce faith. Do you believe that? The culture cannot produce in itself faith.

But that happened so long ago, you say. That happened so far away, you say. How in the world and what in the world does Judges have to say for you and for me in our time?

It might seem to some that Judges is outdated, outmoded, and dead. But that is not so. This is one of the Bible's most loaded books, and we are looking right down the barrel of its moral message this crisp spring Sunday. Hold on, and I'll show you what I mean.

The first verse in the first chapter of Judges reads like this: "After the death of Joshua the people of God inquired of the Lord."

The last verse in the last chapter of the book of Judges—chapter 21, verse 25—reads like this: "In those days there was no king in Israel, and every man did what was right in his own eyes."

That, my friends, is a "new morality" 3,000 years ago. Let us acknowledge that the writer of Judges just might be a monarchist, accounting for the chaos in Israel by the fact that they had no king. But there is still another side to it.

That other side, that dark underbelly, is the sad spectacle of the pilgrimage of these people spiritually. They began in chapter 1, verse 1 inquiring of the Lord about their lifestyles. In 21 chapters they had gone to "doing what was right in their own eyes." That, my friends, is a long way downhill from Moral Mountain at Sinai. That is a slippery, moral slope.

How do you explain that? How do people go from chapter 1, verse 1, inquiring of the Lord to chapter 21, verse 25, everyone doing what everyone wants to do everyone's own way?

The writer of Judges tells us exactly how that can happen in a society. He tells us in chapter 2, verse 10: "And all Joshua's generation were gathered to their fathers; and there arose another generation who did not know the Lord or the work which he had done for Israel."

Do you get that picture? Do you see what happened in Israel? Joshua's generation had been so busy winning the land, building a country, that they neglected to rear a generation to win the faith and put any moral backbone into the country they built. They gave their children Canaan, but not the conscience to possess it. They left their children things, but they did not leave their children values.

That, my friends, is the effect of materialism upon a society whether in the 11th century B.C. or the 20th century A.D. Blame-placers, beware! There are two sides to this story: on the one side there is an older generation who pawned off on their youth a second-hand, second-rate preparation for their lives. But on the other hand there is a younger generation who within themselves decided that their "me, myself, and I" ethic would not poison the people with unbridled pleasure. But poison the people that ethic did.

The old folks knew better, but they did not tell the young people about it. The young folks had no compass, no rudder, no sail but themselves. In time, the sin of "just anything goes so long as everyone does it, and it makes us all feel good" plunged ancient Israel into a moral quagmire.

"They inquired of the Lord" (1:1). "They did what was right in their own sight" (21:25). That is the awesome generation gap chronicled by our book of Judges, and it is the same gap I fear that is chronicled every day now by the local newspaper.

You know what I honestly think? I believe that in our time some people refuse to inquire of the Lord in matters of moral behavior because they actually believe that God is against pleasure. But you see, God made pleasure possible when God made people and the world. In the act of creation, in the dawn of history, God set up a world in which people could enjoy themselves and each other.

Let us set the record straight: We inquire of God and find that certain behavior between persons and by individuals is a forbidden behavior. It is not because God is some sort of "old fogey" or "old meany" who does not want us to have any fun. It is exactly the opposite. It is because God wants us to enjoy the richest, fullest, highest happiness.

But hear this: God knows how we are made, how we function. God knows the world, how the world is made, and how the world functions. God knows how morals fit into the picture and turn us into humans instead of into animals. In short, we inquire of God to find out how life works in a moral universe. The shortest definition of Christian morals you will ever get may be this one: "It works!"

That is not a pragmatic form for a world gone crazy. It works—Christian morals work. That is an honest confession of a good person trying to live right in a moral universe. It works! When persons do not live like that, it just will not work.

Have you ever had a lightbulb to burn out? Perhaps one of those in a string of bulbs around the mirror in your bathroom? You bought a new one, brought it home, and tore up the package it was in. You threw away the sales slip. With a great deal of delight you were going to screw it in, only to find that the bulb you bought had one of those large fittings where you screw it in instead of one of the small fittings. You can spend all the time you care to spend trying to get the electricity to flow, but it will not work. The reason: it is a wrong connection. That is the way it is in this world.

God knows how things are connected morally, spiritually. You and I can connect with those things and enjoy the blessings and benefits and pleasures of this life forever. But when we refuse to connect aright morally, everything goes dark and stays dark.

God knows that the ultimate evil is to love things and to use persons. Sooner or later our exploitation, whether socially or sexually or economically or religiously, makes us wind up in this moral universe with hell on our hands. That is precisely what happened with this deadly "new morality" from the back side of Judges occasioned by every man doing what was right in his own sight.

Not so long ago, one of the editors of one of the weekly news magazines told of receiving a small "assemble it yourself" instrument from a major mail-order house. He tried to put that thing together but got frustrated, could not quite do it, could not make all the pieces fit. He found this message in the box: "If all else fails, follow the directions."

That is the message of Judges. For you and for me, that is the message of these 21 chapters. God has made us. God has sent along moral messages from the manufacturer. And the pieces of our lives simply will not fall into place until we follow those directions. The good news is this: In Jesus Christ, God has sent us more than directions; God has sent us the designer himself. Watch Jesus and we learn how life works. Surrender to Jesus and we have help from the manufacturer. Amen.

March 26, 1995

RUTH

Overcoming prejudice and poverty
Ruth 1:1-9, 16-18, 22; 2:1-2, 8-11; 3:1-5, 8-13; 4:3-6, 13, 17

Never measure the value of a book by either its size or its cover. The eighth book of our Bible is a short four-chapter tract. Its story fills less than three and a half pages; its message fills the whole world with hope.

The book is named Ruth—after its heroine. It is the only book in our Bible, besides Esther, that bears a woman's name.

It is set in the time of the Judges, but students of scripture generally agree that it was written much later than that—perhaps in the fifth century B.C., after the return of the Jews from the Exile. It was certainly written sometime after the career of David. Reading it, one gets the distinct idea that the writer is looking back at a time past from a considerable distance.

Here is historical reminiscence at its best—not fiction, but fact; not nostalgia, but vision.

The story opens like this: "In the days when the judges ruled there was a famine in the land" (1:1).

Upon reading that first sentence it would be easy to conclude that this is just another tale of the times. Some might even suggest that Ruth could just as well be a part of the book of Judges.

But not so! This is not just another earlier version of *Gone With the Wind*, a story detailing a cross-section of the culture.

The book of Judges is uniformly tough, bloody, smelly—almost barbaric. It depicts the growing pains of a people struggling out of the Stone Age toward civilization.

The book of Ruth, in contrast, is tender, charming, pastoral—set in the placid countryside of Bethlehem during the April barley harvest.

In the Hebrew Old Testament the book of Ruth is included in the third division, called "The Writings." But in our canon the book has been drawn forward into the historical section and placed in its appropriate position in the revelation story immediately following the book of Judges.

There is high drama in these four chapters. The script bristles with excitement. Review the little story that packs such a big wallop:

The drama begins with a famine that drives a family of Israelites out of their home in Judah. The story is told from a uniquely feminine slant on life.

Elimelech, whose name meant "My God is king," transported his family to Moab—a land foreign to them in every way. There the unexpected happened.

Elimelech died! He did not mean to make his sojourn into Moab so permanent. Going there was but a temporary respite, fulfilling his responsibility to his family for food.

But when his widow, Naomi, returned from the lonely grave site with a young son clinging to each of her cold hands, the whole thing took on a dreadful note of permanence.

The boys grew up and fell in love with two Moabite women, Orpah and Ruth. These were pagan girls, whose family worship of the gods of Moab was so heathen and sordid that it had best not be spoken of in mixed company.

In 10 years the unexpected happened again: both of Naomi's sons died.

So, in our story we are left with three widows: one old, two young—all bereft of their husbands. And women without men in those times were in desperate straits. What's more, these three were strangers in their own house.

Some months passed. News came that things were better in Judah. Her husband, and her hunger, had carried Naomi into Moab. But now there was no reason for her to remain there. Matthew Henry is right: "When constraint ends, choice begins."

So Naomi laid plans to begin the 60-mile journey back home to Bethlehem in Judah. But an Eastern parting by custom never took place within the house. The parting guest was always accompanied for some distance along the road. So the two daughters-in-law went with Naomi to speed her on her way.

In time the lean, tall, aging widow came to a parting place and invited the girls to return to their native Moab. Orpah did indeed kiss Naomi and part from her. The author says in 1:15, "She went back to her people, and to her gods." Poor Orpah, she steps off the Bible's pages into oblivion. We never hear of her again.

But Ruth flatly refused to go. She kissed Naomi and clung to her—her arms locked liked a ring around Naomi's frail frame. Then she said something that still shakes this world and softens the hardest heart:

> Entreat me not to leave you or to return from following you; for where you go I will go, and where you lodge I will lodge; your people shall be my people, and your God my God; where you die I will die, and there will I be buried. May the Lord do so to me and more also if even death parts me from you. (1:16-17)

Ruth made a six-fold resolve: to travel with Naomi anywhere, to live with Naomi anyplace, to accept Naomi's people as her own, to worship Naomi's God, to die with Naomi anytime, and to rest in a common grave with Naomi and under any sod

With these words, Ruth the Moabite stepped into the biblical hall of fame. She went with her mother-in-law to Bethlehem.

In Bethlehem, Ruth met Boaz, a wealthy relative of Naomi's, who was attracted to the girl despite the fact that she was a foreigner. Naomi, in time, arranged matters so that Boaz offered to marry Ruth, in full traditional Jewish style. He became the kinsman-redeemer.

The marriage was consummated, and eventually a son was born. And now comes the real point of the story: "And the women . . . gave (Ruth's son) a name . . . Obed: he is the father of Jesse, the father of David" (4:17).

In other words, Ruth was the great-grandmother of Israel's hero: King David. And through David she was an ancestress of Jesus Christ. Remember: this happened also in Bethlehem of Judea.

So the story is told. But, you say, it's so ancient, so remote, so far from where we live today. Is it? This story speaks an eloquent word to some of the most pressing issues we face right here, right now. It really is a word for us.

Here is an ancient-modern message on how to overcome both prejudice and poverty. So let's listen to Ruth's word about overcoming prejudice, but first a definition:

Prejudice means pre-judgment, or forming an attitude or embracing an opinion before the facts are in. Prejudice means making up your mind beforehand about a person or a situation.

Prejudice is a great time saver. It is born of attitude, nourished by misinformation, and issues in stereotype. All societies, and all of us, have prejudices in some form or degree. Senator George Aiken may be right: "If we were to wake up some morning and find that everyone was the same race, creed, and color, we would find some other causes of prejudice before noon."

Prejudice has deep and tenacious roots in all of us. The causes are myriad. We are prejudiced because we are naturally centered in our own concerns, limited by our information, bound by our environment, wrapped up in our traditions, jealous over status and power, and gripped by our own irrational superstitions.

In biblical language, this means that we are prejudiced because we are sinners against God and our fellow humans.

So much for diagnoses: What's the cure?

Shape in your mind the situation in the book of Ruth: "So, the two of them [Naomi and Ruth] went on until they came to Bethlehem. And when they came to Bethlehem, the whole town was stirred because of them" (1:9).

Imagine their circumstance in loud-mouthed little Bethlehem—1,000 years B.C. Oh how those people could stare and talk—small-town talk. How they could peer out their windows, jump to conclusions, look only on the surface of things, and make up their minds ahead of time.

There they were: two widows—one Jewish and the other Moabite. One was old: weary, worn, marked, lined by so much sorrow over so long a time. The other was young: attractive, foreign, illegal alien, yet displaying an unbelievable fidelity to her mother-in-law.

The Bethlehemites had to ask: "Is this Naomi?" She had changed so much. Their returning friend gave herself a new name, "Marah," which means "Bitterness." She had gone away at the threat of famine. Now she came home looking hungrier than when she left.

But in time the people of Bethlehem did an amazing thing. They looked below the surface of these two lives and accepted them, differences and all! Naomi, the true Jew, and Ruth, the foreigner converted to Judaism, were seen of equal worth in the sight of God.

Now if you think that insight came easy in ancient Israel, you've got another thing coming. That's tougher than getting pro-life and pro-choice together.

But at this very point the big purpose of the little book of Ruth becomes crystal clear. It was written at a time when the Jews, like Naomi, were returning home again from their exile. The exiles were anxious to purify the land of the foreigners who had infiltrated it while they had been away in Babylon. Some of their leaders established a rigid and narrow policy by which all intermarriage with foreigners was forbidden and all who had already married non-Jewish wives had to put them away.

But there were many among the Hebrews who were appalled at such prejudice and the pettiness of such a policy, along with the heartlessness with which it would be enforced.

So, an unknown one of them wrote the book of Ruth as a clarion call to the universality of the love of God. In writing this story the author was inspired by the fact that David was part Moabite in his ancestry. This writer sought to establish for all time that the exclusiveness demanded of the people of God was based on faith—not race or nation. Both Jews and Moabites were Semites.

The real problem with Ruth was a faith problem. She originally worshiped other gods—gods of Moab rather than Yahweh, the God of Israel. When she accepted Naomi's God—the one she had seen at work so profoundly in her life—as her God, then all reasons to exclude her were gone.

The point could not have been made stronger. If Boaz's foreign marriage to Ruth had been forbidden by a petty prejudice, then there would have been no David. Israel would have missed the source of her highest blessing.

The author's point can be pressed even farther. Through this "mixed marriage," God came centuries later to bless Israel and the world through Jesus Christ—of the house of Jesse, of the house of David, of the house of Boaz and Ruth.

How do we overcome prejudice? Whatever its shape or form, prejudice yields to love. Ruth loved Boaz, the man. Boaz loved Ruth, the woman. Surface differences disappeared. Their faith and their love overwhelmed their prejudice.

This past week rocked our world. The bomb in Oklahoma City maimed our grown-ups, killed our children, and made shambles of our federalism and our sense of safety.

But we learned something in those images that have rolled over us from Oklahoma since Wednesday. When the rescuers pulled a baby from the wreckage, it did not matter whether the little face beneath the blood was white, black, yellow, red, or brown. It was one of our children mutilated, violated, dead.

When a faint cry of life was heard in the rubble, it mattered not whose hands clawed away at the debris—black hands, cowboy hands, Indian hands, Hispanic hands, Oriental hands—all joined to rescue fragile life from the ruins.

For one shining moment in Oklahoma City this week we learned that prejudice yields to a higher affection—and the highest of affections is love. In America, when we hurt we help!

Ruth tried to teach us that a long time ago, but it is a lesson that comes hard.

Now, let's listen to Ruth's word about overcoming poverty.

The bony hand of poverty creeps in through all the cracks of this story. Naomi had left Bethlehem because of famine. Ruth came back with her into abject poverty.

But the old Hebrews had made provision for helping their poor. They left a share for the poor to glean in the corners of all their fields. The procedure had come as a commandment from Yahweh.

The hungry, the poor, the destitute—Israel's street people—were expected to come to the fields at harvest time and glean the leftover grain, take it home with them, and use it as their own.

So a principle emerged in ancient Israel. We overcome poverty best by helping poor people help themselves. They did not give their poor a handout, but a hand.

That is how Boaz first helped Naomi and Ruth. The dignity of their own work was preserved. The way was cleared for these poor widows to help themselves in the fields of Boaz. Their energy and their effort were still required. They invested their own sweat equity.

Now it can be said that Ruth went one step further and married the landlord. But that was an exception and not a rule in overcoming poverty.

I read the strangest thing recently. A ranger in Yellowstone National Park said that every year, after tourist season is over and the cold winds and snows come, bears die by the dozens by the side of the roads. The rangers haul off huge loads of them to a common grave.

Do you know why they die? They are still waiting for the handouts from the tourists—the cookies, the candy, the bread. But the tourists have gone—no more effortless help throughout the long, hard winter.

Yet the bears wait, sitting by the roads for food that will never come. So they freeze and die there. Those bears in Yellowstone are sad sights. They have forgotten how to be bears—foraging, fending, finding food for themselves and caves to hibernate in through the winter.

The word from Ruth sounds loud and clear. No one can do poor people's work for them—not and preserve the dignity of their personhood. Poverty is best overcome by giving the poor a corner to glean in.

The poor need things done with them, not things done for them or to them. Any program for fighting poverty—whether government, church, or community—must eventually involve the poor themselves in its planning and in its implementation.

Otherwise, the poor can actually forget how to be human—fall into a false sense of entitlement. If they do not learn how to help themselves, ultimately they will not be helped at all. Whatever else may be done, eventually the poor need a corner to glean in.

If we are to minister effectively with the poor, we must understand the culture of poverty. Just as some persons have inherited wealth, others have inherited poverty.

Poverty has a culture all its own. It is a culture of isolation. The poor are cut off from economic mainstreams. Opportunities are limited. If you do not believe it, try to operate a family of four on $100 a month.

Living in poverty affects the psyche. Some persons have tried to rise above their circumstances so many times, only to find themselves pushed back down, that they have become psychologically immobilized. It does little good to chide them for their lack of initiative. They simply cannot stand another defeat—and frequently resort to alcohol or drugs.

But just as prejudice yields to love, so poverty yields to sensitivity. Economists tells us that the elimination of poverty is a matter of the will. We have the resources to solve the job problem and the bread problem in this world. It remains to be seen whether we have the will.

If we Christians cannot endorse the current programs combating poverty, then we are duty-bound to develop ministries we can endorse. We can ill afford to neglect the poor or to be indifferent to their needs. Jesus Christ keeps our feet to the fire on this issue. Too much of his teaching reaches out to them, for us to ignore the poor, the hungry, the marginalized.

Ruth's message comes on strong. There is hope that we can avoid prejudice and help the poor. There is a mandate that we must! Amen.

April 23, 1995

1 AND 2 SAMUEL

Renewal through disaster

1 Samuel 1:20, 8:4-7, 10:1, 16:11-13, 17:38-40; 2 Samuel 5:34, 12:24, 18:33

The two books of Samuel, coupled with the two books of Kings, tell one continuous story. They constitute the history of the monarchy in Israel—first as a single kingdom, then as a divided one.

Originally, Samuel and Kings were on two long scrolls. The Septuagint translators separated the two scrolls into four. All four—1 Samuel, 2 Samuel, 1 Kings, and 2 Kings—deal with the monarchy. So we could just as well call these books 1 Kings, 2 Kings, 3 Kings, and 4 Kings.

The books of Samuel bear the name of the last judge and the first prophet in Israel—Samuel, from the tribe of Ephraim. He was a reluctant king-maker.

The books that bear his name relate the careers of the first two kings whom he anointed: Saul and David.

The essential thrust of the Samuel section of our Old Testament is the transition in Israel from theocracy—government under God—to monarchy—government under humans.

Under Moses the people of God functioned as a fledgling nation whose king was Yahweh. This same concept prevailed throughout the career of Joshua and the times of the judges. Then we stumble upon this paragraph in 1 Sam. 8: 4-7:

> Then all the elders of Israel gathered together and came to Samuel at Ramah and said to him: "Behold, you are old and your sons do not walk in your ways; now appoint for us a king to govern us like all the nations." But the thing displeased Samuel when they said, "Give us a king to govern us." And Samuel prayed to the Lord. And the Lord said to Samuel, "Harken to the voice of the people in all that they say to you; for they have not rejected you, but they have rejected me."

You see, during the dark and difficult days of the judges Israel had a heart attack. The people turned from Yahweh—God—as king and desired a king like all the other nations. They wanted to be like their neighbors; to keep up with the Joneses.

Little did they care that their very birthright resided precisely in the fact that they were unlike the other nations. Their destiny lay in their difference. Their king was Yahweh—eternal, immortal, invisible. But they wanted a king they could see.

There is always something sad and historically tragic about a "nation under God" wanting to become a "nation under someone else."

But you know, it is one thing to reject Yahweh; it is quite another thing to try to remove God from the affairs of history. The first is possible among any people; the second is impossible among all people.

The people of Israel denied Yahweh, but they did not dethrone Yahweh! That is the supreme lesson of the Samuel section of our Old Testament.

The historical drama gathers around three central figures in these two books: (1) Samuel, a prophet and frustrated king-maker; (2) Saul, the king after the people's own heart; and (3) David, the king after God's own heart.

With Samuel, the office of prophet emerges in Israel. His office is always superior to that of priest or king. The prophets became the mediators, the messengers, the interpreters of the Word of the Lord. From Samuel to Malachi the prophets stood among the people delivering God's messages.

When God wanted a fresh, relevant, disturbing word said in Israel, God said it through the prophets. Samuel was the premier prophet whose lot it fell to serve as king-maker. He didn't want to do it.

Saul, the first king he anointed, became a sad and twisted revelation to the people indicating what the possession of a corrupt king like their neighbors really meant to them. Saul lived in those days before "Head and Shoulders" became a shampoo. He towered taller than everyone else. He was a big man, a great starter, but a terrible finisher. Once a headlight, he ended up a taillight in Israel; and his suicide marks the low moment of dashed hopes all over the land.

David, the second king Samuel anointed, held out the messianic hope for Israel. We see David in the fields as a shepherd, in the palace as a musician, and in the wilderness as an outlaw—all before we see him on Israel's throne as a king. David lifted Israel to its finest hour. He was important; so was his kingdom. Great were David's sins, but greater still his thirst for the purpose of God.

The theme of renewal through disaster threads through the entire David section of the Samuel books. We see it in every relationship: David and Saul, David and Jonathan, David and Bathsheba, David and Nathan, David and Absalom, David and Solomon.

Nowhere is the Samuel theme of deliverance through disaster more vividly depicted than in the oft-told story of David and Goliath. It appears in 1 Samuel 17, but serves as a summary of this entire Old Testament section. It is to the truth of that time-worn story that I want now to turn.

On the surface it is a record of a 5-foot-tall teenager doing battle with a 10-foot-tall grownup. But at the depths it's the account of youth bursting out of its pitifully small and woefully inadequate world. It is a panorama of young life. Here is restless youth no longer satisfied with sheep-keeping. Here is explosive youth leaping right out of its safe meadow into the midst of a great and worthy and dangerous cause.

It is a reflection of young life in every generation: not a young man putting on an older man's shoes, but a boy seeking out a pair of shoes for himself.

The setting is uncomplicated. The action takes place in the Valley of Elah. Camped on the mountain on one side were the armies of Philistia, led by their champion: Goliath of Gath. Camped on the mountain on the other side were the armies of Israel, presided over by their blundering, ineffective king: Saul.

From the Philistine camp came the taunt: "I defy the ranks of Israel this day; give me a man, that we may fight together." The words were Goliath's, towering 10 feet tall—3 feet taller than basketball greats David Robinson or Patrick Ewing, taller than two Muggsy Bogues stacked on top of each other.

From the Israelite camp came silence. But the record contains a sentence describing their reaction: "When Saul and all Israel heard these words of the Philistine, they were dismayed and greatly afraid."

For a considerable period of time these were the only actors, and this the only dialogue on the mountains towering over the Valley of Elah.

Saul was supposed to be a big man. Goliath's call was for two big men to fight, and Saul knew it. But all the fight had been squeezed right out of Saul.

He was supposed to be a leader in Israel. But now his kingly tent was far from the front lines.

Hear Saul say it: "You can mess up even a big life by aiming it in the wrong direction—away from the purposes of God."

Then enters David. He was the youngest of Jesse's eight sons, the great-grandson of Ruth and Boaz. He had been denied a ticket to see the X-rated violence about to show in the Valley of Elah. His dad had reserved him to keep the sheep safe in their meadows at Bethlehem.

But today he had been commissioned, early in the morning, to take some provisions to his brothers in Saul's army. His errand brought him to the field of battle just as the forces were gathering for a showdown.

See this teenager and you see young adults through all the ages. Here is youth standing in the ranks of frightened, confused, and indecisive adults. Here is youth with both a right and a longing to join a struggle labeled "For Adults Only." Here is youth being told by the most knowledgeable grownups: "You can't do a thing against this Philistine. A David can never win against a Goliath."

But here is youth seeing a challenge that is soul-sized and seizing it. And here is youth asking a question that ought to have been asked: "Who is this uncircumcised Philistine that he should defy the armies of the living God?" At this point the climax of the story nears in 1 Sam. 17:38-40:

> Then Saul clothed David with his armor. He put a helmet of bronze on his head, and clothed him with a coat of mail. And David girded his sword over his armor, and he tried in vain to go, for he was not used to them. Then David said to Saul, "I cannot go with these for I am not used to them." And David

took them off. Then he took his staff in his hands, and chose five smooth stones from the brook, and put them in his shepherd's bag; his sling was in his hand, and he drew near to the Philistine.

The truth hits home: David could not face his challenge in Saul's suit! Imagine how he looked. Since Saul stood head and shoulders taller than everyone else, the surprise is not that David could not wear his armor, but that Saul should think that he could.

But that's the way it is with us grownups. We always think our suits are the best for our youth.

Here on the fringe of the Valley of Elah is unconventional youth preparing for an unusual battle in an unorthodox way. Somewhere, sometime, in some way, every maturing young person stands where David stood: on the fringe of a very personal Valley of Elah. Over there, wrong stands tall against everything you think is right.

Make no mistake: there will always be a Goliath. Oh, he may change his name and address. Neither his shirt size nor blood type will remain the same. Even the calibre of his sword will change. But there are forever giant-sized challenges to be faced, Goliath-tall risks to be run, and decisions as large as life to be made.

The problems of youth today in their Valley of Elah are so often compounded because we adults feebly hand over to them our equipment, insisting they wear it to face their giants. I am certain that no generation has ever sought more diligently to pawn off on its young people a second-hand, second-rate preparation for life.

So, hear the Samuel message of renewal through disaster, teenager, young adult. There just may be some pebbles in the brook that flows through your valley. Under God, find them; take your own gear. Then go! Face the challenges as you see them.

Let me point out a thing or two about your journey: Some of the equipment must be old.

Heritage is still a mighty good word. You cannot take your journey without it. You are plugged into your past. Alex Hailey is not the only one with "roots."

So don't be hoodwinked into what the non-theistic existentialists try to tell you. They are selling the idea that every moment is cut off from every other moment—time before and after it. The present—the existence—is all that matters for them.

That is just not true. You and I bring all the equipment of our heritage into our journey.

Each new generation must try the equipment of the older generation before discarding it. David at least put Saul's armor on before he found out it would not fit.

Some of the problems now are caused by youth discarding old armor on the mere assumption that it will not work for them. Some of the old suit may be the best—not because of its age, but because of its quality.

It is an old world we live in. It's been here a long time. We must bring some tools that have been time-tested and value-tempered to our task.

It is easy for youth to believe that all their problems stem from adult misunderstanding. Could it be that some of the young misunderstand themselves?

Consider your situation: You are less than 20. For years now you have been living in that human game preserve called the teenage subculture. You have been protected and excused under a popular opinion that advises: "There are no good children, just good environments. There are no bad children, only bad parents."

Up to now you have been shielded by all kinds of scapegoats: a dad who curses too much, drinks too much, or prays too much; a mother who works too much or plays too much; parents who were either too dictatorial or too lenient; a community that had too much poverty or too much wealth; a neighborhood that had too many slums and bars or too many country clubs and churches.

In short, you have been encouraged to think of yourself as the products and victims of adult misbehavior. There is some truth in all this. Youth have been exploited by grownups.

Slam goes the door on all the scapegoats. You come to yourselves looking straight down the barrel of responsibility.

Farewell to innocence! Welcome to the real world! From now on, it is your fault! You cannot live a life put together only by Scotch tape or Scotch soda.

What are you going to do about your journey? It is your valley. It is your life. What are you going to put on for the battle?

Equipment that others before you have used will be some of the best fit for your suit. Some of your equipment must be old.

Some of your equipment will be new—brand new.

Observe the sight again: That was a scantily clad, slightly-built, ill-armed youth who strode with his slingshot and a satchel-full of rocks across the Valley of Elah. David was a rebel alright—a rebel with a cause.

Whatever happened to our fine word "rebel"? It has fallen into foul reputation in our time. We have dressed our word wrong. We have made it slouchy and lazy, long-haired and dull; and we have never given it a bath. We have given our word rebel a hamburger heart, a pizza brain, and a hot dog disposition. We have infested our word with a haircut like Samson's and a voice like Delilah's.

But a rebel can be a healthy and helpful nonconformist. The opposite of a rebel is a conformist—a mere carbon copy, one content to live by a stencil someone else cuts. Jesus Christ died far too young declaring his intentions not to live like that.

New challenges, new times require new equipment. Some of youth's gear today has never been worn before.

But have you noticed? Our scene is practically dominated by a certain spirit abroad in the land. It is the "me, myself, I" spirit of the organization generation. This spirit has a credo: "Do not get out of line. Get along. Get ahead. Drink the boss's booze. Share the boss's sex. Conform. Play the game. Climb. Do not rock the boat."

See the results. It issues in persons who never question the system; they merely lubricate it. They are technicians of society, never innovators. They know three words: security, conformity, compromise.

If you are in your teens and have no spark of protest against such a spirit, then you are already diseased and the infection is spreading to the roots of a civilization that is going through a delirious dance of death.

Some of your equipment will need to be brand new—not caught from the culture, but decided upon in your own free conscience and worn though the heavens fall.

All of your equipment will have to be your own.

Laurie Nelson is 15. She has asked a probing question: "What is right? Conforming to conformity, conforming to nonconformity, or conforming to yourself?"

Conforming to yourself . . . That rings real.

You have to look no further than your fingerprint to find God's signature on your life. DNA certifies that you are different—unique. God has a stamp on you. You are the only one just like you God has got.

Conforming to yourself . . . How do you do it? Here is the secret of life in Christ: it is the genius of Jesus to take your life—unique, unrepeatable—and blend all of its ingredients into fullness and wholeness.

God equips us all to live the only life we will ever live. God can make more—much more—of it than we can ever make alone:

The Nine "Do Mores"
- Do more than exist: Live.
- Do more than touch: Feel.
- Do more than look: Observe.
- Do more than read: Absorb.
- Do more than hear: Listen.
- Do more than listen: Understand.
- Do more than think: Ponder.
- Do more than plan: Act.
- Do more than talk: Say something!
- Do something!
- Be something!

April 30, 1995

1 AND 2 KINGS

The sound of silence
1 Kings 19:1-4, 9-10, 18

There is one genuine hazard in reading either a dictionary or a telephone directory: the subject changes so often. This is somewhat the same hazard encountered in reading the massive body of literature in our Bible that bears the name 1 and 2 Kings. In my study Bible this material covers 68 pages, and the subject changes on almost every page—indeed, in almost every paragraph.

These two books contain 47 chapter and equally that many topics. Almost 1,000 persons are named individually in these 68 pages. Trying to compress this material into the compass of a single sermon is like trying to pack a moving van into a pick-up truck: a substantial part of it is going to be left sticking out.

The two books of Kings appear in the Hebrew Bible as one scroll. But because of sheer size/bulk, they were later divided by translators into two books.

Yet they tell one continuous story. They constitute a single historical narrative. In these two books we have the history of just over 400 years.

Compare that with the 375 years of our national history since the Pilgrims landed on these wild New England shores, and you can conceive the fantastic compactness of the material in Kings.

First Kings is bounded by two deathbeds. It opens with the death of David, Israel's second king, and closes with the death of Ahab, Israel's seventh king. It begins in the year 973 B.C. and ends around 823 B.C. Thus it covers about 150 years. Second Kings moves the narrative along approximately 250 years and ends in 586 B.C.

As 1 Kings opens, David, the once rosy-cheeked shepherd lad, has come to the end of his life. His 40-year reign as king over all Israel is coming to a close.

Solomon, the son of Bathsheba and David, after some difficulty with the army and with the priests, is anointed his father's successor.

Israel has now reached a pinnacle of power and prestige she has never known before. Solomon takes his place among the world's monarchs of the first rank. After the bloodshed surrounding his ascension to the throne, Solomon settles into a reign in keeping with his name: Shalom—Salem—Peace.

Yet, in the remainder of 1 Kings there unfolds the story of a nation passing from affluence and influence into poverty and paralysis. Solomon's reign was the climax of early Israelite history, and the building of the temple at Jerusalem was the climax of Solomon's reign.

It was constructed and dedicated as a symbol of Israel's finest hour. But from that point on, the journey was all downhill. Both the king and the country were on a slippery slope toward doom.

Solomon, like his father David, reigned 40 years. He died in 932 B.C. You can mark that date as the last days of the Hebrew empire.

Rehoboam, Solomon's son and heir apparent, possessed a deplorable lack of judgment. He scorned gentle speech and pledged an even heavier yoke for the people.

Israel, consisting then of 10 tribes, revolted in a devastating display of nationalistic fury.

Jeroboam, an Ephraimite who had been exiled to Egypt by Solomon, returned to lead the rebellion and was appointed king of Israel. Thus he ruled in the north, the Galilean sector of the empire.

The split was permanent!

Rehoboam, Solomon's son, was left to be king in the south, with only the tribes of Judah and of Benjamin as his subjects.

The united kingdom of Saul, David, and Solomon had lasted only for decades—from 1006 B.C. to 932 B.C. Now there were two separate kingdoms: Israel to the north and Judah to the south. Israel/Judah now had a Mason-Dixon line.

Bad blood and bad borders abounded. The schism was complete. Warfare was constant. In time, each kingdom separately had 19 kings.

A little more than 200 years after the successful rebellion led by Jeroboam, the Northern Kingdom, Israel, was demolished and brought to a permanent end by the Assyrians under their warrior-king Sargon II. That year was 722 B.C. Samaria, the capital city, was demolished. The leading citizens of Israel were deported. New foreign colonists were brought in. The 10 northern tribes disappeared from the face of the earth. And from that day to this they have been known as the Lost Tribes of Israel.

The Southern Kingdom lasted longer. But in exile the Babylonians, led by their awesome warrior-king Nebuchadnezzar, smashed the remnants of Judah's army, imprisoned and blinded the King Zedekiah, destroyed Jerusalem and Solomon's temple, deported huge chunks of the population, and ushered in the period of the Hebrew exile in Babylon.

The second book of Kings ends here—in exile. There is one note of hope: Even in exile, the deposed king of Judah is treated kindly, and there is a chance for the eventual end of the Hebrews' agony in exile. This hope flowered fully when Cyrus of Persia conquered Babylon, allowing the Hebrews to return to their homeland in 536 B.C.

The period of the kings was also the period of the prophets. The narratives of Hebrew history do not really come alive until we encounter the towering and majestic figures of Elijah, Elisha, Joel, Amos, Jonah, Hosea, Micah, Isaiah, Jeremiah, and Habbakuk.

To read the book of Kings apart from the piercing prophetic messages delivered by these "human thunderbolts and lightning flashes" is to short-circuit the revelation.

The prophets interpreted the events of Hebrew history in light of their white-hot allegiance to Yahweh, the God of Israel.

Both king and commoner came under their fire. City street and country lane resounded with their profound "Thus says the Lord."

So it is to one of them that we turn now for the note of revelance that connects the events of Israel/Judah to the events of our city and our time.

Against a background of political instability, economic insolvency, and religious apostasy there appeared one day—strange and unannounced—an elusive man named Elijah. He emerged from the fringes of the desert and was not at home in any of life's mainstreams flowing through the ninth century B.C. He heard a different drummer. And he marched to the music he heard. Elijah did not jump to the music played by murderous King Ahab, the toad who squatted on Israel's throne, or to his wife Queen Jezebel, the female Phoenician tornado from Tyre.

Elijah was offensive because he did not dress right, talk right, look right. He was offensive because he did not utter the clichés or act nice around the power structures.

He was a troublemaker in Israel, and dared even claim that he made trouble in the name of the Lord. He was offensive because he made so much sense and because he knew the meaning of truth and justice. Even in death he could not be tamed. His countrymen testified that he disappeared in a whirlwind and left no grave.

One incredible day on Mount Carmel this solitary man challenged hundreds of the prophets of Baal—Jezebel's favorite god—to a contest of altars and fire.

Yahweh and Elijah won! The power of the fertility cult—Jezebel's pantheon—was broken. Nature was no longer to be manipulated through sex or magic or ritual. Nature was a creation also—a gift of Elijah's God, beyond the control of mere mortals.

Yahweh—not Baal—was to be God in Israel, and Elijah was to be God's prophet. But right here a strange thing happens. In 1 Kings 19 we watch as the Elijah situation takes a curious turn.

The strange desert man fell into deep depression. He began to think that he was alone in his struggle and became a bit paranoid. He began to fear Jezebel and her ruthless reaction to his victory on Mount Carmel.

He came to believe that he could change his situation by changing his address. So Elijah fled: from his cave on Mount Carmel, far to the north, the length of the entire country, into the wilderness; far south, near Mount Sinai, where long before God had spoken to Moses through an earthquake, wind, and fire.

Elijah's flight was to the womb of Israel's faith. In the face of a frightening, insecure, and threatening present, Elijah is returning to a glorious past. He is gripped by reminiscence. If God visits him here, like he visited Moses years before, then he would be safe from Jezebel just like Moses was safe from the pharaoh.

Elijah's journey is long. It is lonely. It is an awful desert trek from Carmel to Sinai. But after more than a month he arrives at the cave—not just any cave, mind you, but *the cave* where Moses had stood.

There Elijah waits for God to pass by. Surely history will repeat itself, especially for this prophet. But it is a long wait!

To be sure, the old signs do reappear. There is a great and strong wind; after the wind, an earthquake; and following the earthquake, a fire. God had been in these very signs for Moses a long time ago, but not this time—not for Elijah. God is not in the earthquake, wind, and fire.

Poor Elijah . . . here in his ominous present he sought to flee to the past, to get his clues of God's presence from there. But he did not get his wish.

The living God whom Elijah serves cannot be so conveniently predicted, captured, controlled. God comes when and where and how God wills—not just because someone snaps his finger and expects God to appear.

But here the truth in the Elijah situation comes home to us. After the earthquake, wind, and fire there is a *qol demamah daqqah*!

How do we translate that? The most literal Hebrew requires that we render it like this: "a sound of thin silence."

God came in "the sound of silence." The silence was not hollow, empty, void. The very silence was a word of revelation—alive, intense, redemptive.

In hearing the silence, Elijah hears God. Silence becomes the language of his heart, and the prophet communes with God.

After that, there was a word—spoken: "Elijah, what are you doing here?"

It was as if God said: "A retreat to the past is not enough for the stormy present. Go. Return. Live fully, freely, responsibly in your own time. I am with you."

Now, this bit of revelation comes lurching across the centuries to confront us where we live today.

We, too, reel under the blows of our stormy present. We, too, want somehow to stop the world so we can get off:

- Genocide in Bosnia
- Fratricide in Rwanda
- Homicide in Los Angeles
- Suicide in Michigan
- Russians bombing Russians in Chechnya
- Americans bombing Americans in Oklahoma City
- Virus threat from Zaire
- A nuclear threat from Iran and North Korea

Like Elijah, we all ask: "God, why don't you say something?" And we are apt to point out how God has intervened somewhere, somehow in the past.

But the living God will not tolerate historicism. God will not communicate exclusively through memory.

Meaning here and now is not to be found in the rigidity of what was or in the sterility of what might have been. Meaning here and now comes through God here and now—in what is—a transcendent/immanent God at work in the present moment. God comes in present awareness, not only in past recollection.

God's coming is in the unexpected, uncontrolled, unscheduled silence. God just may come most to us when we think God has come the least. Thus is required an openness to the silence.

Just when we think God is saying nothing, God may be saying something. So listen! Listen to the silence! The heart may hear what the ear can never discern.

If God is not saying what we *want* to hear in words, it may be because God is saying what we *need* to hear in silence. It is the lesson Elijah learned.

Some of the most significant things affecting our lives take place in silence. The gravitation that keeps us earthbound comes unawares. The tides churn in upon all Earth's shores in response to mysterious, silent forces. Huge oaks push up from acorns through the soil without a whisper. Massive clouds move swiftly overhead without the slightest swish of sound.

So it is with fearful hearts in the midst of calamitous times. God comes alongside in sheer silence.

When there is nothing we can say and little that we can do, then we can rely upon the silence—believing that, too, is of God.

Listen as Bill Hull reflects on the heart-rending moment of 11-year-old Laura Lou Claypool's dying. She had struggled gallantly for months with leukemia:

> I shall never forget that Saturday afternoon. I sat with my wife in the living room at the foot of the stairs while the family gathered around Laura Lou's bed for a final farewell. When the end came just at sunset, an indescribable silence settled over the house.
>
> Earlier in the day, and so often before, I had heard from upstairs the muffled sobs of pain and the heavy footfalls of parents racing to the bedside to be of help.
>
> And now the sounds of suffering were stilled. But I also knew that I would never again hear that little girl's laughter coming down those stairs or see the dancing steps of a young lady ready for her first date. And so I tested the silence that day to see if it could be endured.
>
> The silence lasted for about half an hour, as the family said goodbye. When they came down, there was really nothing to say, except that the silence could be friendly. For now I know that the silence also belongs to God.

Listen, dear friend, for the "sound of silence." It belongs to God. It must! It can! It does! Amen.

May 14, 1995

1 AND 2 CHRONICLES

Back to basics

1 Chronicles 15:1, 17:1-2, 22:7-10; 2 Chronicles 2:1-2; 7:5, 14; 9:31

The two books of Chronicles are heavy reading—65 chapters in all. They are large, long, laborious. The first person named in this scroll is Adam, tender of the garden of Eden. The last person named is Cyrus, king of Persia. So, you sense the scope of the material.

In a sense these two books recap the entire Bible story from the beginning to the Babylonian exile. That is a lot of history—even if it is "holy history."

The Hebrew title for these two books is *dibre hayyamim*, meaning "records of the times." "Chronicles" is as good a translation as any for that.

The books were written late. In fact, they are the last scrolls included in the Hebrew scriptures. They were written after the return from exile in Babylon—perhaps around 400 B.C.—by either a priest or someone especially sensitive to priestly concerns. Tradition has sometimes labeled Ezra the author of these books. We do not know.

The Chronicles appear in our Bible immediately after Kings—because they repeat so much of that material.

There is one essential difference, however, between Kings and Chronicles. The books of Kings have a *prophetic* outlook on history. The books of Chronicles have a *priestly* outlook on history.

"Adam" is the first word in 1 Chronicles. He is mentioned to establish the genealogy of Judah, Jacob's son. Judah gets the most part of Chronicles' opening genealogies in order to focus on David. David gets the spotlight in these early chapters simply to bring into clearer focus the master passion of his life: the building of the Jerusalem temple.

The Chronicler had a problem: For a long time it had been patriotic to believe that the kingdom of Judah—the Southern Kingdom—and the Davidic line that ruled it would last forever. But the Chronicler and his readers knew that the kingdom of Judah had been destroyed in 586 B.C. by the Babylonians. Their South, too, was "gone with the wind."

No king of the Davidic line had reigned for nearly 200 years. Moreover, there were no immediate signs of the Davidic kingdom being re-established. That which could not happen had happened. Their Titanic had sunk!

It became necessary, therefore, to reinterpret the events of the times. The Chronicler set about writing a history that would offer another interpretation.

His point throughout was that worship is more important than a temple in the lives of the people of God. The people of God can worship God anywhere—with a temple when they have one, without a temple when they have none. The *act* is more crucial than the *place*. He wrote everything that he wrote in order to deliver one flaming declaration—the one the Lord delivered on the day of the temple dedication—2 Chron. 7:14: "If my people who are called by my name will humble themselves, and pray, and seek my face, and turn from their wicked ways; then I will hear from heaven, and will forgive their sin, and heal their land."

For the Chronicler's purpose, it was best to get through the earlier times in the shortest way possible—thus, so much genealogy. Through a listing of selected genealogies the Jews returning from Babylon to Palestine could relocate themselves accurately in the tribal system and society could be renewed. So there follow 10 chapters, stringing together hundreds of names—"so and so begat so and so"—almost without end.

To gather up the history suggested in these genealogies is to see God moving, selecting, changing, forging the history of the Hebrew people. Their history is "holy history." These Hebrews were ruled or ruined according to their reliance on God.

Thus, before the Chronicler tells the story of David, in whose heart was the passion to build a temple to Yahweh, there are these strange 10 chapters filled with hundreds of names.

Then in chapter 11 he introduces David. David is depicted as shepherd, warrior, poet, lover, and king—a man always after God's own heart.

At times he had morals like an alley cat. At others he had values like a saint. He was a brilliant strategist, fearless fighter, faithful friend, ruthless foe, gifted administrator, hard as nails, soft as putty, mystical, devout, demonic, unable to rule his own passions or that of his family. David was saint and sinner locked together in the same manly body.

But for the Chronicler the important thing about David was his commitment to build a temple in Jerusalem. He was thus the father of temple worship and the incarnation of the covenant with Yahweh. The house of David was the symbol of God's promises to the Hebrews. The star of David was their one bright hope.

Next, in chapter 22, the Chronicler introduces Solomon. What David had established on the strength of his personal magnetism, Solomon enlarged by careful alliance with foreign powers and favorable trade agreements. He became fabulously wealthy and took his place among the internationally known monarchs of the times.

But from the perspective of the Chronicler, Solomon's most lasting achievement was neither his wealth nor his wisdom. It was the building of the temple in Jerusalem.

Solomon's temple was to be the spiritual successor of Moses' tabernacle. That splendid edifice was intended to remind the people of their sacred covenant with Yahweh. That is why Solomon's personal failures were so tragic to the Chronicler.

The man violated the temple he had built. His life contradicted the truth his temple expressed. He built something he did not believe in enough to live by.

Solomon played too long on the ragged edge of the awful things that ruined him. Passions ran out of control. His harem abounded with the products of far too many entangling marriages, too many foreign women, and idolatrous allegiances.

So the temple of Solomon became for Solomon just an empty form, signifying nothing—just a beautiful box to put God in. He sowed the seeds of the nation's ruin.

Thus the Chronicler relates the tragedy of the Hebrews after the division of Solomon's empire into the northern and southern kingdoms. In the Northern Kingdom—Israel—Jeroboam began by substituting false forms of worship for the true worship of God. He set up idols at Dan and at Samaria. In the Southern Kingdom—Judah—Rehoboam followed the pattern of his father. He retained the form, but neglected the substance of true worship. Both nations had a heart attack.

Under all of Israel's and Judah's kings—38 in all—there was the observance of the form and neglect of the fact of true worship.

But men and nations cannot long endure on more form. Without substance, formalism perishes. So it was in Judah. Look at the tragic record.

The Chronicler is careful to point out that all the spiritual reformations in Judah began at the house of the Lord. So we see certain of the leaders trying desperately to restore heart and soul and substance to the religion of Judah: King Asa renewed the altar and restored the holy vessels to their place. King Joash restored the temple after rioters had desecrated it. King Hezekiah opened the temple once more and welcomed worshipers. King Josiah repaired the temple as the first step in his massive reforms.

But for it all, form won out over substance. Judah had a splendid temple, but the temple did not have Judah. The people of Judah kept the form, but neglected the fact of pure worship. They had God on Zion Hill; they did not have God in their hearts. Thus, all through the Chronicles we see a people progressing steadily backwards.

Finally there came the ultimate disaster. Nebuchadnezzar of Babylon, with his storm troopers in 586 B.C., burned the temple with fire, killed thousands, and marched the majority of the rest of the people off to exile in Babylon (modern Iraq). It was a holocaust all its own.

So, we see the double-truth of the Chronicles revelation. In Book I we see how important the temple was to Judah's national life. In Book II we see how unimportant the temple was after all to Judah's spiritual life.

That is a gigantic paradox—even a contradiction. But in that screaming contradiction lie the lingering truths of the Chronicles: The first book of Chronicles condemns sheer rationalism in a nation's life. The second book of Chronicles condemns sheer ritualism in a nation's life.

Why? Because rationalism says, "We can manage without God." And ritualism says: "We need God, but not much. We do not have to take God seriously." It is enough to go through the motions. Both are careless. Both are wrong!

So the Chronicle's message comes home to us: "If you think by policy or diplomacy alone to maintain your strength, you are doomed to fail."

A nation cannot be strong and wrong for long. Something in the scheme of things mandates that "might" must be found in "right." Integrity is a matter of right and might blended inseparably into the bloodstream of a people.

That is why we are so baffled in this 20th century by the strange success of the athe-ists—like Communists, the Fascists. Theirs has been the success of the "big lie." But it does seem to work—at least for awhile.

All the while we citizens of this great land say we believe in the power of truth over deceit. We may not always do the truth, but we honestly believe in it as a matter of principle.

We believe that right makes might. But look at our might this morning. It is largely the manufactured might of our farms and factories. It is not so much the moral right from our churches and synagogues.

It is *hand* and *head* might, not heart might. So it troubles us—or it ought to.

What is the future of such might? No one needs to tell us that we have a national moral fever and there is very little medicine left in our bottle. The land mops its brow, sweeps up its blood, and clutches its heart. We have all but fooled ourselves to death.

Instead of a joyful noise to the Lord, there rises the doleful dirge of a people who have no more nerve endings left to stimulate. We have tried everything, and we are still restless.

No one seems to know whether this is the year of the hawk, the dove, or the vulture. In the madness of our overproduced knowledge and underproduced wisdom, many are ready to burn down our cathedrals just to fry eggs.

Huge chunks of the church of Jesus Christ are being dragged, kicking and scream-ing, into another long, hot summer. Maybe Pogo is right: "We have met the enemy, and they is us."

Let's hear one thing from the Chronicler loud and clear: If we are going to chance our lives on Christian and democratic ideals, then we are going to have to get some substance into our souls.

We have not built a thing that cannot be destroyed. That includes our churches. A nation cannot long endure when the lives of its people are put together with Scotch tape and Scotch soda. We must find our might in right.

We are not going to win against any global ant-hill philosophy by merely champi-oning scientific superiority or technological mastery. They are catching up to us on that. No! We must bring upon the whole 21st-century secularism the tremendous presence of a moral oughtness. This they cannot defeat. They have no defense against it.

But in any battle to see who can best barter their souls, our adversaries will always outdo us. The peoples of this earth are standing on tip-toe to see what we in this free land will give in exchange for our souls.

This world is finished with mere formalism. No matter if the landscape is dotted with churches—even splendid mega-churches. What goes on in the house of worship is far more important than the houses.

The peoples of this earth mean business. And a world that means business is never going to be influenced by a church that does not. It was not so in Judah. It is not so in the U.S.A.

The need is for a people of God filled with a presence—flashing their light, communicating their fire. Then we can say to politicians playing statesmen, "You dare not . . ." Then we can say to demagogues in the pulpits of this land, "You are exposed . . ." Then we can confront all kinds of demons in the name of the Lord and say, "Disgorge . . ."

What then is the message of Chronicles for us today? Simply this: There is a moving in the mulberry trees, sifting the merely formal, boiling things down to basics, and howling through the high winds of change. Strengthen the things that remain." That is the age-old message that comes to our country.

It is as old and as fresh as the Chronicles: Get back to basics. "If my people, who are called by my name will humble themselves and pray, and seek my face, and turn from their wicked ways; then will I hear from heaven, and will forgive their sin and heal their land."

The epilogue is there also: if the people do not, there is not the slightest possible chance that the nation will endure. Judah didn't! Why do you suppose we think we can? Amen.

May 21, 1995

EZRA

Old clay—new pot
Ezra 1:1-4; 2:1; 3:8, 11-12; 6:16; 7:16; 9:1-3; 10:1-5

T he book of Ezra cannot be considered alone. We must recognize the connection of this book with those surrounding it. The first three verses of the first chapter of Ezra repeat exactly the last two verses of the last chapter of 2 Chronicles. This is no accident.

In Jewish tradition Ezra was the Chronicler who wrote that whole body of literature, including Chronicles, Ezra, and Nehemiah. This just may be the case.

You see, the Chronicler did not complete his task when he told about the destruction of Solomon's original Jerusalem temple in 586 B.C. by the armies of Babylon. That temple, however, had been the non-human hero of his history.

The Chronicler pressed on then to finish his story—and his story had been from the beginning the history of Hebrew temple worship.

Therefore, immediately after his account of the end of the kingdom of Judah, the Chronicler records a *new* royal proclamation, by a *new* king, in a *new* nation, which led to the construction of a *new* temple. That is why the opening verses of Ezra contain virtually verbatim the closing verses of Chronicles.

About a half century elapsed between Chronicles and Ezra. Yet the story is unbroken.

Ezra opens with a band of impoverished refugees from Babylon trying desperately to go home again and to rebuild their house of worship in Jerusalem.

Chronicles closed a half century before, with the exact opposite situation of a band of impoverished refugees leaving home, on their way to Babylon with the smoldering ruins of their house of worship left behind in Jerusalem.

The first temple was destroyed in 586 B.C. The proclamation that started the process for the second one to be built came in 538 B.C. Within those 48 years Cyrus had conquered Babylon and begun the expansion of his Persian empire throughout the Fertile Crescent.

This empire put together by Cyrus was the greatest that the world had ever seen. It encompassed all of old Assyria, Babylon, Asia Minor, and huge tracts of territory further east. Its remnants remain to this day in modem Iran.

Cyrus was completely unlike the conquerors who had flourished before him. He did not engage in wholesale killings and deportations of conquered people. Rather, he chose to treat them gently, allowing them their self-respect and considerable home rule. The result was that the Persian empire was both a political and a territorial success.

Cyrus' conviction regarding conquered people was simple: "The lighter the grip, the firmer the hold." The Jews were one of those groups who benefited from this policy.

Later Persian kings adhered generally to the Cyrus policy. So, after a lapse of another 50 years following Cyrus' proclamation, Ezra appears on the scene.

The record is that Ezra went up to Jerusalem in the seventh year of Artaxerxes, king of Persia (Ezra 7:7). Since there were two Persian kings bearing that name, scholars cannot be sure as to the precise date of Ezra's journey back to Palestine from Babylon.

If he returned during the seventh year of the reign of the first King Artaxerxes, it was 458 B.C. If he returned during the seventh year of the reign of Artaxerxes II, then it was 397 B.C. This later date would mean that Ezra came to Palestine almost a generation after Nehemiah had returned to initiate his reforms and to rebuild the walls of Jerusalem.

In any case, we can trace the events following Ezra's return fairly accurately. But before we focus on the work, let us meet the man.

Ezra's name is a shortened form of Azariah, a common name carried by at least two dozen people mentioned in the Bible. He was the son of Seraiah, and his proud lineage could be traced all the way back to Aaron, the brother of Moses.

He is introduced to us as a "scribe skilled in the law of Moses" (Ezra 7:6). And with this word we are introduced to a new function in the Old Testament. Up to now we have had prophets, priests, and kings as the emissaries between God and the people. Now, added to that are "scribes."

A scribe is literally "one who writes," that is, a secretary. But during the exile in Babylon scribes became especially important.

The reason: the historical, theological, and legal traditions of the Hebrews had to be reduced to writing and shared by way of handwritten copies with the scattered people, or else the isolated groups would forget their heritage and lose their sense of "Jewishness" during the deportation.

Ezra was one of those scribes who copied, studied, and interpreted the sacred scrolls of scripture dating back to Moses.

There was one basic difference between a prophet and a scribe. A prophet spoke from inspiration, and frequently broke new ground in the proclamation as to the purposes of God among the people.

A scribe spoke from information and was bound to the letter of the law, and had a vested interest in preserving that letter since only by its exact form and precise tradition did he fulfill his function.

There was an inherit peril in this process. It became easy for scribes to overlook the spirit of the law in their rigorous defense of the letter of it. In fact, that is precisely what had happened in Israel by the time of Jesus. Legalism had settled like a fog over the land, squeezing the spirit right out of religion.

So the scribes in the New Testament are generally depicted as arid and musty old men completely inflexible and incapable of moving with the times or updating the purposes of God among the people. However, that unhappy development came hundreds of years later than Ezra. If God were ever to be taken seriously again among the people after the Exile, then it would depend upon people like Ezra. So it is no surprise that this scribe in the line of Aaron emerges.

One flaming purpose motivated Ezra. It is recorded in Ezra 7:10: "He had set his heart to seek the law of Yahweh and to do it, and to teach in Israel its statutes and ordinances."

To highlight this, Ezra recounted in chapters 1-6 how a caravan of immigrants returned to Israel with hopes of rebuilding the temple. Armed with a letter of authorization, along with considerable Persian money and material from King Artaxerxes, governor Sheshbazaar had led a sizable company of about 5,000 pilgrims back to Palestine. Soon thereafter an altar was rebuilt, but construction stalled. A later governor, Zerubbabel, completed the temple in 515 BC.

When Ezra arrived several decades later, he sought to do two things: to bring the people back to the Torah and to re-energize the temple as a center for worship—because it was hard to have one without the other.

Ezra did both these things, and the people responded. The temple he promoted lasted 586 years, until it was destroyed by the Romans in 70 A.D. Thus, the second temple outlasted Solomon's temple by 249 years.

Rigorous though Ezra might have been in enforcing the Torah, he regarded himself as an evangelist. What he brought were words of joy. For him, cooperation with law was cooperation with God in the moral universe.

But, oh, was he severe in pressing for the people to observe God's law and implement it in the practical affairs of their daily lives—especially so in the development of their families, their homes.

Thus Ezra lashed out at mixed marriages between devout Hebrews and the not-so-devout people who had been left in Palestine during the Exile. In Ezra, chapter 10, there is a record of more than 100 such marriages that were actually dissolved, annulled, terminated.

Apparently Ezra demanded and enforced the end of such marriages, along with the ejection of foreign wives and children from the Hebrew community. Although Ezra's scribal policy seems inhumane, strict, and severe, it was seen at the time as the only way to preserve Judaism in its pure form.

Some disagreed with it even then. Chapter 10, verse 15 lists four members of the opposition. Most students of scripture agree also that the book of Ruth was written during this period as a protest against Ezra's narrow policies. The miracle is that Ruth proved so popular that it was included in the Hebrew Bible, even though its heroine was a Moabite woman—not a Jew.

So much for Ezra in history—in the fourth and fifth centuries B.C. Translated, updated, and applied to us, what is his message here, now, today?

The clue to the contemporary message of this rigorous man, whose flaming desire was to make Israel a people of law and order under God, comes in chapter 1, verse 1: "In the first year of Cyrus, king of Persia, that the word of the Lord by the mouth of Jeremiah" that was about be accomplished, the Lord stirred up the spirit of Cyrus, king of Persia, so that he made a proclamation."

What was this "word of the Lord by the mouth of Jeremiah" that was about to be accomplished? Let's review.

Fifty years before, while Judah was sowing the wind to reap the whirlwind, Jeremiah thundered his prophetic proclamation. While one pool of blood bordered another in the streets and his countrymen swayed in a delirious dance of death, the man from Anathoth told his people what to expect.

Jeremiah saw the living God at work in Judah overruling human failure. While his country gasped for breath, Jeremiah made a trip to the potter's house.

He watched the craftsman at work at his wheel. When the vessel he was making got misshaped in his hand, he crumpled the clay and started again. He made another vessel more in keeping with his plan.

So when the prophet left the potter's house, he had his message for Judah: "God specializes in new beginnings."

That is the history of everything from Noah and Abraham and Moses to the captivity. The action of God always involves *old clay* and a *new pot*.

"He made it again another vessel." That is the flaming insight of Jeremiah that burned itself into the Chronicler and became the clue to the messages of Ezra and Nehemiah. These books tell us how God accomplished the words of Jeremiah: he began to make again the vessel that had been marred in his hand.

Judah was beginning again! The purging days in Babylon were done. God was starting over, but the clay was the same.

The Lord of history was beginning a new story. As Ezra saw, Yahweh took hold of mighty kings and their armies and made their very marching a part of God's purpose.

He watched as the God of Judah used the sighs of sobbing captives a thousand miles from home to move the wills of Cyrus, Darius, and Artaxerxes.

So you want to update the message of Ezra? Then write the headlines big and bold and bright: "God makes all things new."

God likes graduations, fresh starts, new beginnings. What is happening for you seniors is correctly named—Commencement: "to begin, to start, to originate; festivities launching, someone/something entirely new."

That is Ezra's final word. It is a different drummer, a strange sound for most of us.

The final word about man's sovereignty is that if you have had a chance in history and failed, then you are finished. The sands of time crush all that will yield.

But the final word about God's sovereignty is that if you have had a chance in history and failed, then God makes it new—a new pot from the old clay.

That is the unquenchable hope that Ezra holds out. When the times are as foul as witch's brew, then God in divine sovereignty begins a new thing.

Of course, if a man/a woman will not have it so, they find a moral universe up in arms against them. And if a nation will not have it so, then its dust and ashes are of its own making.

Let the word of Ezra go forth.

When the times are tough as nails and the nations seem all out of joint, when there is pepper in all the porridge and sand in all the soup, remember: God makes it all new!

Do not step back into these ancient centuries and miss that modern message. Do not imagine that God seized Cyrus and leaves the rulers of today alone. The times are in God's hand!

But have you noticed? The minute it dawns on us that these are times of universal upheaval—almost cosmic convulsions—we start to question the dependability of the moral order. We wonder out loud and quietly to ourselves whether the world is falling apart and the foundations of civilization are crumbling.

They may very well be. But there is one thing sure and certain: The moral order is not falling apart. On the contrary, it is holding together with amazing reliability. Cause and effect—the law of ethical harvest—is operating very well.

What is going to pieces is the immoral order—the false ideas and ideals we are shaping our lives by. Our sheer secularism is failing us, and certain of our behavior is coming to judgment. We are seeing not the collapse of universal moral foundations, but the vindication of them.

The law of harvest has never been more vividly demonstrated. Someday is payday. Dictators still ride bicycles. They stop; they fall. Tyrants still overextend themselves, defeat themselves, and dig their own inglorious graves. Immoral behavior—persisted in, unrepented of—brings life inevitably to ruin.

So every headline seems to be saying "This is God's world, and in the long run it is not a good world to be bad in."

The events of our times are not obscuring God. They are revealing God to all who have eyes and ears like Ezra. The Ezra word is also the Jesus word: "Be not afraid, I have overcome the world" (Luke 16:33).

We have always had trouble believing that it is even harder to grasp in foul weather than in fair. But the New Testament folk caught it—or better said, were caught by it.

This is a visited planet. We can believe and we can trust. *God makes it all new!* Amen.

May 28, 1995

NEHEMIAH

Winning a war of nerves

Nehemiah 1:1-4; 2:1-5, 11, 17-18; 4:1, 3, 6, 15-16; 6:15-16; 13:30-31

The 16th book of the Bible begins at once with the identity of its leading character. In the very first verse it establishes itself as "the words of Nehemiah." Much of the book is autobiographical, consisting of the memoirs of Nehemiah, the layman-governor of Judah. The date of the beginning of the events in the book is given twice—in the first and in the second chapters. It is "the 20th year of Artaxerxes, King of Persia."

If it were Artaxerxes I, the year is 445 B.C.

If it were Artaxerxes II, the year is 385 B.C.

We can most likely place Nehemiah in the year 445 B.C., some 70 years after the completion of the second temple.

There is one very special interest attached to this book. It is the last chapter in the historical portion of the Hebrew Bible. This book finishes the Old Testament so far as historical progression goes.

Everything else in the Old Testament—Psalms, Proverbs, and Prophets—fits into the history we have already traversed.

Originally, Ezra/Nehemiah appeared as one scroll under the title 1 and 2 Ezra. The name Nehemiah was given to the second portion of the scroll in the writings of Jerome in the fourth century A.D. Nonetheless, one continuous story is commenced in Ezra and completed in Nehemiah.

The period covered by the two books is roughly 110 years. It is the rough-and-tumble history of a century that saw a temple rebuilt and walls restored at Jerusalem. Reforms and relapses marked these years also.

The Old Testament book of Nehemiah ends as incompletely and as unsatisfactorily as the New Testament book of Acts. This does not mean that the book is unfinished. It does mean that just when we would like to know more, so much more, the story stops.

As mere history, the material in Nehemiah is a pretty spotty story. But this is not mere history. This is God's story, holy history—the threads of divine economy.

Glance over your shoulder at our pilgrimage thus far: It began with Abraham early in Genesis. Through Jacob and Joseph the story progressed into Egypt, and out again at the exodus under Moses. The Hebrews were forged from a band of former slaves into an organized confederation of tribes following their conquest of Canaan under Joshua.

Then there was the period of the judges, followed by the country's clamoring for a king. Saul was anointed. His blundering ineffectual reign was followed by David and then by Solomon, whose empire was split north and south at his death into Israel and Judah. Then each sector had its own history under 19 kings in each kingdom.

The Northern Kingdom, Israel, was wiped out by the Assyrians in 722 B.C. The Southern Kingdom, Judah, was demolished in 586 B.C. by the Babylonians—and many of its citizens deported out of Palestine. The exile in Babylon was terminated by a proclamation of Cyrus, king of Persia, in 538 B.C. There followed several waves of refugees returning to Palestine. The earliest groups struggled, but rebuilt the ravaged temple on Mount Moriah exactly where Solomon's temple had stood.

Now we are ready for the final page of Old Testament Hebrew history provided by Nehemiah. It is a sad/heroic story of a decadent people, a shattered economy, a band of floundering refugees trying to rebuild their beloved country.

We watch the poor displaced remnant people paying tribute to foreign governments, rebuilding their temple, frustrated in the work, leaving it for long years, taking it up again, and bringing it to such completion that the old men wept when they compared the second temple to their first one's former glory.

Then there develops a formalism, a backsliding, until a new reformation calls the people back to Yahweh—back to faith.

Then a long, long period of silence . . . Eventually Nehemiah emerges to complete the rebuilding of the city walls—a profound piece of work—but it too is followed by a relapse and a new reform.

There the story ends! It is a graphic page of history indeed. But remember, this is not mere history. This is God's story—holy history—the record of the acts of God among the people of God.

So, let's look at the divine economy threading through this final chapter of Old Testament history. What a tiny city the Nehemiah walls enclosed: the rocky heights of Zion to the south, where David 600 years before had built his palace and the temple area to the north. In all, the enclave might have been seven modern city blocks long and about two city blocks wide.

What's more, this little Judean enclave at Jerusalem was surrounded: Samaritans, under the hostile Sanballet, were north of them. The Trans-Jordan tribes, under Tobias, were east of them. The Nabateans were south of them. The resurgent Philistines were west of them.

It is not a safe, secure, substantial city that Nehemiah flings a wall around. It is so poor a city that one of Judah's enemies laughed at the sight of it, saying that a fox sitting on the walls could break them down.

In spite of it, Nehemiah arranged a resolute defense. Half the people built the walls while the other half patrolled the area, armed and ready for battle. Even the builders themselves wore swords. The scene is reminiscent of modern-day Israel where farmers plow their fields with rifles strapped to their backs.

It was indeed a war of nerves. Nehemiah fought and won. The walls were built. Judah's enemies were shut out—or they thought they were.

Yet the real enemies remained inside. The real enemies could not be excluded. They lurked within the hearts of his countrymen.

Now what does all this mean from the perspective of holy history? The New Testament letter of Hebrews years later puts it into perspective: "That which is becoming old and waxing aged is near unto vanishing away" (8:8-13).

The writer is quoting Jeremiah—a text recorded not many years before Nehemiah. Jeremiah envisioned a new glory, a new covenant of God with his people.

This new glory would not be external, but internal. The new covenant of God with God's people would be cut on their hearts. So, in this new arrangement "the old glory, waxing aged" was indeed near to vanishing away! That is precisely the picture that Nehemiah paints of the people of God and the divine economy.

The old glory is gone. But a new glory is emerging, Phoenix-like from the ashes of the old. But how does the new glory come? That is the theme of the entire central section of the book of Nehemiah. After the walls are built, chapters 8-10 record that the law of Yahweh is read one more time and finds lodging in the people's hearts. They made a new covenant—a new vow—to keep that law.

So the last commitment of the Old Testament remnant people is to keep the law, because the law has kept them.

Remember that and read Gal. 3:23-24: "Now before faith came, we were confined under the Law, kept under restraint until faith should be revealed. So that the law was our custodian until Christ came, that we might be justified by faith."

Hear that word again: "The law was our *custodian* until Christ came."

Here is the key to this last bit of Old Testament history: The record ends with people reading/responding to the Torah—the law—in the days of Nehemiah. The last page of Old Testament history points toward the first page of New Testament history with the coming of Jesus Christ who fulfills the law.

In Nehemiah's day—and for 400 years afterward—the law was "the custodian" for the people of God until Christ came. It was their pedagogue, their tutor, their schoolmaster pointing them to Jesus Christ.

So during the days of Nehemiah, the people had miserably failed in their civil and political experiment. They did not have much of a country left. But the Torah remained. So the people had succeeded in their spiritual quest.

The nation had failed under prophet, priest, king, and scribe. Their empire too was gone with the wind. But all this had been external all the time.

Now they had something internal—they had an insides. The law was left, and that gave them a conscience.

Mark one thing well: These wishy-washy, namby-pamby people of God had stumbled in and out of idolatry all their lives through. But after Nehemiah, they never set up an idol again.

They had a lot to learn about the law of Yahweh, written in their hearts, but from that day until this they have not set up an idol again. Call them what you will: Hebrews, Jews, Israelites. But you cannot call them idolaters!

They were left a people bereft—poor in so many ways—failing, crushed, bruised, disciplined. But they became a people who in human history embody the conviction that there is but one God—and Yahweh is God's name.

So the purpose of God in Nehemiah's time emerges. It was to put the people of God back under the law of God—this time, to lock that law up in their hearts. They had survived without much of a country, a flag, a holy city, or a holy temple.

But they could not survive without a conscience. Here, on the final page of Old Testament history, God is giving this people a heart, a conscience, a hope.

And notice the human instrument God used in this war of nerves. Nehemiah was no prophet, priest, king, or scribe. Nehemiah was a layman—a cupbearer in the court of an alien king. He did not reign in Jerusalem as a king. He offered no savory sacrifice as a priest. He thundered no searing proclamation as a prophet. He wrote and preserved no text as a scribe. He was simply a citizen patriot, one of those people with iron in his blood and ice in his veins.

Thus God took a common man—a proud, plain, blunt man who drove a hard bargain, flung up a wall in seven weeks—and saw to it that the people had a new chance to hear the law and to cut a new covenant in their hearts.

The nation had failed. Prophet, priest, and king had left the scene. But here was a man, a holy man. And this man, Nehemiah, in himself embodied the hope of Israel. And that hope was as old as Joshua and is as new as this morning's headlines.

"My righteous one shall live by faith." The way is prepared—400 years later—for the coming of Jesus Christ.

So, the curtain rings down on Old Testament history. But what does all this mean to me, to you?

Without a doubt, some of the former glory is gone from our good land. The "land of the free and the home of the brave" is having heart trouble. It has feet of clay and suffers a serious fever. It is over-drugged and under-medicated.

Nehemiah shows us that we must undertake more than mere external reform. We must probe to the transformation of persons themselves. No band-aid will do. What we need is surgery—moral surgery. We need more than new laws on our books. We need some old laws on our hearts.

Revolutions today are a dime a dozen. We've got big ones, little ones, middle-sized ones, black ones, white ones, red ones, yellow ones; ghetto ones, university ones, city ones, country ones, weekend ones, hour-long ones, bloody ones, bloodless ones, religious ones, and secular ones. Revolutions are a dime a dozen. All of them begin and end the same way.

They set out to alter conditions, inspired by a deep sense of righting wrongs. Then, after much violence, the establishment is disestablished. The purges set in to sweep out everything that looks suspicious.

But even before the shouts of celebration have died down, the new order begins to show an uncomfortable resemblance to the old one. The labels are changed, but not the evils. The top dogs come down, and the bottom dogs go up—without changing the pedigree of either.

Will we ever learn the lessons of history—especially holy history? The only revolutions that have permanence revolutionize not merely human conditions, but human beings themselves. They put a new law in their hearts!

In the old days there was a sanity test for patients in asylums. The patients were placed in a room where there was water spilled on the floor. They were given a mop, a pail, and instructions to dry the floor. However, a faucet had been left dripping in one corner of the room so the patients could clearly see it. If the patients proceeded to mop while the faucet ran, they were considered mentally incompetent. If they turned off the faucet before they mopped, they were considered ready for release.

The test of our sanity as a nation is on the line—it appears that we are continuing to mop while the faucet runs.

The Christian conviction is that the sources of evil are deeper than merely external symptoms—crime, drugs, murder, graft—and they demand a change of heart. All sub-Nehemiah schemes are half-cures at best. What we need is a new law on our hearts.

This land is a pushover for the shortcut. An aspirin is always simpler than surgery. We want to change everything but ourselves.

We scurry for good ends without redemptive means. We want to have stalwart communities without the bother of stalwart citizens.

We are perilously like an alcoholic who wants a cure for drunkenness that will not interfere with his drinking!

What can we do as we face the coming days and the avalanche of problems and possibilities in this land? We can rediscover and re-apply the neglected insight of Nehemiah—and of Jesus Christ.

In any crisis of spirit the worst enemies of all cannot be shut out by any kind of wall. They lurk in the hearts of the countrymen.

To this situation the gospel brings a strong and urgent word. Remember that it was to an imposing society based on servitude and power that Jesus Christ came announcing his kingdom.

He began at the bottom—at the grass roots. That in itself was revolutionary. No one ever thought of beginning a kingdom like that—depending first on the barefoot nobodies. But Jesus went deliberately to people who did not count.

He chose his followers from them. He drummed into their heads the basic ideas of his kingdom—and into their hearts the basic ideals of it.

He taught them what freedom and responsibility were all about, and that death is simply a larger part of living.

It was all so tame, so innocent, so way off over there in Galilee back country. But a convulsion began in those hills. That tempest in a Palestinian teapot endures.

The explosive, redemptive ideals unleashed by Jesus Christ heaved and convulsed, and changed the course of human history. Why? He wrote his law on people's hearts!

This ferment of his has endured because it plunges deeper down than mere externals to transform humankind themselves.

So, we have our clue from both Nehemiah and from Jesus. Write over the ramparts of the land this June morning: "What good to build a nation glorious, if man unbuilded goes?" Amen.

June 4, 1995

ESTHER

For such a time as this

Esther 1:1-3, 10-12, 19b; 2:2, 17; 3:1-2, 6; 4:13-16; 5:1-3; 7:3-6, 10; 8:2b; 10:3

There are two books in the Bible that bear the names of women. One is Ruth; the other is Esther. Esther does not have the gentle charm of Ruth. Instead it is a savage book, filled with intrigue, mystique, and counter-intrigue. The book was written late.

So it breathes the air of nationalism that marked the Hebrews after they were living once more in their homeland following the Exile.

To open the book of Esther is to be plunged headlong into the thick of this morning's headlines. Esther's Persia is our Iran. The country has an unbroken history from Cyrus the Great to the Ayatollah Khamenei; and to the president of Parliament, Mr. Rafsanjani.

The book of Esther opens with all the oriental splendor of a chapter right out of the *Arabian Nights*.

The setting is Persia, fifth century B.C., during the reign of Xerxes I—Ahasuerus— while the Persian empire was still at its zenith—stretching from India in the east to Ethiopia on the African continent. Esther, therefore, becomes the first notable woman of the Bible who lived outside of Palestine.

She was an orphan Jewish girl from a noble family of Judah carried into captivity when Babylon's King Nebuchadnezzar reduced Jerusalem to a wasteland of thorns and briars.

Esther's story is unusual, even controversial, in several ways. For one thing, it has nothing to do with Jerusalem or those Jews who returned to Palestine from Babylon. It is a book about hostages—or if you prefer, captives or refugees.

While the rest of the Old Testament focuses on those Jews who returned to Palestine, led back by Zerubbabel, Ezra, Nehemiah, and others, Esther deals with those Jews who did not come back. They remained scattered—in the Diaspora.

The setting for these 10 chapters then is Persia, not Palestine. Not one time does the name of God appear in this book. There is no reference to Hebrew religion or to Jewish ceremonials. The temple is not mentioned once. No requirement of the Torah is named. Only one reference to a feast or a fast occurs.

Why then Esther? This book became a patriotic symbol for the persecuted people of God. It was their flag in prose.

The religious purpose seems to be to explain the Jewish Feast of Purim that is observed in March every year even now by loyal Hebrews throughout the world.

The author of Esther is unknown. But the writer's estimate of orphan Esther is beautiful to behold. In these 10 chapters her name appears 55 times. The name of no other woman is recorded that many times in the Bible.

Like many great persons in history, Esther had humble beginnings. She was a Jewish maiden in Persia bereft of parents, reared by her cousin Mordecai, a Benjamite official at the palace in Shushan.

In a few swift strokes the fast-moving story is told: Queen Vashti was deposed. This opened the door for Esther, a Jew, to become queen of Persia.

After she became queen she dedicated herself not to the pleasures, comforts, and luxuries of the palace, but to the dreams, hopes, and ambitions of her people—a female Moses! Not long after her crowning she learned that Haman, her husband's favorite Persian official, hated her people—the Jews—and demanded that they bow down and pay homage to him.

Her cousin, Mordecai, refused to do it. And Esther soon received word of a serious rift between him and Haman. She knew she had to act swiftly and decisively.

Mordecai set the situation squarely before her when he sent his cryptic message: "Who knows, whether you have come to the kingdom for such a time as this?" (Esth. 4:14).

Esther prepared to go before her husband, the king, and intercede for her people, the Jews. If the king—a capricious man—was in a good mood, she might gain her point. If not, she could lose her throne and her head.

Her resolve ran deep. She made one of the most courageous statements ever made by any woman—or any man either for that matter. "So, I will go unto the king, which is against the law; and if I perish, I perish" (Esth. 4:16).

She prevailed with her husband, and in time he ordered Haman hanged on the very gallows that had been prepared for Esther's cousin Mordecai. The Jews, then in Persia, celebrated their deliverance from the wholesale massacre that had been planned for them by Haman.

They called the celebration a Purim festival, because Haman had cast a lost—a *pur*—to find the most favorable day to carry out his plot against the Jews.

The Purim festival is celebrated to this day among the Jews on March 14 and 15 when the scroll of Esther is read in synagogues all over the world. Esther lives on in the hearts of her countrymen. She is one of their greatest heroines, because she saved the Jewish refugees in Persia 2,500 years ago.

But that was a long time ago. What is the Esther word for us now?

The first is a strong word about life-changing commitments. This is a word about the calling of God.

You see, that is far more than just a slogan for some Baptist meeting: life-changing commitments. This was a way of life for Esther. Hers was a mission to the power structure. And her commitments shaped her life.

Esther shows us something: *life-changing* commitments can become *life-threatening* commitments, and often become *life-saving* commitments.

Listen: "I will go to the king, which is against the law [custom], and if I perish, I perish." That is one of the immortal resolutions in all the Bible or in all of literature. It was made from the top of the mind to the bottom of the heart.

It reminds me of Paul's "I am ready to be offered," of Carey's "Expect great things . . . attempt great things," of Luther's "Here I stand," of Henry's "Give me liberty or give me death." It strikes the same fire as some words by James Russell Lowell:

Careless seems the great Avenger; history's pages but record
One death-grapple in the darkness 'twixt old systems and the Word;
Truth forever on the scaffold, Wrong forever on the throne,—
Yet that scaffold sways the future, and, behind the dim unknown,
Standeth God within the shadow, keeping watch above his own.

Esther's word to all would-be commitment-makers is this: In the Lord Christ we have already got a bold mission; what we need now is a bold faith for it. ". . . if I perish, I perish!"

Write on the package of that resolution, "Danger: Life-changing commitments can be hazardous to your health." But in them are the seeds of life.

Christian faith is risky business. Deep in the heart of this moral universe is a cross principle.

Jesus spoke of it: Seed. Salt. Leaven. Light.

Suffering can be redemptive. That is what Golgotha is all about. Esther was ready to suffer for her commitments. They may break us! But no commitment is ever really a commitment until we are ready to suffer for it.

What this world needs now, what this country needs now, what this community needs now, what this church needs now are women with an Esther-kind of conviction making an Esther-kind of commitment. In pursuit of the purpose of God, every time a woman breaks a mold and defies a role assigned to her by this world, she is doing an Esther-kind of thing.

It is crunch time, especially for females struggling to find out, deep down, who they really are. In order to live as the persons they were created to be in the '90s, more and more women must challenge the norms that men and cultures have decided on for them. They must break away from some roles this world would impose upon them. They must see that God too has dreams for them.

Observe Esther: ". . . if I perish, I perish!"

Here is a woman deciding that a man—even a powerful one—cannot decide for her either the calling of God or the timing of God. Here is a female bumping up against a glass ceiling; it may be gold-plated, but it is a glass ceiling just the same. Here is a humble human being whose gender she cannot determine, but whose divine calling she can. She is making up her own mind about what God wants from a woman.

And, do you know what God wants from a woman? God wants a woman who will teach, if God calls her to teach—*even* if every man in the world says you should not do it. God wants a woman who will work, witness, and serve through the church, as she is called to work, witness, and serve through the church—*even* if every man in the church says you ought not do it. God wants a woman who will preach, if God calls her to preach—*even* if every man in the SBC says you must not do it. That is what God wants from a woman!

The second Esther word for us comes in the flaming gauntlet thrown down by her cousin, Mordecai: "Who knows whether you have come to the kingdom for such a time as this?" That is a word about the timing of God.

In Christ the mission always begins with the missionary. God does not call sticks or stones or trees or shrubs to do God's mission.

God calls people—not super people, not other people, but people just like you and me. God has pinned kingdom hopes on the likes of us.

You see, God must have purposes for women too. God has made so many of them. God has saved so many of them.

Our modern-day "kingdom" is a tough one to come to. It is tough internationally and nationally.

See the situation in our troubled earth house. "No trespassing" signs are on all the doors. Guards, watchmen, spies, and armies are stationed in all the halls to protect our vested interests.

We harbor all sorts of suspicions and all kinds of hostilities. We have installed hot and cold running wars. We have hung up silk and iron and bamboo curtains to guard our spheres of influence.

We crouch behind trade barriers, a 17th parallel, a 38th parallel, a Jordan River, a Panama Canal, a Mason-Dixon Line.

By now we are learning what law alone can and cannot do. Law can break down barriers, but it cannot prevent polarization. It can destroy walls, but it cannot build bridges. It can cause proximity, but it cannot create good will.

Our people are polarized, segregated, separated into camps—and assault rifles are still our best sellers, legal or not.

Human beings, in laboratory after laboratory, are being studied piecemeal. We are being inspected, bisected, profaned. Bit by bit we are being reduced to levels of life below us. The spiritual is squeezed out, the moral is bleached out; only the glandular is left.

Erich Fromm is frightfully near the truth: "Last decade God was dead. This decade man is dead."

What we believe determines how we behave. The compass is gone. The buoys marking our values are blurred. Our society is careening off course. Our drugged culture is lost in space.

When the roll is called in our U.S. Congress, persons do not know whether to answer "Present" or "Not Guilty."

We cannot bombard a generation with the idea that humans are mere animals or insects without getting animal and insect behavior. We were made for homage! One cannot cut us off from God and have anything left that is human but the gesture.

"Thou hast made him a little lower than the angels," exclaims the Psalmist. "Thou hast made him . . ." Drop God out of one end of that sentence, and human beings drop out of the other.

One of our evangelists is right: "If God does not judge America, then he will have to apologize to Sodom and Gomorrah."

The "kingdom" we are coming to is a tough kingdom indeed. But the challenge now is the same as it was when Mordecai hurled his gauntlet down before orphan Esther: "Who knows whether you come to the Kingdom for such a time as this?"

"Who knows . . .?" The issue is the timing of God. It speaks of something steady, an unquenchable faith for tough times.

This is our moment. The challenge is crystal clear. What we need, what our "kingdom" needs is a faith centered in the life-changing Spirit of Jesus Christ, the Lord.

I heard this week an old story that I had heard before, but had all but forgotten: During the Great Depression in New York's Central Park, a champion of a particular social agenda was expounding the cure-all virtues of his point of view. A sad, emaciated, drugged reject of a man appeared on the scene. The speaker saw his chance to make his point: "Follow my platform," he said, "and we'll put a new coat on that man." Whereupon, a certain listener in the crowd, who had seen and heard the whole thing, spoke up and said: "Follow my Christ, and we'll put a new man in that coat."

Oh God, that is what the world needs now: *new men* in all those jackets, Palm Beach suits, striped shirts, and shorts; *new women* in all those jeans, jackets, designer clothes, and bags. And Jesus Christ excels in providing that.

Today is the first day of the rest of our lives. "Who knows?" Under God, the call to the Kingdom comes for such a time as this.

"Who knows . . . ?" Does it come for you?

Say yes! Run risks! Live—by faith! Amen.

June 11, 1995

JOB

Declaration of dependence

Job 1:1-22; 2:3-13; 5:7; 8:30; 11:5-6; 19:25-27; 42:1-6, 12, 17

The 18th book of the Bible is high drama. It is not a book of solutions, but rather a book of mirrors reflecting basic human experience. The central figure is Job, whose name the book bears. The central fact is suffering, unexplained and undeserved. The central value is the folly of trying to penetrate God's plans and purposes with the limited tools of a human being.

Job is not fictional. He is fact. Job is not an imaginary man. He is real! In fact, he is so real that Archibald McLeish names him J.B. and gives him an address on every street in every town throughout this land.

The circumstances in which we find Job are not illusory circumstances. Rather, they are the ordinary, defining circumstances of human life—sin, suffering, sorrow, and silence.

The experiences of Job, then, are the very real experiences of very real human beings—both long ago and right now. All of us, in some degree, are acquainted with Job. We are his kin.

No one can say exactly when this book was written. It certainly came after the Exile, perhaps about the time Ezra was carrying out his reforms in restored Judah.

The author is likewise unknown. There may be reason to believe that this is an autobiographical drama in which a nameless Jew relates his own struggles through the pen-name of Job.

The book is a drama in both content and form. It possesses a prologue and an epilogue. In between is the meat of the material.

There are three cycles of speeches involving Job and his friends, corresponding roughly to three acts in the dramatic format. These are followed by the monologue of Elihu and the concluding address of Yahweh—always Job's God—and finally, Job's friend.

In order to appreciate the book of Job, we must consider it in light of the backdrop against which it is cast. Most students of scripture agree that it was written as a critique of one of the most fundamental doctrines that prevailed in ancient Israel.

That doctrine, simply put, was this: "In God's governance of us and our universe, righteousness is rewarded by prosperity and wickedness is visited by adversity." It followed that all personal calamity was caused by personal sin.

This doctrine dominates the wisdom literature of Israel and until this day is the most satisfying explanation some people can find for human prosperity and human suffering.

It was against this generalized doctrine of retribution that the author of Job raised his vehement protest. The way he does it is classic. His conclusion regarding the matter of undeserved suffering is still perhaps as satisfactory as any ever reached or written.

No truth as majestic as that shared by Job should be passed over with a lick, a promise, and a rushed-up prayer. So, let us review the process by which Job reaches his conclusion regarding his suffering.

The drama begins with Job, a man in the land of Uz, who exemplified in his own person everything that the wise men of Israel had always taught. The ideal holy man, wise and happy, was likewise the ideal prosperous man.

But suddenly a terrible change took place. In one day Job was stripped of everything. He lost all that he had—wealth, children, friends, servants, and finally his own health and the companionship of his wife. "*Hasatan*" stripped him.

This sudden drastic change in fortune brought Job's three friends to visit him. Thus the stage was set for great dialogue.

For three cycles the speeches proceed: Eliphaz championing the holiness of God, Bildad championing the righteousness of God, Zophar championing the wisdom of God—each in his own way explaining Job's calamity in light of the prevailing doctrine of retribution.

Against all their insinuations and open indictments Job, with increasing fervor, maintained his innocence. Mind you, he did not challenge their assumption that calamity ought to be the punishment for personal sin. Job agreed with that. He even believed that righteousness ought to be rewarded by prosperity, and wickedness ought to be visited by adversity.

But what outraged Job was that God had failed to do this in his own case. Job had lived a blameless and a holy life—and look what had happened to him. The way it was, was not the way it was supposed to be! This gross miscarriage of justice forced Job to grapple with the goodness of God.

We read this book and marvel at the unrestrained freedom with which the hero speaks his mind to God. Job cries, argues, pleads, and on occasion storms out in bursts of wild defiance.

This is no taffy-soft man doing business with a namby-pamby deity. Here is a bleeding man in a crucible. From his perch on the village dump he reaches one flaming conviction: A suffering man must, above all else, be honest with God.

Under the strain of great physical, mental, and spiritual torture, one must not suppress his dissatisfaction with God's handling of things. He ought to come out with it! And when he does, he finds that is precisely what God honors. He discovers that God understands!

Frankly, Job did not deserve what had happened. But in spite of it—with all the material things upon which he had relied swept away—Job reached out for God. And he spoke the deepest things of all to the God he could not find, about the self he could not understand, in the midst of circumstances he could not explain.

Lesser men might have declared their independence from God and come to see themselves as souls naked and alone against the sky—with their lives a meaningless charade of sound and fury signifying nothing.

But not Job! In some of the grandest utterances of all the Bible he made his unswerving declaration of dependence. Let us gather up some of these insights and see Job's conclusion regarding his own undeserved suffering.

In his second speech he speaks like a hurt child to God: "You will be sorry when I am gone" (7:16-21).

In one of his replies to Bildad he utters another childlike cry to God: "Remember that thou hast made me of clay, and wilt thou turn me to dust again?" (10:9).

At the close of the first cycle of speeches he looks for a moment upon what he wants most—not restored health or wealth, but a restored fellowship with God: "Oh that thou wouldst hide me in Sheol, that thou wouldst conceal me until thy wrath be past, that thou wouldst appoint me a set time, and remember me! If a man die, shall he live again?" (14:13-14).

In his next speech Job turns from his friends, who have proved to be "miserable comforters," to God: "Even now, behold my witness is in heaven, and he that vouches for me is on high" (16:19).

This same conviction comes back to him, white hot and in victorious completeness, when he answers Bildad in chapter 19: "For I know that my Redeemer liveth and at last he will stand upon the earth; And after my skin has been thus destroyed, then without my flesh I shall see God" (19:25-26).

No higher hope than that is found in the entire Old Testament. Here, Job knows that it is to God not to men—even friends—that he must look for vindication.

So he turns toward Yahweh in his suffering as champion, advocate, redeemer, and friend. And what Job found in his undeserved suffering was something better than an explanation. He found a presence—a divine partner, a participant in his pain.

Finally Job discovered that God was with him in his anguish, not as an enemy, but as a friend. In that discovery Job gained insight far beyond the popular doctrine of retribution. Listen to the last paragraph: "I had heard of thee by the hearing of the ear, but now my eye sees thee" (42:5).

His vision had replaced his friends' hearsay. His friends had talked as if they knew exactly what God was doing. Little men always do. Their doctrine was exact: the righteous never lose; the wicked never win.

But Job found something far more precious and accurate. Good people do suffer, for reasons they can never know. And when they do, God is not always punishing them. But God is always coming to them—not as a stranger, but as a friend.

Thus, Job cleared the way for persons to love God for God's own sake. He dismissed the idea of reward and punishment as the essential ingredient in the relation of God to man.

This insight became the leaven in the lump of Israel's fresh religious revelation. It remains, however, until this day the solution for the few rather than for the many.

Even now, as in ancient Israel, the many go through life embracing fairly well the old retribution doctrine. But for the few who want a better answer for suffering, Job has opened a window to let fresh breezes blow. What does his message mean to us?

Eliphaz was the realist among Job's friends. He contended that in our evil we bring all suffering upon ourselves. He was long on effect, but terribly short on cause.

Remember how in the fifth chapter he said: "Affliction does not come from the dust, nor does trouble sprout from the ground; but man is born to trouble as the sparks fly upward" (vv. 6-7).

It is the nature of sparks to fly upward. It is the nature of humans to suffer. For Eliphaz, it was as simple as that.

But not for Job! For him there was "a plus" of unexplained—and undeserved—suffering. Job could just as well say: "Man is born to joy, as the sparks fly upward."

Smiles and tears are indeed close friends. That is why we set a face of sorrow and a face of laughter side by side in our symbol of the theater.

Down deep we know that on the stage of this life there is always comedy-tragedy. The two in rhythm constitute the whole human drama.

Every dark moment has its bright twin brother—and we are always forgetting it. Both joy and pain are constitutional in these lives of ours. Without the prior joy we would never recognize the sorrow when it comes. Every sorrow must have a joy to feed upon.

Even cancer presupposes a healthy body to support it. If everything were cancer, there could be no cancer. Thus we confront our suffering, refusing all the while to forget life's goodness.

But the suffering these days seems so overwhelming. I challenge you: read today's newspaper. Catalog the lists of suffering described.

Pain is legion. And it is loose on every street where we live. It enters through every door. And if the doors be shut, then pain creeps in through the windows and the walls.

Suffering of body, suffering of mind, suffering of spirit—self-inflicted, inflicted by others—we face the fact of it. We cannot escape pain. It is the price of admission to life.

The psychiatrist and the pastor may help us "adjust" to our problem, but neither scientist nor surgeon, psychiatrist nor pastor can remove the agony—the pain—the limitation.

Job was right. Suffering goes to the roots of our human situation. It cannot be removed by merely spraying the leaves.

Job's lesson is our lesson. Suffering is more than a problem. Suffering is a happening—an event.

Pain is not theory; it is onslaught. It is not academic; it is actual. An event must be answered by an event.

The "problem of suffering" is always more than a problem. We cannot go on debating our hurting forever with our friends.

We must find a piece of pottery to scrape our sores. We must grapple with the pain—everywhere, always.

Our suffering always wrings from us a triple cry: "Why this pain?" "Why me?" *and* "Where is my salvation?"

Suffering in event requires answer in event. So, let a picture form in your mind. In this world, so disfigured by pain, come stand at a place where pain is the most outrageous because it is the most undeserved.

See: a limp figure, suspended between earth and sky; pierced hands and feet, flies buzzing around a bloody head, sun slashing down like a knife. It is Golgotha! The man on the central cross is Jesus Christ.

Underscore this event in red. Everyone knows that this Jesus was nailed up by soldiers to die as a common criminal. Everyone knows that he does not deserve what he is getting. His suffering illumines his innocence.

There was no martyr complex in this 30-year-old. This man loved life. He spoke deeply of joy, and planned for long years.

This Christ was no Stoic, buckling down to inevitables. He liked dinner parties; he rejoiced in friends. He saw in field and sky and stream a divine signature. He was happy at weddings, and he wept at funerals. But he lived and breathed a presence. So, he set his face like flint and journeyed toward a cross.

In that man, at Golgotha, God suffered too. God pulled no rank on us. In Jesus, God experienced and suffered God's own undeserved divine pain—and triumphed over it.

Jesus Christ walked straight into the teeth of suffering and death—to conquer them. He discovered in his own suffering something better than an explanation. He found what Job found: he found a presence—someone better than an answer.

It is a fact. Sparks do fly upward. But look there against the sky. The event of my suffering—and yours—is met by the event of God's suffering.

See the sign of the cross: it is God's signature on our pain! We were born for that vision—like Job tried to tell us. In that cross, God's pain "makes sense" and God's suffering becomes a sacrament. In that cross, our pain also "makes sense"—and our suffering too can become a sacrament—"a means of grace." And behind the scene—just off stage—Job whispers a line that comes home to us: "I know that my Redeemer lives!"

God is coming! Through suffering somehow, God is coming—never as enemy, but always as friend. Amen.

June 18, 1995

PSALMS

Thou hast made him
Psalm 8:2-5, 23:1-6

The 19th book of the Bible is the old Hebrew hymn book. It opens: "Blessed is the man . . ." It closes: "Praise the Lord." Both God and humans are celebrated in the Psalter.

The book of Psalms consists of 150 devotional poems intended for use in worship. They were written to be chanted to the accompaniment of a variety of ancient musical instruments.

The Hebrew name for the book is *Tehillim*. It means "praises."

There can be no chronological arrangements of the Psalms. They appear to stretch all the way from Moses to Malachi.

It is perfectly evident that the collection has been carefully edited; and the Psalms as we have them are grouped into five distinct groupings. The groups are thematic: 1-41, 42-72, 73-89, 90-106, 107-150.

The individual psalms are superb expressions by many authors at various times under differing circumstances of their consciousness of God: 101 of the psalms have captions stating the traditional names of their authors. In 73 of these David is listed as the author. Since he is traced to so many of them, some people have thought that David wrote all the Psalms.

Of course, he did not. But it is no accident that his name is associated with these poems, for in 2 Sam. 23:1 he is called "the sweet Psalmist of Israel."

Several interesting observations can be made about the collection of sacred Hebrew songs.

For example, at 71 places in the Psalter there appears the strange word "Selah." Have you ever read it and wondered what it means? Well, no one knows exactly what it means. It is an untranslatable Hebrew word presumably giving some sort of direction to those chanting the psalm.

Some psalms give directions as to the musical instrument with which they are to be accompanied. For example, Psalm 4 is for the *neginoth*—"a stringed instrument." And Psalm 5 is for the *nehiloth*—"a wind instrument."

Some of these musical instruments have been lost in antiquity, and today we do not even know what they look like.

There are some striking duplications in the Psalms. For example, the 14th Psalm is virtually identical with the 53rd Psalm. The 70th Psalm and the 40th Psalm are essentially the same in the last five verses.

Certain of the psalms are magnificently constructed acrostics. That is, each verse begins with a certain letter of the Hebrew alphabet. This effect is totally lost in English translation, but it is a masterful literary feat.

Psalms 25 and 34 are acrostics. But the most complex psalm of all is also the longest psalm: the 119th. It consists of 22 sections, one for each letter of the Hebrew alphabet. Each section then has eight lines, and each of the eight lines of that section begins with the same letter. It would be the same as having a psalm with sections A-Z, then sections of eight lines for each letter.

The importance of the Psalter in its entirety has to do with worship. Throughout, the worship—whether of individuals, nations, or the entire earth—is directed toward the personal God of Israel, and Yahweh is God's name.

These ancient songs have endured because they are a chronicle of simple, honest, basic human experience. They record how average, normal, everyday happenings catapult a person into the very presence of God.

These poems record how a person feels and thinks, speaks and acts, when that person is conscious of God.

The Psalms live today because of their revelation of great truths about worship. (And worship is what happens when we bring the gods we have made to confront the God who has made us.)

One student of scripture has well said: "What a record it would be if one could write it down—all the spiritual experiences, the disclosures of the heart, the conflicts and the combats which persons in the course of the ages have connected with the words of the Psalms."

And two psalms above all others, whose words persons have connected with their own combats and conflicts, have been Psalm 8 and Psalm 23. We shared them again today.

Hear Ps. 8:5: "Thou has made him . . ." Drop God out one end of that sentence and man drops right out the other end. The message is loud and clear: man is made for homage. We are made to be led by our maker.

Now hear Psalm 23: "He leadeth me . . ." This is a household phrase. It packs religious dynamite: the Maker leads those who are made.

In these two truths the entire Psalter is summarized: "God has made us" and "God will lead us." We are not orphans in a moral universe.

Sometimes familiarity can breed contempt. Yet I want to turn now with you to focus on the six verses that comprise Psalm 23—the psalm of psalms. The pure gold in these words will plug us into the rich, rare energy of all these ancient Hebrew songs.

If this psalm could write its own autobiography, what a story it would have to tell. There is no sea it has not crossed, no mountain it has not climbed, no road it has not traveled, no land it has not visited.

Treasured by beggars and kings, rejoiced over by saints and sinners . . . The crushed have clung to it. Sheltered and shattered souls have sung it. The battle-weary have quoted it in many a fox hole. The dying have found it a pillow. The living have found it a torch.

It is a poetic gem—perhaps the best-known and most-loved six verses ever written by anyone anywhere. These were the first six Bible verses most of us ever committed to memory.

Alexander McClaren is right: "The world could spare many a whole library better than this sunny little psalm. It has supplied the mold into which many a heart has poured itself."

So let us review this universally favorite song. It is a description of a day in the life of the grace-possessed. Or, better said, it is a thumbnail sketch of an entire lifetime absorbed with God.

Here is a long day's journey into life. It is the brief but vivid testimony of one whom memory has taken by the hand and led gently homeward.

These are the words of one who has now reached life's December, but June is still singing in his soul.

In this six-verse reflection the Psalmist reviews his entire lifetime as if it were a single day in the presence of God. The morning begins: God, the shepherd, awakens the weary human sheep with a familiar call. The heat of the day rises with its fevers and its dangers. God, the guide, leads on, through the rain, through the pain. At day's end, God, the host, welcomes the weary traveler home. Here, then, are the three visions of God in the 23rd Psalm:

- God, the Good Shepherd (vv. 1-2)
- God, the Trusted Guide (vv. 3-4)
- God, the Gracious Host (vv. 5-6)

If this is a summary of one person's experience of bringing average, normal, everyday happenings into the presence of God, then it can describe our own journey also. Let's see!

First, there is reveille: God, the Good Shepherd calls (vv. 1-2).

"The Lord is *my* shepherd . . ." All the blessings of personal religion are packed into that pronoun "my." The figure is fraught with meaning: the sheep need courage, not to battle the wolf, but to trust the shepherd.

The Lord—a shepherd: We would understand it better if the word were captain, foreman, chairman, president, or boss. We would understand it better if the word were cowboy. These are our words—our metaphors for power, authority, associations with clout.

Yet, make no mistake about the Psalmist's insight. God leads. God does not drive. God does not ride herd. Our pilgrimage into life starts with a shepherd's call. There is no beginning, apart from a positive response to that call. The power rests in the call, not in any cheap coercion or trickery to get the journey underway.

A call: that's a terribly fragile thing! Just an invitation—a mere urging. Yet, that is God's only means for getting the journey underway. God is left vulnerable. The call can be answered "no" as well as "yes."

On my desk at home there is an invitation to a wedding. In one corner rests a familiar sign: RSVP. That is the only force the invitation carries: RSVP (*répondez s'il vous plaît*). Invitations are like that: they are only half-finished until responded to.

How fragile, yet how profound is the shepherd's call to follow him into life. The urging goes within. No big stick forces the journey against one's will. But what of those who respond, who come, who follow?

A 5-year-old was quoting these verses and mis-said it like this: "The Lord is my shepherd. That's all I want."

Maybe that says it best of all. For those who respond, the provisions are all-inclusive:

- Shepherd-heart—outliving, outloving all lesser loyalties
- Shepherd-eye—piercing even the deepest darkness with sight
- Shepherd-presence—never serving in absentia, hearing about the sheep in some angelic staff meeting now and then
- Shepherd-knowledge—intimate acquaintance, knowing each by name and by need
- Shepherd-strength—equal to all challenges, whether fang of the wolf or seduction of the sheep-stealer
- Shepherd-tenderness—faithful to the weak and weary, firm to the unruly and the strong

Yet so many refuse to hear and heed the Shepherd's call, fearing the journey and dreading the pace.

And note this: Rest is promised, but it is a rest that replenishes life. Rest is no end in itself.

Follow this Shepherd and you find no retirement plan, but an employment plan. Yes there is rest, but only as an interlude before getting back to work. That is the start, and the pilgrimage moves swiftly through the years.

Second, there at the point of no return is God, the trusted Guide (vv. 3-4).

"He leadeth me . . .": purpose and power for the journey are packed into those three words. Notice the personal pronoun again: "me."

The Psalmist changes metaphors; he no longer sees himself as a sheep being shepherded, but now he is a traveler being accompanied.

And he wants us to know there is no place to turn back. The only direction for the journey is ahead.

By now the day's heat has set in. Still the trusted Guide leads on. But notice, the needs have changed some. Right paths are the chief concern now in the heat of the day. Whatever else, the weary traveler does not need to get lost out here where the roads are confusing and the fever of life is rising.

And the Guide knows that any path will get you there, if you do not know where you are going.

So the truth dawns: God guides in right paths "for his name's sake."

God's honor is at stake too in the paths that the children take. God is involved in our journey—not absentee, but present and personal.

Steady now! We approach that much-loved fourth verse: "Even though I walk through the valley of the shadow of death, I will fear no evil, for thou art with me; thy rod and thy staff, they comfort me."

This sunny psalm faces the darkness to penetrate it with light. And the landscape in the darkest valley is illuminated for us all.

Christian experience has clung to the psalm here. Sick beds have been transformed by this truth. Death beds have been transformed by this hope.

Here is a word about death. There is something steady over all the wreckage. The Guide is there in the valley too. And death is tamed!

The shadow still terrifies. But the substance is such that the traveler journeys on—through death into life!

In his immortal *Pilgrim's Progress* John Bunyan did not put this "valley of the shadows" at the end of the journey. He put the bridgeless river there. He put this valley in the middle of the pilgrim's journey.

The truth is clear: God is the trusted guide through all the valleys that could mean death. God stands ready to guide all those who are fed up with life—but still have some living to do.

One man, at age 42, made a mess of his life, his marriage, his career. He said it aptly as he summed up the situation for a friend. He wept: "Something in me died."

The trusted Guide is desperately needed then, when life caves in halfway through. The Shepherd's tools are still useful to the Guide: his rod and staff bring comfort.

These speak of both a new discipline and a new power ready and available to cope with spiritual emergencies.

Finally, there is journey's end and God, the Gracious Host (vv. 5-6).

Near journey's end, the Psalmist's confidence mounts. Then it soars and eventually explodes. Not just a meal, but a banquet is prepared!

God, the Host, guarantees this traveler refreshment and safety. Looking back now, the Psalmist finds that his only pursuers are "goodness and mercy."

In his final, robustly confident vision, his Bedouin tent becomes a temple and the long day's journey into life leads "into the house of the Lord forever." Day is done! But night does not come. The end is not set in darkness, but in the dawn—not in sunset, but in sunrise.

We would be stopping short of what our hearts tell us if we did not expand the horizon of this final phrase. Tennyson said it points toward the "one far-off divine event to which the whole creation moves."

Those who journey with the Lord Jesus Christ recall his own word about "the place prepared" (John 14). He spoke to his friends just before Golgotha and said, "Let not your hearts be troubled . . . I go to prepare a place for you."

Thus the Psalter is summed up—in all things and in all ways—by our Lord Jesus Christ. Praise the Lord! Amen!

June 25, 1995

PROVERBS

Melting ore into small coins
Proverbs 1:7

Reading the book of Proverbs is like reading a book of quotations. The subjects change often, but each one defines something real and vital. The book of Proverbs gets its name from its very first line. Chapter 1, verse 1 says: "The proverbs." This phrase in Hebrew is *Mishli*. That serves as the title of the book in the Jewish Bible.

The word *Mishli* means "wise sayings." So a proverb is a short, pithy, wise, folk saying that has arisen out of the ordinary experiences of ordinary people. It is generally of unknown origin and frequently used in everyday conversation.

The book of Proverbs is a heterogenous collection of such wise, folk sayings. Along with the books of Job and Ecclesiastes, the Proverbs belong to the "Wisdom Literature" of the Bible.

In the case of the Jews, much of their wisdom literature was ascribed to Solomon. This is natural since we read in 1 Kgs. 4:30 that "Solomon's wisdom excelled the wisdom of all the children of the east country and all the wisdom of Egypt."

Many of the Proverbs are indeed as old as Solomon, and were no doubt developed and collected by him. But what we have in our 20th book of the Bible is a collected and edited book of wise sayings from several sources and from many authors. It probably reached its final form by 300 B.C.

Proverbs addresses a reader personally. For these writers, being human is a great credential. These writers of Proverbs are deeply interested in the sheer marvels of humankind.

They have no ax to grind, no institution to promote, no advantage to seek. They are concerned entirely for the good of their readers and hearers.

They look at the individual—whether a father, a mother, a son, a daughter, a husband, a wife, a neighbor, a friend, a business associate, or a subject—as one to whom they have a responsibility. They want to counsel persons in all their ways so as to make them a blessing to themselves and to others.

These writers make a parental approach to us. They do not command like the legislators. They do not thunder their mandates like the prophets.

These are the philosophers of Israel—their "lovers of wisdom"—and the only authority they claim is that which is conferred by age, experience, and learning. They aim to win their reader or hearer to wisdom by gentle persuasion. They appeal to inherited beliefs, common sense, keen observation, and right thinking.

The method of these Proverbs writers is to assert, not to prove. They begin their pursuit of wisdom not with an investigation, but with an affirmation. Yet the affirmation is born of an investigation of life like an ordinary human lives it.

These pages are snatched right out of everyday life. They are both autobiographical and biographical.

What these writers have to impart is actually the collected experience of humankind caught in the act of being themselves. For them, wisdom is a very practical, everyday, down-to-earth thing. It has to do with life more than thought. The book of Proverbs is the Bible's candid camera.

Dr. Cornill is right: "The book of Proverbs mints the good metal of prophecy and law into current coin." That says it: here is the wisdom of the ages, the best insight of Hebrew prophecy and law, melted down into small coins. Reading them, we actually hold the massive ore of legal and prophetic utterance in our hand. This great currency comes to us in small change.

Compared to the prophets, the Proverbs are a different climate altogether. The emotional temperature is drastically cooler. The prophets of Israel were constantly getting excited. The wise men are calm!

They plead, persuade, threaten, and rebuke with great feeling; but they never lose control of themselves or lash out or weep or hurl denunciations. Life for them is on the whole a placid affair, a stream flowing gently within its banks—not a flooding torrent plunging headlong down a mountainside.

The world of these wise men is rather comfortable where good persons settle down, make money, marry, have children, enjoy their friends, practice philanthropy, live peaceably, and depart in a mellow old age.

Mind you, it is no dream world they paint. It is simply the kind of world they are convinced that wisdom can create. Therefore, the Proverb writers seek diligently to win their readers to wisdom.

At this point we ought to ask what exactly is wisdom. Since the wise men of Israel began their thinking with God, then wisdom began there also.

God has created this world and everything in it with a plan conformable to divine nature. This plan the Proverb writers called wisdom.

For example, in the eighth chapter there is an eloquent passage introducing wisdom: "Yahweh formed me [wisdom] in the beginning of his way . . . before the earth was . . . when he established the heavens I was there . . . when he marked out the foundations of the earth . . . I was by him as a master workman" (vv. 22-30). It is an ode to "Lady Wisdom."

Thus wisdom was formative in this moral universe. Human wisdom then is to know and to order a life by this divine wisdom. For humans, wisdom begins by acknowledging the primary reality in this world: God.

Human wisdom is ethical conformity to God's creation.

Thus the foundational declaration for all the Proverbs rests in chapter 1, verse 7: "The fear of Yahweh is the beginning of knowledge."

A man is wise in the measure that he apprehends and fears God. A woman is wise to the extent that she orders her life after "the fear of Yahweh." But what exactly is a proper "fear of the Lord"?

There are two dimensions in the fear of God: There is the fear that God might hurt me. There is the fear that I might hurt God.

The first is selfish—a cowardly, servile dread that strives to hide from God. It is surely not the beginning of wisdom.

The second is a fear born of love—the recognition of God in the whole of life. It is the ecstasy of a soul in wonder, finding God at work every place.

Thus, "fear" wrought by love is "the beginning of wisdom"—that is the precondition for being wise.

The standards of ethics set by the Proverb writers are especially high. The divine plan—which is wisdom—creates a society in which persons work hard, observe basic human rights, respect each other, have concern for the poor, exercise genuine friendliness, love their families and homes. They are sincere, moderate, modest, self-controlled, temperate, reliable, willing to listen and to learn, forgiving, considerate, discreet, kind to animals, sweet-tempered, generous, and prudent.

Such an ideal is virtually impossible to attain. So the writers urge on us not only their counsel, but also their redemption: "The fear of the Lord is the beginning of knowledge."

The book of Proverbs is not a mere haphazard collection of wise sayings. It has system and order.

Observe: the first verse is the title page. The next six verses are a preface outlining the purpose of the collection and the method of the collector. Finally, verse 7 provides the foundational truth threading through the entire collection: "The fear of the Lord is the beginning of knowledge."

Then there follow three lengthy series of Proverbs collected and arranged by unknown editors.

All this is followed by an appendix containing the words of Agur and the oracles of Lemuel. So the book comes alive—tied to life—in the ancient world and in ours.

It is yet terribly tempting for us to say: "Oh well! So what! All this stuff is awfully old." These proverbs interest us, but how can they possibly assist us? Well, let's see.

Perhaps the very first chapter is as good a place as any to dig in. So get your shovel; let's go treasure hunting. There are lots of rare and valuable coins buried in those 33 verses.

The discourse traces the entire life cycle. It deals first with the child, then with the youth, and finally with the grownup.

The first circle is in the home. Here wisdom must be learned. The next circle is in the neighborhood, where companionships are formed outside the family. Here wisdom must be applied. The final circle is in the nearby city. In the wonderland of life in the city, wisdom must be obeyed.

Remember too that the foundational truth is in verse 7: "The fear of the Lord is the beginning of wisdom." Then that declaration is applied to life wherever it is lived.

First, it begins in the home.

"My son, hear the instruction of your father, and reject not your mother's teaching. For they are a fair garland for your head, and pendants for your neck" (1:8-9).

That is a profound and a beautiful place to start. Here at home the fear of the Lord is taught to children. That seems to be the arrangement for life—building throughout this moral universe. Birds, animals, humans: all these must prepare their offspring for life.

But children are not able to grasp everything said about God in the home. So how do we instruct them?

We do it more by deed than by word; more by how we act than by what we say; more by orthopraxy than by orthodoxy.

For a child, God is incarnate—enfleshed in persons at home. That is the higher meaning of fathering and mothering.

So we need not be anxious to teach our children theology. They will learn it anyway—good or bad—from the examples nearest to them, enfleshed in persons at home. At home we model wisdom or we model folly.

According to Proverbs, wisdom for children is initiated in the instruction of father and the teaching of mother.

This means a very basic and profound thing: parents must be what they want their child to become. Remember the old cartoon character Andy Gump? He would stand aside, button-bustin' proud, and watch his son. Then he would say, "He's a chip off the old block." Somehow all children are. That is why the quality of the block is so everlastingly important. Hear a modern fable:

Once there was a little boy. When he was 3 weeks old his parents began regularly to turn him over to a babysitter at night. When he was 8 months old they did the same thing during the day—and both worked. When he was 2 they dressed him like a cowboy and bought him a pistol. When he was 3 he could curse like a veteran and pleased his parents no end with his vocabulary. When he was 6 his father occasionally dropped him off at Sunday school while he went to the golf course. When he was 8 they bought him a BB gun and taught him to shoot sparrows. He learned to shoot windshields by himself. When he was 10 he had his first smoke, filched from his mother's purse.

The next year he got his first taste of liquor from a bottle his father always kept handy in the cabinet. When he was 13 he told his parents that other boys stayed out past midnight, so they said he could too; it cut down on arguments. When he was 14 he smoked his first "pot." He told his parents they got drugged on nembutal and alcohol, and he got drugged on marijuana and asked them what's the difference. When he was 15 they got a beautiful two-tone, two-ton machine, wrangled a license for him to drive it, and told him not to hurt anybody with it. When he was 16 the police called his home one night and said: "We have your boy. He's in trouble—big trouble." "In trouble!" screamed the father. "It can't be my son." But it was!

Children do indeed demand and deserve more than the devilish advice "Don't do as I do; do as I say." They cannot follow that counsel.

Parents cannot fudge during those crucial formative years and expect miracles later. Parenting is hard work. Parents must be what they want the child to become. That is the ancient/modem wisdom of Proverbs.

Remember: when ancient Rome broke up housekeeping and moved into the care-free apartment era, Rome began to rot. The decay, which eventually led to her destruction, set in when her homes broke down.

The same thing happened in Israel. The homes were charged with the religious instruction of youth. When homes failed, apostasy set in. The nation went on the rocks.

The graveyards of history are filled with individuals and empires that have failed in their homes to impart the spiritual principles that are the ramparts of men and of nations.

So the beginning of wisdom begins in the home, where a child is taught by parents the fear of the Lord. And that teaching comes by modeling more than by lecturing.

Wisdom continues in the community.

The day soon comes when the child in pursuit of his/her own life moves out into wider circles of association and experience.

The Bible has two words about the duty of children to parents at this point: The first word is "obey." That is for the days of childhood. The second word is "honor." That word is forever.

The day comes when children make their own choices, guided by parental counsel, but essentially on their own.

When children enter this stage, wisdom has a special word: "My son, if sinners entice thee, consent thou not" (1:10).

There is no more important moment in the life of a youngster than when he or she begins to choose companions. Wisdom instructs that such choices be made as will contribute to strength of character.

A friend who damages and diminishes a life is not a true friend. That is the word from the wise to the wise.

Finally there comes a day when the youth leaves his own neighborhood to pursue life in the city. Wisdom extends here also, when the address becomes "Elsewhere."

Listen to Prov. 1:20-21: "Wisdom cries aloud in the streets, in the markets she raises her voice. On the top of the walls she cries out, at the entrance of the city limits she speaks."

Wisdom does not call the youth back from the city. Wisdom rather warns the youth of the fate of those who plunge into such things forgetful of God. The sad fact is that if the youngster did not learn wisdom in the home, how terrible is the result in the city.

That is all the more reason why parents must teach their children the way of wisdom *before* they plunge into the topsy-turvy of life—or there they may never practice it.

The counsel with which this first section of Proverbs closes is as practical now as it was when it was first written.

Listen to wisdom speak: "Trust in the Lord with all your heart and do not rely on your own understanding. In all your ways acknowledge him, and he will make straight your paths. Be not wise in your own eyes; fear the Lord, and turn away from evil. It will be healing to your flesh and refreshment to your bones" (3:5-8).

Do you want a motto for living now or 10 years from now or out into the 21st century?

Here is one, time-tested and true: "In all your ways acknowledge Yahweh and he will make straight your paths." That is a word from the wise to the wise. Amen!

July 9, 1995

ECCLESIASTES

Living by a squint or a vision
Ecclesiastes 1:2, 12:13-14

A long with Job and Proverbs, the book of Ecclesiastes belongs to the "Wisdom Literature" of the Old Testament. As usual, the title comes from the first line: "The words of the Preacher . . ."

"Preacher" is a translation of the Hebrew word *Qoheleth*. That word describes a person who convenes or speaks in an open assembly.

The Greek word for assembly is *ekklesia*. And one who addresses an assembly would be an *ekklesiastes*.

A Latin spelling of this word gives us the title of the book. Suffice it to say that Ecclesiastes means "The Preacher." All we know of this preacher must be drawn from this book. He put forth these reflections on life under the great pen name of Solomon.

Students of scripture almost unanimously agree that Ecclesiastes was written after the Exile—sometime between 300 and 200 B.C.—during the period of Greek dominance in world history. The book has many evidences of Greek influence and thought patterns to go along with its Greek name.

The Preacher gives us little autobiographical information. Whether he was young or old or middle age and whether he lived in Palestine or in Egypt, we can only conjecture. But what he does do is bare his soul while sharing his own soul's journey.

His 12-chapter treatise has come down to us both to baffle and to inform. It is one soul's journey through all the varying moods linked up with life.

The method Qoheleth used was different in one important respect from that of Israel's other wise men: They started from belief; he began with facts.

This author had a passion for observation. He insisted on seeing everything, even though some of what he saw could not be reconciled with some of what he believed.

Qoheleth experimented with various lifestyles to get what he wanted. And what exactly did he want?

He wanted to find meaning for his life, his world, and for all the people in it. He sought a moral order that could be depended on and predictable. He longed to outlive himself—to be remembered—and to feel that he and all the rest of us are going somewhere.

But it was such hopes as these that he saw dashed on hard anvils. Therefore, in the opening lines of his message Qoheleth despaired: "Vanity of vanities . . . all is vanity" (1:2).

He was no gentle cynic who could look life in the teeth and smile. He remained the unrepentant rebel—the critic—the hater and the lover of life; the bittersweet seer, hearer, smeller, taster, and toucher of the real-world scene.

Thus there is no author in the Bible who so eludes the reader. He who was the baffled becomes also the baffler.

The book of Proverbs opens with the ringing declaration that "the fear of the Lord is the beginning of wisdom." The book of Ecclesiastes opens with something far different: "Vanity of vanities," says Qoheleth, "all is vanity."

The word vanity implies something as fleeting and as gaseous as air. It means "empty" and can be translated "Vapor of vapors; all is a vapor."

Thus the opening thesis of Ecclesiastes takes shape: Everything sensual is empty, vaporous! In order to impress this fact, Qoheleth—the Preacher—developed his 12-chapter message.

Ecclesiastes is not a diary; it is a sermon. As in most sermons, the first word is not the final word. In fact, the first word sometimes is in direct contrast to the last word.

While in Proverbs the way of wisdom is described at the beginning, in Ecclesiastes the way of wisdom is described only at the ending. So, in this book we have the flip-side of the book of Proverbs.

Here is the revelation of a person who at the outset failed to fear the Lord and therefore lost the key to wisdom. We must keep this fact clearly in mind as we read this sermon. It is a case made by contrast—a positive lesson, negatively presented.

We must also remember the lapse between the time this sermon was written and the time the writer passed through the experiences he describes. He is looking back.

The reflective attitude of this preacher must be grasped and kept clearly in view, or else we miss the value of this book. He looks back on a life he has lived years before. Throughout all his experiences, Qoheleth never lost an intellectual conviction of the existence of God. He was neither atheist nor agnostic.

That was his problem: he believed in God, but tried to live without God. He sought wisdom, satisfaction, "the good life" somewhere/everywhere else except in reliance upon God. Of course, he never found it.

He believed in God, but lacked the fear of God that is "the beginning of wisdom." He did not trust in Yahweh with all his heart. Instead he leaned upon his own understanding, and found out finally that he could not do it.

Consequently his paths lacked direction, and through the years he wandered over trackless and meaningless wastes. He learned something: any road will get you there if you do not know where you're going. He thought through more than he could live through. His head fooled his heart.

Thus the book of Ecclesiastes is a mirror in which we see what a life is like when a person believes in God but lives without God. It is the agony and the ecstasy of a life on the wrong track.

For this reason, perhaps no book in the Old Testament is more contemporary to the religious situation of the 1990s than Ecclesiastes. All over this land there is a form of godliness without the fruits of it.

So let's review some of the insights of this ancient preacher of Israel and apply them to ourselves here and now. In studying this preacher's account of his own experiences we can diagnose for ourselves the emptiness of every life playing games with God.

Here is one of the most intriguing verses in Qoheleth's sermon: "This is all that I have learned: God has made us plain and simple, but we have made ourselves very complicated."

One critic discussing some attitudes of Dr. Hutton, the social analyst, said they were fascinating but useless. When asked why, he replied: "Hutton squinted at everything." He went on to explain that Hutton saw only one aspect of things. He viewed life around him with one eye closed.

The book of Ecclesiastes is much like that. It provides a portrait of a life lived by a squint and not by a vision. And what does this do to a person? Let's see.

One, it leads to a bleak view of the world.

When Qoheleth looked at the universe he saw its machinery, but not its motor. He observed this world's movement and motion, but not its purpose and direction.

He looked intently, brilliantly, and found out some things that it has taken centuries for science to verify: The winds, for him, moved in circles. The rivers rose in the mountains, flowed to the sea, and then through rainfall went back again to the hills.

Here was a man in the engine room of this universe. But it did not help. When he declared that all was vanity he was obsessed with the constant grind of the machinery. He despaired because he had no sense of communion with the master spirit controlling all of this.

Consider this situation: Place a man with no knowledge of machinery in the engine room of a giant textile mill. Here in the midst of the flying pulleys, whirling wheels, speeding motors, he would be oppressed by the sound, the fury, the monotonous motion. Then show him the weaving rooms, the dying, cutting, and sewing processes until he sees the finished product. Now he will discover the music of the machinery—its rhythm, purpose, direction.

Qoheleth, at first, saw the machinery, but his life was not in fellowship with the machinist. Apart from a knowledge of God, his bleak view of the world plunged him into despair: "Vanity of vanities . . . all is vanity."

Two, his squint led to a bleak view of God.

Qoheleth was long on transcendence, but short on immanence. He could conceive of God, safely stashed away in a cloud on the back side of the sky; but it was beyond him to perceive God in the rough and tumble of everyday affairs. He saw God as a summer tourist nosing around in someone else's world.

So, neglecting personal faith in the living God, he plunged into an observation of this world's phenomena, including its appalling human/social conditions, and attempted to deduce, define, and discover God from them. His observations did not allow him to deny divine governance of this world, but he did come to see it as impersonal—only as a governance by so many forces, pressures, and movements.

So God became for him merely the presiding genius maintaining the movement of the machinery without any high purpose—a sort of cosmic executive secretary; CEO of this universe. Looking merely at things in their motions he concluded that there was no more advantage in goodness than in wickedness. All things happened to all persons all the same—whether they were good or bad.

Inexorable forces played havoc with this world and every human being in it. God was too involved in the machinery to draw near to individuals in grace and deliverance. No wonder he concluded: "Vanity of vanities . . . all is vanity."

Third, his squint led to a bleak view of faith.

Qoheleth had considered the mechanism of this universe, observed the social oppression on every hand, and concluded that nothing means anything. Life was all a riddle.

So he tried everything in an effort to find something that had meaning: knowledge, pleasure, passion, and license. Does that sound 1990ish in a culture drugging itself silly?

He could not put God out of his mind, so he would put God out of his heart—out of his life. He would live a lie! No wonder worship was a fearful thing for him.

Remember: there are two kinds of fear in relation to God. One is the fear that what God does will hurt us. The other is the fear that what we do will hurt God. This preacher's fear was all of the first sort. It was all fire and brimstone.

His essential religious response could be summed up like this: it is wise to be careful; God is out to get you. The relentless power of God came to Qoheleth only to threaten and never to comfort. For this reason, he could actually be grateful for the awesome distance between himself and God. It's no wonder he said, "Vapor of vapors . . . all is a vapor."

Wherever Qoheleth looked he saw only the shadow cast by his own mortality. If he had his way, he would make deity out of dirt—just like humanity. He had no vision of anything beyond himself and this present world. Consequently he feared death for the simple reason that it ended life.

His attitude was one of cultivated indifference. His two favorite phrases were "Oh yeah!" and "So what?" He emulated the turtle—grew a hard shell and seldom stuck his neck out.

His vision for life was restricted by the geography that bound him and the parameters of the clock and the calendar. His life was not pursued in any personal, direct, immediate relationship with God. Consequently he squinted at life and lived it without a vision.

This preacher learned a hard lesson: No matter how much a man believes in God in his head, if he puts God out of the everyday affairs of his heart, his life is still smashed.

That lesson, painfully learned, gave Qoheleth his credential to share his final conviction with all of us. He wrote everything in his first 11 chapters in order to write with persuasion the last paragraph in his 12th chapter.

And here is that paragraph: "The end of the matter is this; all has been heard. Fear God, and keep his commandments; for this is the whole duty of man" (12:13).

At last, his squint gives way to a vision. And the vision is precisely the same as the Proverbs.

Here, then, is the living message of Ecclesiastes: Conviction affects character through conduct. Conduct, untrue to conviction, is hypocrisy. Conviction, unexpressed in conduct, is heresy.

So in Proverbs we find a green light indicating the way to wisdom. In Ecclesiastes we find a red light warning against the way to emptiness.

To ignore the living God is to throw away the keys to the good life. A man may try knowledge or mirth or wealth. A woman may chase life without faith, but she will never catch it. It is to chase a vapor. It is a ghost ideal.

To fear God and keep God's commandments is more than to find life. It is to be found by life.

Again the fulfillment of Qoheleth's vision lies in the man of Galilee who said: "I am the way, the truth, the life."

To know and to obey this Christ is to find all the doors to real life flung open wide.

Why don't you enter the open door yourself—now? You can! You must! All else is vanity! Amen.

July 16, 1995

SONG OF SOLOMON

The greatest of these is love
Song of Solomon 2:10-15, 4:1-7, 5:10-16, 8:6-7

There are three books in the Old Testament generally connected with Solomon: Proverbs, Ecclesiastes, and the Song of Solomon. This was completely natural because in 1 Kgs. 4:32 we read: "And Solomon spoke 3,000 proverbs; and his songs were a thousand and five."

This Song of Solomon, as we have it, was finished late—about 300 B.C. The Hebrew title of this 22nd book in our Bible is *Shir Hashirim*.

It means "Songs of Songs" and implies that this was the best and most beautiful of all the ancient songs attributed to Solomon. This was the ultimate song—the *summum bonum* song, "the song of songs."

The Song of Solomon is actually a love poem—somewhat erotic—and perhaps composed to celebrate a wedding. It is in fact a series of songs sung alternatingly by the bride, the groom, and the chorus. It is thus a poetic drama in which several characters speak. Suffice it to say that sorting out the dialogue is anything but a simple art.

The obvious eroticism in the Song of Solomon has caused well-intentioned interpreters to look for hidden meanings; to make more of the book than its simple description of love between a bride and a groom.

So Bernard of Clairvaux, the great preacher of the Middle Ages, interpreted the book allegorically and preached more than 2,000 sermons from it.

Throughout history the book has met with some bizarre headlines at the hands of its interpreters. For some it has become the Bible's *National Enquirer*. Everything that human imagination can devise has been seen lurking in these eight chapters.

For example, Kiri Jewell, a 14-year-old, reported in her recent testimony at the House hearings involving David Koresh and the Waco, Texas tragedy that in 1991 David Koresh had sex with her in a Texas motel. After she took a shower, he read to her from the Song of Solomon. Kiri was 10 years old when this revolting event took place.

Protestants, Catholics, and Jews through the years have made this book a manual of human lovemaking pointing toward divine love in the making.

All of this may be well and good. But I want to suggest that we read these eight chapters today at their face value—simply accepting the words as they stand.

Thus perceived, the Song of Solomon becomes a very human love poem—and a very beautiful one at that. It is the owner's manual for the human heart.

So let's accept one simple rule of interpretation: these poems must be treated first and foremost as simple, yet sublime, songs of human affection. They are about a man and a woman in love.

Taking this view of the Song of Solomon, we recognize in it the supremacy of love. And we find ourselves saying, "If two human beings can love like this, how much more is the measure of God's love?"

We are indebted for this ancient Hebrew insight that on the purely human level our lives find their highest fulfillment in the love of a man and a woman. If we have been loved—really loved—by one person in this world, we have lived well!

So we have here an earthy love song—very passionate and very beautiful.

Yet the journey is not too far from the love song of Solomon in the Old Testament to the love song of Paul in the New Testament: "The greatest of these is love," found in 1 Corinthians 13.

So, in the Song of Solomon let us expect two things: first, a revelation of the true nature of human love; second, a revelation of the highest possibilities of divine love.

In this man-love/woman-love we have a paradigm of God-love. If a man and a woman can love like this, how much more does God love?

The mode of expression in the Song of Solomon is typically Eastern. It is full of human sweat—intense, bold. It is magnificent in its gorgeous color, its racy figures of speech, the sheer abandon of its expressions.

Here is love with muscle to it. The cool, calculating, mechanical person who may dislike this book has forgotten what it was like to be in love.

Lovers will love the Song of Solomon.

So, accepting the book as a cluster of human love songs, perhaps prepared for a wedding day, let's see what it tells us about human affection. Then we can decipher the hints it holds about God's love.

Here the foundation of love is laid.

Through all the songs that these lovers sing, there surges the spirit of mutual satisfaction and fulfillment and commitment. Love's big three: satisfaction, fulfillment, and commitment—each one finds perfect peace and rest in love for the other.

Here then is the superlative power of a supreme affection.

This becomes the sure foundation for the love between this woman and this man. In all the songs they sing there surges one supreme affection.

They are not playing games. They are not making trial runs. This is not Hollywood. This is not tabloid or TV soap. This is *love!*

They do not come to their marriage altar simply to undress each other. Neither desires merely to consume the other—sensually. They come to marriage—as they come to life—in love to fulfill and fully to satisfy.

Joseph Cook has said it: "A supreme affection is the only natural basis of marriage, and that supreme affection can only exist between two persons in love."

A whole parcel of lesser affections can be spread among many lovers. But the supreme affection is possible only for one. And that is the foundation for marriage love.

Exactly what is a supreme affection? Well, let's let the Song of Solomon tell us. Here is a bit of the second chapter: "As a lily among thorns, so is my love among maidens."

That is the language of a man in love. "As the apple tree among the trees of the wood, so is my beloved among young men." That is the answering word of a woman in love.

These two bits together illustrate the meaning of supreme affection between these two. Their love is absolutely exclusive. Each sees the other as the only one.

By the side of his lily, all others are thorns—so sings the man. To the woman, her one apple is supreme; all other trees are full of worms.

This kind of love is not born amidst the feverish promiscuity of a mating season. Neither is it nourished by sophomoric triflings at a singles' bar.

This is love at its highest, noblest best. This is a supreme affection. It yields absolute mutual fulfillment and satisfaction and commitment. This is the kind of love to build a marriage on.

But what of so much "loving" without commitment these days? It is the stuff of fickleness and flirtation. Any male/female can have an affair. Only special males and females can have a marriage.

This is the fallacy in the average office wolf who huffs and puffs around many a water cooler. For him, every woman is new territory to be taken, a challenge, an object to conquer.

His line is always the same: "I love you. I want you. I need you." Translated, that means "I love me; I want you." There is not the slightest inclination in the direction of a commitment that extends beyond momentary pleasure.

There is sadness and tragedy in "love" like that—insulated/isolated from commitment. Yet the essence of life is love—not selfish or exploitive, but giving and growing love.

This is love that is God-made and God-like. It blends couples through commitment into marriage.

Let the word go forth from here: the starting love of a courtship and the staying love of a marriage are not the same thing. What most couples call "love" at the outset is a far cry from what love must become to ensure and to enhance a marriage.

That which is so glibly sung about, written about, talked about in the name of love is often at best a sort of romantic bubble that can burst at the first pin prick.

Now, no one will ever hear me raise an objection against romance. I'm all for that. It is one of the things that makes the world go round.

But romance must be part of a larger experience; and the larger experience is love backed up by commitment.

This is the love that Paul says "*bears* all things, *believes* all things, *hopes* all things, *endures* all things." No couple ever starts off with that quality of love at their wedding. It grows along the way beyond the wedding into marriage. In this way the intimacies of real romance can be sustained.

The image of love in the 1990s, packaged and marketed especially to people in their teens, is usually inadequate, often distorted, and frequently obscene. It is treacherous to believe that an infinite number of capricious relationships can better prepare a young person for the mature love of marriage.

In fact, the exact opposite is true. Infidelity does not lead to fidelity. Wholesale lovemaking without commitment bears strange fruit.

Persons who practice it sometimes find themselves content to use people and to steel themselves against any real intimacy.

Thus they discover that they cannot love, nor can they risk ever being really loved. They are condemned to a life forever full of a thousand trifling affections and can never know the one supreme affection defined in the Song of Songs.

Hear Mike Tyson, heavyweight champion of the world, quoted in newspapers sometime ago: "I love to hurt a woman, hear her scream, see her bleed." That, my friends, is not macho; that is animal—and such a man will never know love like human beings were meant to love.

So, the truth of this ancient Old Testament book comes home to us. Love at its highest is a supreme affection between two persons. Love at its highest, deepest, and best is the uncalculating and absolute mutual satisfaction of a man and a woman in each other forever.

Sure, that is an ideal! But whoever said ideals ought to be easy? We can be grateful that something this severe is expected of us.

It is the uniquely human challenge of true love. All the animals can emulate everything less.

Here too the strength of love is shown.

Hear the song of the lovers in chapter 8: "Set me as a seal upon your heart, as a seal upon your arm; or love is strong as death, jealousy is cruel as the grave. Its flashes are flashes of fire, a most vehement flame. Many waters cannot quench love, neither can floods drown it. If a man offered for love all the wealth of his house, it would be utterly scorned."

That is to say, love cannot be destroyed if present; love cannot be bought if absent.

Here is a clear and forceful proclamation of the vast and all victorious strength of true love. It fits perfectly Paul's classic statement in 1 Corinthians 13: "The greatest of these is love."

In the presence of the glory of love, this writer warns us not to trifle with the most sacred thing in this life. Thus, if Solomon's song is sung only of human love, it is nevertheless sung before Yahweh—and reflects supremely God's love. It flashes its light upon the vaster range of God's love for us all.

Human love harmonizes with the pattern of God's love. And what is that pattern?

It is focused in the person of Jesus Christ. He was "the happening" of God's love in history. Through this Christ, God accomplishes "the happening" of God's love in us.

It must fill us with perennial astonishment that our human loves at their best point us to the vaster love of God for all of us.

The energy of God's love is far beyond any love we can ever know. Yet the fact of our human love provides clues to the power of divine love.

My cousin, Ruth—battered, abused in her hospital bed—said: "I guess I'm afflicted with an incurable condition. I love him." Finally, my cousin left the one who abused her. But she went to her grave—an early grave—loving that man.

So is God "affected with an incurable condition." God loves us. God showed us how much—in Christ. God in Jesus went to an early grave also, loving persons who abused his love.

So hear the Song of Solomon's word for us: When it is real and for keeps, our human love models God's love. When it is cheap and selfish, our human love betrays God's love.

There are both truth and poetry in these lines scribbled on an asylum wall:

Could we with ink the ocean fill,
And were the skies of parchment made,
Were every stalk on earth a quill,
And every man a scribe by trade,
To write the love of God above,
Would drain the ocean dry.
Nor could the scroll contain the whole,
Though stretched from sky to sky.

The Song of Solomon is a song of love—our love and our God's love!

Love divine, all loves excelling,
Joy of heaven to earth come down;
Fix in us thy humble dwelling;
All thy faithful mercies crown!
Jesus, Thou art all compassion,
Pure unbounded love Thou art;
Visit us with Thy salvation;
Enter every trembling heart.

Amen!

July 23, 1995

ISAIAH

I saw the Lord

Isaiah 6:1-8, 9:5-7, 11:1-2, 40:1-5, 53:1-7

The last half of the Old Testament records the works of 16 prophets. These flourished during the three-century span from 750 to 450 B.C. The books are not placed in any chronological order. Rather, they are divided into two sections on the basis of length. Fully two-thirds of the material in these 16 prophetic books is to be found in the first three: Isaiah, Jeremiah, and Ezekiel.

These three do appear in chronological sequence: Isaiah lived during the period of Assyrian ascendancy as a world power (eighth century B.C.). Jeremiah lived during the period of Babylonian ascendancy (early sixth century B.C.). Ezekiel was a prophet of the exile in Babylon (late sixth century B.C.).

Perhaps the best known and most loved of all the prophets is Isaiah. It is from that matchless book that we share some insights today.

All we know of Isaiah is provided autobiographically in the book that bears his name. His father was Amoz. So far as we know, he is mentioned only this once in the Old Testament. So who he was, we can only conjecture.

There is a rabbinic tradition that Amoz, Isaiah's father, was a brother of Amaziah, Judah's former king, and Uzziah's father. If this were so, then Isaiah would be a member of the royal family and a first cousin of King Uzziah, whose death marked the date of Isaiah's call to be a prophet.

Students of scripture judge from Isaiah's writing style that he did indeed belong to the upper class in Judah. If this is so, here was an aristocrat who lived and worked on behalf of the dispossessed masses in his homeland. Few men in history have ever championed more eloquently the cause of the poor and the disfranchised.

Like most of the prophets, Isaiah was radical, insisting that ritual was no substitute for true religion in Judah or anywhere else.

The general period in which Isaiah carried out his prophetic mission is given in the first verse of the book: "The vision of Isaiah . . . which he saw in the days of Uzziah, Jotham, Ahaz, and Hezekiah, kings of Judah."

Remember that by this time in Hebrew history, Solomon's empire had been divided in both land and leadership. Israel, in the north, had her kings. Judah, in the south, had her kings.

Isaiah's work was directed in the main to the Southern Kingdom—Judah. His life extended through the reigns of four Judean kings: Uzziah, Jotham, Ahaz, and Hezekiah.

Since Uzziah came to Judah's throne in 780 B.C., and Hezekiah died in 642 B.C., this makes Isaiah a man of the eighth century B.C.

For the actual year of the beginning of his prophetic career, we turn to the sixth chapter. It begins like this: "In the year that King Uzziah died, I saw the Lord, sitting upon a throne, high and lifted up."

Uzziah died in 740 B.C., a time when Judah's power and prosperity were at their peak. Isaiah could not have been much more than 20 years old when he experienced the vision that launched his prophetic career.

We might expect the record of his call to come in the first rather than the sixth chapter. But what we have here is a prophetic remembrance—the beginnings looked back upon from well into the journey.

Success came hard for a prophet in Judah. Not everyone came running to join his crusade. Isaiah's call had not ended; it had begun his struggle against overwhelming odds.

So, well into the journey he sought to vindicate the results—or lack of them—to his own heart. Thus, he hearkened back to the beginnings.

You see, ministry does not chronicle by time but by experience. So this sixth chapter is a cardinal event—an experience often reflected upon and frequently referred to during Isaiah's lifetime.

Let's review it for some insights that apply to us here and now.

Isaiah's sixth chapter is autobiographical. It is the most detailed and vivid account in scripture of the making of a prophet. The miracle is that the prophet was fashioned out of an ordinary human being—a mere man who had a soul-shaking experience of the reality of God.

"In the year that King Uzziah died, I saw the Lord . . ." This strange sentence becomes even more intense when you consider that his king was dead, his countrymen were mourning, his flag was at half mast, and his nation was ready to grasp at straws.

See this young man in the Jerusalem temple—the one Solomon had built. See him well. Let him teach us some things we can do in times when the land wipes its brow, mops up its mess, gasps for breath, and grapples on the brink of a national nervous breakdown. When the flag flies at half-mast and the country has a fever, what then? Isaiah tells us.

The first thing faith does is survey the field for evidences of God.

Uzziah had been a good king in Judah. His death had smashed the citizenry. He had ruled 52 years, 16 of which were from his isolated infirmary where he had suffered leprosy.

He brought military prowess, political stability, and economic prosperity to his people. He put Judah back on the map during his 52 years.

Fifty-two years: that is a time as long as the combined U.S. presidencies of Truman, Eisenhower, Kennedy, Johnson, Nixon, Ford, Carter, Reagan, and Bush. The empire was at a peak it had not known since Solomon.

Uzziah conquered the Philistines toward the Mediterranean, the Ammonites to the south, and the Edomites in the wastes of Arabia. He substantially improved the walls of Jerusalem, his capital city. He built a port city on the gulf of Akabah and a number of storage cities in the southern deserts. He championed agriculture and taught his countrymen how to improve the strains of their sheep, horses, and cattle.

Uzziah increased his nation's water supply by digging many wells and developing a system of aqueducts. His reign had been punctuated by both peace and prosperity. But now, King Uzziah was dead. The people were smashed; especially the young felt a light had gone out. And for young Isaiah, it was a time for the searching of soul.

Isaiah had loved Uzziah. Chances are, they were cousins. In all likelihood, his king had appointed Isaiah as a member of the court. He had watched the affairs of state unfold from the inside.

Now the news of his monarch's death fell with a thud upon him. In Judah, too, there had been a time of lightning and a day of drums.

See young Isaiah: First, he went to the palace where he recalled the stirring speeches and wise decisions he had come to expect from his king. Now the palace was beautiful, but empty. The throne room was gilded but untenanted. Next he visited the infirmary where for months his king had battled the dreaded leprosy. Here the fearsome disease had won the long battle and robbed the nation of its leader.

Then he visited the cemetery where they had left the remains of his friend. Even here the beauty of the funeral memories, in their coldness, left him numb.

The king was dead! The nation mourned. Young Isaiah was crushed.

Then Isaiah did a most significant thing. He returned to the temple—to the very place where the priests had intoned their funeral dirges for the king. He recalled all the sights and sounds that ended in a requiem. He knew too that at this very place, shortly thereafter, Judah would crown herself a new king. And then it happened! But let him tell us in his own words:

> In the year that King Uzziah died, I saw the Lord sitting upon a throne, high and lifted up, and his train filled the temple. Above him stood the seraphim . . . and one called to another and said, 'Holy, Holy, Holy is the Lord of hosts, the whole earth is full of his glory.' And the foundations of the threshold shook at the voice of him that called, and the house was filled with smoke.

The moment of truth in that experience breaks through. The king who was gone was replaced by a vision of a king who was always there, always had been, and always would be.

In the aftermath Isaiah saw God and sensed something steady over all the wreckage.

Now that's what a man of faith can do when his situation gets desperate! When the flag won't fly and the country hurts, a man of faith can survey the field for evidences of God.

But I warn you, it is a difficult discipline. It is far easier to become frightened, frustrated, suspicious, and sick. For when something precious in the nation dies, it is easy to conclude that God has abdicated also.

Jesus Christ, in the days of his flesh, had a word about precisely this crisis: "Blessed are the pure in heart, for they shall see God."

There is a vision born of a pure heart. It depends totally upon the right equipment for seeing. Eyes can't do it. Mind cannot do it. It is a vision of the heart. Such a vision of God does not stem from standard human equipment. It is the vision of proper worship. It is the vision of confrontation, encounter, exposure.

One who does not worship right can hardly expect to see God at work in this troubled world. But hear young Isaiah at the toughest time in his life

"I saw the Lord"—in correct perspective ("high, holy, enthroned"). The God he saw was one worthy to be worshiped. He was no superhuman big brother who could be maneuvered or manipulated. God was no toothless, clawless lion of Judah.

Isaiah was no longer restricted by having no one larger or nothing stronger than himself upon whom to depend. The God who came to him was larger than the temple. His train filled it. The smoke of his holy presence cascaded all out of doors. The whole earth was full of God's glory.

"I saw the Lord"—in correct proximity ("train filled the temple"). Imagine that: the Lord God of Judah—high, holy, enthroned—was yet in the very place where Isaiah was. In the rough and tumble of his right-now experience he sensed the awesome presence of God. This was no absentee deity a thousand layers of clouds away. Here was God in his world—not as a tourist seeing the sights, but as a redeemer putting things right.

Isaiah found that it is not the office of faith to seek out a God who is hard to find. Rather it is the task of faith to be found by a God who constantly seeks his own.

It is not terribly difficult to believe in God, unless we try to define God.

"I saw the Lord"—in correct proportion and power. "At his voice the foundations of the threshold shook."

This is not the power of a dotty grandfather deity who will shut one eye and approve us just any old way. Here is the tough and persistent power of redemptive love—*hesed,* the Old Testament calls it. God's is not so much the power to blast humankind into eternity as it is the power to bring eternity into humankind.

"I saw the Lord . . ." That confession of Isaiah at the front door of his mission raises a good question: When our situation becomes desperate, what do we see? Our answer to that question says volumes about the quality of our worship.

Have you noticed? Our Sunday services at 11 o'clock have come to be called "preaching services" rather than "worship services." This means that if for some reason we do not resonate with the preacher, then we do not resonate with the worship.

Now, I am a preacher and deeply appreciate the place of the sermon in worship. But suppose you do not like the sermon? Suppose you do not appreciate the preacher? Is the hour wasted?

Note this well: Isaiah does not say, "In the year that Uzziah died, I heard a sermon with which I totally agreed." Rather, he said: "I saw the Lord." As devastating as it is to the preacher in me, there was no sermon preached in the temple that day.

Yet, worship happened—gloriously happened! A young man ceased to be a spectator in the temple that day. He became a participant. When your situation becomes desperate, what do you see?

Andrew Johnson, vice president of the U.S., was in a New York hotel when Abraham Lincoln was assassinated. He was 34 years old and faced with the awesome responsibility to be president. The crowd outside his hotel was shocked: angry, restless, thirsty for revenge.

When Johnson finally came out to make a statement, he chose a biblical text: "'Justice and judgment are the habitation of God's throne. Mercy and truth shall go before God's face.' My fellow citizens, God reigns, the Republic yet lives, and life will go on." In the nation's darkest hour, young Vice President Johnson saw God.

Yet, faithless little men live as if God were never there, and as if it does not matter whether God is. But God is there—and here—and it does matter. It matters supremely! It remains for us in faith to see God and lead others to know of God's presence for those who have the vision for it.

Remember the experience of the two men exploring the same strange new world of outer space? Russian cosmonaut Yuri Gagarin said, "While I was circling the world in space I did not see anything to make me believe in God." American astronaut John Glenn said, "The God to whom I address my prayers is not so small that I would expect to see him on a few clouds or even in the mighty oceans of space."

It is more than a point of view. It is a matter of being equipped to see. "The pure in heart see God" —in proper perspective, proximity, power.

It remains for faith to see God. Isaiah shows us one thing more that a person in crisis can do: he can identify with his countrymen's sickness and dedicate himself to bringing them wholeness and health.

Again, hear the young prophet in the temple: "Then said I, 'Woe is me! For I am undone, because I am a man of unclean lips, and I dwell in the midst of a people of unclean lips,' When we see God aright, then we correctly see ourselves!

For the most part, a man is content with himself. He seldom deals frankly in self-analysis. He is not too often bothered by conscience. He compares himself with other men and persuades himself that he is as good or better than they—just as he is.

And then something happens—something bad! It shocks him out of his complacency and gives him occasion for appraisal. We need one and all the Great Physician and that very real redemption from ourselves, and the deliverance from the unsavory brew we always cook up when left alone in the kitchen.

Here is the good news of both Isaiah and Jesus: "We are *not* left alone in the kitchen." We can each one feel the live coal from off the altar of God and its searing, cleansing in Jesus Christ.

Remember Tess, the tragic, twisted girl-woman created in one of Thomas Hardy's novels? Hardy left her dying amid the eerie ruins of Stonehope with a bitter word: "Justice was done and the President of the Immortals had finished his sport with Tess."

Hardy was wrong—all wrong! Heaven is not ruled by some irrational clown who in his caprice does sport with us. In our tragedy, God engages not in sport but in deliverance.

And in that process we see ourselves—unclean, undone; commissioned to minister to an unclean and undone people. So the truth from this page snatched out of Isaiah's prophetic pilgrimage comes home to us.

And here is the truth: in our crises, God engages not in sport but in deliverance. Cal Smith has said it:

Peace must start within you.
There is no other way.
It does not start with someone else
In places far away.

Don't say, "They ought to bring peace."
Or, "Someone should stop war."
You are the one to do that job
Right at your own front door.

If you want peace in this old world,
I'll tell you where to start.
Forgetting "they" in distant places,
Let peace start in *your* heart.

I haven't got this thing quite right.
Where can my judgment be?
I should not say peace starts with you;
It's got to start with me.

And you know something? He's right! Amen.

August 13, 1995

JEREMIAH

Cutting a covenant where it counts

Jeremiah 1:1-2, 4-12, 13-14; 8:4-7, 20-22; 9:23-24; 18:1-6; 31:29-33; 52:3-7; 10-16, 27b

J eremiah is the second of the Major Prophets, both chronologically and in his position in the Old Testament. He comes right after Isaiah according to the Canon, but 75-100 years separate the two prophets according to the calendar.

By the time of Jeremiah, the Northern Kingdom—Israel—was gone, wiped out by Tiglath-pileser of Assyria in 722 B.C.

The opening lines of Jeremiah establish the date of his call to be a prophet. It was during the 13th year of the reign of Josiah. That was 626 B.C. Jeremiah launched a prophetic ministry that carried him through almost half a century, including the final fall of Jerusalem and the beginning of the Babylonian exile.

It was a time of gathering doom, moving toward a climax of total disaster. This is stated vividly in Jeremiah's writings, where page after page there is an unmistakable rhythm of delight and despair.

These 52 chapters were wrung out of the very life of a timid, fierce, emotional man of Anathoth.

Anathoth, Jeremiah's birthplace, was a small Benjamite village about four miles northeast of Jerusalem. Here for three centuries, descendants of Abiathar, the high priest deposed during Solomon's reign, had lived in relative obscurity. But they never forgot that they had the blood of Eli in their veins. Jeremiah was one of them when he met God face to face during the 13th year of Josiah's reign.

Jeremiah, like Isaiah, could not have been much more than 20 years old at the time of his call. Students of scripture delight in contrasting Isaiah's call—related in his sixth chapter—to that of Jeremiah—related in his first chapter.

Jeremiah's call is described vividly in his own words. It is one of the most intimate self-revealing texts in all the Bible. Beyond the record we sense the man, his character, and conviction regarding his life's work.

The secret of this somewhat timid, provincial man's invincible courage and universal impact is early established by Jeremiah himself in verse 9, chapter 1: "Then the Lord put forth his hand and touched my mouth, and the Lord said to me, 'Behold, I have put my words in your mouth.'" Jeremiah was marked forever by this intimate moment with his God.

Unlike Isaiah—who was touched by a hot coal from the altar on the wings of a seraphim while the ineffable mystery of God remained high and lifted up, filling the temple—Jeremiah's experience was simple, direct, personal. The man and his God met face to face, heart to heart, hand to hand, and the man never forgot it. His modest, withdrawing, tender, sensitive nature was set to flame. And always on the pages of his prophecy, behind the print, we sense the person: God-touched, yearning, uncompromising, unsilenced. He had a word in his mouth, and he had a fire in his bones.

The sequence in the book of Jeremiah is incredibly tangled. The events are not related in any chronological order. Therefore, it is imperative that we understand the times in order to unravel the puzzling chronology of the prophecy and to grasp the varying moods of the prophet.

So, let's briefly review the situation surrounding Jeremiah and Judah during the latter seventh and early sixth centuries B.C.

Remember: Isaiah lived through the reign of Hezekiah in Judah. These were the times of Assyrian dominance on the world scene (modern Iraq). Hezekiah's successor was Manassah, who is dubbed in Jewish history as "evil Manassah." During his reign of nearly 55 years he virtually reduced Judah to an Assyrian puppet state. He paid tribute to Assyria and transported its idolatries into the land.

By the time Jeremiah was born in 650 B.C., however, Assyria was on her amazingly swift descent downhill as a world power.

Josiah, Judah's boy king—who came to the throne at age 7—had launched a vigorous religious reform following Manassah.

Chances are the circumstances might have been different in Judah if two things had not happened: One, Josiah was killed in a battle against the resurgent Egyptians in 608 B.C. at age 39. Two, the Babylonians who had chipped away at the Assyrian empire became the new, fast-rising world power.

So when Jeremiah launched his prophetic career, Judah was affected outwardly by two threats: Egypt to the south and the fast-coming Babylonians to the east. During the years of his ministry Judah attempted either to play these off one against the other, or was hesitating as to which she should make an alliance with in order to protect herself against the other. It was high-stake political roulette.

The people's vision of God was dimmed, if not lost altogether. Their hope, as they saw it, lay in pitting Egypt against Babylon or in securing the aid of one against the other. So the swift-moving, dangerous game of international intrigue polluted the land.

Simply to name the kings who ruled during Jeremiah's 46 years as a prophet is enough to understand the darkness of the days.

Jehoahaz followed Josiah. He was a popular appointee, the youngest son of Josiah. But his three-month reign proved that insofar as the people generally were concerned, Josiah's reform attempts had been purely on the surface of their lives. There had been no change in national character since "Evil Manassah."

Jehoiakim, a puppet placed on Judah's throne by Egypt, presided over the further deterioration of the nation.

His association with Eygpt brought reprisal from the Babylonians and a deportation of many of Judah's finest citizens to Babylon in 597 B.C. Things were going from bad to worse. No wonder Jehoiakim cut up the scroll containing the prophecy of Jeremiah with a pen knife!

Jehoiachin reigned only briefly—for three months—and was deposed, carried captive to Babylon by the marauding Nebuchadnezzar.

Zedekiah came to Judah's throne. He meant well. But he proved perilously weak and a total mismatch in the Babylonian-Egyptian power struggle. At the slightest word of disorder anywhere in the Babylonian world, he would quickly get Egypt's ear to form a coalition against Nebuchadnezzar. Egypt was always long on promising help, but short on delivering it. In time, Zedekiah used up his string. Nebuchadnezzar marched westward.

His armies sacked Jerusalem, burned much of it, broke down the walls, demolished the temple of Solomon, executed Zedekiah's son before his very eyes, then blinded Zedekiah and carried most of the elite of the nation off to Babylon as captives. That was 586 B.C.

Never for one single moment during those more than 40 long, dark years did Jeremiah arrest the downward plunge of his people or his nation. Never once by anything he said, by anything he did, by anything he suffered could he check that awful deterioration. It was as stormy a half century as the people of God in the Old Testament ever knew, in spite of one of Judah's greatest prophets.

It is little wonder that Jeremiah is remembered as the prophet with a broken heart. His intensely sensitive spirit was open to divine influence, but his countrymen did not care.

Judah was caught in a delirious dance of death.

Dr. Moorehead is right: "It was Jeremiah's lot to prophesy at a time when the people would not listen. Judah was rushing down to a final catastrophe. Political excitement was at its height, but there were no statesmen. Passions swayed the various parties and the people. The most fatal of counsels prevailed. It was Jeremiah's lot to see his own beloved countrymen plunge over one precipice after another into wide, weltering, wholesale ruin."

Jeremiah bared his soul to Judah. The very muscle and nerve and bone of the man appear in his prophecy. The portrait of the prophet is vividly stamped upon every line of his scroll.

The last thing he ever wanted was to be isolated, much less hated. Yet he was both.

His message of doom was not of his own choosing. He would have much preferred to prophesy of hope. But he had been called to speak the Word of the Lord. That he did!

Is it any wonder that six centuries later when some people of Galilee saw in Jesus Christ the reincarnation of "one of the prophets," it was to Jeremiah that their thoughts went most readily (Matt. 16:14)? Behind the voice from these pages, we feel and sense the pulse of the man.

It is next to impossible to select a single passage that summarizes the thrust of a man and a message like Jeremiah. But there is one section where the whole scene does seem to come into focus. It's chapter 31, verses 31-33:

> Behold the days are coming, says the Lord, when I will make a new covenant with the house of Israel and the house of Judah, not like the covenant which I made with their fathers when I took them by the hand to lead them out of the land of Egypt, my covenant which they broke . . . But this is the covenant which I will make . . . after those days says the Lord: I will put my law within them, and I will write it upon their hearts; and I will be their God, and they shall be my people.

Jeremiah spoke of cutting a covenant where it counts—not on stone, but on the people. He spoke of cutting a covenant where it hurts—not on paper, but in the heart. Jeremiah's covenant is a cardiac covenant.

Judah traced her troubles to the difficulty of her position sandwiched between Egypt to the south and Babylon to the east.

Jeremiah declared instead that their troubles were within themselves. They had dismissed God from their concerns and were discussing policy and logistics instead of putting away evil. Judah had to repent! The people could never expect a better political order without a better spiritual order. They required open-heart surgery.

Their threat was inward before it was outward. Their problem was not so much Egypt or Babylon. Their problem was Judah.

Jeremiah's message then went out for a radical conversion of the inner person—a new covenant with God cut in the heart.

The aging prophet dreamed a great dream. He conceived a new covenant between Yahweh and the people.

It would be inward, not outward; marked by a changed nature; something at the heart of humankind. It would be immediate like Jeremiah's call, coming directly from God without intermediaries—whether prophet, priest, or king. It would also be universal—that all should know God.

It was a covenant of forgiveness. The sins upon every page of every person's life would be wiped clean forever. Each life would get a fresh page upon which to write a better story.

Jeremiah opened new windows on the Godward-side, and let fresh breezes blow. Here was a revolutionary insight into the affairs between God and man. His insight has never been superseded or surpassed. Nothing in the Old Testament matches it.

Is it any wonder that on the night before his death, Jesus Christ, in a Jerusalem upper room, said as he lifted the Passover wine at the Last Supper: "This cup is the new covenant in my blood." Jesus lifted the "Jeremiah cup."

In his own death the next day that same Jesus revealed the cost and the consequence of a covenant cut in the heart.

But what does all this mean to us?

We too are God's people of covenant. Almost concurrent with its founding in 1859—136 years ago—this congregation adopted its first covenant. It has been revised only slightly through the years. Today, we have it copied and attached in our hymn book.

First Baptist Church
Greensboro, N.C.
Church Covenant

As we trust that we have been brought by divine grace to embrace the Lord Jesus Christ, and by the influence of His spirit to give up ourselves wholly to Him, so we do now solemnly covenant with each other that, God helping us, we will walk together in Him in brotherly love;

That, as members one of another for the glory of Christ in the salvation of men, we will exercise a Christian care and watchfulness over each other, and as occasion may require, faithfully warn, rebuke and admonish one another in the spirit of meekness, considering ourselves lest we also be tempted;

That we will willingly submit to, and conscientiously enforce, all wholesome discipline of the church;

That we will uphold the worship of God and the ordinances of His house by regular attendance thereon, search diligently the scriptures, observe closet or family worship, and seek to train up those under our care to the glory of God in the salvation of their souls;

That, as we have been planted together in the likeness of His death by baptism, and raised from an emblematic grave in newness of life, especially will we seek divine aid to enable us to walk circumspectly and watchfully in the world, denying all ungodliness and every worldly lust;

That we will remember the poor, and contribute cheerfully of our means for their relief, and for the maintenance of a faithful gospel ministry among us, and for the spread of the same to the ends of the earth;

That we will endeavor, by example and effort, to win souls to Christ; and,

Through life, amidst evil report and good report, seek to live to the praise of Him who hath called us out of darkness into His marvelous light to whom be glory and honor and power forever and ever, Amen.

Our covenant is anchored in grace, energized by Spirit, soaked in love and trust. It commits God's people to care, to worship, to pray, to bear their burdens together. It binds us to mission and to ministry—to evangelism and social concern. It commits us to pay the bills and to be good stewards of our money. It is clothed in a vision of peace.

Now our task is to get that covenant out of our hymnal and into our hearts. We must transform it from cold print on a paper page to a set of convictions/commitments that shape our lives.

Ours is the Jeremiah task: to have God cut a new covenant in our hearts. Amen.

August 20, 1995

LAMENTATIONS

Strong men do cry
Lamentations 1:1-3, 12, 18, 20-22

The 25th book of the Bible is one, long, five-chapter sob. It is best called "a lament." Webster defines a lament like this: "A dirge, mourning some loss or calamity; an expression of deep sorrow." Actually, the book of Lamentations consists of five separate laments—five poems, each comprising a separate chapter.

All five of them deal with the same central theme: the destruction of Jerusalem and the desolation left after the Babylonians got through with the city in 586 B.C. In these pages are lightning, thunder, and a river of tears. Swords flash. Armors clash. Spears crash.

In the Jewish scriptures this scroll is a part of the third division of the Canon called "The Writings." It is not among the Books of Prophecy.

As usual, the Hebrew title is taken from the first line in the book. The book opens: "How lonely sits the city." The Hebrew word "how" is *ekhah*. Therefore, the name of the book for the Jews is *Ekhah*.

However, in our English versions the laments follow Jeremiah and the full traditional title of the book is thus: "The Lamentations of Jeremiah." Hence is established the tradition that Jeremiah was the author of these laments.

This is natural for two reasons: First, Jeremiah did compose certain laments (2 Chron. 35:25). Second, Jeremiah was the most prominent prophet in Jerusalem during the days of its great disaster at the hands of Nebuchadnezzar and the Babylonians in 586 B.C.

All five of the poems are acrostics. Remember, in our review of the Psalms we came across our first acrostics. Such poetic literary form was popular among the Jews because it was easier to recall and recite.

In an acrostic each line begins with a different letter of the Hebrew alphabet. The first line starts with *aleph*, the second with *beth*, the third with *gimmel*, the fourth with *dalath*, and so on throughout the poem. It is the same as if an English poem were written with the first verse beginning with a word starting with an A, the second a B, the third a C, the fourth a D, and so forth.

Now notice the arrangement of the five chapters of Lamentations. Some of the acrostic effect carries through even in English translation.

There are 22 characters in the Hebrew alphabet. Note, the poem's comprising chapters: 1, 2, 4, and 5 have 22 verses—each one starting with each Hebrew letter in the alphabet. Poem (chapter) 3 has 66 verses because each grouping of three verses begins with the same letter.

Some students of scripture, recognizing these highly stylized forms of acrostics, doubt whether Jeremiah, in the aching and breaking of his own great heart, would have sat down to work out slowly, laboriously, a set of acrostic poems. They propose that these poems bear witness to Jeremiah's pain in retrospect.

I find myself wanting to believe that Jeremiah wrote them. Although ordinarily, breaking hearts do not cry out in painstaking acrostic fashion, Jeremiah's was no ordinary breaking heart.

He was a most extraordinary man who bared his soul to Judah. Why shouldn't he have composed his laments in a most unusual way?

Let's review for a moment the bad scene marking Judah, Jerusalem, and Jeremiah during the last years of the nation's mad dash toward doom. With each king, Judah sowed a little more of the wind to reap the whirlwind. Things moved fast and furiously—and all the motion was downhill.

Remember: a swift-moving, dangerous game of international intrigue pervaded the land. Judah's hope, as her leaders and her people saw it, lay in pitting Egypt against Babylon and being shrewd enough to know which one to join when.

Jehoahaz followed Josiah and proved that so far as the country was concerned, Josiah's reforms were only skin deep. He lasted only a very few months before he was deposed.

Jehoiakim was a puppet king enthroned by Egypt. He would not listen, and cut Jeremiah's scroll up with a pen knife. The Babylonians swiftly cut him down.

Jehoiachin fared no better. He reigned only three months before Nebuchadnezzar and the marauding Babylonians carried him out of the country captive.

Zedekiah was Judah's last king. He was a total mismatch in the Middle East power struggle. His intrigues with Egypt brought the Babylonians down on him. And Nebuchadnezzar marched westward.

His armies smashed Jerusalem, broke down the walls, demolished the temple, slew the royal family, blinded the king, and carried off most of the nation's elite to Babylon as captives. That was the dark year, 586 B.C.—all this while Jeremiah had sought to check the awful deterioration. But Judah was heart-sick and hard-headed, caught in a delirious dance of death.

Dr. Moorehead is right: "It was Jeremiah's lot to see his own beloved countrymen plunge over one precipice after another into wide, weltering, wholesale ruin." It's no wonder that Jeremiah's large, sensitive heart broke.

One thing we learn from all this: "Strong men do cry." Their tears are signs not of weakness but of strength.

Frederick Buechner has said a significant thing in an article titled "Whistling in the Dark":

You never know what may cause tears. The sight of the Atlantic Ocean can do it, or a piece of music, or a face you've never seen before. A pair of somebody's old shoes can do it. Almost any movie made before the great sadness that came over the world after the Second World War, a horse cantering across a meadow, the high school basketball team running out onto the gym floor at the start of a game. You can never be sure. But of this you can be sure. Whenever you find tears in your eyes, especially unexpected tears, it is well to pay the closest attention.

They are not only telling you something about the secret of who you are, but more often than not God is speaking to you through them of the mystery of where you have come from and is summoning you to where, if your soul is to be saved, you should go to next.

It is the role of tears!

The last thing Jeremiah ever wanted was to be left alone—solitary— abandoned, hated. His message of doom and the river of tears were not of his own making. He was a mere reporter, speaking "the Word of the Lord." So kings, princes, priests—along with most of his countrymen—turned against him.

Behind these Lamentations we feel the anguish of the man—Jeremiah, the "weeping prophet."

Let's explore in some detail the first of these "Songs of Sorrow." Perhaps chapter 1 is the best known of the five laments. It divides rather simply into two main sections: the prophet's lament over Jerusalem (1-11) and the people's lament over their capital city (12-22).

In the process of lamenting the fallen city, the causes of its condition are described. That is the living message of these Lamentations for us.

See/sense the lonely city in verses 1-7. Jerusalem was the capital city of Judah, the center of commerce and worship. Her markets were always open for business. Her temple was always crowded.

Now, all that is past. The streets, what's left of them, are empty. It is a lonely city, like a widow bereft of husband and children—solitary, deserted. Jerusalem has been deserted by her friends, especially those nations like Egypt who had been long on promises and short on deliveries.

Night has descended upon the holy city—perpetual night, when the lonely seems most lonely and even slight sounds are frightening. Even the roads leading into the city, as well as the great spaces around her gates, are empty—none wish to visit her. No one comes to worship, to buy, or to sell. No tourists are in sight.

The temple is leveled. So the priests probe among the debris and weep. All the single women grieve because there are no prospective husbands in sight. Even the children are gone. No cries of laughter are heard in the streets.

No longer is the royal court, in all its splendor, an attraction for travelers. It is all ruin. The king is a captive, and the princes are dead.

What a contrast was all this to the prosperous and happy city that thrived only months before. What went wrong with Jerusalem's former glory?

Well, the poet tells us in verses 8-11: "Jerusalem sinned grievously, therefore she became filthy . . . Her uncleanness was in her skirts, she took no thought of her doom. She has no comforter . . . her enemy has triumphed."

In other words, Jerusalem is desolate due to her evil. She has committed moral suicide.

I wonder whether we see what the prophet wants us to see: The city was not punished so much *for* her sins, as *by* her sins. There was an awesome built-in judgment to the kind of evils embraced by Jeremiah's countrymen.

The conduct of their lives simply ran its natural, inevitable course. Their pattern of life simply suffered its unavoidable consequences. Their "chickens came home to roost."

That is the way it always is in this moral universe. God does not so much punish a people. God does not have to. Their own evil punishes them.

All God did was leave the country to its own designs. History gave them the rope, and Jeremiah's countrymen hanged themselves—personally, nationally, internationally.

My friends, that is the pattern that judgment most often takes in this world. Ask Beirut in Lebanon or Medellin in Colombia or Washington, D.C. Observe the signs of it all over this land. It is an inexorable law that evil brings its own consequences upon a people and a society.

See this recent summer headline: "Scientists Measure Arctic Ozone Losses." Scientists have now found an "ozone hole" over the Arctic not unlike the one discovered earlier over the Antarctic. Ozone is a form of oxygen, found high in Earth's atmosphere, that blocks ultraviolet rays from the sun. These are the rays most likely to cause skin cancer. Manufactured chemicals called chlorofluorocarbons are blamed for the ozone destruction. And every one of them is man-made.

Now, set the scene: In years to come, our children's children and their children will be unable to play in the sun except at a grave risk of skin cancer. Our "sin" against the precarious ecological balance on this planet bears its own awesome fruit.

God has not "caused" our judgment. We have! Rebellion in God's kind of world provides its own built-in sort of suffering.

So Judah's essential problem is stated in verse 9: "she took no thought of her doom." She did not give a second thought to the damaging, destructive effects of her way of life.

How often we all live like that! In everything from dietary habits to sexual habits, we rebel against the designs of God for us, flagrantly violate the very ways that we are made, and do not give a second thought to the eventual effect of it on us or on our children.

See that young man of 20, living on a steady diet of "crack." He is a momentist—settling for the split-second of pleasure he momentarily possesses, with no thought of its consequences for the future.

A society that shoots prejudice, poverty, pollution into its bloodstream is thoughtlessly doing this same thing. That is why it is so crucial in a moral universe to look beyond the moment to the longer consequences of an action. Ask Mickey Mantle. Ask Larry Hagman.

Back to the poem: The people are affected—deeply affected—by their smashed, lonely city (vv. 12ff.) So, in time, they cry aloud for themselves. They break in on the prophet's lament with a panting cry of distress: first to the passers-by (vv. 12-17), then to the surrounding nations (vv. 18-19), and finally to God (v. 20).

The sequence of the people's cry is all wrong. Of course, they should have begun with their repentant cry to God, and then, having started there, confessed to their neighbors and friends.

But how tempted we always are to start every place else except at the right starting place—in the pilgrimage of faith.

We scratch and paw for someplace else to start, except the point of repentance—facing our evil, confessing it, asking forgiveness for it, and changing our lives. But there is no other starting place—not in the life of faith.

There is a story out of the Lancashire cotton mills decades ago: On the wall above each machine was a sign: *"If you get your threads tangled, call for the foreman."* One new girl at the mill got her threads badly tangled. She tried to untangle them herself, only to make matters worse. Then she called on the operator at the machine next to hers. The mess got messier. Finally, she sent for the foreman. The girl explained immediately, "I did my best. I tried to untangle the mess myself." To which the foreman replied, "No, you did not do your best. Your best would have been to send for me."

Jerusalem's best, in the days of Jeremiah, would have been turning to Yahweh. Our best, as we face the growing tangles in our lives and in our world, is to begin with Jesus Christ. We must! We can! Will we?

August 27, 1995

EZEKIEL

Knocked down but not out
Ezekiel 1:1-3; 2:1-5; 3:15-17; 18:1-4, 19-20; 37:1-6

Ezekiel was a younger contemporary of Jeremiah. It is therefore chronologically fitting that his prophecy should follow that of Jeremiah. There are 13 datings in the scroll of Ezekiel, each one providing a year, a month, a day, varying from the first in 592 B.C. to the last in 570 B.C. Thus, this is the most dated book in the Bible.

Ezekiel's name means "God strengthens." The three opening verses of the book that bears his name furnish considerable detail of God's strengthening. For one thing he was called during his 30th year while a captive among his exiled countrymen in Babylon. For another thing the vision that marked his call to be a prophet occurred during the fifth year of the captivity of Jehoiachin, king of Judah.

This means that Ezekiel had been carried off with the puppet king Jehoiachin after Nebuchadnezzar's first siege of Jerusalem in 597 B.C. The fifth year of that captivity was 592 B.C. At that time the kingdom of Judah still existed, and the city of Jerusalem still stood.

Zedekiah was the king in Judah, still playing his dangerous game of international roulette. Jeremiah was the lonely prophet warning the unheeding people of their approaching doom.

If the 30th year in verse 1 is meant to be Ezekiel's age at the time of his call, then he was carried off to Babylon when he was 25 years old. The year of his birth would be 627 B.C., during the reign of Josiah in Judah. This would make him at least 20 years younger than Jeremiah. In fact, he would have been born the year before Jeremiah received his call.

There is a strong possibility that young Ezekiel was a disciple of Jeremiah in Jerusalem. Furthermore, the opening verses of the scroll establish that Ezekiel was a priest, perhaps of the line of Zadok. For this reason he gives himself eventually to the minute details of a re-established temple worship.

George Herbert once sang: "A man who looks on glass, / On it may stay his eye; / Or, if he pleases, through it pass / And thus the heavens spy."

Ezekiel saw the glass, but he looked right through it, and everything on his horizon was magnified. Here is how it happened:

During the final dismal years of Judah's deterioration, he was just a teenager in Jerusalem. His father, Buzi, was a priest in the splendid temple Solomon had built.

Jeremiah, the older prophet, was a familiar figure to Ezekiel. On the whole, he sympathized with this lonely man of God. He drank in Jeremiah's teaching and caught the fire of his uncompromising courage.

Then in 597 B.C. there came an abrupt change in Ezekiel's life. The Babylonians invaded Jerusalem and rounded up the best of the citizenry for deportation. Young Ezekiel was among these spoils of war.

So far as we know he was never to return to his native land. After a long, exhausting march of more than three months across the parching desert wastes, he was settled with his fellow captives in the heartland of Babylonia. Here, five years later in 592 B.C., he appears to be living by the River Chebar. That "river" was, in fact, one of the larger man-made canals that interlaced the Babylonian plains. It conducted the Euphrates River water in a long loop from the east bank by the ancient city of Nippur, back into the Euphrates further downstream.

Here, Ezekiel and his fellow Jews lived in a sort of captive colony. He dwelt with his wife in a house of sun-dried brick. Surrounding him was a considerable community of Palestinian exiles.

They were allowed to have their own tribal organization with elected elders. They practiced their ancestral religion and met freely for worship in their homes. They retained their native Hebrew language.

Thus the policy of the Babylonian government toward the deported Jews seems to be generous. But for it all, Ezekiel viewed another horizon. The influence of that lonely man, Jeremiah, was too indelible upon him. Therefore, his body was in Babylon, but his heart was in Jerusalem.

He knew that in spite of all the punishment his countrymen had received, still they had not repented. Indeed their evil was increasing continuously. So, in his 30th year he felt the "hand of the Lord upon him." He was called to be a prophet!

His prophetic messages were addressed first to the exiles on the banks of the River Chebar. And yet through them he spoke to all of Judah—and to all of us.

The details of Ezekiel's call are related in the opening chapters. Here is the same mystical, overpowering, vision of God—like Isaiah's, but with even more vivid detail.

Ezekiel's psychic nature is immediately underscored. He saw many "visions of God." In fact, no writing prophet in the Old Testament was so prone to vision, ecstasy, and trance as was Ezekiel.

Again and again we encounter him seized by the hand of God, taken possession of by the Spirit, struck dumb, lifted up, shown things taking place at a distance, carried back and forth in a trance, all the while executing inspired signs and wonders.

In time, he says that he was sent to "them of the captivity." It was among the exiled Jews that he was to labor, although at first sight it might seem that his message was addressed to the Jews still in the homeland.

The 48 chapters of this book fall rather conveniently into three sections:

1. Utterances *before* the final siege of Jerusalem in 586 B.C. (chs. 1-24): These came during the decade between Ezekiel's call and Jerusalem's complete destruction.

2. Utterances *during* the siege of Jerusalem (chs. 25-32): Here, Ezekiel turns on those nations surrounding Judah who had promised so much and delivered so little. They too would be destroyed by the marauding Babylonians.

3. Utterances *after* the siege of Jerusalem (chs. 33-48): This final third of the book contains much material apocalyptic in nature, foretelling first a future invasion of Israel by the hordes of a mysterious ruler from the north, and after their final defeat, foretelling the re-establishment of an ideal Israel. In this section he outlines not only the structure of the restored temple, but also the meticulous details of a re-established ritual for worship.

Thus Ezekiel is sometimes called "the father of restored Judaism." In all probability he died before the final defeat of Babylon by Cyrus the Great in 538 B.C. But his vision of restoration was carried out by such men as Ezra, Nehemiah, and Haggai. The city and the temple were rebuilt.

But all of this was so long ago and so far away. What about us—here, now? What is the Ezekiel word?

I am glad that you asked, because Ezekiel does have one word that is critical just now. It is the unquenchable word *hope!*

Throughout the book of Ezekiel hope rings clear and jubilant. Here was a man, along with a displaced group of God's people, knocked down but not out.

Ezekiel could sing in the darkest night. Why? Well, part of the reason was his call related in chapter 1.

From the north in a storm cloud, pierced by constant flashes of fire, his complicated call-vision came. He saw a fourfold living creature, combining human with animal faces, winged, with wheels within wheels, full of eyes, moving hither and yon like a flash of lightning. And over the head of the living creature there was the likeness of a firmament, and above the firmament the likeness of a throne, and upon the throne a likeness of a man. Hear the prophet relate his impression:

> When I saw it I fell upon my face, and I heard the voice of one speaking. And he said to me, "Son of Man, stand upon your feet, and I will speak with you." And when he spoke to me the spirit entered into me, and set me upon my feet; and I heard him speaking to me. And he said, "Son of Man, I send you to the people of Israel, to a nation of rebels, who have rebelled against me. . . ." The people are also imprudent and stubborn: I send you to them and you shall say to them, "Thus says the Lord God." And whether they hear or refuse to hear (for they are a rebellious house) they will know that there has been a prophet among them. (2:1ff.)

So, Ezekiel himself describes his call. Here was the secret of his unquenchable hope. He had experienced a vision of God and accepted a call to be a prophet among God's people. So with his feet in Babylon and his heart in Jerusalem, he went to work.

Ezekiel in Babylonia, like Jeremiah in Palestine, saw Judah die. Like Jeremiah, he refused to take that death as final.

He met history's momentary "no" with God's everlasting "yes." He believed more in God than in calamity.

When those around him perceived only dry bones, he beheld also the Spirit of God who would make them live. He was knocked down, but not out.

This conviction climaxes in a bit of high drama in chapter 37. It is that eerie and spectacular episode of the valley of the bones.

Overcome by an awesome sense of the presence of God, Ezekiel sensed himself set down in the midst of a valley full of sun-baked, parched, dry bones—a portrait of devastated Judah. Admonished by the divine Spirit, he prophesied, and the bones suddenly formed into bodies, muscles, and nerves—bones and ligaments coming together without movement or motion. Admonished a second time, he called for the Spirit and now the newly formed bodies lived—stood upon their feet, an exceeding great army!

So, to the helpless, hopeless, captured people of God came an unmistakable word of energizing—of reviving, renewing. Perhaps that is Ezekiel's strongest and most timely word for us.

In times like ours it is a simple thing for the whole horizon to become a quagmire of despair. The slough of despondency could claim us all.

But Ezekiel hands us the scope and asks us to look through the glass. When we do, there comes into focus not a closing time for our hopes, but an opening time; upon a world full of miracles God has not used up yet.

Ezekiel's hope is a prototype of that fuller hope that skips and sings all through the New Testament. Paul's invincible surmise is that faith, hope, and love endure when all else is smashed in this world.

Over and over there is a recurring conviction: "The God of hope fill you with all joy and peace in believing." Banish that conviction from life and you have severed the jugular vein of Ezekiel's prophecy and of New Testament faith.

As long as persons hope, realistically anchoring their hopes in the presence and work of the living God, they can live abundantly—even in the toughest of times.

But that is precisely our problem. The ring of the real is missing from so many of our hopes.

So many of our hopes are false, because they are geared to all sorts of artificial stimuli.

But let the word of Ezekiel go forth. Tough times are not times for the people of God to want out of life; that is the time for them to want to get in deeper. Instead of shouting for the world to stop so we can get off, Ezekiel urges us to look for places to get on.

That is the good news affirmed and enfleshed in Jesus of Nazareth. In that one man, God uttered the final "yes."

So, Christians fulfilling the Ezekiel vision become equipped to celebrate life—in all ways and in all things. Life, and life abundantly, is what being in Christ is all about.

Whatever else we may say about the resurrection of Jesus Christ, it was God's great affirmation of Ezekiel's vision of dry bones alive. It underscores the worth and meaning of our existence right here, right now. And it shouts God's word for our lives. That word is "yes!"

This does not mean that our faith knows nothing of life's dark side. After all, hope is born not in ivory towers, but in shades and shadows. Our Christian hope was born out of an experience of abandonment, rejection, even a cross.

Ours is not a faith that fakes blindness when the chips are down. It faces the inevitabilities of death, but life is its theme. It knows full well the tragedies of evil, but deliverance is its song.

Our faith lays bare human weakness, but our hope proclaims the final power and goodness of God. Our hope is the Ezekiel hope, frequently knocked down but never knocked out. For it is a hope in Christ! Amen.

September 24, 1995

DANIEL

Man's dark—God's light

Daniel 1:1-6, 8; 3:1, 4-6, 14-15; 5:1-5; 6:10, 16-17, 21-25

In our Old Testament, Daniel follows Ezekiel as a fourth major prophet. Since the events related in the scroll took place during the Babylonian exile in the reigns of Nebuchadnezzar and his successors, that is the place for it.

In the Jewish scriptures, however, Daniel is not found among the prophets. Rather, this scroll appears in the third section of the Jewish canon called "The Writings."

There are thus several significant things to be kept in mind as we approach this 27th book of our Bible. For one thing, most students of scripture agree that this was one of the last books of the Old Testament to be written. Almost six of the 12 chapters were originally written in Aramaic, not in Hebrew. This means that by the time of its writing, Aramaic had become so much the common language of many people in Palestine that it was readily understood. Such was not the case until well into the second or third century B.C.

For another thing, a variety of features of the Hebrew language portions of Daniel reflect the Greek period of Hebrew history rather than the Persian period. So there is considerable reason to believe that this book might have been written to send a signal of hope into the midst of the awful persecution of the Jews under Antiochus Epiphanes and the Seleucid kings in the second century B.C.

In an effort to strengthen his countrymen during that desperate time in the second century, this author dipped back into the history of his people, dusted off a page of that history, and reminded them of Daniel during the days of the exile in Babylon in the sixth century B.C.

So we have in these 12 chapters a heroic and comforting message for the faithful in every age.

The book of Daniel is certainly unique in the Old Testament. It is sad that it has become the happy hunting ground for all sorts of hucksters making charts and setting dates for the end of time. Other than possibly the book of Revelation, no book in the Bible has fared worse at the hands of its interpreters.

Daniel is rich in both the usual and in the unusual. Some of the most famous episodes in the Bible are found within its pages: the three Hebrews in a fiery furnace, the handwriting on the wall, the den of lions and Daniel, and in the final six chapters no less than five famous visions of the governance of God over all the events of history.

These were all reminders out of their past that the people of God needed then and still need now.

This author was a true messenger, with a true message about a true God and a true hope in the toughest of times.

Without a doubt, Daniel was a well-known figure in Jewish history. Ezekiel mentions him three times in his book.

Quite expectedly, when the people of God during the second century B.C. needed a rallying point against the Seleucids, this inspired unknown writer reminded them of some illustrious pages out of their past. His ringing message was that the Seleucids in all their glory were, after all, like a lion in a den-full of Daniels.

Then in six chapters at the end he provided them, in highly apocalyptic fashion, visions of God's future purposes in history.

So, in this book we have a rhythm: six chapters of historical reminiscence and six chapters of apocalyptic vision for the future. Here is a balanced record of man's dark and God's light. Through Daniel, the man of God, the people of God heard a trumpet blow loudly and clearly.

Now let's sketch briefly the background of the awful situation surrounding the Jews in Palestine in the second century B.C. during the Seleucid persecution. Remember that in Isaiah's day the Assyrians dominated the world scene. In Jeremiah's and Ezekiel's time it was the Babylonians who were the scourge of history. Hard on their heels came the Persians, led to prominence by their king Cyrus. This brought to an end the period of Jewish exile outside Palestine. The temple was again built in Jerusalem.

By 338 B.C. another world power began to emerge. This time it was the Greeks guided first by their masterful warrior-king, Philip of Macedon. He was murdered in 336 and succeeded by his 20-year-old son, Alexander.

Within 13 years Alexander, whom history has dubbed "The Great," subjected almost all the then-known world under his rule. Persia, Tyre, Gaza, Syria, Egypt, Babylon, India: all these fell in his wake.

Alexander died just before he was 33 years old. He left no heir to his throne, so his generals divided the empire four ways. Two different dynasties were established: the Ptolemies in Egypt and the Seleucids in Asia.

Both these kingdoms were intensely Greek in culture and content. This meant that Greek civilization was superimposed, sometimes graciously, sometimes ruthlessly, but always persistently, upon all the conquered peoples of that world.

Alexander actually thought that to be Greek was to be great. This is the feature of his empire that left its indelible mark upon all the rest of history. He sought to revitalize, by the alchemy of Greek culture, all the countries he conquered.

This Grecianizing (Hellenistic) campaign embraced a language, a body of ideas, and a way of thinking that had an unparalleled impact upon the nations and ushered in an absolutely new era. At its heart lay the great Greek appreciation of man and of human capacities—especially our reason and intellect and sense of beauty—our art and architecture. These were the legacies of Socrates, Plato, and Aristotle that Alexander left in his wake.

As this Greek culture rolled its bright waves over the world, it was inevitable that it should dash itself against the structures of life and thought that had for centuries lodged within the Hebrew people.

The humanistic/rationalistic outlook of the Greeks remained blinded to the corruptions of human nature. So the Jews turned swiftly from it. Although some Jews were profoundly marked by Greek influence, most of them were not.

That is where the Seleucids came in. Under their infamous king, Antiochus Epiphanes, these Hellenizers undertook to stamp out Judaism and replace it with the religion of the Greeks. Thus throughout Palestine there swept a furious persecution. A fort was built south of the temple area in Jerusalem and from there the Hellenizers sallied forth from time to time to attack those engaged in worship at the temple.

Blood flowed freely. The situation was intolerable. It was horrible!

The climax came in December, 168 B.C., when a small heathen altar was actually erected on the altar of the temple at Jerusalem, thus defiling it. Pork sacrifices were offered to the pagan gods of Greece on that holy altar.

The temple itself was rededicated to Zeus, the chief god of the Greeks. Throughout Palestine, anyone confessing allegiance to Yahweh and loyalty to the Torah was promptly persecuted and often executed.

Some Hebrews complied with the demand of the Seleucid Grecianizers. Others fled Palestine, becoming religious refugees. Still others chose to stand firm even in the face of death.

In time, a resolute band of Hebrews revolted. From then on, it was war.

Eventually Rome conquered Greece and the conditions were established that prevailed when Jesus Christ was born during the reign of Caesar Augustus. The Seleucid period was brutal and bloody just like the earlier Babylonian period for the people of God.

Early in the days of the Jewish revolt against Antiochus Epiphanes, the writer of Daniel put forth his scroll. He was one of those resolute Hebrews who had watched the growing menace of Hellenism with horror. When the persecution broke out, he resolved to remain true to Israel's God and to Israel's past—come what may.

But his heart broke for his countrymen who, like himself, had come under the shadow of instant death. They needed encouragement—the blowing of trumpets. They needed a vision of God for this awful time.

This author provided that! He put forth the book of Daniel. It was the message out of the dangerous past from God almighty for the dangerous present. He wrote of Daniel—the man of God—during the times of Babylon's blood baths.

His scroll did two things for the people: It rallied them to remember some illustrious pages out of their past. It provided hope for God's presence with the people now. He blew the trumpet!

The Seleucids were nothing compared to the terrible Babylonians. He reminded his countrymen how mighty kings long ago shrank before the awesome majesty of Israel's God. He established that through faith in Yahweh, Daniel and his friends faced death in their times and overcame it.

In his message one thing is central: God never fails nor forsakes God's own. The faithful believers are never alone. They are in the midst of friends they cannot see.

Here is the key: "But Daniel resolved that he would not defile himself" (1:8) . . .

- Physically: a different *diet* than the one from the royal table
- Mentally: a different *vision* than the one seen in the captors' eyes
- Emotionally: a different *peace* than the false one afforded by his pagan peers
- Spiritually: a different *God* than the idols of the royal pantheon

Without a doubt, this confidence gave his countrymen hope. But what of us here—now? What is the message of the book of Daniel for us?

Amidst the history and the imagery of this book we catch sight of something steady over all the wreckage of time. Empires rise and fall. Great kings come and go. Yet Daniel shows us something that does not pass—something faith thrives upon. It is the "scenery of eternity," set solidly in time.

Imposing indeed are the colossal nations of our own day: Russia, China, Japan, India, Brazil, the U.S.A. Resistless seems their power, miltarily and economically. This world is shaped by their hand.

Yet, here in Daniel we see something else. We behold the four winds of heaven breaking forth upon the great seas of the earth. Thrones are smashed! And one like the Son of Man takes his place beside the Ancient of Days.

Then we remember that, after all, these nations too are but a passing procession before the reviewing stand of history. Once it was Assyria, then Babylon, Persia, Greece, and Rome. Later it was England, France, Germany, and Spain. Now it is our country, the U.S.A., along with Russia, Japan, China, India, Nigeria, and Brazil. In time, it will be someone else, somewhere else in this world. History marches on.

But Daniel sees it correctly: The awesome forces of this world, which seem to carry everything and everyone in their wake, can never have the final word. The Living God, creator of us and our universe always has the last word.

You do not have to be a theologian to believe that. You do not have to be a historian. You only have to be a Christian.

Painted heavily upon the canvas of time, Daniel depicts "the scenery of eternity": Assyria swallowed by Babylon, Babylon smashed by Persia, Persia humbled by Greece, Greece conquered by Rome, Rome topped by Barbarians. So is the course of history.

Western empires colliding with Eastern empires, Third World nations setting their sights on New World nations and on Old World nations . . . Time marches on!

And in it all there is the Lord of history "whose throne, unlike Earth's proud empires, shall never pass away." Really! History is "HIS-STORY."

Looking through the visions of Daniel at the governance of God, we see one imposing thing: the constant and unavoidable mixture of good and evil in every age.

Evil today may appear worse than it ever has been—more massive, more subtle, more refined, and therefore, more dangerous.

But good today is also more abounding than ever before. We have fuller revelation of our possibilities and potentialities than ever before.

The book of Daniel promises that these two realities will ever remain. There can be no reconciliation of good and evil. There will be no weakening of good until there is nothing but evil. There will be no weakening of evil until there is nothing but good.

The crises will mount. The conflicts will rage and break and dash people and nations upon hard anvils. But in God's own time and in God's own way, divine purposes will prevail. That is the Daniel promise. That is the Daniel hope.

It is our business to make calendars, because we are creatures of time. God has no calendars. God has no computers. God calculates by eternities.

I warn you: any attempt to predict with chronological precision the things Daniel saw and heard and said were coming to pass will be frustrated. There are too many gaps, too much space for which we cannot account, too many unmeasurables, too many unponderables.

Let us let Daniel be Daniel—brimming with courage, shrouded in mystery, blowing the certain sound of his prophetic trumpet. He wants one thing of us: to believe that, in the best of times and in the worst of times, God reigns!

We can enjoy fellowship with the Lord of history. Through faith in Jesus Christ we can know the God who split history in two. And this will enable us to live according to divine purposes in this portion of A.D. that falls to us.

That is what Daniel did. He lived faithfully through the portion of B.C. that fell to him. That is what he urges us to do in our time. Let's!

Majesty, worship His majesty.
Unto Jesus be all glory, honor, and praise.

Majesty, kingdom authority
Flow from his throne unto his own; his anthem raise.

So exalt, lift up on high the name of Jesus.
Magnify, come glorify Christ Jesus, the King.

Majesty, worship his majesty;
Jesus who died, now glorified, King of all kings.

Then sings my soul, my Savior God, to Thee,
How great Thou art, how great Thou art.
Then sings my soul, my Savior God, to Thee,
How great Thou art, how great Thou art!

God will make a way,
Where there seems to be no way;
He works in ways we cannot see,
He will make a way for me.

He will be my guide,
Hold me closely to his side;
With love and strength for each new day,
He will make a way, He will make a way!

October 1, 1995

HOSEA

Recovering a false start

Hosea 1:1-3, 3:1-5, 4:1-3, 6:1, 14:1-3

The final 12 books in the Old Testament are a dozen relatively short prophetic messages. For convenience sake, in ancient times these 12 books were combined into a single scroll. Thus we speak of the "roll (scroll) of the 12."

These 12 writings are sometimes called the "Minor Prophets." This is not at all because their messages are less important. The reason is simply that these books are much shorter than the prophecies that precede them in the Old Testament.

These 12 books do not occur in any chronological order. Indeed, they span from the eighth to the fifth century B.C.

Hosea, who heads the list, is one of the earliest of the 12. He is the only one of them to be a native of Israel, a northerner, rather than a citizen of Judah in the south. In fact, Hosea is the only citizen of Israel whose utterances are collected into a formal and separate book. All the other prophets are men of Judah.

Hosea is one of the Bible's greatest books because it was written by one of the Bible's greatest men and concerns one of the Bible's greatest themes. Students of scripture describe this strange 14-chapter document as a "succession of sobs." Since men do not weep in orderly sequence, and since breaking hearts do not cry out in painstaking logical fashion, this book is a puzzle, a patchwork of magnificent prophetic utterances.

The message is jumbled, garbled, disconnected, and sometimes resembles the diary of a soldier written in the thick of battle with shells whistling overhead and the shrieks of the dying mounting nearby. These chapters are some pages snatched out of one man's spiritual autobiography.

The opening verse places the book firmly within its historical context: "The word of the Lord that came to Hosea . . . in the days of Uzziah, Jotham, Ahaz, and Hezekiah, kings of Judah, and in the days of Jeroboam, the son of Joash, king of Israel."

This was the last half of the eighth century B.C. It means that Hosea was an older contemporary of Isaiah.

He preached from the last years of Jeroboam II until the total destruction of the Northern Kingdom by the Assyrians in 722 B.C.

Out of the cauldron of his nation's darkest hour Hosea outlined the shape of the grapes of wrath stored in his culture and in ours. The times were tough as nails then.

Israel's Indian summer under Jeroboam was almost over. Already the haze was on the horizon and the nights were crisp with a touch of winter without end. The season was far spent. Hosea lived during the last days of his beloved little nation—Israel.

The signs of the times were written in shifting sands. They were written largest in the sudden starts and stops of the nation's foreign policy.

Caught between two great powers—Assyria to the east and Egypt to the south—the uneasy kings of Israel played a fast and dangerous game of political roulette. Theirs was the age-old tactic of playing "both sides against the middle." Now little Israel was caught in the middle and about to be crushed.

Within 10 years the tiny country crowned five kings. Man-made and man-murdered, they came and went in sound and fury. One pool of blood bordered another in Hosea's beloved homeland.

The monarchy was an erratic weathervane, turning willy-nilly with every wind that blew! The nation neared the brink.

The instability of the throne was simply a symptom of the instability of the people—a nation without soul, without root, without direction. Hosea's countrymen had sown the wind and were about to reap the whirlwind. They were "trampling out the vintage where the grapes of wrath were stored."

And Hosea, whose heart was as big as all outdoors, had one profound problem: too many eyes and too few hands. He could see what was happening, but could do next to nothing about it. Hosea could not get anyone to care. Besides this, his own life was seared, scarred, and shaped by the infidelity of his beloved wife Gomer.

Right in the thick of things—"with three hungry children and a crop in the field"—she left him for other lovers. She put her body on the market, and in time Hosea had to buy her back out of prostitution with a considerable portion of his life's savings.

But his tears became telescopes. He gained his gospel through his grief. The tragedy of his hearth taught him the tragedy of Israel's altar. As Hosea sat amidst the shambles of his own dreams, he heard the distant rumblings of his nation falling apart.

The reason for it became crystal clear: Israel had done toward God exactly what Gomer had done toward him. So, in Yahweh's name sad Hosea set out to bring Israel back to her first love. He charged his countrymen with breaking a covenant as sacred as marriage.

He told them that they were acting like a young woman who had murdered her parents and now was beseeching the judge to be merciful with her because he was dealing with an orphan.

With a pounding in his heart and a lump in his throat, Hosea told unheeding Israel just how sick she really was. And in the process he made some points that apply right now to all of us. Let's review the words of Hosea for our own time:

First, there is the warning.

Familiarity can breed contempt. Israel had seen it happen. She had handled her religion fast and loose for a long time.

The nation should have been in its spiritual maturity. Long ago, when the nation was very young, it relied upon Yahweh—God of their fathers. But that was long ago.

Now, Israel was older and, as the people thought, wiser. As the nation had grown fat and lazy and gray-haired, the people had lost their sense of reliance.

For long years God was a part of the furniture of their mind, but alongside God there were no other pieces. Frankly, some of them had grown more attractive and predominant in Israel's mind than that old antique called Yahweh—handed down, generation to generation ever since Abraham.

As a matter of fact, God was not nearly the most important reality in Israel anymore. Familiarity had bred contempt! Israel had bogged down in the mire of indifference toward Yahweh.

Our hearts tell us that this is not only possible, but indeed probable, here and now. We too face the "peril of the proximate."

The reality of faith has lost its hold on us not just because God is too far away, but because God is too familiarly known.

So the first fine reveille of our faith dies for want of air. Routine and familiarity are even now deadly foes to vital faith. Let me illustrate.

One of the fine British novels of some years ago describes it: Little Bron is 5 years old. He goes to church for the first time in his life with his governess. He watches intently every part of the worship, and when the preacher stands in the pulpit, Bron hears him give out a piece of terrible news. It's all about a brave, kind, good man who was nailed to a cross, ferociously hurt a long time ago. It's about that same man who wants us to respond to him here—now.

Little Bron thinks the preacher is relating that story because there are lots of people there, and they will do something about it. He is impatient, almost on the edge of his seat. He can scarcely wait to see what the first move will be to right this terrible wrong. But nothing happens!

Bron weeps. But no one seems to care. No one does anything. The service is over. The people walk away as if they had heard nothing. Bron is trembling when he leaves the church. His governess looks at him and says, "Bron, don't take it to heart. Someone will think you are strange."

That says it! Such overfamiliarity with religious reality until it produces indifference: Hosea warns against it—then and now.

To be careless about spiritual things is the first storm warning. Whether in a marriage or in a church or in a nation or in a life, it is a sign of danger.

We cannot be presumptuous in our relationship with the Living God and have anything left but the shell of vital faith. When the substance is gone, only the form remains!

Following the warning, there is the promise.

Hosea addressed himself to a people who had long since taken God for granted. The cutting edge had been knocked right off their relationship to the Holy. They had already sown the wind; now the deadly spiral of the whirlwind loomed on their horizon.

But Hosea mounts a higher plane than mere warning. He holds out hope. He understands that out of tragic mistakes and failures some good can come.

Not even our wrong steps are a total loss. God sees to it that we learn from our false starts. So Hosea affirms that the Living God has a special treatment for good intentions gone awry, for holy dreams defiled, for lives that get all messed up.

Just because we have sinned, it does not mean that we abandon all hope. There is the promise.

God knows the pain of stifled things. That is God's promise through Hosea to us. Dorothy Quick has summed it up like this:

God has a special place for still-born things
The things that never were and should have been.
The little songs no singer ever sings
The beauty of a picture hung unseen.
A noble heart that loved with no return
And deeds well meant which somehow turned out ill.
A lovely flame that vainly tried to burn
But could not last, though all the winds were still.
The early flower that no one ever sees,
Making its way through ground iced hard with sleet.
A Caesar to whom no man bends his knees,
The Christ-like smile that meets each fresh defeat
God treats them very tenderly, for God
Knows what the pain of stifled, aborted things can be.

That says it! The glad good news is that even our sin need not be fatal.

The promise of Hosea is that God's love reaches even our sin—and forgives. For God knows the pain of stifled things. Hosea's wayward wife taught him that.

Perhaps the crux of Hosea's whole prophecy comes in chapter 6, verse 1: "Come, let us return to the Lord, for he was torn that he may heal us; he has stricken, and he will bind us up."

God never, never, never gives up. Divine love will have its way at last. Even our suffering can be redemptive.

"Return" is Hosea's big word. He uses it 15 times in these 14 chapters.

Let the word go forth: there is always "another time" with God's love. God's love is expansive enough to recover all our false starts and to cover all our broken chances. God gives us new ground on which to stoop and to begin building again.

So Hosea has a right-now word for all of us depressed, confused, smashed: For those who return to the Lord and honestly seek to build their broken dreams, God flings open a door of hope.

This, after all, is the message incarnate—seven centuries later—in Jesus Christ: "Come to me, all you who are weary and heavy laden . . . and I will give you rest." Amen.

October 22, 1995

JOEL

The day of the Lord

Joel 1:1-4, 6-7, 15; 2:1-2, 12-13, 28-29; 3:14-16

Any civilization that scaffolds right and enthrones wrong must do so by accomplishing two things: They must scuttle the prophets, and they must crucify the Christ all over again. These two infamous deeds accompany each other. In fact, one issues directly in the other.

Jesus of Nazareth perceived the peril in disregarding the messages of the Old Testament prophets. He addressed Jerusalem sadly, as the city that had killed the prophets and stoned the heralds of God (Matthew 23). In his most scathing denunciation of the hypocritical scribes and Pharisees, he labeled them as persons "who build the tombs of the prophets and adorn the gravestones of the righteous saying, 'if we had lived in the days of our fathers, we would not have taken part in shedding the blood of the prophets.'"

This, Jesus added, was an indictment against them because they were "sons of those who murdered the prophets."

Jesus Christ delivered a scalding indictment: "sons and daughters of those who murdered the prophets." Here is an ever-contemporary complaint. In ancient Israel they slew them with swords and staves and stones. Today we smother them more subtly, with vicious indifference, and bury them beneath the dust we allow to collect on the books that bear their names.

Perhaps the handiest way of all to silence the prophets is to picture them as decrepit old men who—with flowing white hair, crystal balls, and musty old scrolls—reamed their way through history, muttering nonsense that applied neither to their countrymen nor to us. This, many of us have done! Why?

Why do model Americans today believe that we can be both well read and well behaved when we know Freud, Darwin, Marx, and even Jefferson, and neglect the Old Testament prophets? Perhaps it is because, if aroused, these prophets of the Old Testament just might cause us to see how far we are falling short of the purposes of God and thereby are crucifying Jesus Christ afresh everyday.

Let's hope that is the result as we turn to review the men and the messages of the last 12 books in the Old Testament. Hosea is the first of these. We met him last week.

Today we meet Joel. He comes first in the line-up of 11 prophets from Judah, the kingdom in the South.

Unlike some of the early books, Joel provides no hint at all as to the exact time he lived and worked. The book simply opens like this: "The Word of the Lord that came to Joel, the son of Pethuel . . ."

Therefore, his name and that of his father are about all we know of Joel.

His name in Hebrew means "Jehovah is God"—*yo-el*. That conviction, caught even in his name, runs white-hot throughout his message.

Joel was a passionately earnest man who stepped upon Judah's scene during a particularly difficult time. The locusts had hit! And in those sober-toothed little bugs Joel saw a paradigm for his prophetic message. The locust plague hitting Judah was but a preview of coming attractions.

Joel is unqualifiedly the prophet of the "Day of the Lord." The phrase occurs seven times in his three chapters. This means that for him there was a constant and unavoidable intervention of God in the affairs of history. Now, this intervention did not always come through usual, expected, or orthodox means.

Joel's God was a God of surprises. But when God's intervention did erupt on the scene, it always had two components: judgment and deliverance. God intervened to judge, *and* God intervened to deliver. This is the dual thrust throughout Joel's three chapters, and we must always keep both realities in mind as we read his word.

Joel appears to be a native son of Jerusalem. He loved the holy city, the temple, and the Jewish religious system. He was a vigorous nationalist.

In fact, Joel has been criticized by some because he saw Judah's sins so small and the sins of the neighboring nations so large. Unlike Amos, he found it hard to rebuke his own countrymen for their evil.

However, his spiritual discernment was remarkable. He was always seeing the Eternal at work in the temporal. Even in the coming of a locust plague he could see signals of the inevitable Day of the Lord.

Joel's book is a vivid proclamation of what to him constituted the supreme duty of his countrymen. That duty was repentance, in face of God's impending judgment that would divert disaster and open the way for God to come in deliverance.

He was convinced that if and when such repentance came, it would bring an amazing inward change of heart immediately marked by outward changes of life and conduct.

Joel's prophecies could have been early or late: during the reign of Joash, about 837 B.C., or during the restoration at the end of the Exile, about 350 B.C.

The truth is, his message is always contemporary. His immediate interest was to draw a spiritual truth about the Day of the Lord from a locust plague and a drought that had swept his land. Since these were fairly common occurrences in Palestine, it was not the event that was important. It was rather the meaning of the event that Joel wanted his countrymen to discern.

He began by describing a swarm of locusts, and then moved to consider that disaster as a symbol of much more awful events to come in God's judgment against the people's evil.

So for Joel, the Day of the Lord was any day that marked vividly the activities of God in human affairs. Such a day was always present, and it was always coming—both at the same time. For Joel, the future was always now; and it was always open to the surprises of God.

But you know that is not in vogue in religion today. Someone has said that anything will sell in America if it glorifies the past, sanctifies the present, and petrifies the future.

This means that we want a future that is nailed down, zipped up, is totally predictable. We are tired of change, surprises, unpredictables.

But not Joel. He served a God of serendipities. Any day could become the "Day of the Lord." Any event could be fraught with great meaning—if God were seen at work in it.

Readers of the book of Joel are sometimes confused by the variety and scope of his prophetic vision. The man did indeed provide for both his countrymen and for us a "plan of the ages." Naturally, such scope confuses and baffles us.

Observe what Joel has done. He has assured us that there is an amazing consistency in the way that God works in the *immediate*, in the *impending*, and in the *eventual* affairs of history. Let him illustrate:

The first part of the message concerned things that were nearest to him. An actual plague of locusts had struck, devastating the land. So the first portion of his message drew lessons from that. In it God was accomplishing two things: judgment and deliverance.

The second part of his message concerned judgment of a more serious nature threatening the people. He envisioned a hostile army marching on Judah, leaving devastation far beyond anything in the locust plague.

But even in the impending invasion, God would be present and active accomplishing the same two things as with the locusts: judgment and deliverance.

The third portion of his message is cast well beyond his own day and generation. Climbing to a yet higher vantage point, Joel saw things to come at far distances. Thus he spoke of the coming "Day of the Lord" when God's Spirit would be poured out upon all God's people. And again he spoke of a time far beyond that day of the outpoured Spirit when history would be ended in some great catastrophic fashion and the "Day of the Lord" would come in final judgment and deliverance.

Now, get the picture! Here is a keen-visioned sensitive prophet of the Living God who wants to make one thing very clear to his countrymen and to us: *We do not escape God simply because we deny God!*

That would be the same as "defeating by denying" gravity, while jumping out a 10-story window to our death.

In all the affairs of history—whether a swarm of locusts right now or an invading army threatening soon or a far-distant cataclysmic event—God is at work, present and active in the affairs of men and nations.

"Jehovah is God" and as long as the world stands, God will be accomplishing two things in it: judgment and deliverance. And always, God's grace acts as a counteragent upon God's judgment.

God's ultimate attitude in judgment is not that of a conqueror who rejoices that he has broken and crushed, but that of a sovereign who rejoices that he has brought health, peace, and justice and another chance to the vanquished. This is the Joel call to Judah: "return to the Lord, rend your hearts and not your garments" (2:12-13). This is also the Joel call to us: "repent."

Every day for this prophet was the Day of the Lord. Joel is both far-sighted and near-sighted. He sees nearer at hand and farther ahead than any of the Old Testament final 12. For him, the final Day of the Lord is postponed, but it is absolutely sure and certain.

Meanwhile, Joel stakes down one central thing: with God, the present and the future are always filled with surprises. Nothing is petrified, fossilized, set in concrete. God is free and loose in the world, filling all time with serendipities.

Listen: "And it shall come to pass afterward, that I will pour out my spirit on all flesh; your sons and your daughters shall prophesy, your old men shall dream dreams, and your young . . . men shall see visions. In those days I will pour out my spirit" (2:28-29).

To deal with Spirit is always to deal with surprises. Unchained, unfettered, unpredictable—God's Spirit moves like the wind among God's people. Trying to tame Spirit is like trying to tame wind.

Peter, in his Pentecost sermon, proclaimed God's great surprises of the descending Spirit as "that which had been spoken by the prophet Joel" (Acts 2:16). Thus, what Joel saw in dim outline became reality hundreds of years later.

Do you want another surprise? Listen: "Your sons and your daughters shall prophesy." Some Christians I know are not ready for that—even yet.

"Prophesy" means "preach." Joel says both sexes will preach. Sons and daughters will preach—and be ordained and get called into missions. Then what? When the God of surprises collides with men whose minds are set like concrete, sparks always fly. But God always prevails. And sad little men who try to keep the surprises from happening grow sadder still.

It's tough business trying to keep a lid on the religious situation when you have a God like Joel's—or like ours. God unzips the zipped-up and un-nails the nailed-down. God dares let women preach!

Do you want another surprise? Listen: "And God will give portents in the heavens and on the earth, blood and fire and columns of smoke. The sun shall be turned to darkness and the moon to blood, before the great and terrible day of the Lord comes. And it shall come to pass that all who call upon the name of the Lord shall be delivered" (2:30-32).

Here is more than mere apocalyptic poetry. It is Joel's vision that one day all of history will end in a flaming atomic fireball. It has not happened yet. Nor do we have the final clue when it will come—in spite of all our date-setters.

But this Joel word is a somber word. He saw Pentecost hundreds of years before it happened. Who are we to deny that he has also seen the endtime and has told us how it will be on that great and final "Day of the Lord"? We are going against overwhelming odds when we doubt this inspired seer.

None of us escapes God simply because we deny God. Everything from pollution to drug traffic, the whole gamut from nuclear war to germ warfare is wrapped up in Joel's vision.

You see, he said a long time ago that physical and social disaster always accompanies moral disintegration. Doubt that if you choose. But read the tombstones in the grave-yards of history and argue with the facts.

How a society lives in relation to God indelibly flavors the political, social, and economic history of that society.

As Joel sees it, we are punished more *by* our sins than *because* of them. The judgment of God most often comes by God's simply letting our own evil run its natural and inevitable course.

That is the irony of our times. Through our own insensitive sinning in creating our scientific and technological wonderland, we are sowing the very seeds of our judgment.

God will never pull the trigger to launch a nuclear holocaust; some human will. Then all that is left for God to do in God's great love is to pick up the pieces. "All who call upon the name of the Lord shall be delivered" (2:32).

That is why repentance is so everlastingly important. It puts a person in such relation to God that God at any time can start picking up the pieces. And that is what repentance means: letting God pick up all the pieces in the spiritual puzzles of our lives and, in Christ, to put them together again!

Remember: Joel said it. God always comes in judgment and in deliverance.

Maranatha. Come Lord Jesus! Amen.

October 29, 1995

AMOS

Privilege means responsibility
Amos 1:1-2; 2:6-8; 3:1-2, 12; 5:18-24; 7:12-15; 8:1-3

Amos is the third prophet in the Old Testament "book of the 12." In actual fact, he appears to be the oldest of the group. Indeed, Amos seems to be the very first prophet whose words were written down.

The book of Amos is dated in the first verse: "The words of Amos, who was among the shepherds of Tekoa, which he saw concerning Israel in the days of Uzziah, King of Judah, and in the days of Jeroboam, King of Israel." This means that Amos worked about 760-750 B.C. He was a contemporary of Hosea and Isaiah, perhaps a little older than either.

Amos was a native of Judah, but his chief prophetic target was Israel. He grew up in the Southern Kingdom, but delivered his message to the Northern Kingdom. He was a southerner who went north to prophesy. His home was Tekoa, a small mountain-top village about 12 miles south of Jerusalem.

The village was hemmed in on all sides by dense wilderness and precipitous limestone cliffs, except on the east where there was a massive slope from Tekoa dropping almost 4,000 feet in the 18 miles it plummeted to the Dead Sea. The name Tekoa means "to pitch a tent." Perhaps at first the village was only a camp for shepherds and traders.

Amos was a layman. He was neither a son of a prophet nor a graduate of any school of the prophets. He was a herdsman, keeping a rare species of desert sheep noted for their tiny size and high-quality wool. He also dressed sycamore fruit. This means that at the right season he pinched the small fig-like lumps on the trees around Tekoa, allowing a bitter fluid to drain out so the fruit would ripen.

These two pursuits made Amos a man of moderate means. He was not wealthy. But he was far from the illiterate, uncouth hayseed some people think of when they hear his name. Some of the finest grammar and literary style in the Old Testament are to be found in the book that bears his name.

There at Tekoa several influences converged upon him. One was the discipline of the desert.

Amos knew the lonely life of a shepherd. He had lots of time to ponder and to meditate. Here in the "university of hard knocks" he learned to discern quickly between the real and the sham. He attained an alertness that marked his life forever. Here too he gained the courage and the determination to share his convictions.

Another thing that influenced Amos was his trips to national markets. Bethlehem was only six miles from Tekoa. Jerusalem was 12 miles; Bethel, 22. Samaria was only a two-day journey.

While in these trade centers, selling wool or sycamore fruit, Amos gained a first-hand view of life in his time.

He saw the golden calf set up at Bethel and worshiped by his countrymen in Israel. On his journey home he had time to ponder what his desert eyes had seen and what his desert ears had heard.

Something was wrong—bad wrong—with Israel and Judah. They were rotting like the other nations surrounding them.

So, in his soul mounted a struggle issuing in his call to be a prophet. This was no routine call, mind you. The presence of God split the desert stillness with a series of special visions. Amos mentions five of them in his book: He saw a locust plague (ch. 7), a great fire (ch. 7), a plumb line (ch. 7), a basket of summer fruit decaying (ch. 8), and a destroyed house of worship (ch. 9).

His dynamic sense of call never left him. In 3:8 he recalls the flame God ignited in his soul: "The Lord God has spoken. Who can but prophesy?"

However, he hotly rejected being labeled just another of the popular court prophets who "preached for pay." Indeed, upon being questioned by Amaziah, the priest at Bethel, he denied that he was a prophet or the son of a prophet in the "usual" sense. He was a lone wolf cut from a different mold. He had no fits or seizures, but spoke in plain language on what he considered to be the burning issues of the day.

In order to understand Amos' message, we must understand historically the situation in which it is couched. It was the mid-eighth century B.C., 750 years before Jesus Christ was born. Jeroboam II was in the midst of his 41-year reign in Israel.

Politically, he had masterminded Israel's finest hour. The borders had been extended to include more territory than ever before. To the north, Syria was smarting from recent defeat. To the east, Assyria was languishing in the mire of weak leadership. To the south, Egypt was content with her existing boundaries.

It had been hard "to start a war" in Israel. The land was enjoying "the best of times." The people were euphoric, optimistic. They reclined on ivory beds in fine houses, stretched out on velvet couches scarcely recalling the tough times that used to be.

The country was full of yuppies. If God were on their minds at all, it was on the back side of them. It would not have been hard to get a large audience for a lecture on "God is dead" in Israel. It was "Indian summer."

Amos saw the impressive exterior of Israel, but he perceived just how bad things were internally. Morally, the land was diseased. The rich were infatuated with power and satiated with perverted pleasure.

Faulty weights and measures marked their commerce. The rich were getting richer; the poor, poorer. Bribes were many and varied. Land grabbing was rampant. The courts were corrupt. Justice was hard to come by.

The middle class was fast disappearing. Ask anybody, nobody's word was their bond.

The women were the ring leaders in Israel's evil. Liberty had become license for them. Fornication was committed in the name of the Lord. Worship had given way to the wildest of orgies.

Religion ran shallow. It consisted of meaningless ceremonials conducted by priests more interested in their salaries than in their messages.

Israel was morally bankrupt. Entrenched evil, like some terrible moral malignancy, gnawed away at the muscle and nerve of the nation.

As things turned out, Israel had less than 30 years left on the world map. By 722 B.C. she was wiped out—gone forever!

Into this kind of sick society Amos stepped to prophesy. He came as the eloquent herald of a God with a conscience. For Amos, God was a thoroughly righteous being who was not taken in by religious sham.

The gospel of Amos was the gospel of a lion's roar. He heard the rumblings of Assyria on the plains to the east. He knew that "only two legs and a piece of an ear" would be left of Israel when Assyria got through.

Every time he saw a palace he snorted. The leaders were not leading Israel. They were simply letting the people go over the precipice into the graveyard of history. His countrymen were marching off the map.

His God could come to this kind of society only in judgment: this was Amos' conviction. So he said it in 5:24: "Let justice roll down like waters, and righteousness like an everflowing stream."

Amos came onto the scene when there was one surpassing need: a clear, crisp, fearless statement of the character of God and God's relationship to all humankind. So, he said it. But his countrymen would not listen.

Israel had been blessed to be a blessing. The people were not pets of providence. Their special relationship to Yahweh laid special duties upon them (3:2). Privilege meant responsibility in Israel 750 years before Christ, as it does in our city 1,900 years after Christ.

Those who have the clearest light experience the profoundest judgment.

So Amos came to Bethel in midsummer preaching. And he had no soft drink in his hand. He did not stutter, nor did he stammer.

He came to Israel's most splendid city, not as a fresh and stimulating summer breeze. He came as a hurricane. And before the eye of that storm had passed through Israel, everything false had been exposed. Israel stood naked and condemned before Amos' God.

But it is so easy for us from our own vantage point to say, "So what?" "Amos came to Bethel, not to our city." "He came to Israel, not to us!"

Yet, did he? I have an uneasy feeling that Amos has come to us also. He is a man for our time.

So, hear the herdsman from Tekoa as he thunders over the wrecks of time. Let him tell us of one of his visions. Then note whether what he says is so far removed from where we are.

I speak of Amos' vision of the basket of summer fruit. It brought into focus Israel's real situation (ch. 8). It was a big-gun parable, and its fire ball reaches us all.

Get the picture. Summer fruit has been plucked from the vine. It is lovely to look at, pleasing to smell. But already the fruit gnats are buzzing. Already the flesh of the fruit is unfirm.

It is only a matter of time until the entire basket of summer fruit will mold, sour, rot. It is a vivid picture of decadence.

If Amos were to come to our city, he would press that vision upon our lives also. So many of us are trying to live on spiritual fruits gathered earlier. So much of our meaningful religious experience is in the past tense.

We have so little fruit gathered fresh just this morning. In our generation of pleasant diversions and bright distractions, decay runs deeps in our basket of summer fruit.

No wonder—now as then in ancient Israel—Amos' parable drives home its truth of inescapable judgment. He deals not with lavender and old lace, but with blood and smoke. He thunders judgment, but it is the kind that comes from nature simply running its course. The fruit rots—quietly, naturally, inevitably—because nothing is done to keep it fresh.

Judgment: what in the world does the word mean? We tend to think of judgment as some "far-off divine event toward which the whole creation moves."

Not so, not necessarily, with Amos or with us. Judgment is here, now—inherent in the way things are.

Decaying fruit reeks with the stench of its "judgment" long before it is thrown out of the basket, rotted and destroyed. Yet we have ingenious ways of reducing the sting of such a sharp truth as that. Our merry-go-round starts on Monday morning and does not run down until late Saturday night. Even if we do go to church on Sunday, most of the sobering thoughts we have just sit there on the tops of our minds and never soak in.

Like Morley's *Old Mandarin*, we can manage some sort of distraction. Judgment seems so far off. We never think of it coming quietly, silently, naturally—rotting our insides out.

For most of us, it is sufficient judgment for our spiritual nature to take its inevitable course in these lives we live.

That was Jesus' point in one of his most poignant parables. He told us of "a rich farmer" who learned what Amos was talking about too late (Luke 12:16-21). When we meet him he is already gray around the temple. He is what we would call a successful, self-made man—a sightly basket of summer fruit. He has worked hard, made no significant mistakes, been successful.

But Jesus saw in him a fatal flaw. There was a strange confusion in that man's mind. He thought of all the symbols of his success—his barns, his fields, his grain.

He saw these as mere extensions of himself: He was as tall as his barns were tall. He was as big as his fields were big. He was as full as his bins were full.

His life and his possessions were one and the same thing. And his judgment lay precisely not in what he had accumulated, but in what he had lost. Somewhere along the way the farmer lost his identity as a man—he forgot what his life was all about.

Little did he know—this rich poor man—that an inevitable judgment coursed through every one of those 40 to 50 years that he had filled his barns and emptied his soul. Finally, his barns had consumed him.

Now, as he approached the end of his time, there had been nothing of God in his life; so there was nothing of God in his death—except judgment. The summer fruit had rotted! His grave bore a tragic epitaph: "Foolish mortal human—born a man, died a farmer."

So Amos and Jesus both jolt us awake with the arresting fact that all our tomorrows taste of all our yesterdays. Judgment threads through all our days. It is never something "to come." It is always something already here.

Spirituality soon spoils if it is cut from the Vine, if it is not made fresh every morning.

Our summer fruit is decaying in its basket. If we are ever going to make any changes, now is the time to do it. Now is the time for change—inside out.

And right here is where the gospel comes in. Jesus Christ has permeated time with eternity, mortality with immortality, corruptibility with incorruptibility.

He is himself the Living Vine who will guard all our summer fruit from decay.

Jeroboam and his countrymen would not hear Amos. They had the priest to run him out of town. But they had not rejected the prophet; they had rejected the God who sent him.

Within a generation the jackals were howling in what were once the streets of Bethel, and the proud throne room of the king was a haunt for lizards basking in the sun.

Somehow I perceive Amos once more boiling things down to basics:

The clock of life is wound but once,
And no man has the power
To tell just when the hands will stop
At late or early hour.

The present only is our own,
So live, love, toil with a will,
Place no faith in "Tomorrow,"
For the clock may then be still.

The man from Tekoa has come to tell us all two things: Change is inevitable; progress is not—spiritually or otherwise. Judgment is inevitable; it's not coming. "Judgment is already here," even now in the basket of summer fruit we have picked with the labor of our lives.

"Let justice roll down like waters, and righteousness as an everflowing stream." And let it begin right here, right now—in me, in you, in us. Amen.

November 19, 1995

OBADIAH

Evil is a boomerang

Obadiah 1:1-4, 10-18, 21

The book of Obadiah is the shortest scroll in the Old Testament, consisting as it does of a single chapter with 21 verses. Along with Jude in the New Testament, this is the most compact message in the Bible.

Obadiah starts off with nothing about the author—just his name. We do not know anything more about him, except that there are a dozen Obadiahs mentioned in the Bible. This popular Hebrew name means "Servant of Yahweh."

The most notable Obadiah was a court official in the palace of Ahab in Israel, and his exploits are recorded in 1 Kings 18. Later Jews took this Obadiah to be the author of our present book. But that would date it about 860 B.C., which seems improbable.

The main thrust of the book is against Edom for its crime in joining some invaders who destroyed Jerusalem.

Therefore, most students of scripture agree that the book came not too long after the destruction of Jerusalem by Nebuchadnezzar and the Babylonians in 586 B.C. Since Obadiah seems to expect a return of the 10 northern tribes, as well as the two southern ones, it may well be that it was written before the return from exile in 536 B.C. or so early after the return that the final demise of the Northern Kingdom had not been accepted.

This page out of our Old Testament was not written by a man sitting quietly under his grapevine in a camel skin chair. Obadiah was on his soapbox, and he was fighting mad. So put away your sweet-syrup and soft-taffy concept of a prophet as you read these 21 verses. This man was incensed, outraged, indignant, and mad as a wet rooster. Here is a stem, pious, patriotic prophet whose paramount conviction was that God is in command of the affairs of men and nations.

In Obadiah the great prophetic faith in God's righteous judgment is expressed in its most fierce, most nationalistic form. For this reason, some say that the book of Obadiah marks a sad decline in Hebrew prophecy.

Be that as it may, here is one page marinated in the crucible of a white-hot indignation. The bubbling, boiling cauldron that is the Middle East of today is reflected here 500 years before Christ.

Obadiah was armed and angry. He did not hesitate to let either his countrymen then or his readers now know it.

The holy city, Jerusalem, had been smashed by ruthless invaders, and the Edomites had displayed the most unbrotherly kind of attitude toward the Hebrews, actually sharing in the plunder of the city as well as the ravaging of the refugees. It is to this immediate situation that Obadiah thunders out his brief word: he predicts the overthrow of Edom and the eventual restoration of Judah.

Actually, the broader background of this prophecy extends all the way back to Jacob and Esau. Remember, these were the twin sons of Isaac and Rebekah. They were likewise the founders of the brother nations of Israel and Edom. In the book of Genesis a most suggestive comment is made: "The children struggled within her" (25:22).

So, even before their birth, the antagonism between Jacob and Esau is anticipated. The brothers remained hostile to each as long as they lived. Their offspring kept up the feud. In the one brief page provided by Obadiah the hostility between Jacob and Esau is brought into clearer focus than anywhere else in the prophetic literature.

Jacob is always in the background of this book, while Esau is in the foreground. A Jacobite is saying this scorching, searing red-hot word about an Edomite. The sons of Isaac are having it out again.

The Edomites were direct descendants of Esau. They were a proud, haughty people who lived within their rocky fortress at Petra, carved out of the solid rock, on a caravan route from north Palestine to the Red Sea. They were great traders and accomplished bandits. From their rocky fortress in what is now south Jordan, they could swoop down on trade caravans—mostly Jewish—and then retreat swiftly to their rock-ribbed stronghold.

Petra could be approached only one way: through a narrow ravine, terminating in a gorge where only two horsemen could ride abreast. On either side of this entryway called "the siq," massive cliffs rose 700 feet high.

They literally were, as Obadiah says, "like eagles with their nests snugly built in the crags of the mountains, among the stars" (v. 3). The Edomites naturally felt secure behind such an impregnable barrier. For centuries they lived there in this natural fortress, preserving a somewhat primitive culture and adding insult to injury in their dealings with their cousins in Judah.

During the siege of Jerusalem by Babylonian troops in 586 B.C., the Edomites joined with Nebuchadnezzar. They occupied the hill country south of Judah when many of the Jews were carried captive into Babylon. This aroused afresh the long feud between the nations of Judah and Edom.

Feelings of revenge overflowed their banks, and in the scroll of Obadiah we have some results of the flood.

The historical fate of the Edomites is interesting. By 312 B.C. the doom predicted by Obadiah began to befall Edom by way of invading Nabatean Arabs. Their mountain stronghold was overrun by hordes from the deserts to the east.

The descendants of Esau, the remnants of Edom, were chased out of Petra to settle in the region just south of the Dead Sea known as the Negeb. Here, by intermarriage with other peoples of this locale, they became the Idumeans.

In New Testament times we encounter the Idumeans in a most significant way. Herod the Great, king of Palestine at the time of Jesus' birth, was an Idumean. He built Masada down by the Dead Sea.

When we watch Herod trying to wipe out the infant Jesus, we see once more the flames of the ancient feud: Jesus—offspring of Jacob's branch—*versus* Herod—offspring of Esau's branch!

In A.D. 70 Titus, Rome's conquering general, destroyed the Idumean power completely—storming Masada, and causing the suicide of all the defenders. The Edomites, as an identifiable people in history, disappeared off the face of the earth.

It took more than 500 years, but Obadiah proved correct: the "proud eagle" got its wings clipped. "For the day of the Lord is on its way . . . As you have done, it shall be done to you. Your deeds shall return on your own head . . . The house of Jacob shall be a fire . . . and the house of Esau stubble; they shall burn them and consume them, and there shall be no survivor to the house of Esau, for the Lord has spoken" (vv. 15, 18). Thus, Obadiah issues his somber warning to entrenched evil everywhere.

This moral universe arrays itself against men and nations who persist in their rebellion against God.

Evil is always a boomerang! Eventually it turns back to cut down the persons or the societies who harbor it. Consider poor, sad, besieged little Colombia where drug lords have turned a country into a wasteland.

Edom is Esau enlarged into national scale. His essential evil, and theirs, was pride demonstrated by the violence done to others.

Obadiah puts his finger on this evil of evils in verse 3: "The pride of your heart has deceived you, you who live in the cleft of the rock . . . and say in your heart, 'Who will bring me down to the ground?'"

Here is an attitude of heart that declares its ability to go it alone without God.

Such a person, proud as Esau, is one who has no spiritual sensitivity, who sets no value on a birthright and will sell his soul for any bowl of hot pottage. Such was the sin of Esau. Such was the sin of Edom—proud, haughty, acting as though they were general managers of the universe—thoroughly independent of God's control of history.

While Jacob at least stumbled toward some far-off spiritual ideal, Esau enjoyed his entangling alliances with evil—never praying, never repenting, never worshipping anyone beyond himself.

Obadiah would have the word go forth that every such confederacy with evil works toward eventual ruin. For evil is a boomerang. Eventually "as you have done, it shall be done to you; your deeds will return on your own head" (v. 15).

So this ancient prophet, trembling with rage, reminds us that there is a dark sentence written large in the stuff of history: "What you sow, you shall also reap." Or as we might say today, "Chickens come home to roost."

Why does this have to be? Well, no one seems to know exactly. No more so than one can explain precisely how *Voyager II* can bypass Neptune with uncanny precision—4 minutes off in 4 years, 20 miles off in 4 billion years—and spin free into the cosmic regions of outer space.

The dark line on history's brow, the fearsome blotch at history's heart is there to testify that judgment is as predictable in the moral universe as mathematics are in the physical universe.

Let one generation sow the wind; the next reaps the whirlwind. The newborns are never really given a clean start on an unmarked page. We all write our lines in this life on pages already soiled.

Honestly, we have not done too well in figuring out why it works this way. But no one has to tell us that it does. The evidence is all too convincing.

An infection has entered the bloodstream of things as they are, and all of us share the sickness. But worse still, all of us pass it on.

Tell me, if you were in control of this world, how would you run it?

Would parents pass on such dark legacies to their offspring?

Why should a child be blinded because of his father's sexual promiscuity, contracting syphilis?

Why should a baby's chromosomes be broken up by a mother's thoughtless cocaine-high during pregnancy?

Why should a young man's early years be smashed because his teenage mother bore him out of wedlock just to spite *her* parents?

Why should children of this generation suffer from the political and ecological madness of the former ones who have raped the earth and opened international hostilities that even now bathe the newborn and the unborn in bad blood?

Why should the slum dwellings built a generation ago now invite rats and threaten to explode every day into violence?

Why should fathers and mothers eat their stomachs out with ulcers, trying to amass financial security when their sons and daughters blow it almost before their parents' corpses are cold?

Of course, it's because history is continuous, and it bears on every page our soiled fingerprints. All our tomorrows taste of all our yesterdays. Obadiah was right: "Your deeds do indeed return on your own head."

Hate begets hatred. Greed begets greed. Ignorance begets ignorance. Violence begets violence down through all the years.

History harbors a recurring refrain: "Things are out of sorts. Something has gone wrong at the core of things."

And all Obadiah could do about that was to hold out a hope. He accents it in his final verse 21: "Saviors shall go up to Mt. Zion . . . and the Kingdom shall be the Lord's."

So, let the Obadiah word go forth: Evil is a boomerang! So is hope!

It is inconceivable on the stage of history that wrong can ultimately triumph over right—not so long as the universe is moral.

God is sovereign. To God goes the governance over everything and everyone forever and ever. God has put evil under house arrest. It can no longer have the final word.

History holds one incontrovertible fact: evil can only destroy; it cannot redeem. It is an imposter. Evil has no creative power. It is deceitful and must always pose as good to get anywhere.

Thus, evil is always inferior: it can exist only by imitating the good. The Living God of us and our universe has evil under control. Yahweh gives evil just enough rope to hang itself. That is Obadiah's hope, and it is ours.

That is what Golgotha is all about. Here at the cross of Jesus Christ evil was cutting its own throat, gloating over its best effort, but all the while paving the way for God to forgive. And forgiveness is the one force that evil cannot withstand.

Forgiveness, then, is God's ultimate answer to evil, whether in history or in me—or in you. And God's forgiveness through Jesus is an answer about my redemption from me and about your redemption from you so we can rise above pride and selfishness to enjoy being the sons and daughters of God forever. Amen.

November 26, 1995

JONAH

Beware, even prophetic exclusiveness
Jonah 1:1-3, 15, 17; 3:1-5; 4:1, 9-11

The book of Jonah is different in several ways from all prophetic literature in the Old Testament. For one thing, it is not a book of utterances by a prophet. It is rather a book about a prophet. It is not a sermon. It is a story—a gripping short story. It is not a story about a whale, but a whale of a story. It is written about Nineveh and the Assyrians, but it is written to Israel and the Jews. Thus, it is about one group—but for another group. Besides all that, the book of Jonah ends with a question (4:11).

In fact, the Jonah message is both prophecy and a critique of prophecy. It affirms that for a person of faith, attitudes and words and actions must all be one. In short, Jonah is a cure for prophetic schizophrenia that would love God and despise people.

Jonah is included among the Old Testament prophetic books because the story is about a man mentioned in the historical section of the Old Testament as a significant prophet during the reign of Jeroboam II in Israel. Thus we read in 2 Kgs. 14:25: "Jeroboam II restored the coast of Israel according to the word of the Lord . . . which he spake by the hand of his servant Jonah, the son of Amittai . . . of Gath-hepher."

Gath-hepher was a village about three miles northeast of Nazareth. The traditional tomb of Jonah is there even now. The prophet Jonah, mentioned in 2 Kings, lived during the early part of the reign of Jeroboam II in Israel. He apparently predicted the successful outcome of the king's plans for his territorial expansion.

This would make the prophet active about 780 B.C. Most students of scripture agree that our present book of Jonah was not written that early. Therefore, it is not a story by the prophet Jonah, but a story about him.

For example, in 780 B.C., while Jonah lived and worked during the reign of Jeroboam II, Assyria was in a period of decay and was no threat to anyone. Nineveh was only a small provincial town on the banks of the Tigris River in Mesopotamia. The capital of Assyria in Jonah's day was Calah, as it had been for 500 years.

It was nearly 100 years after the time of Jeroboam II—and Jonah—that Sennacherib established the royal residence at Nineveh. Nineveh then became the infamous capital city of the Assyrians—who for three quarters of a century were "the scourge of history." They became the most dreaded and powerful military machine in the world.

It was these very Assyrians who destroyed Samaria and the Northern Kingdom in 722 B.C., and who became the masters over the Southern Kingdom until 612 B.C. when the Babylonians destroyed Nineveh and wrestled the Assyrian empire to its knees.

In Jonah 3:3 the writer refers to Nineveh in the past tense and gives some indication throughout that the memory of his readers needs to be refreshed concerning how great and wicked a city Nineveh actually had been.

So much for the historical situation concerning Nineveh . . . After all, it is only the backdrop against which the book of Jonah is cast. In order to find the essential message of this book, we must look for the revelatory features in the story. In doing this it is crucial to distinguish between incidentals and essentials.

The incidentals are the ship, the ticket, the storm, the fish, the gourd, the wind. If we focus on these, we miss the essential message. Now let me hasten to say that just because they are incidental, that does not make them unimportant. I am not prepared to say that these existed only in the imagination of the writer.

This is no fable we are dealing with. This is rather a four-chapter section of our Old Testament alive with a burning message about the love of God. Jonah is about a prophet trying to get across a message about God. The fact is, Jesus Christ himself sought to witness to the same thing in Matt. 12:39-41:

> An evil and adulterous generation seeks for a sign; but no sign shall be given to it except the sign of the prophet Jonah. For as Jonah was three days and three nights in the belly of the fish so will the Son of Man be three days and three nights in the heart of the earth. The men of Nineveh will arise at the judgment with this generation and condemn it for they repented at the preaching of Jonah, and behold something greater than Jonah is here.

So there are essentials in this book far greater than the incidentals. The message depends upon our grasping these essentials.

The surpassing essentials of the book are the transactions between Jonah and Yahweh. When our attention is focused here, then we begin to discover the living message of this story.

Here are a man and his God having it out with each other. The attitudes and actions of both of them toward Nineveh constitute the permanent value of this book.

The book of Jonah is perhaps the highest peak of the missionary thrust that threads throughout the Old Testament.

This writer is dealing death blows to racial and religious bigotry. He is delivering a blistering broadside against the threatening exclusiveness of the chosen people of God.

Jonah, like the book of Ruth before it, exposes the sin of imagining that if we have received light, it is for our lamps only.

The man around whom the events in this story revolve represents the whole of the Hebrew contempt for and antagonisms toward neighboring nations. He harbors a horrible four-letter word: THEY.

The God around whom the events in this story revolve depicts the whole of the divine pity and patience toward Israel's neighboring nations. God operates off a beautiful two-letter word: WE.

This rhythm is the high drama and the living message wrapped up in this immeasurable little scroll. It is the story of a man struggling with the love of God. Jonah is trying to get across to us that the love of God is indeed broader than the measure of man's mind.

Observe how the writer does it. First, he tells us some things about Jonah. Here is anyone, anywhere, anytime who stands with a ticket in hand seeking passage away from the purposes of God.

Jonah is a troubled man facing a difficult and dangerous new territory into which the love of God is about to plunge him.

So he made a decision: he would go west, even though the call of God was to go east. He would sail to Tarshish, a Phoenician colony, at the opposite end of the Mediterranean Sea from Palestine. He would put the sea between himself and his God. He would change his situation by changing his address.

But Jonah learned something! His problem was an inside one. He was trying to run away from something that was deep down within him. It was like trying to escape his shadow in broad daylight.

No change of scenery—not the mountains or the sea, not the desert or the sky, not altitude or longitude or latitude—could make him escape something inside that was compelling him.

God was there, not just in Palestine or in Tarshish, but besieging Jonah from within. Jonah was called to represent God to Nineveh. But he was not willing to do it.

So, we have a conflict of wills: "*my* will be done" or "*thy* will be done."

That is why Jonah ran. That is why he rebelled, and that is why he sat in heated anger on the rim of the city under his gourd vine.

Now, it would be easy to say that Jonah acted like he did because he really did not know God. But that was not the case. In fact, right the opposite was true. Listen to these words, spoken after Nineveh had been spared:

> But it displeased Jonah exceedingly, and he was angry. And he prayed to the Lord and said, "I pray thee Lord, is not this what I said when I was yet in my country? That is why I made haste to flee to Tarshish; for I knew that thou art a gracious God and merciful, slow to anger and abounding in steadfast love . . . Therefore, now O Lord, take my life from me, I beseech Thee, for it is better for me to die than to live." (4:1-3)

Jonah acted like he did precisely because he did know God. The things he knew of God conflicted with the things he knew of Nineveh.

Down deep, Jonah did not want Nineveh to be spared. Those hard-to-love Assyrians had been merciless and cruel. Their reputation was such that no one could admire
them, much less want them to be spared. They had made a hard bed and ought to have
to lie in it.

Jonah's prejudice had to be overruled by God's purpose. And that is always a painful
process. But Jonah could never come into a missionary enthusiasm until he came into
fellowship with the love of God for Nineveh—the world's most wicked and untouch-
able people.

So a question is shaped for us: Why do we fail so frequently in our mission to the
hard-to-love? For exactly the same reason that Jonah did: because we also dodge our
Ninevehs.

It is easy to ignore our mission to the hard-to-reach, the hard-to-teach—as if there
were actually some people whom God does not want to be redeemed.

Take for instance, the very hardest to love here in our own city. Are we really ready
to cooperate with God in reaching the unreachables right here where we live? Or, are
there some people simply too hard to love and thus too far outside the circle of our
concern to be redeemed?

The fact is, there are a great many people in this city who repel us. They turn us
off—frighten or threaten us.

We do not want to get near them. We are not really anxious that they be saved. And
if they ever are, it will be by someone else. We are reluctant to stretch out a hand to help
them. In short, we have the Jonah problem.

And sometimes we are moved to say, "I ought to love them; I am going to try to do
it." It is impossible! We cannot simply love someone by trying harder to do it.

So what can we do? We can fall in line with the purpose of God. We can let God
love them through us.

In obedience to God comes the capacity to love even those we cannot compel
ourselves to love.

So let us begin not out of our effort to love the hard to love, but out of our effort to
love God. Love God! God will lead us to find that others are lovable through that love.

And thus we learn one lesson from Jonah. The truth about Jonah is the truth about
us also.

Finally, the story tells us some things about God. We do not find the deepest revelation of God until we come to the very end of the book. The story begins with God
commanding Jonah to go to Nineveh. The story ends with God revealing why Jonah
should go. The last paragraph marks the climax of the revelation:

> And the Lord said, "You pity the plant, for which you did not labor, nor did
> you make it grow, which came into being in a night, and perished in a night.
> And should not I pity Nineveh that great city, in which then are more than
> 120,000 persons who do not know their right hand from their left?" (4:10-11)

"Should not I pity Nineveh?" Here is the foundational truth of the entire book. God loves Assyrians, the modern people of Iraq. Everything else is an outcome of this divine concern. The command to go to Nineveh, the patient, persistence with which God compelled the reluctant Jonah to obey—all stem from that reality: "I pity Nineveh!"

God is trying to give Jonah the courage to care!

Thus Jonah completes the Old Testament prophetic picture of God's international/universal concern. In Amos, God's sovereignty over the nations is revealed. In Obadiah, God's judgment of the nations is revealed. In Jonah, God's mercy toward the nations is revealed. All of it is a devastating blow against exclusiveness—even prophetic/preacher exclusivism.

That word "pity" is a significant one. Literally, it means "to cover." The idea is the same one Jesus embraced toward Jerusalem: "How often would I have gathered your children together, even as a hen gathers her brood under her wings . . ."

So God asks, "Should not I cover Nineveh? Brood over her, protect her, feel her sorrow as my sorrow?"

In that word "pity" we have God's attitude toward sinning people/cities everywhere—us/ours included. God's anger with sin is always born of God's "pity" for sinners. Thus, even God's judgment is love-inspired!

So the Jonah message comes home to Greensboro and to us: We must go to our Ninevehs, because God commands it, whether the going falls in with our prejudices or not. And as we go, we will come into fresh fellowship with God and find a new comradeship with all humankind—even the hardest to love. Amen!

January 21, 1996

MICAH

Remember the grassroots

Micah 1:1, 6; 2:1-3; 3:1-3, 12; 4:1-4; 5:2-4; 6:6-8

Micah came from the hill country. He snorted every time he saw a city. He was a rustic son of the soil; more comfortable in overalls than in business suits; a sentimental man whose loyalties never ranged far from the country people who were his chief concern.

His home was Moresheth in Gilead. It was a small rural village in the foothills of Judah near the borders of Philistia, and 25 miles northeast was Jerusalem where the great Isaiah was a prophet at the same time as Micah.

The geographical distance from Moresheth to Jerusalem was but a few miles. The social and economic distance was vaster by far. These two places were in two different worlds.

In Jerusalem lived the absentee landlords, the bankers, the loan sharks, the rulers who ruled for hire, the priests and the prophets who preached for pay. Micah's sympathies were not there—or in any other city he had ever seen.

His loyalties lay with the laboring peasant people and their problems. He would have agreed wholeheartedly with Bobby Burns who said in "The Cotter's Saturday Night": "Princes and lords are but the breath of kings; in honest common man is the noblest work of God."

Micah had his doubts whether an honest common man could ever live in a city.

Although Micah never tells us his occupation, it is almost certain that he was a farmer. He was an unadorned rural man—"of the people . . . and for the people."

Essentially, Micah was a poet. His approach to life was lyrical and emotional. His words were always heavy with feeling. He could rage one minute like a tornado and babble the next like a brook. He used strong words because he was swept by strong feelings.

Micah's name means "who is like Yahweh." It is a popular proper name in the Old Testament.

Micah was the fourth of the great prophets during the eighth century B.C. He was a contemporary of Isaiah, Hosea, and Amos. While Hosea was a Galilean and Isaiah was an aristocrat of Jerusalem, Micah, like Amos, came from the rural pasturelands and farmlands of Judah.

According to the first verse in the book that bears his name, he lived and worked during the reigns of Jotham, Ahaz, and Hezekiah—kings of Judah. This would place his ministry roughly from 735-700 B.C.

His prophecy is addressed to both Israel—to the north—and Judah—to the south. In the main, however, it centers around his associations with the peasant people of Judah. Although he spoke often of cities, there is no evidence that he ever lived or preached in one.

He stayed near his rural roots—and delivered his blistering broadside at the wickedness in the cities from the outskirts of town.

Students of scripture tell us that Micah's writings may be divided into two parts, each coming from a different period in his lifetime.

Chapters 1-5 are "Micah mad." They come from Micah's earlier years and are aflame with a prophetic word on the burning social issues of the time. To read these texts is to feel growing indignation at the economic and social injustices that his friends and neighbors "down on the farm" were suffering. Micah lived on the land and was outraged at the injustice of absentee landlords, living idly in Jerusalem and taking half the farmer's toil in rent. They had forgotten the people at Judah's grassroots, and for Micah that was fatal.

Chapters 6 and 7 are "Micah sad." In this section Micah feels more sadness than outrage. His spirit is mellower, though his passion still runs strong. The reason for his sadness is that his countrymen are so blind to their real needs and so resistant to the grace of God.

The man from Moresheth simply cannot understand it. The closing sentences of his scroll, uttered in broken sobs, express his wonder at the amazing love of God: "Who is a God like thee, pardoning iniquity and passing over transgressions . . . He (God) does not retain his anger forever because he delights in steadfast love . . . He will cast all our sins into the depths of the sea."

So, from youth to age, Micah is the strongly feeling man who speaks straight from the heart. In his youth he was outraged. In his maturity he was saddened, simply because he was a champion of the poor and a spokesman for God all in one process.

Like Isaiah, Amos, and Hosea, Micah lived through tragic days. Both internally and externally his countrymen were threatened.

The social and religious abuses of Hosea's and Amos' day in Israel had moved southward into Judah with alarming swiftness.

The political plight of both northern and southern segments of the people in Palestine had grown steadily worse. Assyria was on the loose! And it appeared that only time stood in the way of her warlords completely demolishing Palestine.

In turn, Micah saw Damascus, capital of Syria, fall in 732 B.C.; Samaria, capital of Israel, captured in 722 B.C.; and Jerusalem besieged in 701 B.C.

Yet, through it all, his chief concern remained religious and social rather than political. His rather uncomplex message had one recurring refrain: *Do not forget the grassroots!* Thus, pinched peasant faces peer from every page of this prophecy.

Underlying Micah's feelings, whether of outrage or of sadness, are certain presuppositions. Without these presuppositions his feelings might have run wild. But with them his feelings run true, straight to the heart of life itself.

Through these basic presuppositions Micah speaks his strong word to us. They focus his message for us. The first is a word of right and wrong.

Many of us subconsciously have our definitions of right and wrong. They are relative to all sorts of things—our feelings, our location, our age, our circumstances, our strain and stress.

But Micah causes us to sharpen our definitions. He believes that wrong and right are not relative to anything. There is a wrong, and there is a right. And if we respond to God as children—not as rebels—and if we respond to our neighbors as brother/sisters—not as strangers—then we can find the right and avoid the wrong.

Juliet Lowell wrote a book a few years ago titled *Dear VIP*. It was a series of letters written by children and youth to prominent persons on a variety of subjects. One of the letters, addressed to the late President John F. Kennedy, went like this:

Dear President Kennedy:

My name is John, too, and I'm president of my class. Please write and tell me what things a good president shouldn't be caught dead doing.

Signed, John S

We smile at such innocence! But Micah thunders his reply: there are some things that a good president, a good citizen, a good landlord, a good tenant, a good preacher, a good deacon, a good laborer, a good boss, a good secretary should not be caught dead doing. Most of man's rebellion against God and much of man's inhumanity to man stems from a fuzzy, dim, light-grey-colored ethical relativism. "Situation ethics" sounds better than it turns out to be.

A perfect example has been cited by a friend of mine in *Plumb Lines and Fruit Baskets*. A neighbor took his car to the garage for a little work on the electrical system. It was under warranty, so he expected no bill. But a bill did come, for $5.00, labeled "not covered by warranty." In the meantime he had discovered that the mechanic had left a pair of electrician's pliers in the car. Until he got that bill, he had fully intended to take those pliers back. But after receiving the bill, he just somehow never got around to taking the pliers back.

You see what happened: that man decided he had been overcharged. So to rectify the situation, he just kept the pliers that belonged neither to him nor to the owner who overcharged him—but to the poor mechanic who did the work.

In this case, right and wrong had become completely relative. Here was something he could do without getting caught; his ethic had become shaped by his situation.

Now you and I may understand what he did. We might even be able to rationalize it, justify it, admire it, or duplicate it. But Micah warns us that such ethical relativism is cancerous. It is corrosive. It is moral quick sand. It eventually consumes all of a life and applies not simply to a pair of pliers. There is a treachery in calling wrong "right"—and thinking that makes it so.

Yet we have all done things like that. But it fogs up our sensitivity and makes it easier to justify any kind of behavior. The embezzler never intends to be a thief; he only intends to borrow the money for a while.

The adulteress never intends to break up a marriage and smash other people in the process; she only attempts to do the most natural, loving, and friendly thing toward the guy at the party.

The landlord never intends to condemn the tenant to sub-standard housing, infested with rats and roaches; he is simply trying to turn a profit on the rent.

The employer never means to pay less than a livable wage, and the laborer never intends to steal his company blind; they are simply reacting "normally" in their situation. They are both victims of circumstances.

So the crazy, mixed-up logic of ethical relativism goes.

Micah warns that there is a right and there is a wrong, and in our own lives and in public affairs we can usually find it if we want to. But that is the problem! We do not always want to.

We act! Then we arrange our reasons for acting as we do. We shoot first, then draw our target around the bullet hole.

And we find that reason is a faithful servant. It will support any position, any decision, any choice we wish to justify.

Micah, this feeling man, knows how feelings can betray us. He also knows that underpinning life there is an absolute God-given ethic—a definite right and definite wrong. And simply calling wrong "right" does not make it so.

Wrong and right in human relations do not shift places so blithely. Sooner or later wrongdoers get caught up in their own web of rationalizations, half-truths, and false-hoods by which they have called wrong "right"—and they stand judged and condemned by their own actions.

That is Micah's first word to his countrymen and to us. His second is a word about forgiveness.

There are two ways to handle our wrongdoing: try to cover it up or own up to it. These are our alternatives: cover it or confess it.

What saddened Micah was that his countrymen chose the cover-up. In their foolish rebellion they refused to face up to their guilt. Ethically, the land was sick and refused to go to the doctor.

In covering up, they refused the gift of God's forgiveness and sooner or later the storm of Yahweh's judgment had to fall.

At this point Micah provides for us the clearest, most crisp and concise definition of true religion anywhere in the Old Testament. It is 6:8: "He has showed you, O man, what is good; and what does the Lord require of you, but to do justice, and to love mercy, and to walk humbly with your God."

Here is actually a blend of the elements championed by the other three great eighth-century prophets: the justice stressed by Amos, the love preached by Hosea, the humble fellowship with a holy God urged by Isaiah. All these are stirred into Micah's succinct formulation.

But even such a classic definition of the essence of true religion contains no gospel. Within ourselves we simply cannot do justice, love mercy, and walk with God. It depends on empowerment—beyond/within.

It only prepares us for the gospel—the empowerment—the good news that "while we were yet sinners, Christ died for us" (Rom. 5:8).

Therefore Micah, on the far distant side of history, marveled at the provision and the forgiveness of God.

Listen to Micah 5:2: "But you, O Bethlehem Ephrathah, who are little to be among the clans of Judah, from you shall come forth for me one who is to be ruler, in Israel, whose origin is from of old, from ancient days."

Thus the Messiah is foretold 700 years in advance. And those of us on this side of Bethlehem and of Golgotha marvel at the peasant-prophet's insight.

But we marvel even more at the peasant-prophet's God: the grace, the forgiveness, the limits to which God will go in order to pardon—even to the point of visiting this planet enfleshed in the man of Nazareth, Jesus Christ the Lord!

A friend of mine has done an interesting thing. He has taken a stop watch to a football game. He asks, "How long is a football game?" "One hour, two hours, or more?" Would you believe just eight minutes?

Regardless of how long the game lasts, the time actually involved in running the plays is about eight minutes. The rest of the time is spent huddling, calling signals, shifting, calling time-outs, getting ready to execute the plays that consume about eight minutes of time.

"The getting-ready time"—that is mighty important in football. I do not know what you are "getting ready for"—business, profession, career, study, marriage—but this I do know: Not one of us is ready for life until Jesus Christ is Lord.

Today is the best time ever to "get ready" for the rest of your life by accepting Jesus Christ as Savior and making him Lord. Amen!

January 28, 1996

NAHUM

The wrath of God's love

Nahum 1:1-3, 7-8; 2:8-10, 13; 3:1-7, 18-19

One can hardly read the book of Nahum without a pulse beating faster. Its solemn message is full of trumpets and the roll of drums. The theme of these three chapters in the 34ᵗʰ book of our Bible is the complete destruction of Nineveh and with it the fall of the Assyrian empire as a world power.

The name Nahum appears nowhere else in the Old Testament. It means "The Comforter." It is apparent that such a blistering broadside against hated Assyria was indeed comforting to the harassed Hebrews.

Very little is known about Nahum. His home was Elkosh. The whereabouts of that village is uncertain. Some say Elkosh was on the site of modern Capernaum—the city of Nahum. Others say it was southeast of Jerusalem near Moresheth, Micah's birthplace.

Wherever Elkosh was in Judah, it spawned among its citizenry one amazing man. Nahum is perhaps nearer to Isaiah in sheer literary ability than any other Old Testament author. He was a poet of major magnitude. He was also a consuming patriot—a nationalist in love with his country.

With a lively imagination and superb poetic powers, Nahum pictured the conquest of Nineveh in such terms that a reader can almost see the smoke and smell the burning corpses. His book resounds with the thunder of horses' hooves and the whir of chariots' wheels. His language rumbles, rolls, reverberates much like the battles he describes.

Nahum nowhere points out the sins of his own people. He is too busy cataloging the sins of Nineveh. In this respect he is different from other Old Testament prophets.

His three-chapter monologue is one long cry of fierce joy and savage exultation over the hated, fallen foes who are finally getting exactly what they deserve. There is no love lost in this book.

There is not much pity in it either. In fact, some interpreters have called it a "hymn of hate." It is militant from start to finish. Nahum was neither an owl nor a dove; he was a hawk. His hand was on the trigger, his missiles in the air.

The book itself sets its date somewhere between 663 and 612 B.C. Thebes was destroyed in the earlier year, and Nineveh in the latter one. The book mentions the sack of Thebes in past tense and the destruction of Nineveh in future tense. Thus, Nahum wrote his scroll somewhere in the 50-year span between these two towering historical events.

During the seventh century B.C. the Assyrian empire reached its peak as a world power. History has never known a more cruel, proud, or defiant force than the Assyrians. Nineveh was the formidable capital of Assyria. Old Testament history has much to do with this city.

Both Jonah and Nahum focus on Nineveh in their writings. Sennacherib made the city his Assyrian capital, and assembled a great library there. To the Jews, Nineveh symbolized the ultimate in deceit and treachery. It was Tehran and Baghdad all wrapped into one. The mere mention of the place sent a chill through a Hebrew. It was not so affectionately called "The Tiger of the Tigris" reposing as it did along the banks of the Tigris River.

The Israelites had been helpless to deal with the Assyrians. What the Assyrians wanted the Assyrians got—and little Judah could do nothing about it.

There stood Nineveh, glittering and strong, stretching for several miles along the river banks. Her bulwarks were formidable. The city walls, built entirely by slave labor, were 7.5 miles in circumference and wide enough for three chariots to drive abreast on the roadway atop them.

Her people were proud and her heritage rich. Under Esarhaddon and Assurbanipal, for more than half a century, Nineveh served as the hub of the empire that history knows as the "Scourge of Nations."

But long before these kings, the mighty nation began to have internal difficulties that eventually led to its collapse. Upon the death of Assurbanipal, Assyria rapidly deteriorated.

Nineveh fell in 612 B.C. before the combined attack of the Medes and the Babylonians. Never was destruction more complete. Alexander the Great marched over the ruins of the city 300 years later and never even knew they were there.

In 1842 the two great mounds marking the site of ancient Nineveh were opened by archaeologists. For the first time we began to discover the facts about that great mass of human evil that was Nineveh. The ruins are in Iraq, not so far from Baghdad.

In what some would call "a verbal overkill" Nahum levels his big guns at Nineveh. He bombs the rubble. Yet he does not give vent to mere personal passion. He speaks not as a patriot, but as a prophet. In a strange twist, his message is a missionary message. The thrust of his message is essentially twofold.

First, Nahum insists that God is an avenger of evil wherever it is found. And Nineveh represented everything that Nahum could imagine of evil. His passionate conviction was that God is in control of history and of nations. God's moral government will be manifest in the ultimate punishment of tyranny wherever and whenever it appears.

Entrenched evil, though defended behind fortresses and moats and walls, must give an eventual accounting to the sovereign God of this universe. Nahum would say that this fact holds true whether the situation applies to Nineveh or to Moscow or Peking or London; to Paris, Manila, Bogata, or Washington, D.C.

Second, Nahum asserts that God is the refuge of oppressed people wherever they are found. He speaks not only for Judah, but also for oppressed people everywhere.

Of course, he assumes that the oppressed people will maintain their faithfulness to Yahweh. Therefore, he nowhere accuses his own people of their sins. This is admittedly an extraordinary omission.

But be that as it may, Nahum bears witness to a great spiritual truth: This moral universe is so created that kingdoms based on force and fraud will eventually fall. Dictators, given time, will dig their own inglorious graves.

God's nature is righteous. God's universe is orderly and moral. In the destruction of Nineveh, Nahum saw the inevitables of this moral universe being worked out.

The law of harvest was at work. What had been sown was now being reaped. "Chickens were coming home to roost."

And in his strong three chapters, Nahum of Elkosh is bearing testimony to what he saw and what he believed.

The permanent value of his message so far as we are concerned is the single, white-hot, vivid truth he imparts about the wrath of God's love. Think it not strange that I say it this way. That is precisely how Nahum sees it. God's wrath is God's love experienced by rebels. And nowhere in the Old Testament is it elaborated more clearly.

In the very first passage of his prophecy Nahum uses seven different and distinct words to describe the awesome anger of God. Listen to the whiplash of the words: jealous, avenging, wrath, anger, indignation, fierceness, fury.

These are biting, stinging, slashing words. In fact, every Hebrew word found in the Bible suggesting anger is packed into the compass of Nahum's brief and awful first chapter. Nahum saw his God angry!

These three pages out of our Old Testament are not simply a matter of heated rhetoric in which a man under the sway of some personal feeling of vengeance attributes to God the things that are in his own heart. These pages contain rather a careful and profound theological description of the anger of God.

We would be wise to linger long enough to let Nahum instruct us upon this important theme. So let's convene the class, open our books, and get down to business.

Nahum of Elkosh, what is your living message for our times? First, there is this: God is slow to anger. So let us never imagine, when we consider the anger of God, that it is anything like the hot, passionate, blind, and often foolhardy blundering of humans in a temper tantrum or a rage. Dean Pusey has observed: "In the case of man, wrath becomes his master, and uses him; whereas in the case of God, God is the master of wrath and uses it."

God is slow to anger. Yet, having once crossed the threshold into the presence of persons who persist in rebellion, God is as irresistible as the hurricane that beats the sea into fury along the shoreline.

Nevertheless, God is forever a stronghold for those of faith; an avenger who calls all nature to rage against those who rebel. Now, just before we mismanage this truth, let us hurry on to Nahum's second insight.

Second, there is this: to believe in God's love is to be certain of God's wrath. Nahum insists that if you can persuade him that God is never angry, then he can persuade you that God never loves. God's anger is the wrath of God's love experienced by a rebel.

Let us for a moment assume the stance of trying to interpret God from a human point of view. Can you look at flagrant, obvious, cruel wrong—even abuse and oppression—without being moved?

Listen to an all-too-human happening, paraphrased from a report by the *Washington Post* and the *Los Angeles Times*:

"Daddy," a battered, half-dead 5-year-old told his stepfather, "I don't want to live anymore."

'Then why don't you just die?" asked the stepfather.

"Alright," said the frail youngster, "I will."

And the next day, Jeffery died.

This was the version of the youngster's death given to investigators by his mother, Betty Johnson Berry:

Jeffery accidentally knocked one of his stepfather, Ronald Berry's, shoes out of a second-story window at their residence.

Jeffery had set his shoes on the window sill to allow them to dry after pretending to polish them as he had seen his mother do.

She could not retrieve the shoe because she was not allowed to leave the apartment while Berry was gone. When he returned, the shoe had disappeared.

When Berry learned of the shoe incident, he beat the boy relentlessly with a belt and ordered him to stand in a corner.

Feeling sorry for Jeffery, Mrs. Berry allowed him to leave the corner as soon as her husband left again, but he then accidentally tipped over a can of paint she was using to paint a baby crib.

Berry was enraged when he returned home, beat the boy again, and refused to allow him to eat dinner.

In the days that followed, Berry pounded Jeffery with his fists and whipped him with a belt, forced him to stand in the corner, to miss meals, and to crawl around on the floor until his knees became raw.

He also kicked the boy and, at times, tied Jeffery to a door knob at night so he could not lie down to sleep.

By the day the boy died, Jeffery had bruises all over his hands, face, legs, and body.

On that day, Berry gave Jeffery a shower and when he finished, Berry half threw and half pushed the helpless boy into the living room.

While the youngster lay there, Berry stepped on his stomach while going into the kitchen for a beer.

A short while later, Berry told her Jeffery was dead. He asked her to get a large suitcase.

Mrs. Berry put the boy's body in the suitcase herself, because "every time he touched Jeff, he wouldn't pick him up; he would just drag him from one place to another and just drop him."

They drove to the area where the boy's body was found more than a month later. Berry took Jeffery's body from the suitcase and threw it over the embankment.

Mrs. Berry said that her husband threatened all the children, but Jeffery and the others fathered by her first husband in particular.

Once, she said, Berry told the boy that someday he would kill him. Asked what Jeffery said in reply, Mrs. Berry sobbed: "Jeff just told him that he loved him."

As a human being, have you never longed to lay hands on some devil incarnate who has wronged someone like that? If not, could it be because you do not have the courage to care?

A God who cannot get angry would be a God incapable of love! Jesus showed anger at the temple as he chased the moneychangers out. To believe in God's love is to be certain of God's wrath.

Finally, from Nahum there is this: the wrath of God must always be seen as the love of God wooing the rebel.

We can bog down in bad theology by thinking of God as petulant, selfish, ill-tempered, capricious. Behind the wrath is the infinite mystery of God's love.

God's activity in judgment, in the final analysis, indicates the depths of God's love. We must always remember that for God, judgment comes as retribution and never as retaliation. It is always redemptive in motive and design.

God's wrath is forever discerning: "God knows them that put their trust in him . . . But with an overrunning flood God will make full end . . . and will pursue his enemies into darkness" (1:7-8). There is a wideness in God's mercy; God graces us through God's judgment.

So, Nahum's word goes forth to all the Ninevehs of today: "The living God is slow to anger and given to patience; but to believe in God's love is to be sure of God's wrath." And not even the living God can work the same work in a rebel as in an obedient child. Amen.

February 11, 1996

HABAKKUK

What if the bad guys win?
Habakkuk 1:1-11; 2:1-4, 6, 9, 12, 15, 19-20; 3:1-2

The 35th book of our Bible bears the name Habakkuk. That name with all those Ks looks like a throat disease, a new Hebrew breakfast cereal, a terrorist outfit in the Middle East. The truth is, we know nothing about Habakkuk except his name. It means "The Embraced One."

Habakkuk marks a very important transition in Hebrew prophecy. He was the first genuine prophet-philosopher. The former prophets had addressed the people on behalf of God. Habakkuk addressed God on behalf of the people. For the other prophets, their chief concern was human sin. For Habakkuk, the chief concern was divine indifference.

God was unavailable for comment. Yahweh would not come at the snap of the prophet's finger, and that—to say the least—was a bit inconvenient.

Habakkuk was a keen thinker whose giant heart was breaking over problems he could see and solutions he could not discern. He marks the beginning of prophetic speculation in Judah. His pilgrimage marks a passage from faith's agnosticism to agnosticism's faith. He could not hem God in so he could conveniently believe, nor could he squeeze God out so he could conveniently disbelieve.

So, Habakkuk passed through doubt's dark waters into the light. He learned that doubts are the ants in the pants of faith, keeping it itchy, alert, alive.

These three chapters consist of a dialogue between the prophet and God. They are some pages snatched out of one man's spiritual autobiography.

Habakkuk was the younger contemporary of the great Jeremiah. His prophecy came during the reign of Jehoiakim of Judah, between the fall of Ninevah and the Assyrians in 612 B.C. and the Babylonian invasion of Judah in 597 B.C. Perhaps 600 B.C. is a near date for Habakkuk.

This was a turbulent time in the Middle East. Conditions in Judah went from bad to worse following the death of Josiah. His successor, Jehoahaz, lasted only three months. He was deposed by Pharaoh Necho of Egypt and replaced by the Egyptian puppet King Jehoiakim.

The situation became intolerable under Jehoiakim. Remember, this was the king who cut Jeremiah's scroll into bits with a pen knife and threw it into the fire (Jeremiah 36). God once again had been squeezed out of the affairs of the country. Blood ran free in Judah. Habakkuk's countrymen were sick inside out.

Moreover, danger threatened the nation from the outside. To the east, beyond the borders of Judah, the Babylonians—Chaldeans, Habakkuk calls them—were rattling their sabres and getting restless. Flushed with the spoils of their victory over Assyria, they were on a rampage of carnage and conquest.

The Babylonians had already "let the blood" of dozens of tiny kingdoms around Judah. Besides that, Palestine lay directly in the path of marauding Babylonian troops marching on Egypt. It was like a hurricane making landfall.

Habakkuk feared that his country was next. In the topsy-turvy Middle East it looks like someone's country is always next. The news in Judah was bad, getting worse daily. There was no one to change the channel. And the people did not seem to care.

For years Habakkuk had warned his countrymen that if they failed to clean up their lives and turn to Yahweh, the judgment of God was sure to fall. Now that the judgment was coming, Habakkuk could scarcely believe it.

What shook him was not the *fact* of judgment, but the *form* of judgment. It would not have seemed so unreal, so incredible, if the enemy had been a God-fearing people who lived more decently than his own people.

But the enemies—the instruments of judgment—were the Babylonians, haters of God, without faith or conscience. They would scour the countryside with their disbelief. It looked for the world like the bad guys were about to win!

Suppose that you should become solidly convinced that the Chinese—officially atheists—were going to conquer the U.S.A. during your lifetime. Then you would have the Habakkuk problem.

Habakkuk suspected that his own people deserved to lose, but he knew also that the Chaldeans did not deserve to win. And where was God?

God seemed so absent, so remote, so inactive in Judah. So Habakkuk climbed his tower to watch and wait and worship (ch. 2). Hot and fierce were his thoughts! You can almost hear him now: "God, why don't you do something to check this awful evil in Judah?"

And, God's reply: "Habakkuk, get your head out of the sand. I am at work right now. Don't you hear the distant rumble of the Babylonians marching west?"

Now, Habakkuk's second problem is bigger than his first: "But, but, but, God! Are you going to sit by, remain silent while violent evil swallows up everything good? These people you are able to let beat your people not only hate us, they hate you. Granted, we have sinned. But look at the Babylonians: they are the bad guys. We are saints compared to them."

Does that sound like a familiar dialogue? It is a watch being kept by a great many people. It is a cry being raised globally right now.

Like Habakkuk, we need a tower too—a place to wait, to watch, to worship. Let us share two things that he learned from his tower.

First, he got perspective—perspective on his world and of his work. From his tower reflecting, Habakkuk gained the advantage of the longer, wider look. When a man gets lost in the woods, he always does well to hunt a hill or climb a tree. Here, on a high spot, he can recover direction and see how the land really lies. "Even a dwarf on a giant's shoulders sees the farther of the two."

So Habakkuk climbed his tower and listened in the great silence for God. He went from the underbrush to let the winds of this moment in history blow fresh through his mind. Things came back into focus again.

That is always the way with real worship. Since we stand so close to our moment, we cannot readily decipher either the signs of the times or the meaning of our struggles. Here in this space-time world we are much like men and women trying to see a landscape through the small peephole in a $10 camera.

We need a tower! We are made for it. It lifts us out of all the boxes/ruts that our particular moment tends to put us into. How terribly we need the longer, wider look.

Among the rides at the North Carolina state fair one year was a miniature diesel train that circled a tiny track, sounding an eerie horn as it rounded the turns. The driver was a fascinating study in boredom. Why not? His day and much of his night were spent sitting cramped in his compartment, riding endlessly and aimlessly on his track with no variation except starting, stopping, and pressing that ghastly horn!

It occurs to me that for many persons life has degenerated into a pattern much like that. Someone has labeled the difficulty "chronic spherical circulitus." Those who suffer this malady mistake their monotonous track for the whole of reality.

The missing ingredient is the perspective of the tower. It was here that Habakkuk got his clues for assessing what he saw. He saw the apparent victory of the "bad guys" in perspective.

In his second chapter, 20th verse, he shaped in his heart and with his pen an utterance that believers in this world can never forget: "The Lord is in his holy temple: let all the earth keep silence before him"

Many times we have heard his words. Many times we have printed them on our church bulletins. Many times we have misunderstood them. The Lord's temple is no building with Gothic arches and stained glass windows. These can be pulled down and destroyed, like the Babylonians did to the temple Solomon built in Jerusalem.

If that is the only temple God has got, then God is always just one bomb blast away from having no dwelling place at all. The Lord's temple is God's world, God's word, and God's people.

"For the earth shall be filled with the knowledge of the glory of the Lord, as the waters cover the sea" (2:14): We worship God aright when we respect, God's creation, reverence divine handiwork, and preserve this earth's irretrievable resources.

"Write the vision, make it plain upon tablets, that he may run that reads it. For the vision is yet for an appointed time, but at the end it shall speak, and not lie, though it tarry, wait for it, because it will surely come" (2:1-2): At other times we Christians have wrestled with the meaning of the Word of God made flesh. Now we wrestle with the meaning of the Word of God made words. We love God aright when we love God's Word, learn it, and live it! The Bible is not a weapon; it is a resource for our growth.

"Thou wentest forth for the salvation of thy people, for the salvation of thy anointed" (3:13): We worship God aright when we love God's people and serve them with our hearts, our heads, our hands.

The Lord's temple, then, is God's *world*, God's *word*, God's *people*. God's presence in these, before whom the whole earth is to keep silence, is an eternal force—an energy—in history.

The Lord's presence to be celebrated is God's reign in everything from an atom to a star. That divine presence can no more be destroyed than the elements can dissolve—although there always seems to be some Henny Penny telling some Ducky Lucky or Cocky Locky that the sky is falling.

This is the sturdiness and the perspective to be gained when we come to the tower to watch, and wait, and worship.

Finally, Habakkuk gained insight. The insight came out of the perspective. His amazing insight was this: there is a self-defeating force always at work in evil. In a curious way evil overreaches, overextends itself and ultimately destroys itself. Evil cuts its own throat!

Habakkuk came to see that there was a certain profound moral oughtness in what was about to happen in his country. His people refused to face the consequences of their evil. They kept on sowing the wind. Now they would reap the whirlwind and be cleansed by a violent hand.

So Habakkuk came to see the Babylonians, evil as they were, as instruments in the hand of God to accomplish a moral purpose. Terrible as the chastening would be, the people of God were to be cleansed, scoured, aroused, awakened—and finally redeemed.

Yet, in that process was the certainty also that the Babylonians themselves would be smashed against the same laws of rightness that they so ruthlessly defied. Their very success would have in it the seeds of their failure.

Who was the general who led the Babylonian blitzkrieg across Judah? Scarcely anyone knows. And he probably thought he was immortal—poor ole' "General What's His-Name." (In case you want to know, he was Nebuzaradan [2 Kgs. 25:8].)

And where are the Babylonians now? They are the third strata, beneath the sand and silt of the Middle East. Only the glories that were Persia/Greece/Rome are nearer the surface than they.

As Habakkuk predicted, the Babylonians flared up for one brief moment, took some land, rattled some sabres, and then went on to smash themselves by the same brutal methods they had fashioned for others. They lived and they perished by the sword.

More and more, here is the Habakkuk insight: History has its own way of burying its bad guys. Evil cuts its own throat in God's kind of world. That is what Golgotha is all about.

Vegetation may die every autumn, but nature does not die. Creeds may change, but belief never perishes. Social orders may come and go, but persons in relation remain. Civilizations rise and fall. Tyrants start for their little violent hour and die, but the reign of God in this world holds fast.

That is the perspective and the insight from Habakkuk's tower. He summed it all up in a text that became the ground swell of the Protestant Reformation. Paul received it from Habakkuk and wrote it in Rom. 1:17. Luther received it from Paul and turned his world upside-down with it in 1516 at Wittenburg: "He whose soul is not upright in him shall fail, but the just shall live by faith" (2:4).

The wicked exist. The righteous live. This is so because only those who live by faith in God have lined their lives up alongside the laws for life-building in God's kind of world.

It is not our role to make our city a nicer place to go to hell from. Our role is to make it a better place.

Goodness is always simple. It is evil that is complex. It is always more difficult to deal with a crooked thing than with a straight thing.

Suppose I said to you that I have two sticks in my hand: one is straight, the other is crooked. Which can you imagine best? The straight one! Because a straight stick can be straight only one way. A crooked stick can be crooked in a hundred different ways.

So with our lives: we can be evil in a thousand complex ways. Goodness comes through the simplicity/the profundity of faith that lines a life up with all the laws for growth in a moral universe. This is the Habakkuk insight at the very heart of Christian faith.

Dietrich Bonhoeffer was a young university professor when Hitler began his rise to power in Germany. He was one of the first to perceive where Hitler was headed. He was likewise one of the first to oppose him. He returned from America to his beloved Germany, flying into the very teeth of the Nazi menace. In time, he was put in prison. And ironically, on the day before the Allies overran his prison, he was executed.

While a prisoner, everything he had counted on spiritually, theologically, philosophically came under the severest possible test. In one of his letters and papers from prison, Bonhoeffer gives this magnificent opinion about it all: "For the Christian it is essential to have a hope that is based on a solid, uncomplex foundation of goodness. However, potent a force evil and illusion may be, the influence of a sure and certain hope is infinitely greater, and the lives of those who possess it are invincible. Christ our hope: this Pauline formula is our life's inspiration."

No one can deny a life! That is what God has given us in Christ: a life. No matter what difficulty we encounter in committing ourselves to him, Christ is our hope! Evil did all that it could do to him, and yet could not win. He is our life's inspiration! Jesus Christ is Lord! Amen.

February 18, 1996

ZEPHANIAH

Love is blue—and golden
Zephaniah 1:1-3, 14-16; 3:14-20

Zephaniah is given the longest genealogy of any of the prophets. In the opening verse his family tree is traced through four generations. No doubt this is done in order to reach an important person in his background. And before you know it, that is exactly what happens: "Zephaniah, the son of Cushi, the son of Gedaliah, the son of Amariah, the son of Hezekiah."

This Hezekiah was in all likelihood the king of Judah during Isaiah's lifetime. Zephaniah is therefore the great-grandson of the king, in the third generation following Isaiah.

This would fit the date of the book, given also in the first verse, "in the days of Josiah . . ., king of Judah." Josiah was also a great-grandson of Hezekiah.

It appears then that Zephaniah was a member of the royal family in Judah, a second cousin of the reigning reformer king, Josiah. Thus the prophecies of Zephaniah must be viewed against the background of Josiah's reign in Judah about 625 B.C.

This was a period of Jewish religious reform. This was also the period of Assyria's rapid fall on the world scene and of Babylon's rapid rise. Quickly gathering anarchy was sweeping over Western Asia, compounded by the hit-and-run raids of the nomadic Cimmerians from the north.

Zephaniah sees in all this turmoil a foretaste of the coming day of the Lord and a sample of its nature. This is why Zephaniah, more than any other prophet, is the herald of the day of the Lord.

He did not coin the phrase or invent the concept, but he did gather up into one great climax the many ingredients that the other prophets had included in their idea of that day.

Zephaniah uses the phrase the Day of the Lord 19 times in his three brief chapters—almost as many times as all the other prophets combined. It was his burden, his obsession, his consuming passion.

Thus, we should expect to find here a fuller explanation of the meaning of the phrase than in any other place in the Old Testament. And that is precisely what we do find. It is Zephaniah's most lasting contribution to our prophetic understanding.

We may not understand what we hear, or like what he tells us, but we had best listen to this fervent voice out of the past. He provides us neither an almanac nor a calendar. But Zephaniah does tell us two superlative things about the Day of the Lord.

First, God's love is blue, moving toward terrible judgment. The day of the Lord will be a day of searing judgment.

Perhaps no passage in the Old Testament surpasses the words of Zephaniah describing the judgment that is to come. He never says *when*, but he sure says *what*.

His words are consuming, scorching. Listen: "I will utterly sweep away everything from the face of the earth, says the Lord. I will sweep away man and beast. I will sweep away the birds of the air and the fish of the sea. I will overthrow the wicked; I will cut off mankind from the face of the earth, says the Lord" (1:2-3).

No wonder some students of scripture say that this part of the prophecy of Zephaniah is all desert—completely barren. There is no life, no flower, no fruit, no forest; nothing left. It is a world swept clean by a cosmic hurricane—or is it a mushroom cloud, a firestorm?

We read him and weep at the devastation. We catch an ancient glimmer of a charred, reeking, radioactive cinder that once was a world.

Here is the Old Testament's strangest and strongest word about "the last things." Here is eschatology at its white-hot peak.

As we read this terrible passage, we want to ask so many things: When? Where? How? But Zephaniah leaves us in the dark on all such matters. He simply provides the picture after the fact. He is a reporter filing his story from the scene.

The nations seem to have disappeared. It is a world without borders. History seems to be on hold. Time stands still. All the clocks are stopped. Everywhere is ground zero. Devastation is total. Judgment is complete. The landscape is like a Salvador Dali painting: everything is melted down.

Kings and countries, as instruments of the judgment, are no longer found here. No great armies clash. God is sweeping this earth with a divine broom. And God is doing it directly, absolutely, finally.

Zephaniah affirms that the Living God will act in human history suddenly, swiftly, decisively—visiting this planet with direct, positive, irrevocable judgment. So, the great Day of the Lord is a time when God invades human history and ends it.

On that Day of the Lord, God personally will come directly, supernaturally, and finally into human affairs. The earth is sucked in by the *sun*! And there is nothing mere mortals can do to forestall it.

No wonder Zephaniah's countrymen could not contain these words. They simply could not comprehend or take them in. They would not compute. Zephaniah describes their lazy, luxurious, dizzy, indifferent response: "At that time I will search Jerusalem with lamps, and I will punish the men who are thickening upon their lees, those who say in their hearts, 'The Lord will not do good, nor will He do ill'" (1:12).

Get the picture: whole populations of cities and of nations—cold, indifferent, agnostic—denying any intervention of God, saying "Why ole what's-his-name up in the heavens would not do that. He is the neutral, nice God, not known for doing much of anything—completely indifferent toward us/toward earth."

How tragically wrong the people were. Here are a people, purely secularized, materialized, and mesmerized. Their rulers, judges, princes, prophets, preachers, and priests are all corrupt. Here is moral chaos! And God comes to sweep the landscape clean. No wonder Zephaniah's countrymen could not or would not take all that in.

But still the prophet pressed his point. The extent of the judgment on that great and terrible Day of the Lord is complete. Human beings and everything they have polluted will be swept away.

Yet, there is another note struck by this prophet amidst the gathering doom: It comes in Zephaniah's third chapter.

Second, the love of God is golden, moving toward wonderful deliverance. Additionally, the Day of the Lord will be a day of resounding joy.

Hear the joy bells ring as Zephaniah pulls the ropes: "Sing aloud, O daughter of Zion; shout O Israel! Rejoice and exult with all your heart . . . the Lord has taken away the judgments against you, He has cast out your enemies . . . He will rejoice over you with gladness. He will renew you in *his love* . . . At that time [God] will bring you home" (3:14ff). Here is a rainbow at midnight!

The prophet who sees most clearly the fierceness of God's wrath also sees most clearly the tenderness of God's love. The Day of the Lord is a day of destruction for all things that destroy life. It is a day of beginning again for all things that bless life. The love of God is blue—and it is golden!

This resounding joy projected by Zephaniah reached its peak during the reign of Caesar Augustus when God walked down Bethlehem's stairs. Listen to Paul: "When the fullness of time was come, God sent forth His Son, born of a woman" (Gal. 4:4).

That strong Son of God—Jesus Christ of Nazareth—marked the beginning of a new era. B.C. became A.D.! The earth was sucked into the *Son!* Songs replaced sighs. Service displaced selfishness. Solidarity transfused the scattered people of God across the earth and across the centuries.

So, today we need to hear Zephaniah's trumpets, as well as his cannons. He renews in us the passion that truly expects God to judge things that are wrong in this world, and truly expects God to bless those things that are right. God will in time end the wrong and establish the right—and God will do it God's way.

This is Zephaniah's contemporary message to us, uttered a long time ago, during the reign of Josiah.

Modern Maturity has recently surveyed hundreds of its readers. In this election year: "Is America in moral/social decline? If so, how would you address it?"

Not one person surveyed—our oldest citizens; our most astute citizens—disputed the premise that American society is decaying. Also, what came across was a sense of urgency that we get back to basics, to virtues, to values. Some things noble have been lost: integrity, responsibility/respect, selflessness.

Results of the survey included these answers to the question, "What are the best ways to halt the downward course?"

- Shore up personal responsibility (35%)
- Strengthen families (20%)
- Recover vital religious faith (18%)
- Clean up the media (9%)
- Get tough on crime (4%)

The bottom line? Albert Schweitzer said it years ago: "Humans must cease attributing their problems to their environment and learn again to exercise their wills—their personal responsibilities in the realm of faith and morals." Zephaniah would agree!

Surely Charles Kingsley had been reading Zephaniah when he wrote his powerful verse, "The Day of the Lord."

The Day of the Lord is at hand, at hand:
Its storms roll up the sky:
The nations sleep starving on heaps of gold;
All dreamers toss and sigh;
The night is darkest before the morn;
When the pain is sorest the child is born,
And the Day of the Lord at hand.

Who would sit down and sigh for a lost age of gold,
While the Lord of all ages is here?
True hearts will leap up at the trumpet of God,
And those who can suffer, can dare.
Each old age of gold was an iron age too,
And the meekest of saints may find stern work to do,
In the Day of the Lord at hand.

Love is blue—and it is golden too. That is what God's breakthrough is all about. It is the great, glad day of the Lord!

God's Son has come! All of us are even now being *judged* by God's Bethlehem breakthrough. We are also being loved and being *rescued* by that breakthrough. Come; be rescued by God's love! Amen.

February 25, 1996

HAGGAI

Word to flesh to word
Haggai 1:1-6, 13-15; 2:1, 3-9

The book of Haggai is dated very specifically in the first verse: "In the second year of Darius, in the sixth month, in the first day of the month . . ." Darius ascended to the throne of Persia in 521 B.C. Haggai's prophecy was therefore centered in 520 B.C. It, along with Zechariah and Malachi, is a message to the people of God following their exile in Babylon.

The book of Haggai contains two chapters with 38 verses, and consists of four distinct prophecies—or sermons—delivered in the autumn of 520 B.C. In order to understand and appreciate the thrust of this significant page out of our Old Testament, we must take a look at the times of new beginnings faced by Haggai and his countrymen.

Remember, Babylonian policy toward conquered countries was to deport their leading citizens. This policy deprived the conquered state of those who would naturally preserve and rebuild their shattered systems.

Also, the Babylonians made it a policy to reduce to ruins any temple, palace, or public building that might keep up the morale—especially the religious spirit of the people who remained in their conquered homeland. Along with this they carried away the gods of the conquered country to Babylon, thus insuring that the former temple sites would no longer be centers for recovery.

In the case of the Jews, there were no idols or icons to Yahweh to be deported. So the conquerors had to content themselves with smashing the Jerusalem temple and taking away to Babylon all the sacred vessels they could find.

This policy proved quite successful! Rapidly, the leadership of the Jewish religious community shifted from Palestine to Babylon. Here, by the Euphrates River in southern Mesopotamia, the Jews formed a new religious, intellectual, and economic center for their colony.

The ruins of Palestine were complete! For a half century Judah and Jerusalem lay a wasteland. In the minds of many Israelites, Yahweh had departed from the land of Israel and God's favor was no longer directed that way.

When Cyrus the Great led the Persians in their conquest of Babylon, he changed all this. It was his policy to conciliate vassal states. One chief way to do this was to recognize and to sanction their national religions, even bringing their gods—idols—back where necessary to their religious centers of worship. This policy carried with it permission for political exiles to return to their homelands.

Thus, in the first six chapters of Ezra, in the Old Testament's historical section, we are told that Cyrus, the Persian king, issued a decree concerning the Jews about 538 B.C. He permitted them to return to Palestine and to rebuild their temple. This indeed marked the dawn of a new day for the beleaguered people of God. They dreamed a new dream. They hoped a new hope.

Cyrus' permission sparked immediate response. Instantly, many hundreds of the Jews in Babylon began the long, hot, desert-journey back home to Palestine, following their leaders such as Zerubbabel.

This second exodus was a metaphor of the first one. Like the first exodus from Egypt, this one from Babylon was a courageous journey. The people had to leave a life they had grown accustomed to in Babylon—a life of comfort and relative ease. For 50 years they had reared their families in this strange land.

Yet they abandoned their businesses and left houses and lands that had supported them in Babylon. They turned their backs on the rich cultural and economic opportunities to be enjoyed in this center of the world's civilization.

Besides all this, these first returnees severed their connection with the established Jewish community in Babylon. The pull of Palestine was too much! These were pioneer types. So they set out, heading for home.

They would rebuild their country, their temple, their houses, their land. You might suppose that a robust and spirited group like this would meet with immediate success. But such was not the case. Far from it!

Consider what they found back home in Palestine: For one thing they found some people inhabiting the country, but they were scant and dispirited. Houses were dwelt in and some land and vineyards were cultivated, but for the most part the landscape was desolate—still devastated from Nebuchadnezzar's scorched earth policy 50 years before. The "cities of Judah" had been permanently abandoned.

Demolished stone houses, orchards, vineyards, and ancestral fence lines stretched for miles in ruins. Many fields were grown up in thorns and briars.

For another thing, the territory of Judah had drastically shrunk during the interval. Gone were huge chunks of territory to the south, along with much land to the north that had belonged to the kings of Israel. This had now been claimed by others.

In fact, there remained for the returnees only a small area of land around Jerusalem, including Jericho—in all, estimated to be 40 miles square. How pitiful a contrast to the former empires of David and Solomon!

Another reality that greeted them was the unimaginable poverty. The luxury and magnificence that had increased during the last gasps of Judah's grandeur—before the Exile—was gone with the wind. All the great houses lay in rubble heaps where lizards bathed in the sun. The peasants who had been left in Palestine were fortunate if they had been able to keep body and soul together.

To be sure the returning exiles brought with them some of the wealth of Babylon, but it was by no means enough to raise the economic level to anything like comfort.

Another thing that greeted the returnees was the absence of a king. Ever since Saul, the Jews in Jerusalem had been ruled by a king of David's line. Now, no king of the Davidic line or any other line ruled in Jerusalem.

Instead a Persian governor sat in the seat of power, a symbol of the people's servitude. The temple too lay in ruins. It would have to be rebuilt from the foundation up.

A final misery lay in the attitude of the neighboring people, who came to be called Samaritans. These were persons who had remained in Palestine, intermingled and intermarried with pagan foreigners, and reduced whatever Judaism that remained in both quality and content. They were quick to interpret to the returnees their own opinion for the desolation of Jerusalem. It was proof that Judah had been cut off and forsaken by Yahweh.

This attitude was a constant irritant and caused no small discouragement in the months immediately following the arrival of the people from Babylon.

Yet, in spite of all these problems, the returnees had some things going for them. They had the long, hard discipline of the captivity behind them. This had put iron in their blood. Their enthusiasm for Yahweh had deepened.

Moreover, the most powerful government in the world, Cyrus and the Persians, was favorably disposed toward them. Imperial oppression had disappeared!

One thing now was uppermost in their minds: they had to rebuild the temple. They had to restore their worship. That is why they had come back home.

Soon after their arrival in early autumn, the whole populace assembled in Jerusalem to map strategy for their task. The next spring, construction actually began on the temple, overseen by the Levites.

This happy inauguration of the work was soon to be abruptly halted. A grave problem developed.

When the news that the temple was being rebuilt spread through the northern districts—among the Samaritans—it roused the people to want a share in the work. So they converged on Jerusalem, apparently friendly enough, asking permission to help. After all, they were descendants of Abraham also!

Their request opened two possible courses of action for the restored community. They could be either inclusive or exclusive.

Apparently they did not debate the matter for long. They gave a prompt and abrupt response: "Nothing doing!" "Thanks, but no thanks." "You have nothing to do with us in building a house unto our God" (cf. Neh. 2:16-20).

As might be expected, this rebuff turned friendliness into hostility. So the inhabitants of the land made the going rough for the newcomers from Babylon who were about to rebuild the temple. They stood by, watched and ridiculed, arguing against the project, making threats, using political pressure, and at times resorting to violence (cf. Nehemiah 3-6).

And there was no strong leader to defy them. The effect was immediate. The workers became frightened and discouraged.

After all, why should they neglect their own houses? They could turn to rebuild them and to cultivate their own fields.

Let the temple wait! So they stopped construction on the house of God and went to work on their own houses and fields and vineyards—and 15 years passed!

It looked as if the great dream of a restored sanctuary was fading. The high hopes of the returnees were running into swamps.

The people were settled down into a feeble acquiescence. What they were doing was a far cry from what they had come home to do. It looked for the world like the religion of Israel might disappear as a force off the face of the earth.

Then comes Haggai! We know next to nothing about this man who intervened to redeem the situation. Not even the name of his father is given.

He comes before us simply as "Haggai, the prophet, Yahweh's messenger" (1:1). He steps upon the stage of Israel's history at a moment of crisis, speaks four brief times within five months, and disappears.

What is most impressive about Haggai is that he is a man possessed of one idea—one objective. And he is convinced that his is an idea whose time has come.

Remember: these were the days of the theology of a "resident deity." God required a place—a space—to be present in; at least, God did in the minds of the people!

The whole future of Jewish religion was being held up for the lack of a temple for God to dwell in. This was the main tenet of "the restored temple theology."

Haggai did not ask his countrymen to make any radical changes in their own lives, but only to throw off their lethargy and start rebuilding the temple. That was the one right thing that needed to be done. Nothing else could be right until the temple was finished.

So in the second year of Darius' reign, on the first day of the sixth month, Haggai strode forth to tell his people:

> Consider your ways. You have sown much and bring in little; you eat, but you do not have enough; you drink, but are still thirsty; you put on clothes, but none is warm; and he that earns wages earns them to put into a bag with holes...Consider your ways. You looked for much, and lo, it came to little; and when you brought it home, I blew it away. Why? Says the Lord of hosts. Because of my house that lays waste, while you run every man to his own house. (1:7-9)

Wow! What a chairman for a building committee! So, with thunder and lightning in his voice, Haggai connected every calamity of the past 15 years since the people's return with the fact that there was no temple for God to tabernacle in.

Three weeks after his electrifying challenge the work of rebuilding got underway. It was interrupted twice, each time prompting an evermore stem and blunt word from Haggai.

Until on the 24th day of what is our 12th month, December—the ninth month in the Jewish calendar—he spoke his final word: "From this day will I bless you, says Yahweh" (2:19).

After this we hear no more from Haggai. He spoke his Christmas Eve message and disappeared. But thanks to his urging, the temple was rebuilt. So, it is no wonder that there is an old Hebrew proverb that began to circulate in the sixth century B.C.: "No Haggai—No Temple."

Observe the miracle process: the Word of the Lord had been enfleshed for a season in the man Haggai, and the temple for God to tabernacle in was rebuilt!

But what does this mean for us? Think it not strange that the last word we hear from Haggai, the prophet in the day when the Lord's temple lay smashed at Jerusalem, came on December 24—Christmas Eve. From that word—enfleshed in Haggai—a new temple was built for God to dwell with God's people.

My people, do you know what that means? It was a prototype of Advent—of Christmas—520 years before Christ.

We cannot embrace Haggai's "temple theology." But we can let John tell us the new revelation in this matter. Listen to John 1:14: "The Word became flesh and tabernacled among us, full of grace and truth; we have beheld his glory, glory as of the only Son from the Father."

That is what the new Christmas breakthrough is all about: Immanuel—"God with us." In Jesus Christ, God has a new temple for tabernacling among God's people. Once again the Word has become flesh and a new temple has been built. This time the temple was Jesus—the God-Man in history in whom God took up residence among God's people.

On that first Christmas the people of God still had their holy temple on Zion Hill, remodeled and refurbished by Herod. But it was not sufficient for God to tabernacle in. It was too unholy a box to put God in.

God chose another dwelling place. And the angels sang "Joy to the world." And shepherds were startled. And the cave where cattle were kept behind a Bethlehem inn became the focus of history. God became flesh—from word to flesh to word.

God has forever another temple in the midst of the people: Jesus Christ the Lord, and since then his Spirit. Gene Owens says it beautifully:

"In those days" people stood in line to catch a glimpse of God. Most often when they saw him, they couldn't believe their eyes.

"What did you see?" asked one of another, as the line passed the place where God was.

"I'm not sure," was the reply. "I think it was a man."

"That's what I thought," observed the questioner.

"But it couldn't be," declared the observer.

"We were told that we would see God. Think I'll get my money back. I can see a man anywhere, anytime.

"In those days" people stood in line to glimpse God. It was a man.

They were sure of it.

A God-man.

Now the people wondered, not whether they had seen God; but whether they had ever really seen man before.

A funny thing happened on the way to see God. They met man for the first time.

Could they ever be happy with this God-in-man?

Faith answered with a community and a commitment.

Church was born!

And you can be a part of it—through Jesus . . . word, flesh (yours), word. Amen.

March 3, 1996

ZECHARIAH

An unquenchable hope
Zechariah 1:1-3, 8:1-5, 9:9

Zechariah was a contemporary of Haggai. In fact, the two began their prophetic ministries the same year—520 B.C.—just after the first Jews had returned to Palestine from Babylon following their half-century of captivity.

Haggai and Zechariah are mentioned together in the fifth chapter of the book of Ezra. So their lives overlapped. Also, the last prophecy in Haggai and the first prophecy in Zechariah overlap by a month in 520 B.C. Together these two became the champions of restored Judaism. They wanted things in the holy land to be reconstituted just as before the Exile. Their dream was to restore the old vision of God and country.

In one way they differed: Haggai's work ended the same year it began. Zechariah continued to work at least three years until 518 B.C.

It was Zechariah, therefore, who continued the task of encouraging his countrymen until the job of rebuilding the temple was complete.

We actually know very little about this puzzling man Zechariah, except that he was the grandson of a prophet. His name means "Yahweh has remembered." His father was Berechiah. His grandfather was Iddo. He was himself a priest. Zechariah had either recently returned from Babylon or he returned with the original refugees in 538-536 B.C.

When the word of the Lord came to him in November, 520 B.C., it produced one of the strangest conglomerations of prophetic utterances anywhere in the Bible. His 14 chapters are chock-full of material that virtually defies interpretation. There are eight visions, written largely in code and strongly apocalyptic.

Then there are six chapters of oracles that students of scripture see so disjointed in the historical background that some suspect them to have come from different hands at different times altogether. These chapters are difficult to decipher.

The people to whom Zechariah delivered his message were looking backward, conscious of a history at once glorious and shameful. The history of God's dealing with them was full of glory. The history of their dealing with God was full of shame.

Their immediate outlook was one of depression, despondence, and discouragement. The hope of ever restoring their holy nation in their holy land was indeed bleak.

Hemmed in by opposing forces, they were a rag-tag people on a postage stamp-sized piece of real estate in what used to be Judah.

They were without constitution, king, parliament, army, or political power base. It certainly seemed to this feeble remnant that there was very little reason for hope in their future.

So the peculiar task of Zechariah was to launch a ministry of encouragement—to inspire an unquenchable hope in the hearts of his discouraged countrymen. His job was to get them to stop looking backward and to start looking forward. Their future was in front of them—not behind them. He was an Old Testament Barnabas.

He went right to work. His messages encouraged them not only to follow Haggai's urging and rebuild their temple, but to press on until they had rebuilt their country also.

Zechariah called them to a gigantic physical, spiritual, and economic task. You might say he had his own "Marshall Plan."

He called them by way of apocalyptic, much like parts of Daniel in the Old Testament and parts of Revelation in the New Testament.

He provided his countrymen with visions and voices both remote and near. He took the lid off. He was the great unveiler of God's activity in the world.

He was also the great prophet of the "Lord of Hosts," using that term 53 times in his 14 chapters. The idea behind that term is that God is the Lord of massed armies, just ready to march through history to accomplish divine purposes.

There can be no mistaking his essential message. Haggai had charged his people: "Be strong . . . and *work*." Zechariah charged them: "Be strong . . . and *hope*."

He urged them to see the unseen, for he knew that the secret of strength is vision and the proof of vision is strength. He was forever blowing the trumpet of encouragement. He was the people's cheerleader during the painful period of restoration.

From amidst the jumble of his apocalyptic visions and voices come some of the living messages that saw his people through the turbulent 500 years until Jesus Christ was born.

For example, in his third chapter is this promise of a fresh branch rising out of the withered stalk of the Davidic line: "Hear now . . . Oh high priest, you and your friends who sit before you, for they are men of good omen; behold, I will send my servant, the Branch" (v. 8).

And in the ninth chapter is this arresting promise: "Rejoice greatly, O daughter of Zion! Shout aloud, O daughter of Jerusalem! Lo, your King comes to you; triumphant and victorious is he, humble and riding on an ass, on a colt, the foal of an ass" (v. 2).

And in the final chapter is this: "And the Lord will become king over all the earth; on that day the Lord will be one and his name one" (14:9).

Thus, Zechariah's living contribution to his times and to our own is his ringing declaration to "take heart and have hope." God is not finished yet, either with us or with our world.

The core of his message and his ministry of encouragement comes in chapter 1, verse 3. It is the cornerstone of the "Zechariah Plan" for recovery—then and now: "The Lord was very angry with your fathers. Therefore, say to them, 'Thus says the Lord of hosts: Return to me, says the Lord of hosts, and I will return to you, says the Lord of hosts.'"

First he glances backward to sum up all of Judah's former experience with Yahweh in a single sentence: "The Lord was very angry with your fathers."

God's anger, poured out on the people, was climaxed by the great destruction of Jerusalem and the deportation of its best citizens to Babylon. Zechariah did not need to expand on the idea. The ruins and rubble on all sides were ample evidence of it.

Then the prophet gazes ahead and delivers to the people the good news of a new divine invitation: "Return to me and I will return to you."

Here is God's love, the other side of God's anger. The past judgment has given way to the present opportunity and to the future hope. The message is simple, direct, appealing—an invitation to an estranged people to be reconciled with their God.

There is no mention of past sins. This invitation cuts through all the guilt to shout "Welcome Home!" Repentance is complete.

That, my friend, is the ultimate word of encouragement. And it is the heart of the Zechariah Plan for us in our times—right now. "Turn to me and I will turn to you." This is the way "back home" no matter how far we have roamed.

There is a cardinal rule about encouragement in every age: Stop using words that hurt; start using words that help. This, Zechariah did masterfully.

Watch his process of encouragement at work. It is inspired by love and designed to uproot fear. Real encouragement occurs when words are spoken from a heart of love to another's recognized fears. When my love hooks up with your fears, encouragement happens.

In Romans 12 all of us are told—Zechariah like—to rejoice with rejoicers, weep with weepers, restore the spiritually bereft, admonish the undisciplined, strengthen the weak—in sum, by word and by deed to encourage others to press on in their pursuit of holiness.

The only motivation that will stir us to reach into another's life with encouragement is unfeigned love—genuine care.

But we hold back. Like the frightened witness to a crime, we seek to remain uninvolved. We maintain a comfortable distance by withdrawing behind our excuses. We do not demonstrate the kind of involvement modeled for us in the incarnation.

In Christ, God forsook the comfortable distance between divine and human and became completely involved with us/in us/with-in us. God, in Zechariah's words, "turned to us." Our love promotes another's healing, but it involves exposure at close range: the courage to care.

Words aimed at another's fear always bring encouragement—if they are delivered from a heart of unfeigned affection.

Encouragement, then, is not a technique to be mastered. It is a sensitivity to persons and a confidence in God that must be nourished and demonstrated.

Not surprisingly, the perfect example of encouragement is found in Jesus Christ, the Lord.

Note the soul's journey to Jesus: In our evil we come to him. He declares us sinners all; the diagnosis is worse than we feared. Like the wretched woman in John 8, we are "caught in the very act" of all kinds of evil. With Paul we realize that "nothing good dwells in our flesh" (Rom. 7:18).

We cringe in Christ's presence, afraid to look into what we are sure will be an angry face. We await the pronouncement of our well-deserved rejection. Yet we hear words that dance in our minds, words so unexpected that we blink with astonishment. We listen. We dare even to look. Then we see the warm, gentle, loving smile of God, and we hear Jesus say: "Of course, you are guilty. Go. Sin no more. I forgive. The Father has purposes for you."

We are eternally encouraged! Christ has spoken from his love to our fear. That is the way of Christ's redemption.

The Zechariah Plan is repeated again and again in our time—in our lives: "Turn to me, and I will turn to you."

A seminary student turned in his very first-ever written sermon to his teacher in a homiletics class. He was fearful beyond words when he received the manuscript back. Here is what his teacher wrote on his paper:

> I will not attempt a formal critique of your sermon. After all, preaching ought to be a wedding of substance and form. The sermon is of great interest to me because of what it tells me about you personally. I welcome the opportunity through the remainder of this academic year to talk at length with you about your inner aspirations, problems, and questions. I can bring no ready answers. But I do promise you an interested and concerned spirit. What is happening to you and within you is of much greater importance to me than any formalities of homiletics.

That teacher is dead. But that preacher will never forget that man and that message. Encouragement . . . All of us crave it. All of us are called to it! Amen.

March 10, 1996

MALACHI

Externals without internals
Malachi 1:1-2a, 13-14; 2:1-2, 17; 3:1-3, 7-10

T he last book in the Old Testament begins like this: "The burden of the word of the Lord to Israel by Malachi . . ." The word Malachi means "my messenger." It may, therefore, be taken as the prophet's name or his title.

In any case, we know absolutely nothing more about this last Old Testament writer except what we find in this book that bears this word.

But in the four brief chapters he serves us considerable clues concerning his own spiritual temperature and temperament. Malachi was a man who simply could not stand mere show. He was interested in style, but his consuming concern was substance.

So he came to speak a strong word of the Lord to his countrymen whose lifestyle consisted of a well-upholstered exterior without any kind of real interior.

Malachi lived and worked during the Persian period of Old Testament history. He was a prophet of the restoration. The precise time of his ministry appears to fall about the mid-fifth century B.C.—around 460-450 B.C., to be exact.

Since this is our last opportunity to do so during our journey through the Old Testament, let's review the sweep of history that leads up to Malachi's time—and the close of the Old Testament revelation.

Genesis 1-11 gives an account of beginnings: the world and everything in it—man, woman, family; the seasons; the cosmos—evil, redemption, judgment.

Genesis 12 and following tell of the patriarchs of God's particular people, Israel, including Abraham, Isaac, Jacob, Joseph, Moses, Joshua/the judges, and Samuel.

The people of Israel clamored for a king, so Samuel anointed Saul.

The consolidated Hebrew empire had three kings: Saul, David, and Solomon.

At Solomon's death the empire was divided into North—10 tribes—and South—2 tribes.

Israel, to the north—in Galilee/Samaria—had 19 kings and endured until 722 B.C., when Samaria and the nation of Israel were obliterated by the Assyrians.

Judah, to the south—centered in Jerusalem—also had 19 kings and endured until 586 B.C., when the Babylonians destroyed Jerusalem, obliterated the temple built by Solomon, and carried the people captive.

In 538-536 B.C. Cyrus the Great, king of Persia, conquered Babylon and decreed that all subject peoples exiled in Babylon could return to their homelands.

Shortly thereafter a considerable contingent of Hebrews who had been refugees in Babylon for 50 years returned to Palestine. Sheshbazzar was the leader of the first wave.

A year later they laid the foundation and began to rebuild their cherished temple in Jerusalem.

Remember their motivation: to have a temple was to have Yahweh in their midst. Place and presence went together. But the reconstruction was abandoned. The people turned to other tasks.

Fifteen years passed. Haggai and Zechariah came thundering their messages, and as a result the building of the temple was resumed. By 516 B.C. the work was done.

The new temple did not compare with the glory of the old one Solomon had built. But it did suffice. It had to suffice.

With the restored temple came restored Judaism.

Still more time passed, and a sort of spiritual malaise seemed to settle over the land. Back home in Judah the people fast forgot the lessons of the Exile.

So in 458-459 B.C. Ezra returned to Jerusalem from Babylon to initiate the religious reforms that came to be associated with his name. In 445 B.C. he was joined by Nehemiah with his project to rebuild Jerusalem's city walls.

Shortly before the reforms of Ezra and Nehemiah, Malachi delivered his blistering broadside against the lethargic restored nation of Judah.

He came to tell his countrymen—and us—that there are lots of things that are thievery that never get called that. There is sometimes theft at the very heart of religion.

And that is where Malachi comes down—hard! His ancient words are thunder and lightning, treating painful themes.

Here is a camel driver with something to say—to God's people who tend vineyards or drive Cadillac cars.

He unleashes his "burden" on the back side of the Old Testament. His countrymen were majoring on externals and minoring on internals when Malachi got there. They were trying to kindle the fires of faith with wet wood.

So he sharpened his pen and went straight to work. Malachi snorted every time he saw sham—and he saw a country full of it in 450 B.C.

Judah had come back home from Babylon 85 years earlier, ending her exile. Now, once more, in Palestine the people had a holy *land*, a holy *city*, and a holy *temple*. There really seemed no need then for them to have holy lives also.

It was a time of economic depression in Palestine. Farming and vineyard-keeping were bad and getting worse. The economy was agrarian. The people depended on their farms, their vineyards, and their flocks. Insects ingested their crops. Their vines dropped their grapes prematurely. Their flocks were ravaged by disease.

The people could explain these things only one way: Yahweh was being harsh with them.

But why? After all, they were doing all the "right things"—going through the right motions, being religious. But that was precisely their problem: they were *religious*, but not *righteous*. They had a form of godliness without the substance of it. They had a fine showroom, but no storeroom in their lives.

They were guilty on all counts of fraud and greed. They performed the externals of their religion, but were utterly devoid of the internals of it. They maintained the machinery, but had lost the meaning of their faith. They were lamps with no light.

So Malachi came to this nation of grumblers and malcontents. His message is packed into 55 verses on the last three pages of the Old Testament.

The major thrust of his word is the constancy of God's love in contrast to the fickle faithlessness of God's people. In four chapters he charges his countrymen with seven glaring sins. They deny them every one. Listen:

1. "How has Yahweh loved us?" (1:2)
2. "How have we despised God's name?" (1:6)
3. "How have we polluted God's plan?" (1:7)
4. "How have we wearied God?" (2:17)
5. "How shall we return?" (3:7)
6. "How have we robbed God?" (3:8)
7. "How have we spoken against Yahweh?" (3:13)

The spark of Malachi's burden catches fire in his very first sentence: "I have loved you, says the Lord" (1:2).

It does no violence to the action of the verbs in that sentence to translate Malachi like this: "I have loved you; I love you now, and I always will love you, says the Lord."

It is a ringing declaration of the constancy of God's love. That, my people, is Christmas Eve, 450 years *before* Christmas morning. The next voices we hear from scripture are the herald angels announcing Messiah's birth.

From Malachi to Matthew is a mighty long way, but the bridge between the Old Testament's ending and the New Testament's beginning is this: "I have loved you, says the Lord." It is the Old Testament's final word in preparation for Jesus Christ.

That is why Malachi's charge in his second chapter is so serious. It was a charge about priesting. The people's and the priest's sins were sins against love—against the awesome trust of standing in the breach between God and humankind.

Their profanity, sacrilege, greed, and indifference wounded the great heart of God. Sin is never just against law. It is always ultimately against love.

God loves people. And God longs for people to love back. Malachi knew that it was possible to attend the temple, bend the knees in prayer, go through the religious rigamarole; but unless there was love in it, there could be no communion with God. The call was for religious integrity, for substance not style.

And Malachi knew another thing. The very moment people cease to love God, they begin to wonder whether God loves them. Thus the grumbling and the coldness and the callousness that led to form without faith, practice without piety.

Listen to Malachi's word of the Lord about priesting:

And now, O priests, this command is for you. If you will not listen, if you will not lay it to heart to give glory to my name, says the Lord of hosts, then I will send the curse upon you and I will curse your blessings; indeed I have already cursed them, because you do not lay it to heart. Behold I will rebuke your offspring, and spread dung upon your faces, the dung of your offerings, and I will put you out of my presence.

So shall you know that I have sent this command to you that my covenant with Levi may hold, says the Lord of hosts. My covenant with him was a covenant of life and peace, and I gave them to him, that he might fear; and he feared me, he stood in awe of my name. True instruction was in his mouth, and no wrong was found on his lips. He walked with me in peace and uprightness and he turned many from iniquity. For the lips of a priest should guard knowledge, and men should seek instruction from his mouth, for he is the messenger of the Lord of hosts. But you have turned aside from the way; you have caused many to stumble by your instruction; you have corrupted the covenant of Levi, says the Lord of hosts, and so I make you despised and abashed before all the people, inasmuch as you have not kept my ways but have shown partiality in your instruction. (2:1-9)

The word "priest" comes from the Latin *pontifex*, that is, "bridge." A priest is a bridge—one who stands in the awesome breach between God and man, heaven and earth.

Priesting has two sides to it. One is buttressed firmly in this world: completely earthy, this-worldly, material; the commerce of the human side. The other side is anchored in factors beyond this world: entirely spiritual, heavenly, other-worldly, supernatural; the commerce of the Godward side.

To balance these sides, to connect them, to live and to serve in both these worlds: that is the genius of priesting.

We Baptists, free-church Christians have a foundational commitment to a concept of the priesthood of every believer. We believe that no one must or can stand in the breach between ourselves and our God.

But we believe just as profoundly in a concept of ministry. We believe that God calls some persons to specialized, vocational ministry. And we set such persons apart to their ministries. We ordain them, thus recognizing their gifts and their calling.

What Malachi says about priests applies among us to our ministers, whether laypersons or clergy. It is always: "like priests, like people." It is often just as true: "like ministers, like people."

There are at least two occupational hazards for ministers/priests, according to Malachi. First is overfamiliarity with the darkness.

You have done it, as well as I: You go into a restaurant, dark as if it were underground. You can scarcely see the menu, much less read it. Finally, you order. When the food arrives, you eat it by faith and not by sight. Then before you leave, you notice that you have become acclimated. Your eyes adjust to the dark and you can actually see in the dimness.

It is so in life, especially so in the life of faith. In priesting, especially, we must be ever alert. We can become entirely too familiar with the dark.

Most of us, after all, live hard by "vanity fair"—the headquarters of the world, the flesh, and the devil.

Lucille Ball, that wonderful, winsome redhead knew the situation well. She said once: "I am shocked because I am *not* shocked." Tragedy has become comedy, and it all starts innocently enough. It slips up on us, especially the priests. Here a compromise, there a broken confidence, someplace else a promise not kept. In no time at all we have come to terms with the darkness.

The Swaggert sin, the Elmer Gantry sin is not the sin of us all. But their overfamiliarity with the darkness does beset us all. It is an occupational hazard of priesting.

Another hazard is overfamiliarity with the light.

The task of priests, especially, is to carry the light—not their own, but the reflected rays of the light of Christ. But we can get used to good things. We can, and we do, grow stale.

Nice is enough. We become habituated with holy things. Routine grabs us until we settle for playing "Jesus games" with the truth.

We approach our priesting task bored at the prospect of coming to the meeting of persons with God for authentic worship. That is the worst kind of boredom.

Vance Havner used to say that every time a preacher preaches, it should be as the *first* time, as the *best* time, as the *last* time. Iis just as true every time a worshipper worships.

Now we have a new phenomenon, electronic priesting. These remain remote and build their bridges on the waves in the air. They broadcast their "ministries"—rely on performance not experience. Amusement replaces amazement. It all boils down to show.

One cardinal rule for those of us who handle holy things: *Never lose the wonder!* Orthodoxy must be matched with orthopraxy, or else the priesting aborts.

Malachi cuts deeply: "You have turned aside from the way." One remedy: change ways! Jesus helps us to do precisely that. Let him!

March 10, 1996

MATTHEW

Something more than Caesar's taxes
Matthew 9:9-13

The New Testament begins with four different biographies of Jesus. Strangely, not one of them bears his name. Instead, these biographies bear the names Matthew, Mark, Luke, and John. We call them Gospels. That means "news"—"good news." Thus the term Gospels, as applied to the first four books of the New Testament, applies not only to the facts about Jesus Christ, but also to the higher meaning of those facts.

It is about the "good new things" that have broken in on this world through Jesus Christ. In a time when all the news was bad, these four Gospels "changed the channels."

The first three Gospels—Matthew, Mark, and Luke—are very similar, but by no means identical. They are "synoptic"—that is, they "see with one eye." Place them side by side and they view the Jesus story in focus. John, as we shall see, looks at the whole thing differently.

The first of our biographies of Jesus bears the name Matthew. The story behind that story is a warm human drama. In order to understand it, we must go back aways—to Capernaum, a seaside village, 20 miles northeast of Nazareth, on the shores of the Lake of Galilee, around the year 30 A.D.

Rome ruled all the real estate. Her imperial heel was on the necks of all who lived in Palestine.

The caesars realized that commerce was the blood of the empire and that roads were the arteries through which that blood flowed. So Rome built one of the finest systems of roads that the ancient world ever knew. One of the great east-west arteries of that system of roadways cut right through Capernaum, making it an important town with a Roman military garrison attached and a district collector of internal revenue.

That's where our Gospel comes in. Here at Capernaum a man named Levi headed an office collecting taxes for Rome.

His duty was to extract the revenue for Caesar's roads, soldiers, markets, town halls, public buildings, baths, and stadiums throughout the empire. Even the temple at Jerusalem refurbished by Herod came from taxes collected by men like Levi.

Caesar did not spend his taxes on public health, education, and welfare except in the city of Rome itself. There was no Department of Health, Education, and Welfare for the provinces. But he did spend vast sums for the Department of Defense and the administrative affairs of government.

To finance these programs, Caesar had an elaborate system of taxation, a system he bequeathed to the Western world: duties on imports and exports; taxes on property, land, business, sales; a modest tax on income of one percent

In order to assure tax collection, Rome appointed provincial tax collectors and invested them with such authority that their word was law. These people in Palestine were called publicans.

Therefore, in Capernaum, Levi had his power—backed by all the force, pomp, and red tape of Rome. However, in spite of his high office, Levi was despised by his countrymen—especially the Jewish religious leaders. Scribes and Pharisees would cross the street to avoid having to look at him. Children tossed stones at him and spat at him before dashing down some narrow alley out of sight.

So Levi was loathed in his hometown because he levied taxes for hated Rome.

To patriotic Hebrews, Levi was an enemy agent, a turncoat, a traitor who sold his countrymen for considerable sums of silver. For, you see, to a substantial degree the tax rate was set by the tax collector rather than by Roman law. Frequently also the privilege of collecting taxes was a political plum purchased at great price.

To the tax collector went all the profits over and above the tax amounts required by Rome. The system invited graft galore. Tax collectors were all considered thieves—and in fact some of them actually were.

So when Levi opened the door to his tax office at Capernaum, he closed the door on most of his Jewish friends and family. No respectable Hebrews would have him as a guest in their home. His money was tainted money—and unacceptable in the synagogue. His word was a distrusted word—and could not be used in a Jewish court of law.

Thus, in the scriptures we see tax collectors—i.e., publicans—almost always linked with sinners. So unfolds an age-old principle: a society enforces its standards by casting out those who ignore them. Somehow, Levi just did not fit!

No doubt, sometimes in the still of the night he asked himself whether he had made a good bargain. Donald Trump-like, he could buy everything except respect. His tax collecting had feathered his nest while ruining his reputation. He was a stranger in his own house—Capernaum's richest up-and-out.

In some discontent, therefore, we can imagine that Levi turned often for solace to the Holy Scriptures—his Old Testament, and ours. Here he pored over the Law, the Prophets, and the Writings—reviewed the faith of his fathers.

After all, his name was Levi—a son of the Levites, the tribe of priests. How ironic that he had priestly blood in his veins, and yet he could not even worship in the Capernaum synagogue. He was an outcast to the faith of his countrymen.

These were the days when John the Baptizer was going everywhere preaching his arresting message: "Repent for the kingdom of heaven is at hand." Levi was strangely struck by this man.

Besides, John welcomed publicans and had some rather harsh things to say about scribes and Pharisees.

Levi was encouraged by the manner and message of this scantily-clothed man from the Judean desert.

But before Levi could adjust to John, a new and even more pulsating voice was heard in Capernaum. Jesus of nearby Nazareth began to stir the people with words and deeds more remarkable than anything John ever said or did. In Levi's hometown, Jesus Christ came through like a fresh summer's breeze. In a flurry of activity the man from Nazareth healed Simon's mother-in-law of a fever, cast an unclean spirit out of a man, reached out and touched a leper, and forgave the sins of a paralytic as he cured him from what crippled him.

The scribes and Pharisees whistled through their teeth. They called all this a scandal, an outrage, and labeled the man from Nazareth a blasphemer.

But Levi looked and listened. His heart raced fast. Could there possibly be a place in the purposes of God for a publican like him? With mounting hope, he heard the man from Nazareth every time he could.

Then one day it happened! The whole world changed for Levi. The spiritual quake that hit him was a 10 on the Richter scale.

Jesus came by the Capernaum tax collector's district office. Matthew writes about it in his own words in his ninth chapter: "Jesus saw a man . . . sitting at the tax office; and he said to him, 'Follow me.' And he rose and followed him" (v. 9).

Where others in Capernaum had seen a despised little publican collecting Caesar's taxes, Jesus saw "a man." He knew the hidden hungers, the awesome estrangements, of that man. And the record is: "Levi got up and followed him."

The simplicity of the Gospels—including Matthew's own account of this—conceals the radical dimensions of what Jesus Christ did. Here is risk-taking with a capital "R." To plunge his youthful "kingdom of heaven moment" into association with such questionable company was to take quite a chance.

Today it would be the same as if the United Way elected as its chairman a felon just released from prison for embezzling funds from NationsBank. It would be the same as the Ayatollah Khoumeini's successor inviting Salman Rushdie to join him in his Islamic Revolution in Iran.

Many in Capernaum snorted: "Oil and water just do not mix." They could tell Jesus Christ a thing or two about choosing disciples. He might know how to forgive paralytics their sins, but he did not know how to protect his reputation.

The Capernaumites saw trouble ahead. The public relations department pulled out its hair. The spin doctors lost sleep.

But Levi was overjoyed at the call to be a disciple, so much so that he prepared a feast to celebrate. He invited the only guests who would eat in his house: other tax collectors and sinners—outsiders all to the Jews.

Jesus joined the festive occasion with Levi and his guests. Possibly at this very feast—recorded by Matthew himself in his ninth chapter—Jesus announced that Levi would have a new name to match his new life. Henceforth he would be called Matthew, which in the language of his countrymen meant "Gift of God."

The scribes and Pharisees were shocked! To them the whole affair was a scandal—unholy men in an unholy house, at an unholy table, eating unholy food!

But in almost all cultures the readiness of people to eat together signals the removal of barriers. Jesus knew this. So he smashed barriers all over the place with that meal at Matthew's table.

No wonder the scribes and Pharisees sought out some of Jesus' friends and asked: "Why does your Master eat with tax collectors and sinners?" Frankly, the friends did not know, because Jesus often puzzled his friends just as much as his foes.

But the inquirers really did not want an answer. They wanted to make a case against him, for "proper people" like them could never understand improprieties like this. For them, Jesus' friendship with Matthew merely confirmed their prejudices: "A man is known by the company he keeps. This man Jesus is wild-eyed and radical—a long-haired, unbathed sinner—and no good will come from him."

But just about then, Jesus intervened to make one of the most revealing statements he ever made. He gave his reason for loving sinners: "Those who are well have no need of a physician, but those who are sick. Go and learn what this means, 'I desire mercy, and not sacrifice.' For I came not to call the righteous, but sinners" (9:12-13).

While so many in Capernaum preferred to gather their robes about them to avoid pollution from the masses, Jesus Christ declared his intentions forever.

The tragedy is that his followers today often find it easier to serve the saint than the sinner, the well rather than the sick.

But the issue raised at Matthew's house will not go away. It is the crux of the gospel. Will this be the year we break through the rules for being nice with a vision, a warmth, a courage to care for even the not-so-nice?

The Capernaum tax collector became a disciple—a man with a gospel. Alex Whyte stated it this way: "When Matthew rose up and followed Jesus the only things he took with him were his ink and his pen." The first book of the New Testament bears his name and the mark of his hand.

It was just like Matthew to write a gospel bridge between the Old Testament and the New. He quotes the Old Testament profusely, showing how it came to its fulfillment in Jesus.

Tradition has it that for 15 years Matthew preached to Jews scattered in Asia, in Persia, and in Syria. His gospel is definitely the most "Jewish" one of all—as if he wrote it with his own countrymen in mind.

The Gospel of Matthew contains practically all the material in the Gospel of Mark, plus about 200 verses not found in any of the other three Gospels.

His writing is characterized by a careful arrangement of materials and an obvious interest in numbers. These are precisely the kind of things we would expect from a bookkeeping tax collector turned Gospel writer.

Matthew alone records the parables of Jesus about the treasure hid in the field and the pearl of great price. He alone tells of the visit of the magi from the East bearing their gifts for the newborn Jesus.

These records would be very precious to the ex-tax collector who gave all his wealth and all his heart to the Christ.

Matthew's Gospel probably reached its present form about 70 A.D.—the very year Jerusalem was destroyed by the Roman general Titus. The last words in it are Christ's great commission, concluding with this promise: "Lo, I am with you always, to the close of the age."

What music to the ears of a tax collector once shut out from the congregation of Israel. He was included. He was needed. He was loved. He was family.

Matthew has left his own legacy for all the ages. It is the good news of God's great love for sinners—up and out, down and out.

The poet Francis Thompson understood the truth of it firsthand. While a medical student in London, he became a victim of drug abuse. He got the opium habit. He lost contact with his parents, sold his books, slept on park benches by the Thames. He became a bootblack. In his destitution he contracted tuberculosis and hovered between death and life. Doctors thought he would die. Yet, loving people nursed him back to health, helped him with food and clothing. By God's grace he survived. His mind cleared once more, and he wrote what many consider one of the finest pieces of verse in the English language, "The Hound of Heaven." From his own experience he says:

I fled him, down the nights and down the days;
I fled him, down the arches of the years;
I fled him, down the labyrinthine ways
Of my own mind; and in the midst of tears
I hid from him, and under running laughter
. . .Those strong Feet that followed, followed after
. . .Deliberate speed, majestic instancy.
They beat—and a Voice beat
More instant than the Feet—
"All things betray thee, who betrayest Me."

Matthew-like, after his long, wandering, suffering flight, Thompson surrendered to the voice that summoned him like a bursting sea—and was found by the Hound of Heaven. His story can be our story also! Amen.

April 14, 1996

MARK

Something more than running away

Mark 14:51-52; Acts 12:12, 25; 13:13; 15:36-41; 2 Timothy 4:11; 1 Peter 5:13

In our New Testament the second biography of Jesus bears the name Mark. Most students of scripture agree that Mark's Gospel was the first one written. It is certainly the shortest: its 16 chapters are crisp, cryptic. Mark does not waste a word in telling his story of Jesus. For example, he begins his Gospel with a quotation from Isaiah 40:3. Then he moves immediately to introduce John the Baptizer.

When we meet him first in Mark, Jesus is a full-grown man appearing at the Jordan to be baptized by his cousin John. Mark's purpose thus is to tell the story of Jesus as the Christ, the Suffering Servant Son of God.

This first written Gospel might well have come to encourage Christians who were being vigorously persecuted by the half-crazed emperor Nero following the great fire in Rome—64 A.D. It was a turbulent time in the Middle East during those days. In Rome, Nero's mad thrust was designed to wipe out Christians. In Palestine, Titus—Rome's counterpart to General Sherman—was already putting his campaign together to burn Jerusalem.

Behind these pages that bear the name and reveal the hand of John Mark stands a story warm and human in its weakness, lofty and soaring in its strength. Threading through five books of the New Testament are bits and pieces that, when put altogether, relate to us the checkered career of John Mark.

So let's review these chalk marks in Acts, Colossians, Timothy, and Peter—as well as Mark—in order to sketch the portrait of a man who found something more than running away.

Have you ever hacked your initials on a failure tree? Then take heart: John Mark has a word for you.

John Mark was a native son of Jerusalem. There in a great house he was born and he grew up. He must have been quite young—certainly no more than teenage—at the time of those topsy-turvy events in Jerusalem that led to Jesus' crucifixion.

There is an incident described in Mark—but not in any of the other Gospels—that most people think is autobiographical for Mark: his signature on his Jesus story. Remember, all these biographies of Jesus include autobiographies of the evangelists whose names they bear.

Mark's incident comes in 14:51-52. It was Thursday night in the Garden of Geth-semane. Jesus had just been arrested around midnight by the posse from the temple. The disciples who had been with him in the garden had, for the most part, fled.

Then Mark describes an unidentified young man, perhaps a teenager, who had quite a memorable experience: "And a young man followed Jesus with nothing but a linen cloth about his body; and they seized him, but he left the linen cloth and ran away naked" (14:51-52).

Nothing follows from this event. It is isolated. The young man is never named, nor does he anywhere reappear. It sounds autobiographical. Most students of scripture agree that this was Mark's subtle way of mentioning that he was in the garden the night Jesus was arrested.

If this is the case, then the first time we see John Mark he is a teenager running naked from Gethsemane—heading for home.

Now, from all we can surmise, that home of his in Jerusalem was quite an impos-ing place. It appears that his family enjoyed considerable wealth and status. They were cultured and refined—the hub for religious and social activities.

We know nothing of Mark's father. But his mother, Mary, early emerges as one of the leaders among the cluster of Christians at Jerusalem. Their house in Jerusalem became an early gathering place for the disciples. Chances are that it was here, in a great upper room, that Jesus shared his last supper with his friends.

Here, too, the disciples probably returned after Jesus' burial, after Jesus' resurrec-tion, after Jesus' ascension. And it was likely that they were in this same house when the "Day of Pentecost" burst upon them.

We know for sure that it was to John Mark's house that Peter went directly after his escape from Herod's prison in Acts 12:12. Here he found "many gathered together praying"—perhaps for him.

So, the case seems to be that John Mark's Jerusalem house was the gathering place, headquarters, sanctuary for the first Christian congregation at Jerusalem.

Besides this remarkable family influence, young Mark was early enriched by devout Christian friends. He had more than casual contact with both Peter and Paul, the two premier leaders of the early church. In fact, Peter in chapter 5, verse 13 of the book that bears his name refers to Mark endearingly as "my son."

Besides all this, Mark was a kinsman—a cousin—of Barnabas, that dynamic and magnanimous Christian from Cyprus.

So he got a good start! But it's not the start that makes a journey complete. It's the finish that counts!

Mark's checkered journey resumed when still as a young man he went from Jerusa-lem to Antioch with his cousin Barnabas and Paul.

He was thus in Syria at precisely the time when the Christians at Antioch con-cluded their plans to send Paul and Barnabas on their first mission tour. He went along! But he did not last out the journey. Luke records in Acts 13 that Mark left the tour, forsaking Paul and Barnabas at Perga in Pamphylia and returning to Jerusalem.

So the second time we see John Mark in the New Testament he is fully clothed, but again running for home. Why did he do it? Well, we really do not know.

Some say Mark got homesick. Perhaps he did. It does take a certain self-reliance to be on long and dangerous journeys far away from home.

Others say Mark was too dependent on his mother. There were apron strings he had not cut back home.

Still others think John Mark simply "chickened out"—grew fainthearted on the journey. After all, out there ahead from Perga in Pamphylia to Antioch in Pisidia lay the rugged Taurus mountains. Across those ranges one had to ascend 3,600 feet along one of the most treacherous roads in Asia.

Besides, the route was notorious for bandits; and beyond the mountains in the cities of Galatia, hostile crowds awaited to do battle with these bearers of a strange new gospel. So young John Mark was weary with the journey, and headed for home.

What's more, some believe that Mark left the mission tour because he disagreed with Paul's leadership. He was perhaps more accustomed to Barnabas' methods or Peter's. Paul was more rigid, authoritarian. He ran a tighter ship than the others had run. So John Mark, having problems with such authority, hit the road—home.

In any case, the die was cast. Mark's relapse caused a rupture in the relationship between the two leaders after that first tour.

For when Paul and Barnabas began planning their second mission tour, Barnabas again wanted to take Mark along with them. Paul flatly refused!

But Barnabas, Mark's kinsman, felt so strongly about taking him that he broke up his partnership with Paul.

The word is that there was "sharp contention" between them (Acts 15:39). So Paul and Barnabas separated, each going his different way. Paul took Silas and went through Syria and Cilicia. Barnabas took Mark and sailed home to Cyprus.

No details are given as to what happened on this second tour. But Mark must have come through, fully justifying Barnabas' confidence in him.

And the word reached Paul. Mark was completely reinstated and restored in the confidences of his earlier Christian mentors.

The New Testament record closes with Paul and Mark in a warm, affectionate partnership in ministry. In Col. 4:10 Paul tells the Christians at Colossae to "receive Mark." Then in Philemon, Paul describes Mark as a "fellow laborer" (v. 4). Just before his death, Paul wrote for Timothy to "bring Mark with you (to Rome) for he is very useful in my ministry" (2 Tim. 4:11). So at long last, John Mark found something better than running away.

This one-time timid kitten became the lion that roared. And until this day the lion is the image of Mark in Christendom. That is why that magnificent regal lion graces St. Mark's Square in Venice until this day.

Now we have a Gospel—our first Gospel—that bears the name of a quitter who made good. The very existence of this Gospel with Mark's name on it bears witness that even the most cowardly and immature Christian among us can come back the second time around.

All we need, in Christ, is someone to have confidence in us and the conviction that no failure is final or fatal.

Back of this Mark-Gospel is a method to redeem a person for usefulness. The method: to believe in that person and to give that person another chance.

Thus it is no accident that in his brief, crisp biography of Jesus, John Mark depicts Christ again and again as the forgiving servant of the most High God who busies himself giving persons second chances. Thanks to that Christ—who forgives 70 times 7— and to his earliest followers, John Mark found something better than running away.

What a discovery! So many people in our time are on the run—on the lam— running out on life.

Tradition has it that Mark became a bishop in the early church, and while yet a young man was martyred for his Christian faith. But before he died, the lion roared, and provided all Christendom with its first written Gospel.

Papias, the second-century Christian bishop, suggested that Mark composed the Gospel using eye-witness information provided by Simon Peter. This could explain Peter's affectionate reference to his young associate as "Mark, my son" (5:13).

Ironic, isn't it? Both John Mark and Simon Peter were restored after a false start: Mark escaping Gethsemane, naked; Simon, denying in Caiphas' courtyard that he ever knew the Galilean.

In some respects Mark's Gospel is a reflection of Mark's life. He presents a cryptic, graphic picture of "the Christ on all the roads" giving "whosoever" will second chances. Mark's 16 chapters are the nearest thing we will ever get to an unembellished report of Jesus' life. Its great characteristic is its realism. Mark's story of Jesus is his story of his best friend.

It is sometimes said of a story that "it marches." But Mark's Jesus story does not so much march; it dashes along, in a kind of breathless wonder. There is no Gospel that gives a more human picture of the divine friend, Jesus Christ.

Matthew and Luke must have had Mark's Gospel with them when they wrote theirs. They both follow Mark's outline and order of events. Mark has 661 verses. Matthew reproduces 606 of these—more than 300 of them in Mark's exact words. Luke reproduces 320 of Mark's verses—more than 150 of them in Mark's identical words. In fact, there are only 24 verses of Mark that do not occur somewhere in Matthew and Luke.

It is a thrilling thing to remember that when we are reading Mark we are reading the first biography of Jesus ever written—and it was compiled by a quitter who made good on later commitments.

Kipling has said a classic word for all the John Marks in this world—and for all of us lesser lights also—who do not quit before the journey is done:

If you can keep your head when all about you
Are losing theirs and blaming it on you,
If you can trust yourself when all men doubt you,
But make allowance for their doubting too;

If you can wait and not be tired by waiting,
Or being lied about, don't deal in lies,
Or being hated, don't give way to hating,
And yet don't look too good, nor talk too wise:

If you can dream—and not make dreams your master;
If you can think—and not make thoughts your aim;
If you can meet with Triumph and Disaster
And treat those two impostors just the same;
If you can bear to hear the truth you've spoken
Twisted by knaves to make a trap for fools,
Or watch the things you gave your life to, broken,
And stoop and build 'em up with worn-out tools:

....

If you can fill the unforgiving minute
With sixty seconds' worth of distance run,
Yours is the Earth and everything that's in it,
And—which is more—you'll be a Man, my son!

Amen!

April 21, 1996

LUKE

Something more than a fine medical practice

Luke 1:1-4, Acts 16:10, Colossians 4:14, Philemon 23, 2 Timothy 4:11

The third book in our New Testament bears the name of Luke. It is not a name we have heard before anywhere else in the Bible. He was never one of the famous, towering figures in the early church. If he had not written this Gospel, we would no doubt have ever met him. But write it he did, and along with it the companion fifth New Testament book: the Acts of the Apostles.

Luke was a Gentile. This means that he was the only New Testament writer who was not Jewish. His name is Roman—Lucas in Latin. It is a shortened form of either Lucius or Lucanus, both fine Roman names.

Luke's Greek, grammatically and syntactically, is some of the best in the Bible. So he must have had a thoroughly Greek education.

Some physicians appear to take courses in non-writing, but not Dr. Luke. He writes with the best of them. His flair for beauty and detail is profound.

Outside the personal introductions to his Gospel and to the book of Acts, Luke appears four other times in the New Testament. Let's check these four places and piece together the information they afford to paint a portrait of a man who had a head for history and a heart for his Savior.

We meet Luke first with a jolt when suddenly in Acts 16:10 the narrative takes a shift from a third-person account to a first-person record. Luke writes: "After he (Paul) had seen the vision, immediately we endeavored to go into Macedonia."

This sudden and unexpected change into the first person, this use of "we" instead of "he" must mean that the writer—i.e., Luke—was with Paul on his second journey. Luke was with Paul at Troas, trying to arrange passage across the Aegean Sea to Philippi in Macedonia. They were in Asia trying to go to Europe.

The other three times we meet Luke, Paul mentions him as one of his traveling companions. In the letter to the Colossians, Paul brings his messages to a close by mentioning those around him. He says, "Luke, the beloved physician . . . greets you" (4:14).

Later, in writing to Philemon from Rome, Paul says: "Luke, my fellow worker sends greetings to you" (v. 23).

Finally, in perhaps the last letter he ever wrote—only weeks before his execution by Nero—in 2 Tim. 4:11, Paul speaks with unmistakable pathos: "Luke alone is with me."

The situation, as we can best piece together this autobiography threading through Luke's biography of Jesus, goes something like this:

The Christians at Antioch in Syria were largely of Gentile extraction. This was the congregation that first sent Paul and Barnabas, and later Paul and Silas, on those three missionary thrusts into the Gentile territories of Galatia, Asia, and Europe.

Paul, according to his own testimony in his writings, was often sick—and even at times threatened with having to abandon his career for reasons of health.

Remember, he spoke in Galatians 4 of his "bodily ailment" and of his "thorn in the flesh"—the buffeter of Satan that kept him physically weak and depleted.

Luke must have been a native of Antioch in Syria—of Syrian extraction—and a recognized trained physician. It seems only natural that Luke joined Paul and the others, if not on their first tour, then certainly on their second one, in order to give Paul much-needed regular, personal attention as his doctor.

That explains the close connection of the two and the Apostle's appreciation for Luke's fidelity as the "beloved physician." So, in his Christian missionary task, Luke found something better than a fine medical practice. To him goes the distinction of beginning first-century medical missions in the name of Christ, in the company of Paul, for the whole world as he knew it.

Maybe the fact that Luke was trained as a physician gave him the great sympathies he possessed. It has been said that a minister sees persons at their best, a lawyer sees persons at their worst, and a doctor sees persons as they are most honestly themselves. In any case, Luke saw real persons, and he loved them every one.

But Luke was something more than a Syrian doctor who could write. He had a penchant for history. His writings bear almost a scientist's concern for precision of detail.

For example, he dates the emergence of John the Baptizer by no fewer than six contemporary checkpoints (ch. 3). "Now in the 15th year of Tiberius Caesar, Pontius Pilate being governor of Judea, Herod being tetrarch of Galilee, and his brother, Philip, being tetrarch of Itureaea, and Lysanias, the tetrarch of Abilene, Annas and Caiphas being the high priests . . ."

It was the same as Luke saying: "It was the fourth year of Bill Clinton as president of the U.S. and of Al Gore as vice president, the fourth year of Jim Hunt as governor of North Carolina and of Dennis Wicker as lieutenant governor. It was while Newt Gingrich was Speaker of the House in Washington and Harold Brubaker was Speaker of the House in Raleigh. Burly Mitchell was chief justice of the North Carolina Supreme Court, and Carolyn Allen was mayor of Greensboro."

Here is a man who writes with great care, and who intends to be just as accurate as he possibly can.

Luke based the outline of his biography of Jesus squarely on the outline of Mark, but he added a substantial amount of additional material. Luke wrote later than either Matthew or Mark. Students of scripture generally agree that Luke wrote sometime after

70 A. D.—the year Jerusalem was conquered, burned, and the temple destroyed by the Roman armies under Titus. Perhaps around 80 A. D. is when Dr. Luke put his hand to this scroll.

Both Matthew and Luke add their own material to that of Mark. But what Luke adds is vastly different from what Matthew adds.

In all likelihood the difference in the materials arose out of their difference in purpose. Content was affected by intent.

Mark produced a simple, fast-moving, uncomplex, brief, crisp life of Jesus Christ intended to set forth the good news of Jesus—the Messiah finally come.

Matthew crafted his Gospel for the eyes of those steeped in Jewish Old Testament teachings. He included many references to the Hebrew prophecies that Jesus fulfilled.

Luke recast Mark's Gospel in a way particularly to appeal to Gentiles—especially those who were gorged with paganism, and sympathetic with the fresh good news of God in Jesus Christ.

The Roman authorities are treated more gently and humanely by Luke than by either Matthew or Mark. And Jesus himself is portrayed as far more sympathetic to Gentiles in Luke than in the other Gospels.

Luke knew that he was not writing the first biography of Jesus. In his opening line (1:1) he notes that "many have undertaken to compile a narrative of the things that have been accomplished among us."

If Luke could not write the first Gospel, then he could write the most complete Gospel. It was to that end that he set his heart, his head, and his hand.

Mark began with Jesus' baptism by John at the time Jesus was already a full-grown man. Matthew went back to the birth of Jesus to start his story. But Luke went farther back still: to the birth of John the Baptizer, Jesus' cousin and his forerunner. Thus he begins with Zacharias and Elizabeth, the parents of John, persons not mentioned anywhere else in the Bible.

He does this, he says, in order further to inform a "most excellent Theophilus"—apparently some Roman citizen, a God-fearer, who received the dedication for both Luke's Gospel and his book of Acts.

So Doctor Luke, M.D., the only Gentile writer in the New Testament—and for that matter in the entire Bible—wrote to instruct Gentiles like Theophilus—and like you and me—about Jesus, the Son of Man, the Son of God. And instruct us he does!

The overriding theme throughout the 24 chapters that bear his name is this: "Jesus Christ is Savior of the whole world"—not part of it, but *all* of it.

Luke's is the great universal gospel! We Christians need desperately to hear the ring of that. The Old World/New World/Third World are all really one world. And that world is overwhelmingly lost.

In this book all the barriers come down. Jesus Christ is for all persons, without distinctions, without exceptions.

How is humanity divided in our time? By race, by class, by gender, by region, by religion, by ideology.

Mark these divisions, then read Luke to see how in Christ everyone of them is smashed. Neither race nor place; neither class nor cause; neither sex nor opinion matters one whit.

Jesus Christ comes to everyone, every type, every class, every circumstance, every possibility, every phase of human life. There is nothing a human being can do to disqualify for Christ's grace—except to refuse to accept it.

Matthew traced Jesus' family tree back to Abraham. Luke traced it back to Adam. Jesus Christ is New Man—God/Man—for all mankind.

This universal note is especially sounded when "the beloved physician" turns to write about Jesus' treatment of this world's outcasts—the disfranchised, the marginalized, the desperate in society. For example, women were treated like dirt all over Palestine. They were the property and the playthings for men. Even good, godly men prayed: "Thank God I am *not* a Gentile, a slave, or a woman."

But Luke in his Gospel gives a very special place to women—and to children. The birth story of Jesus is told from Mary's point of view, as if Luke's information had come straight from the young virgin's lips. In Luke we read of Elizabeth, of Anna, and of the widow of Nain. It is Luke who paints such vivid portraits of Mary Magdalene and of the Bethany sisters, Martha and Mary.

He depicts tenderly the narrative of the woman from Syro-Phoenicia and the woman who anointed Jesus' feet and dried them with her hair.

As Luke tells it, when the man of Nazareth arrived, the women of this world were set free to be themselves. And no man could put them back into chains. They were last at the cross and first at the tomb.

Luke's is a Gospel with all the barriers to Jesus broken down. This Jesus Christ is Savior for everyone—the down and out, the up and out; the sick, the well.

Not even the half-breed Samaritans are shut out. As Luke alone tells it, Jesus made one of these despised mulattos a hero in one of his best-loved parables: "the Good Samaritan" (Luke 10). Let John record that "the Jews have no dealings with the Samaritans." Leave it to Luke to show that Jesus does: he shuts the door on no man/no woman.

Lepers are welcomed! So are widows and orphans; Romans, publicans, soldiers; sinners of every sort and type.

Luke's Jesus is supremely interested in every person. Especially does he come to the poor. In fact, Luke alone relates Jesus' story of the rich man and the poor beggar at his gate.

Luke's Gospel is good news for the underdog. His heart aches for everyone who has had a bad break, who has been dealt a loaded deck.

The rag-tag, the bobtail, the smelly, barefoot nobodies: they skip and dance throughout the pages of Luke's universal Gospel. Dr. Luke's Jesus makes house calls.

And above all, Luke presents Jesus Christ as the friend of sinners! He alone tells of the penitent thief on the cross as well as Jesus' immortal story of the prodigal son (Luke 15).

Luke, of all the four Gospel writers, saw no limits to God's great love. It ripples, flows, cascades, and floods over all the lives all over this world.

Taylor Caldwell has said it well in the foreword to her classic novel about Luke, *Dear and Glorious Physician*: "The story of St. Luke is the story of every person's pilgrimage through despair and darkness, through anguish, doubt, and rebellion to the very feet of God . . . without this search, a person lives only as an animal. With it, persons become the sons and the daughters of God."

So, in the third book of our New Testament we meet the universal Jesus introduced by the universal physician. We also meet Luke, M.D.—"beloved physician" who found something better than a fine medical practice. His Gospel reflects the facts so vividly captured in Faber's classic lines:

> There's a wideness in God's mercy,
> Like the wideness of the sea;
> There's a kindness in His justice,
> Which is more than liberty.
>
> For the love of God is broader
> Than the measure of man's mind;
> And the heart of the Eternal
> Is most wonderfully kind.

So it is! Amen.

April 28, 1996

JOHN

Something more than fishing
John 3:16; 13:23-25; 18:15-16; 19:25-27; 20:1-8; 21:7, 20-25

The fourth book in our New Testament bears the name of John. Fred Craddock has said, "The Gospel of John is so vast that a child can wade in it and an elephant can swim in it." It is at once very simple and very profound. These 21 chapters speak to all ages, all groups, all centuries. They bear the name and address of every person on the planet. Those who go to this book with their hearts breaking come away again and again strangely comforted. Who can ever forget it? John 3:16—the one fragment that sums up the whole Bible.

In Christendom the symbol for John is the eagle. The eagle can fly higher than any other bird. Of all the creatures, only the eagle can look straight into the sun and not be dazzled.

John's is the eagle Gospel. Its flights of thought soar higher than any of the others. Its penetrating gaze extends into the very mind of God.

John has not written so much an historical Gospel as a theological one. For this reason, the fourth Gospel is different.

It omits so much that the other three include: the birth stories of Jesus, accounts of his baptism, his temptation, the Last Supper, the agony in Gethsemane. It also contains so many things that the other three leave out.

More than one half of John's Gospel sets the scene in Judea/Jerusalem during Jesus' last journey there. Five chapters capture events in the upper room the night before he died.

Who is this John whom tradition gives credit for these 21 chapters in our New Testament? Let us collect some things we know about him.

In Mark 1:19-20 we learn that John was the younger son of Zebedee, who possessed a fishing boat on the Sea of Galilee and was well enough off that he employed other persons to help him with his fishing business. His mother was Salome. And there is some reason to believe—from Matt. 27:56—that she was a kinswoman of Mary, the mother of Jesus.

John had an older brother James who was also a fisherman. These two boys appear to have been in partnership with Simon Peter and his brother Andrew in their fishing business (Luke 5:7-10).

Mark tells us in 1:20 that with his brother, James, John obeyed the call of Jesus to leave his fishing and follow him. At that time John was probably in his late teens.

As a young man, John was clearly a turbulent and ambitious person. Bishop Francis McConnell calls this the "green apple stage" in his life.

In Luke 9:49 Jesus gives to John and James the name Boanerges, which means "Sons of Thunder." So violent were their tempers that they were prepared to blast a Samaritan village right off the map because it refused them hospitality when Jesus was on his way to Jerusalem.

Later, either they or their mother, Salome, registered the request that when Jesus finally established his kingdom that they be given chief seats in its government.

So, in the Synoptics, John is presented as a strange mixture: tough/tender; tempestuous/ambitious; gentle/stormy. Yet, for it all, Jesus saw pure gold in this young fisherman. And in Jesus, John found something more than fishing. He became one of Jesus' closest companions, even enjoying a place within the inner circle. The "green apple" ripened.

In the book of Acts, John appears again. Here he is always the companion of Simon Peter, but never speaks a word in the entire book.

He was with Peter when a lame man was healed at the temple gate. With Peter also he was hauled before the Jewish high court, facing his accusers with astonishing courage and confidence.

With Peter also he went from Jerusalem to Samaria, confirming the new converts gained by Philip, the deacon. Strange irony, isn't it? This very Samaria was the spot where only months before he suggested that Jesus call lightning down from heaven to demolish everything. The "green apple" kept on ripening.

In Paul's letters John appears only once. In Gal. 2:9 he is named as one of the pillars of the Jerusalem church—along with Peter and James. Paul suggests that John thoroughly approved his work with the Gentiles.

Now, if you have followed the references closely, you have noticed that all our information about John thus far has come from the first three Gospels, Acts, and Galatians. The fourth Gospel never mentions the name of John in its 21 chapters.

But the fourth Gospel does do an interesting thing: it threads an autobiography of a certain disciple throughout its moving biography of Jesus. Someone called "the disciple whom Jesus loved" is mentioned five times. Observe:

1. He is first mentioned in the upper room at the Last Supper when Jesus told the men that one of them would betray him. Peter told "the disciple whom Jesus loved," seated next to Jesus in the seat of honor, to ask him who it would be (13:23-25).

2. This "beloved disciple" is mentioned again at the trial of Jesus. Here he is called "another disciple" who was well known to the high priest and helped secure Peter's entrance into Caiphas' house (18:15-16).

3. He is mentioned a third time at the cross on Golgotha. In his suffering, Jesus turned to "the disciple whom he loved" and entrusted his mother into the disciple's care and keeping (19:25-27).

4. The next time we see "the beloved disciple" is on the first Easter morning. Mary met him and Peter first after her discovery that the tomb was empty (20:1-8). The two men raced to the open grave. He outran Peter, and the two of them became the first persons inside the empty tomb.

5. The last time we see "the disciple whom Jesus loved" is on the beach, by the lake, in the early morning at the last breakfast Jesus prepared for the weary fishermen following his resurrection. It was this disciple who first recognized that the strange figure through the fog on shore was Jesus (21:7).

You see, the situation in the fourth Gospel is that John is never mentioned. But five times there is mention of this "disciple whom Jesus loved." Tradition has never really doubted that this "beloved disciple" is John. It is his autobiography within Jesus' biography.

According to the early church fathers, John, after he stepped off the pages of Acts, went to live at Ephesus on the coast of Asia Minor. During the reign of Emperor Domition (81-96 A.D.), when Christians were severely persecuted, he retired for safety to the Island of Patmos, about 50 miles southwest of Ephesus. After Domition's death, John returned to Ephesus, where he was inspired to produce this Gospel sometime during the reign of Trajan (98-117 A.D.).

If John were near 20 years old at the time of Jesus' crucifixion, this means that he could well have been in his 90s by the time this fourth Gospel was written.

The actual penman may have been one of John's closest associates at Ephesus, but the mind and the memory behind these chapters is the aged apostle John himself.

What we have here in our fourth Gospel is a first-hand, eye-witness word right out of Jesus' empty tomb. This is the testimony of a man who was there. He stood in the open grave to make this proclamation.

Here is an eagle, looking straight into the sun and telling us what he saw. Here is a "green apple" fisherman who ripened to find something better—far better—than fishing.

But why would John write a fourth Gospel? The church already had three, and in all likelihood John knew about all of them.

Shape the situation: Jerusalem had been totally destroyed by the Romans in 70 A.D. Christians had scattered to the four winds. The church grew, becoming every year more Greek and less Jewish.

The new centers of Christianity were Antioch in Syria, the cities of Galatia, Philippi, Corinth, Rome, Alexandria, and Ephesus.

This being so, the Jesus story needed to be retold. The truth had not changed, but the ways for telling it were drastically altered.

Let me illustrate. A Greek-oriented person might take up the Gospel of Matthew. No sooner had he opened the scroll than he was confronted by a lengthy genealogy tracing Jesus' family tree back to Abraham.

Now, genealogies were familiar and precious things to a Jew but quite unintelligible to a Greek.

He would read on to confront a man named Jesus who was the Son of David, a king about whom a Greek had never heard. He would be faced with the concept of Jesus as Messiah—another term with which the Greek was totally unfamiliar.

You see the problem: Must a Greek who wanted to know about Jesus Christ, perhaps who even had an interest in becoming a Christian, change all his thinking into Jewish patterns? Must Greeks, in effect, become Jews before they could become Christians?

John's answer was a resounding "No!" So he handed over to the world our fourth Gospel, an incredible handbook on who Jesus actually was. It is a manual for the human spirit. Listen to the first line, a genius line: "In the beginning was the Word (*logos*)."

He hooks his good news of Jesus both to "Genesis" for Jews and to "Logos" for Greeks. Then for 21 breathtaking chapters he opens all kinds of windows and doors to let the fresh winds of revelation blow through.

John lights up the pages of Matthew, Mark, and Luke with new lanterns. For him, God has no grandchildren!

There is not a parable in the entire Gospel of John. Instead he records signs—seven of them. They are acted-out parables pointing toward who Jesus is. Each one is followed by a lengthy discourse on some theme in John's Jesus story. John's signs, signals, witnesses to the Word include:

- changing water into wine (2:1ff)
- healing an officer's son (4:43ff)
- healing a paralytic at Bethesda (5:1ff)
- feeding the multitude with a boy's lunch (6:1ff)
- walking on the sea through a storm (6:16ff)
- healing a man born blind (9:1ff)
- raising Lazarus of Bethany after being dead four days (11:1ff)

And if that were not enough, John helps us to draw a portrait of our Lord's own self-understanding with his seven amazing and beautiful "I AM's" of Jesus:

1. "I am the Bread of Life" (6:35).
2. "I am the Light of the World" (8:12).
3. "I am the Door of the Sheep" (10:7).
4. "I am the Good Shepherd" (10:11).
5. "I am the Resurrection" (11:25).
6. "I am the Way, the Truth, the Life" (14:6).
7. "I am the True Vine" (15:1).

Paul was the tentmaker theologian who spoke to the early church's mind; John was the fisherman theologian who spoke to their heart.

John outlived 12 Roman emperors from Augustus to Trajan. Two of these committed suicide. Seven were murdered. Almost all of them were persecutors of the truth that set John's great heart aflame.

The man himself is the miracle of this Gospel, the miracle of a life whom Jesus Christ has touched and redeemed. John lived out John 3:16!

Jerome recounts one of the most beautiful stories ever to circulate in the early church. He writes that one Sunday the aged John, now highly respected as the only apostle still alive, was invited to preach to the church at Ephesus. A huge congregation assembled to hear him, filling all available seats and spilling out into areas around the building.

When John arrived he was so feeble that he had to be carried into the building. After eloquent words of welcome the aged John was lifted to his feet to speak. A great hush came over the congregation. Everyone strained to hear each word. The old man said: "Little children, love one another, love one another, love one another."

And he sat down. His sermon was done. None went home disappointed that day. None saw an old man in his dotage.

That 11-word sermon is the heart of the Gospel. It is the insight of the saint, not the infirmity of the senile: "Little children, God is love! Little children, love God; love each other." Amen!

May 12, 1996

ACTS

They too were human
Acts 1:1-5, 2:1-4, 6:7, 8:1-3, 9:31, 13:2-3, 16:5, 28:28-31

The four Gospels in our New Testament are in fact four biographies of one life: Jesus of Nazareth. Following them is a 28-chapter scroll that traces the growth of Christianity for the first 50 years following Jesus' lifetime. It bears the name Acts of the Apostles. That may be as good a name as any for it, but the plain fact is that only three apostles appear with any prominence on its pages.

James is mentioned in one sentence that records his execution by Herod Agrippa (12:2). John appears twice (chs. 3, 4), but he never, one time, speaks a word. Peter is on the scene prominently in the early pages, but by chapter 12 he is gone from the story.

Other personalities punctuate these pages. There is Stephen, who lived at floodtide and died under an avalanche of stones for saying what he believed. And there is Philip, the deacon, man of fire and ice, who turned Samaria upside down with his gospel. And there are Silas, Mark, Luke, and that lovable believable man from Cyprus: Barnabas. There are Aquilla and Priscilla, Rhoda, and Lydia.

But the most imposing person on these pages is Paul—formerly named Saul—tent maker and rabbinic student from Tarsus. He towers so tall over everything and everyone else that the second half of the book of Acts is essentially a biography of Paul.

Be that as it is, however, the real actor in the book of Acts is not any one of the apostles or the deacons or the missionaries or even the dauntless Paul.

The real actor in the book of Acts is the risen Christ, active in his young church through his Holy Spirit. Thus the best possible name for this book in our Bible might be "The Acts of the Holy Spirit."

The writer of Acts is almost universally agreed upon. It was Luke, the same Gentile physician and traveling companion of Paul who wrote the third Gospel.

Indeed, in all probability, Luke wrote his Gospel and the book of Acts as a single scroll, which was divided later either for convenience of handling or after it was decided to gather the four Gospels into one group.

Every page of this manuscript evidences a physician who worked and thought and wrote like a historian. The first 15 chapters read almost like a collection of the church minutes from local Christian congregations at Jerusalem, Caesarea, and Antioch.

But from chapter 16, verse 10 onward, Luke makes a dramatic shift. He draws from what appears to be his own "travel diary" as he accompanies Paul on their journeys carrying the gospel all over the then-known world. From that point on, he speaks in the first person—the historian is himself making history.

Acts traces the remarkable spread of Christianity from its Palestinian beginnings in Jerusalem to the faraway heart of the empire at Rome.

The hero of that shift is Paul, the indomitable little man from Tarsus. Luke wrote Acts around 80 A.D., just after the blood bath precipitated by Nero in 64 A.D. and the destruction of Jerusalem by Titus in 70 A.D.

In these 28 chapters he has built a bridge that connects the life of Christ in the Gospels with the work of Christ in his church.

Pentecost is the watershed (Acts 2). Previous to Pentecost, the living Christ was enfleshed—localized, limited; one person at one place in Palestine. After Pentecost, the living Christ was inspirited—loose in the world indwelling his people, the church, at all places during all times.

Everything in the book of Acts is unfinished. It is a book of beginnings—start-ups, processes. Nothing is finished. Everything is to be continued.

And that beat goes on! The Lord Christ is still doing through his people, the church, in the world, the same things he did during the days of Acts. He is yet the living center, the head, the energy of his church.

He is bringing to fruition *now* everything that he began *then*, completing *here* what he started *there*. And that is the essential message of the book of Acts for us in our time.

Yet, you see, we must never try to go back to the first century and duplicate the details. Rather, we must go back to the book of Acts to discover the essentials. And when we do, we find that these essentials are with us still—presently, continually, perpetually.

This book is crucial for us because it reveals to us the possibilities and the perils of the people of God for all places, for all times. Through the details of the first century we see the essentials of the 20th century—in Christ.

Here we discern three abiding realities. First, the church originates in the Lord Christ. In Matthew's Gospel Jesus says: "I will build *my* church." In Acts 1:8 Jesus says, "I will empower *my* church."

The most crucial thing in Jesus' special called-out group—*Ekklesia*—is the personal pronoun "my." The church is *his* church. He lived and died it into existence.

Its first members were people he handpicked. He filled their minds with his truth, which they could not understand. He baffled them with his presence, which they could not comprehend.

He lived and he died, and he arose from the grave—right before their very eyes. It was for them, as it would be for you, if your best friend stormed out of his tomb. They were transfixed in amazement.

Then he poured out his Spirit upon them, energizing them to out-live and to out-die their opposition.

This handful of ordinary Spirit-filled people planted the church in the then-known world. Their unity is our unity. They were together, although not alike—in Jesus Christ.

They were church—Christ's church—and they originated in him. This the book of Acts affirms on every page.

We do not have Christian churches all over this earth today simply because someone decided that it would be nice to have them. We have Christian churches because Jesus Christ lived and died and lived again to create them. The Christian church originates in Christ!

Second, the church endures in the Lord Christ. In the 28 chapters of Acts we see the church facing the world: Christ and culture collide. Sometimes the Christians are flimsy, faulty, feeble, fumbling, failing. They bumble, mumble, stumble along their way. Sometimes the Christians are magnificent—loving the hard-to-love, reaching the unreachables, touching the untouchables, teaching the unteachables—making somebodies out of barefoot nobodies.

But always the Christians are sustained by an incredible conviction: their life is Christ's life. They are men and women "in Christ."

So you never hear them grumbling, "Look what our world is coming to." Instead you hear them shouting, "Look what has come to our world."

Just about every month for the past 1900 years, someone, somewhere has volunteered to serve as pallbearer at the funeral of the church. Scores of capable people have misread the signs and declared that the church is dead.

Quite confessedly, the people of God have frequently not breathed very hard, and have been dragged kicking and screaming to face fresh challenges in their changing world.

Yet, we mourn the wrong corpse. It is culture, not the church, that is sick unto death. By now we ought to know that the church endures in the Lord Christ.

It never has nor will it ever endure in any specific form, shape, structure, or institution. All these pass with time. It may have inordinate vested interest in some of these, but its life lies elsewhere.

That is why every form, shape, or structure; every precedent, tradition, or ritual may perish or change—while church lives on! No one can ever crush the Rock of Ages into a pile of assorted gravel. It endures in the Lord Christ!

Third, the church functions in the Lord Christ. The people of God are the instruments—the incarnations—of the living Christ in the world. They carry on his work by the way they do their own. Their life is the Christ life.

Watch the Acts drama unfold: the Spirit chooses persons, indicates places, initiates processes. See the persons: Simon Peter for Cornelius at Caesarea, Philip the deacon for Samaria, men of Cyprus and Cyrene for Antioch, Saul of Tarsus for Europe and Asia.

Note the places: Jerusalem, the holy city of the Jews; Antioch, the gateway to the Gentiles; Corinth, the marketplace of Greece; Ephesus, the center of teaming Asia Minor; and Rome, the central city of the first-century world.

Observe the processes: The very minute someone tries to cramp the church's free spirit, boxing it in with rigid forms and structures, it slithers away like a moonbeam in their hand. In Acts one fact is nailed down forever: the church functions in the freedom of the Lord Jesus Christ.

But right here is where the crisis mounts both in the first century and in the 20th century. The peril always is that the church originates, endures, and functions in the Lord Christ; but the decisions as to its shape and its strategy rest with more mortals.

The men and women in Acts were human also. We too are human. They, like us, were mere men and women—nothing more, nothing less, nothing else.

At least twice in these 28 chapters we hold our breath while these mere mortals hammer out decisions about the shape of the church in the world. In both instances the decision could have gone differently and altered the whole course of history.

Let me illustrate, first from Acts 15. The first Christian missionary tour through Cyprus, Pamphylia, and Galatia was finished. Paul and Barnabas were back home in Antioch rejoicing in the way Gentiles had responded to the gospel of Jesus.

Some brethren from Judea—Judaizers—showed up. They insisted that Gentiles had to be circumcised before they could be accepted as Christians. Paul hit the ceiling!

He saw what this meant. It meant that a man, virtually, had to become a Jew before he could become a Christian. They had no small debate. Luke describes their heated argument as "dissension" in Acts 15:2.

Paul insisted that every person on the face of the earth could come to Jesus Christ on their credentials merely as a human being. Faith, not circumcision, was the key to salvation for Paul. It was a work of the Spirit, not a work of the flesh. He argued for inclusiveness, not exclusiveness, as the shape of the church.

The controversy raged fiercely at Antioch. So much so, that the congregation insisted that Paul and Barnabas go to Jerusalem and have the apostles and elders in that revered first Christian congregation hammer out a decision on the matter.

So they journeyed the difficult and dangerous 200 miles south from Syria to Jerusalem. In Acts 15 Luke tells us the outcome. And in Galatians 2 Paul gives his own assessment of "the Jerusalem Conference."

Suffice it to say that while the world held its breath, mere mortals decided the shape and strategy of the church in its world. Would Christianity be just a slightly revised version of Judaism? Was the gift of God's Son for only a select few or for the whole world?

The debate was heated. The division was sharp. The dissension ran deep. The Judaizers were not bad; they were simply wrong. And these Jerusalem Christians could have made the wrong decision, but they did not!

They cut the gospel loose from its legalistic umbilical cord forever. Peter and James, two pillars in the Jerusalem church, led the way, stood tall, and led the church to decide that persons are saved by grace through faith and not by circumcision, baptism, or any other outward ceremony, sign, or symbol.

But don't ever forget: they, too, were human and could have made a monumental mistake. The entire mission to the Gentiles was at stake.

Mere mortals held in their hands the destiny, the shape/strategy of the church. That is forever the glory and the agony of Christendom—first century or 20th century. The treasure is in earthen vessels.

Let me illustrate once more this reality, this time from Acts 16.

Paul had returned to Antioch. He was elated at the decision confirming his mission to the Gentiles. He and Silas had prepared to revisit the churches in Pamphylia and Galatia.

Now Paul was at Troas on the Aegean Sea. Where would he go from here? If he went north, he would evangelize Bithynia and perhaps push farther east into what is now Russia. If he went south, he would plunge into Asia Minor and perhaps spend the rest of his life in the provinces of that dark subcontinent—in India.

In Acts 16:9 Luke tells us what happened. Paul had a night vision—perhaps a dream. A man from Macedonia appeared, urging him to come westward and share the gospel with Europe. So to the west Paul would turn.

And from that moment on, the future course of Christianity was set. It would move westward rather than eastward.

I cannot help but wonder what differences would there be in our modern world and in all our lives if the East—India, Orient, and Russia—had become Christian rather than the West—Europe, Americas.

Once more, a mere mortal hammered out a decision that has affected the history of Christendom for all time. So it has always been in the wild, wonderful economy of God.

A church depends for its structure, shape, and strategy upon persons just like you and me.

The world still awaits our choices that will affect their lives. We can no longer equate attending services with performing services. The title of our book is "Acts," not "Intentions."

James Pleitz tells a story out of his Arkansas rearing: Times were tough. He and some neighbors were going on a hike. He took his picnic lunch bucket: biscuit, fatback, molasses. They took their picnic lunch: baked bread, cake, cookies, chicken. By 9:30 someone suggested, "Let's eat!" They shared their lunches. At that moment he learned the meaning of sharing: "When all that I had became theirs, then all that they had became mine."

It's the wild, wonderful way with God's people in this world. It is the way of God in Acts and where we live also. Amen.

May 19, 1996

ROMANS

Keep the faith

Romans 1:1-7, 14-17; 2:1; 5:1; 8:1; 12:1-2

Following the book of Acts in our New Testament are 21 letters written by various persons at various times to a variety of individuals and churches. The majority of these—as many as 14 by some counts—were written by Paul, within a span of 10 years during his busy life, and the letters as a whole are the earliest writings in our New Testament.

Some of them were written as early as 17 years after Jesus' death/resurrection and 20 years before Mark's Gospel. These letters do not appear in our Bible in chronological order. They seem, rather, to be placed in order of length—with the longest first.

Thus the first and the longest letter is a 16-chapter scroll simply called Romans. Perhaps its length, coupled with its address to Christians in the capital city of the empire, accounts for its place of prestige in the New Testament.

We must remember that when we are reading these letters in the New Testament we are not reading scrolls that were meant to be either academic exercises or theological treatises. Rather, these are warm human documents written by friends to friends, and for the most part they are designed to deal with some particular immediate situation.

Therefore, we have to seek continuously to reconstruct the situation against which the letters were originally cast. We read the New Testament letters much like we would listen to one side of a telephone conversation. We do not know what the people at the other end are saying or asking.

We can only deduce the situation that prompted the correspondence from the material in the letters themselves. Thus when we turn to Romans we must shape the situation behind it.

But first, let us meet the man who is responsible not only for this letter but perhaps also for a dozen others in our New Testament.

We need at least a thumbnail sketch of Paul's life. He was a Greek-speaking Jew. His father was an ardent son of Israel and also a Roman citizen. He was descended from the favored tribe of Benjamin and was given the Hebrew name Saul, the name of Israel's first king.

His Roman name was Paul. Thus Saul/Paul was a man with two great heritages flowing in his veins: a son of Israel and a son of Rome. He was not born in Palestine, but in Tarsus, a Greek-oriented city in the Roman province of Cilicia.

He was born in Tarsus about the same time Jesus was born in Bethlehem. The two were practically the same age. Paul's native city was an important cultural and commercial center on the main trade route midway between Europe and the Orient.

Following the wise Jewish custom of the day, his father saw to it that Paul learned a trade. The one he chose was the time-honored, practical manual craft of tent making. However, the young man was an aristocrat socially, intellectually, and religiously.

At age 15 he began his training to become a rabbi. He went to Jerusalem, where he sat at the feet of one of the most famous open-minded and large-hearted rabbis of his day: Gamaliel.

So this young man with a Roman citizenship came from his Greek hometown to Jerusalem and to a famed Jewish rabbi where he became absorbed in the law and tradition of the Hebrews. In time he embraced a set of beliefs that identified him most closely with the party of the Pharisees in Jerusalem.

Then came an episode in his life from which he never recovered. It was the murder of Stephen in Jerusalem by stones thrown from some of the very persons he had come to respect most highly.

Paul could never get away from the way Stephen died—that light on his face, that complete absence of retaliation in his heart. These were in such marked contrast to the strained, twisted, bitter faces of his countrymen who threw those stones.

But as is so often the case, Paul overcompensated for the terrible tug that Stephen's death had upon his heart. For a time he gave himself with abandon to a frightful, murderous hostility against Christians. It was bloody. It was brutal.

He became a scourge of the small band of Christians in Jerusalem and was about to extend his infamy to Damascus, the capital city of Syria, when in the fierce sun at midday on the road he was confronted by the spirit of the living God. There on the plains, outside Damascus, God in grace did what Jewish law, Greek learning, and Roman citizenship could not do. This rigid, bitter, young man, breathing fire and slaughter, making cruel havoc of Christians, was converted. He became more than a changed man!

He became another man, a different man, "in Christ." And later, as he wrote to the Corinthians, Paul said, "If a man is in Christ, he is a new creation" (2 Cor. 5:17). He wrote that out of experience. From that time on, Paul pursued his task in this world as a Christian with just as much fervor as he had pursued his task as a persecutor of Christians.

In an amazing way he combined physical weakness and spiritual strength. Paul limped and wheezed across the Graeco-Roman world, proclaiming a gospel that had made him its slave. Throughout the rest of his life he suffered an incurable disease. He spoke of it as "a thorn in the flesh."

Biographers of Paul have diagnosed it as everything from dysentery to malaria, insomnia to migraines, palsy to epilepsy. In spite of it he undertook three missionary tours that all together kept him on the road for eight years—living out of a suitcase, traversing thousands of rugged miles.

He endured incredible hardships: On at least five occasions he was whipped with 39 lashes that brought blood with every lick; three times he was whipped with rods. He was stoned at Lystra and left for dead. Four times he was shipwrecked. And he knew the insides of at least a half-dozen jails.

By A.D. 60, persecution closed in on him and, as in the case of Jesus before him, it was perpetrated by his own countrymen. As a Roman citizen he appealed to the emperor Nero for that justice of which Rome was famous.

For two years he languished in jail at Caesarea on the Mediterranean coast. Then he sailed for Rome, was shipwrecked on the voyage, but finally arrived there in A.D. 62.

It was his first visit to Rome. When he got there the city was great and prosperous —the most important city in Paul's world. It was midway of Nero's reign. He was half-crazed by now. Paul had to wait, under house arrest, until the emperor got around to hearing his appeal.

At this point the New Testament record fades out and tradition moves in. The word tradition bears is that Nero went off on a trip while Paul was in prison—either a first or second time. One of his favorite mistresses was won to Christ by Paul's dynamic witness.

When Nero got back, his concubine was gone and he was infuriated. He ordered Paul taken out on the Appian Way to a special spot where the soldiers cut off his head with a sword. That was the year A.D. 67.

But to behead Paul was not to stop him. It was to release him into a new, enduring vibrance and vitality. The man lives on in these ageless letters in our New Testament.

So, look to the situation that shaped his letter to the Romans and to us. His reasons for writing the Romans were somewhat different from those that prompted his other letters. Ordinarily he wrote because there were problems or concerns in the churches. Since he organized most of the churches, their leaders naturally came to Paul for advice and counsel. But Paul had never been to Rome. Someone else had organized that church.

So why would he write to these Christians? For one thing, he had always wanted to preach the gospel in Rome. It was, after all, the center of the civilized world. The Christians there had never met him, so he wrote firsthand just what he believed and preached.

For another thing, he longed to gain support from the Christians at Rome for a mission to Spain. Paul was always haunted by distant horizons. He never saw a ship at anchor, but he wished to board her and carry his good news of Christ to the people on distant shores.

He never saw a range of mountains, blue in the distance, but he wished to cross them and stake the claims of Christ on the regions beyond. Palestine was the eastern boundary of the empire. Spain was its western boundary, and Paul yearned to go there.

Besides, Paul had been delayed in his plans to visit Rome. His third missionary tour had been complicated by the fact that he was raising an emergency relief fund from the Greek-speaking churches of Europe and Asia to help the church at Jerusalem that was experiencing genuine financial hardship.

Raising money always takes time. So he was being held up, and the church at Rome needed to understand this delay.

Besides, his opposition had picked up considerably and there was some reason to believe that he might not live long enough even to make it to Rome. For 10 years he had been a man on the go—a busy pastor, missionary, church planter, an administrator. There had been no time to think through and to write out with care his full understanding of the gospel. The Holy Spirit impressed Paul that this was the time to do it!

So he wrote his letter to the Romans. It was the last letter that he would write as a free man and as an active missionary. All the rest of his letters came from prison. Romans was written at the height of his powers while he was at Corinth in A.D. 58. Apparently Phoebe was the bearer of the correspondence from Corinth to Rome.

She was, Paul says, "a deacon of Cenchrea," a suburb of Corinth, five miles east of the city (16:1).

What a document these 16 chapters comprise! Martin Luther believed it to be the heart of the New Testament. It became the hallmark of the Protestant Reformation. Every great spiritual awakening in Christendom has been associated with this letter.

From these pages goes forth the word that for every sin there is pardon, for every hurt there is healing, for every weakness there is power, and for every trouble there is peace.

Here is good news of release from the sin-guilty heart, the divided mind, the warring will, and from cosmic loneliness. In these pages Paul strikes four great themes that are at the heart of the gospel then and now.

First, he talks about a great deed on the part of God: "God has done what the law could not do, sending his own Son in the likeness of sinful flesh . . . he condemned sin in the flesh" (8:3).

The gospel means the power of God's great love. It means the rightness of God has come to earth through Jesus Christ.

No wonder Paul is proud to bear such good news, as he says in 1:16. But how do we know about God's great deed?

God has shown it to us. God has pulled back the curtain to let us see for ourselves. Jesus Christ has come to make things right again between God and humankind.

We mortals did not figure this truth out. We did not invent it or arrive at it through trial and error. It was not a matter of reason or feeling or intuition. God did it!

God took the initiative. The first step was a divine step. Jesus Christ came to this world. This right relation to God can now be obtained through our faith in Christ. It cannot be earned, bought, merited, bargained for, traded for, or worked out.

Not one of us can be good enough to obligate God to bestow this rightness on us; it is a gift. It comes as a sheer act of grace. That is the great Christ-deed of God.

Second, Paul speaks of a great need on our part. Read chapter 3 of Romans and you will say it is the most pessimistic page of literature upon which your eyes have ever rested: "All have sinned and come short of the glory of God" (v. 23)—not some, but all! One man—Adam—falls and fails. The whole creation falls and fails with him—creaking, groaning, sighing, sobbing. All is lost! There is no good in us. Everything we touch we soil, pollute, distort.

Some lose patience with Paul at this point. They say he is too severe, hopelessly pessimistic, narrow, outdated. So he is.

But look at the scene today. See modern man set up his democracy. Watch him try to operate it on his own. Graft and greed and corruption creep in through all the cracks. Lobbies, pressure groups, vested interests rip and tear the beautiful dream to shreds. Man knows better than he is able to do.

Observe modern man trying for decent relationships with others of his kind. He tries to bring the races together and they end up polarized, segregated, separated. He fights his war to end all wars and hurls the whole world ever after into an armed camp.

Humankind has a great, personal, incurable problem. We are sinners! All of us are! And our evil brings moral, mental, and spiritual death.

Third, Paul speaks of a great offer on the part of Christ. Read chapter 8 of this letter and you will say it is the most optimistic statement that has ever fallen before your eyes. Hear Paul say it: "Let us grasp the fact that we have peace with God through our Lord Jesus Christ" (vv. 16-19).

Following his straight, fearless, daring look at the human heart, Paul takes a clear look at the heart of God. Our awful helplessness has been met by God's awesome provision in Jesus Christ. And we appropriate that provision through our faith.

Finally, Paul emphasizes a great opportunity on the part of believers.

The last four chapters of Romans are ethical in content. Now that God has done a great thing for us; now that we are conscious of our great need; now that we have accepted the great offer of Christ, we are empowered to live the Christ life daily.

Paul says it this way in chapter 12: "With eyes wide open to the mercies of God, I beg you . . . to give your very selves as a living sacrifice, consecrated to him, and acceptable by him. Don't let the world around you squeeze you into its own mold, but let God remold your minds from within."

There are four great therefores in the book of Romans: 2:1, 5:1, 8:1, 12:1. On these four pivots Paul's ideas all hang. The result is his own definition of his own vision of the gospel and his faith in it.

Luke records in Acts 26:19 that as Paul faced the pagan king Agrippa, he said: "I was not disobedient to the heavenly vision."

And later Paul himself writes to Timothy as he faces the steel of Nero's sword: "I have fought the good fight, I have finished the race, I have kept the faith" (2 Tim. 4:7).

He did not speak of just any vision, just any faith. He speaks of the vision and of the faith that he has outlined so carefully for the Romans and for us in these 16 chapters.

So let us come with our weakness or incompleteness, our inability and awful helplessness, and let us put our confidence in Christ who will blot out our sins through the mystery of his grace. In his peace we can live. He will quench the fires, break the chains, and lift us into fellowship with himself. And through us his love will flow to all persons and to all creation for their health and healing.

Here is Paul's bottom line in Romans: "The wages of sin is death, but the free gift of God is eternal life in Jesus Christ our Lord" (6:23). Amen!

May 26, 1996

1 AND 2 CORINTHIANS

Together but not alike

1 Corinthians 1:1-3, 10-11; 3:9; 13:1-3; 2 Corinthians 5:16-21; 11:4-6

Following the book of Romans in our New Testament are two volumes of correspondence between Paul and the Christians at Corinth. We refer to these as 1 and 2 Corinthians. Both of them were written before Romans. The first of them is almost the length of Romans, and the second is not much shorter. Altogether there are 29 chapters.

Thus it can be said that in our New Testament we have a record of more correspondence with Corinth than with any other people at any other place in the world.

Paul wrote to the Corinthians during that interval of three years he spent at Ephesus from 55-57 A.D. The church at Corinth was only five years old then. Paul founded it around 51 A.D. in the course of his second missionary tour.

Let's get acquainted with this city and these people who received so much attention and got so much mail in our New Testament.

A glance at the map of Greece will show that Corinth was made for greatness. The southern part of Greece is very nearly an island, indented on the east by the Saronic Gulf and on the west by the Gulf of Corinth. All that is left to join the two parts of Greece together is a narrow isthmus only four miles across. On that narrow neck of land Corinth stood—much like an oil-rich desert sheik astride his choice camel.

Such strategic position made it inevitable that Corinth should be one of the greatest trading and commercial cities of the ancient world. All the traffic of Greece, north and south, had to pass that way, and most of it east and west came through there rather than to sail around the treacherous southern tip of Greece.

Corinth was the wealthiest city in Greece. It sported between 750,000 and 1,000,000 people when Paul got there.

The people came from all over the Mediterranean world: Jews from Rome, Orientals from Asia Minor, Africans from Egypt, Occidentals from Europe. Corinth was the empire in miniature.

The new city had been built on the ruins of an older one upon orders of Julius Caesar in 46 B.C. Now Corinth was a Roman colony and the capital city of Achaia. The official Latin had given way to Greek as the common language.

Corinth was nestled beneath a sheer cliff towering 1,800 feet above the azure Corinthian Gulf. Those entering the city from the east traveled a colonnaded road that led to the marketplace. This crowded thoroughfare was lined with shops, temples, and baths. It terminated with a massive arch crowned by two bronze chariots driven by the sun god and his offspring.

Passing the arch, visitors found themselves standing in a central square as wide as a football field and twice as long. To the south was the awesome Stoa with 71 columns.

This was swinging Corinth in the first century A.D., a city with a mass of country clubs and slave quarters. This was the site of the famed Isthmus games, so Corinth boasted a stadium seating 20,000 and a roofed theater seating 3,000.

The Corinthians were a pleasure-loving, proud, and religious people. Temples, shrines, and sacred sanctuaries dotted the landscape. The stately temple of Apollo supported by its 38 massive columns, each one more than six feet in diameter, was one of the most imposing places of worship in the world. Shrines, altars, and images to Zeus, Isis, Aphrodite, and Dionysius abounded all over town.

Yet, for all these religious forms there was a woeful absence of ethical substance. So, Corinth had the worst reputation for debauchery and immorality in all the ancient world.

If ever a Corinthian were depicted upon the stage in a Greek drama, he was drunk. Corinth has been designated the "vanity fair" of the Roman Empire. It was the London, Paris, New York, Hollywood, Hong Kong, and Singapore of the Greek world.

Above the city towered the hill of the Corinthian Acropolis. On it there stood the great temple of Aphrodite, the goddess of love. To that temple were attached 1,000 sacred prostitutes, and at eventide they would descend from the Acropolis to ply their trade on the streets of Corinth. No wonder there developed a Greek proverb, "It is not every man who can afford a journey to Corinth."

Here in Corinth business was at its highest, greed was at its coldest, passion was at its wildest, and arrogance was at its boldest. Corinth had a beauty, but it was the beauty of a cut flower. There was no heart, no roots, no soul in the sad city.

Into this most unpromising hot bed of every vice, Paul came to plant an outpost of Jesus Christ. He stayed longer in Corinth than in any other city except Ephesus. He was there 18 months, and Luke relates the whole story of that stay in 17 verses of Acts, chapter 18.

Seldom had the gospel ever been planted in more hostile soil. Yet, Paul saw the good news of God in Jesus Christ as an urban as well as a rural message.

Where Jesus had described people as sheep without a shepherd, Paul saw them as newcomers to town without an apartment. So naturally he went to Corinth. He got there in 51 A.D. following a disappointing stop at Athens.

To support himself he gained employment in the local tent-making establishment of Aquila and Priscilla, a Jewish couple recently exiled from Rome. Paul went right to work as usual, and began to preach in the Jewish synagogue.

Before long he ran into such intense opposition that he moved next door to the house of a god-fearer named Titus Justus. Here he so effectively preached that Crispus, the ruler of the synagogue, became a Christian.

Incensed at this loss of so important a person, the Jews in Corinth brought Paul before the Roman governor of the province. Apparently Gallio refused to render an official verdict. A riot followed, and indications are that the populace sided with Paul.

In spite of all this opposition, a flourishing church was founded at Corinth. It had immense vitality and variety.

The Corinthian congregation was indeed a melting pot. It included men of means like Crispus, artisans such as Aquila and Priscilla, Italian colonists like Justus and Fortunatos, officials such as Erastus, the city treasurer, and a considerable company of slaves.

So the gospel took roots in this urban jungle. The Christians began to out-love, out-live, and out-die the pagans. But Paul could not stay in Corinth. He had to travel on to his other duties.

Almost five years passed. Paul was in the midst of his ministry at Ephesus. He got bad news about the church at Corinth.

He received the news both in a letter from the church and from some members of the church who came over to Ephesus to see him. It was to deal with what he learned from these sources that Paul wrote the material in our New Testament known as 1 and 2 Corinthians.

The arrangement of our Corinthian letters is such that it appears we have only two. But remember, Paul's letters were collected and arranged without any chapter or verse divisions. In fact, the chapters were not divided until the 13th century and the verses were added in the 16th century.

What we have appears actually to be four letters instead of two. Let's review the situation.

In 1 Cor. 5:9 Paul says, "I wrote you a letter not to associate with fornicators." This obviously refers to some previous correspondence, and many students of scripture believe we have that letter contained in 2 Cor. 6:14-7:1. If so, we can call that section "the previous" or "the first" letter (Letter 1).

Then news came to Paul at Ephesus about the factions developing in the Corinthian church, along with a campaign mounting to question Paul's own preaching and apostleship. In response to all the information and to some questions the congregation asked him directly, Paul wrote 1 Corinthians (Letter 2).

He dispatched that to Corinth from Ephesus by Timothy. The result was that things got worse instead of better. Paul got so concerned that it appears he made a quick visit to Corinth. After all, it was only two or three days sailing from Ephesus.

We have no record of such a short visit, but in 2 Cor. 12:14 Paul writes: "The third time I am ready to come to you." We know of one time before that, but there must have been a second time.

His visit did no good. So Paul wrote afterwards an exceedingly stern and severe letter. He says in 2 Cor. 2:4, "Out of affliction and anguish, I wrote to you with many tears." And in 2 Cor. 7:8 he speaks of a letter "that made you sorry though it were but for a season."

Most students of scripture believe that we have this "severe letter" in 2 Corinthians, chapters 10-13 (Letter 3). Here is the most heart broken cry Paul ever made.

These chapters reveal that he had been hurt, insulted, and slandered. His appearance, his speech, his apostleship, and even his integrity had all come under attack within the Corinthian congregation. Thus we think we have this severe letter that he sent to Corinth by Titus. If so, chapters 10-13 of 2 Corinthians were actually written before the first nine chapters.

Paul was extremely worried about his stern letter. He could not wait until Titus returned. So in 2 Cor. 2:13 and 7:5 we learn that he set out to meet him.

Somewhere in Macedonia the two met, and Paul found that things had improved at Corinth. His letter had helped!

So, probably at Philippi, he set out to write a letter of reconciliation. We have that letter in 2 Corinthians 1-9 (Letter 4).

Thus what appears to be two letters in our New Testament are perhaps actually four. In all this correspondence Paul actually lifts the roof off the church at Corinth and lets us see what is going on inside.

And what we see looks awfully familiar. That first-century, large-city church was marked by so many of our current problems and possibilities.

In fact, right here we see some of the ever-contemporary things that threaten the gospel whenever it confronts an urban culture.

The Corinthians were giving first-class loyalty to second-class causes. And so are we!

The first four chapters of 1 Corinthians deal with the divided state of the church of Jesus Christ in Corinth. Instead of being united in Christ, they were split into quarreling camps. The "rock of ages" was about to become a pile of assorted gravel.

This letter begins with a foreboding sentence: "It has been reported to me by Chloe's people that there is quarreling among you, my brothers. What I mean is that each one of you says, 'I belong to Paul' or 'I belong to Apollos' or 'I belong to Peter' or 'I belong to Christ'" (1:11-12).

See the sight well: one woefully small Christian congregation in all the teeming pagan city of Corinth. Nowhere did Christians more desperately need to be united.

But instead of unity there were factions, cliques, parties. Does the situation ring real?

Nowhere does the church need more to be an integrated, unified Christian community than in an urban culture. And nowhere is it more seldom united. The city seems to divide the church into awesome cliques and camps.

Here, people have no established sense of community. They need one. So they come together in church to create family. That is the ideal.

The actual is far different. Here, communication comes hard. It is easy to distrust someone you do not know.

The problem of the church at Corinth is the problem of the church today. It is a church divided—broken into factions.

All the while a confused, lost world listens in vain for some strong word of the Lord.

Listen. Hear what the Christians say: "I belong to Wesley. I belong to Luther. I belong to Calvin. I belong to the Vatican."

In the same congregation many Christians say: "I belong to this tradition. I belong to that issue. I belong to this preacher. I belong to that teacher."

But Paul delivered his blistering broadside against all such factions that split and divide Christians.

"Is Christ divided?" he asks in 1:13. And then he proceeds in four chapters to answer that question with a resounding "no!"

Divisions emerge because persons begin to think too much about purely human matters and too little about the sheer grace of God—just as they did in Corinth.

Paul's solution for factionalism reaches its climax in 1 Cor. 3:9: "For we are laborers together with God." It is no accident that Paul said this first to a diverse, cosmopolitan congregation.

"Laborers together" never has, never will, never could, never should mean "laborers alike." Unity in diversity: that is the wild, wonderful way with the grace of God. It is the genius of the congregation that keeps its priorities straight.

So let the word go forth. There is not an issue or a challenge big enough to split a church whose first and highest loyalty is to Jesus Christ before it is to anyone or anything else. We are together, but not alike—all under the Lordship of the Christ, who alone matters.

Fort Alcan was torn down a few years ago. They found huge doors, two-inch rods over windows, massive padlocks. They found walls of thin plywood, even cardboard, painted to look like pig iron. The prisoners through the years had hacked away at the doors, bars, locks. It never occurred to them that the walls were so flimsy, so thin.

So with us: the walls are flimsy that divide us when our supreme loyalty is to Jesus Christ. Amen.

June 2, 1996

GALATIANS

Passion and principle

Galatians 1:1-2, 6-9, 11-12; 2:20-21; 3:1-5; 5:1, 6; 6:11-14

Someone has said that a good story begins with an earthquake and works toward a climax. If this is true, Paul then wrote at least one good story. It was his letter to the Galatians. In these six chapters he writes with explosive, white-hot passion. His language flows like molten lava. He scolds and scalds, pleads and exhorts, denounces and argues—all in an explosion of emotion.

The whole letter flashes and crashes like a verbal earthquake. Until, in his third chapter Paul actually says: "Oh you dear idiots of Galatia, who saw Christ the crucified so plainly, who has been casting a spell over you?" (3:1).

In reading these six chapters it is especially important to set the record straight as to how Paul produced his letters. See the situation:

Paul did what most people did in his day. He did not normally pen his own letters. Rather, he dictated them and then added his own authenticating signature. Such was the case in Romans, Corinthians, Colossians, and Thessalonians.

But with Galatians, Paul did a very unusual thing. He wrote a concluding paragraph of this letter in his own hand, using extremely large letters. He even calls attention to it in 6:11.

Make no mistake about it: Paul intended to get his point across in no uncertain terms.

So here we must not picture Paul sitting quietly at a desk carefully polishing each sentence he wrote. Rather, we must see him striding up and down some little room, pouring out a torrent of words, while his amanuensis—secretary—races furiously to get them all down.

Thus this letter is no carefully polished theological treatise. It is rather a living, moving, vibrating torrent of words poured straight from Paul's heart to the hearts of his readers in Galatia.

Actually, he was writing to friends, not foes. Paul had evangelized these people.

From the record in Acts we know that Paul visited the churches in the Roman province of Galatia at last three times—once upon each of his missionary tours. On his first journey with Barnabas they founded these churches.

Remember, they went first to Cyprus, Barnabas' island home. Then they crossed the Mediterranean over to the southern tip of Asia Minor. There Paul got sick!

In order to get him out of the hot, sultry, coastland climate, friends took him to the more promising climate in the highlands of Galatia.

Here, thanks to his illness, Paul first preached to the people of Iconium, Lystra, Derbe, and Antioch in Pisidia.

Paul knew these churches well! These people were his first converts. They represented his first Gentile fruits of the gospel.

A little later Timothy, his trusted young associate, would join him from this region. His home was Lystra. All these things added up to a very deep love and attachment for the churches in Galatia.

It was precisely this deep affection that caused Paul to react so violently to the word of their deviation from him and his message. But deviate they did!

And Paul saw it as serious. In fact, it was so serious as to evoke his most violent literary outbursts. So is born the letter that begins with an earthquake and moves toward a climax.

Someone has likened Paul's Galatian letter to a sword flashing in a great swordsman's hand. When he wrote it both he and his gospel were under attack.

If that attack had succeeded, then Christianity might well have become just a polished and enriched sect of Judaism.

Here is how the attack took shape: For centuries the Jews, Paul's physical and spiritual ancestors, had believed and firmly taught that they were God's chosen people. This conviction sprang from God's covenant with Abraham and was sealed in the Torah—that is, the law delivered through Moses at Sinai to Israel.

Thus God had given the Jews the one true way of redemption. And that way was through loyalty and fidelity to the Torah, including all its precise ritualistic and ceremonial requirements.

Now, other people were not cut off entirely from God. They had access to God, but only through the law, the ritual, and the ceremony of Israel.

Practically speaking, this meant that the door into the Kingdom of God was through the Jewish synagogues and the Jerusalem temple.

In time, some of these hardline Jews became Christians. They accepted Jesus Christ as Messiah. But remember, as they saw it, Christianity was from its beginning a movement within Judaism. They thought that the purpose of Jesus was to polish and enrich the religion of Israel.

To them it was necessary, absolutely essential, for a person first to become a Jew before that person could ever become a Christian. These people were called Judaizers.

And it seems that a particularly strong contingent of them had slipped in through the cracks at Galatia. While Paul was away, they made haste and havoc. The Galatians, who were never very stable anyway, became confused.

Who exactly was right anyway: Paul or the Judaizers? To be sure, their positions were as different as night and day. For Paul, to be human was all that was required to be Christian. For the Judaizers, to be Jewish first was required to be Christian. Who could, who should the Galatians believe?

It was to clear up this confusion and to confront the teachers of this false doctrine that Paul wrote his blistering broadside letter to the Galatians.

Interpreters differ in their opinion about the date of the letter. Some think Paul wrote it from Antioch in Syria as early as 47 A.D., right after his first mission tour to Galatia. If so, it was before the Council of Jerusalem convened in 48 A.D. to deal with the same thing. Others think Paul wrote Galatians in the course of his second tour while at Corinth in 51 A.D. Still others propose that he wrote it during his stay in Ephesus on his third tour in 56-57 A.D.

In any case, when he wrote it, both he and his gospel were under attack. The Judaizers insisted that Paul was not a true apostle. After all, he had not been actually hand-picked for apostleship by Jesus, nor was he an eyewitness to the resurrection, nor had he been ordained by the Jerusalem council of original Christians.

Obviously, Paul failed to fulfill any of these essential qualifications to be an apostolic preacher or teacher. Besides, he had been a notorious persecutor of Christians, trying to stamp out the fledgling Christian movement before it got started.

But right off the bat, Paul proudly insisted that the source of his apostleship was not a human source. No human hands ordained him to his office. No man or group of men gave him his credentials. Rather, he received his call and commission directly from God. Listen: "Paul, an apostle, not from men nor through men, but through Jesus Christ, and God the Father, who raised him from the dead . . . to the churches of Galatia" (1:1).

In spite of it, the Judaizers turned up the heat. Their message was crystal clear: if a Gentile wished to become a Christian, then let that Gentile first become a Jew. This meant that a man must be circumcised and that he must take the whole burden of the Torah upon himself.

That, for Paul, was wrong—dead wrong! It meant that a person's salvation depended upon what that person could do under the law. It meant that persons by their own unaided efforts could earn their salvation.

To Paul, salvation was a very different thing. It was entirely a work of grace. God bestowed grace upon persons, and those persons accepted the love of God through an act of sheer faith. It was a gift.

For Paul, the essential thing was not what a person could do for God, but what God had already done for that person in Jesus Christ. His argument was that faith, not works, brought a person into right relation with God. And in these six chapters to the Galatians he reiterated that argument in a dozen ways.

Paul's great principle throughout was the glory of the sheer grace of God, and the necessity of our realizing that by our own works we can never save ourselves, but can only rely in utter faith upon the love of God offered in Jesus Christ.

And he defended that principle with white-hot passion. Yet, even within this passionate defense of his principle of salvation by grace alone, Paul realized that a very serious question arose: "What then is the place of the Torah, the law of God for God's people?"

Paul recognized that the law had its place in the scheme of things. In fact, the Torah does two things.

First, the law shows us what sin is. Without the checkpoints provided by the law, we could never know the true dimensions of our rebellion. If there were no law to break, there would be no parameters, no law-breakers. So, the Torah reveals the source and the seriousness of human evil.

Second, the law really drives a person toward the grace of God. It is a custodian, a guardian, a schoolmaster that constantly shows us our weakness. The struggle to keep every jot and tittle of the law is always a losing one.

In effect, then, law drives us to despair where we see that there is nothing left for us to do but to throw ourselves in one great act of faith upon the mercy of God.

Complete obedience to the Torah is impossible. Our helplessness, our insufficiency in the end compels us to admit that there is only one thing that can save us—and that is the grace of God.

So Paul in six chapters defines for the Galatians, and for us, the Magna Carta of Christian liberty. Listen: "For freedom Christ has set us free" (5: 1).

> Nothing in my hand I bring,
> Simply to Thy cross I cling;
> Naked, come to Thee for dress;
> Helpless, look to Thee for grace;
> Foul, I to the fountain fly;
> Wash me, Saviour, or I die!

But what does all this mean to us? Simply this: there are always the Judaizers. Their names and their addresses change. The style and content of their attack may shift. The locale for their mischief may transfer from Galatia in the first century to our city in the 20th century, but the thrust of their effort always remains the same.

They insist that becoming a Christian is something you do, rather than something you let God do in Christ for you. Perhaps it is something you say or feel; a certain action, a certain statement, a certain sensation, a certain dogma. These things make you Christian, and without them you cannot ever know Jesus Christ. That is the Galatian heresy all over again.

Whenever someone puts the clamp on free access to God by faith in Jesus Christ, adding this or that to the process, there are the Judaizers at work all over again. And they receive Paul's scorching scorn; and they ought to receive ours.

One popular Judaizing tendency just now would have us believe that we can accept our freedom in Jesus Christ, but reject his freedom in the church. Take a look at the mushrooming movements that reject Christ's freedom in his church. They take many forms: a certain creed, a certain liturgy/music, a certain form or structure.

The demand is that we "do church" this carefully prescribed way, or we do not do authentic church at all. Many are the prescribers; many are the Judaizers, peddling their particular wares: language, creed, dogma, feeling, or form.

But being an authentic Christian is far more than a matter of feeling something, getting high on a wave of religious emotion, or mouthing a certain cliché or shibboleth. Being a Christian is a matter of surrender to the Lordship of Jesus Christ and to the nitty-gritty business of getting involved in the discipline of Christian discipleship. Being Christian means bearing the fruit of the Spirit (5:22). And it never comes by way of cheap grace.

Dietrich Bonhoffer, that gallant German, coined the phrase "cheap grace." It is the preaching of forgiveness without requiring repentance or church discipline. It is communion without confession. Cheap grace is grace without discipleship, grace without a cross. It is the grace we bestow on ourselves.

Costly grace is the gospel that we must respond to again and again, the gift we must ask for and receive all our lives through. Such grace is costly because it costs us to surrender, and it is grace because it compels us to follow Jesus Christ.

Such is the grace that Paul offered the Galatians—and that he offers us. Come to the Christ. Come to the grace. Come to the freedom! Amen.

June 9, 1996

EPHESIANS

Building bridges, smashing walls

Ephesians 1:1-10; 2:8-10, 13-16; 4:1-8, 11-12; 6:10-20

Legend has it that there was once a king who liked to hear a story so much that he wanted an endless story. He offered a generous reward to any subject who would tell him one continuous, unending story. Storyteller after storyteller tried for the lucrative reward, but none could tell a story without end. Finally, one day there came a man to the castle with a story about the locusts and the corn.

After an elaborate introduction he said: "Another locust came and took another grain of corn; and another locust came and took another grain of corn; and another locust came and took another grain of corn." On and on the story went, until past midnight. The king became so tired, he fell asleep.

Next morning when the king awoke, the storyteller was still going strong: "And another locust came and took another grain of corn." The king gave his subject the handsome reward and sent him on his way.

That king discovered something: there is no satisfaction in a story that has no end, no purpose, no point, no goal. A story ought to head someplace, wind up somewhere.

Paul the apostle would say a hearty "amen" to that. So, in his letter to the Ephesians, he retells the "greatest story ever told" with a special reference to where it is headed and how it is going to end. He retells the Jesus story!

By common consent these six chapters in our New Testament rank at the very top of the theological and devotional literature of Christendom. Ephesians has been called "the queen of the Letters"—perhaps rightly so.

Yet this is at heart a circular letter. In fact, the earliest and best manuscripts do not contain the word "Ephesus" in the opening verse at all.

Thus, many conclude that this letter was intended for a number of churches in Asia, not just the congregation at Ephesus.

Remember, Paul spent three years at Ephesus during his third mission tour. It was his longest personal ministry—outdistancing his stay at Corinth by 18 months.

It does seem a bit strange that in the letter there are no words of endearment, no personal greetings, no "local color" at all. There is without a doubt a sort of "official distance" here that is not found in any other Pauline letters.

Besides, there are more than 70 words in the vocabulary of Ephesians that are not found in any other letter written by Paul.

These facts taken together have caused some students of scripture to conclude that Paul did not write Ephesians. I think he did. Several things set the context.

Paul was in prison at Rome when he wrote these six chapters. It was the year A.D. 62. Measured by the expected life span of the first century, Paul was an old man.

For more than a quarter of a century he had worked and spoken and written boldly in Jesus' name.

He had never ducked a fight or shunned a controversy when it meant defending the cause of Christ.

He had already condemned schisms at Corinth, defended his apostleship in Galatia, battled the Gnostics in Colossae, warned the Thessalonians not to misunderstand his eschatology, and written his love letter to his soul brothers and soul sisters at Philippi.

Now he could look upon his work as a whole—he could see the forest as well as the trees. What is the meaning of it all? Where is the whole thing going? How are life and history to end?

Ephesians is a serious and thoughtful religious meditation, a kind of theological tract on the purpose of life and history.

Now we ought to remember that Paul wrote most of his letters in the midst of a busy ministry. He was on the road, living out of a suitcase, and wrote to meet some immediate and desperate need. His letters had been responses to 911 calls. Torrents of words were evoked. In almost every case he was racing against time.

But Paul wrote Ephesians while he was in prison. He had time on his hands. He did not have to race against the clock and the calendar. It is no wonder that the style and the vocabulary of Ephesians are different from his other letters.

These six chapters bear a striking resemblance to the letter to the Colossians. In fact, there are at least 55 verses in the two letters that are practically identical in thought.

Tychicus was apparently the deliverer of both letters. He was a native of the province of Asia, and might well have been an Ephesian. If so, he was taking Paul's letter from Rome back home.

The key thought in this well-thought-out letter is the gathering together of all things in Jesus Christ. Listen: "For he has made known to us in all wisdom and insight the mystery of his will according to his purpose that he set forth in Christ as a plan for the fullness of time, to unite all things in him, things in heaven and things on earth" (1:9-10).

For Paul, there is a purpose threading through all of history. It is God's purpose for both heaven and earth. And the agent for fulfilling that purpose is Jesus Christ working through the church.

Thus the six chapters fall roughly into two sections. Chapters 1-3 are a lyrical prayer celebrating the unity of all things in Christ. Chapters 4-6 designate the Christian church as the practical agent and arena for achieving that unity.

There is a battle in nature—"red with tooth and claw." There is a battle within human nature—and between human beings. Every person is a walking civil war. Worse still, there is a separation between God and humankind.

For Paul, this disunity can become unity only when all things and all persons are united in Jesus Christ.

Christ is God's instrument of reconciliation. Church is Christ's instrument of reconciliation.

Through Christ and his church, God is always at work building bridges and smashing walls. That is the central thrust of Paul's letter to the Asian churches.

But what is his message to us now? Exactly the same exciting thing!

Our world is a divided world. Barbed wire entanglements of clan and class and color and creed keep human from human, and humans from God. But all along God has planned to smash every barrier that separates, cut every curtain that divides, and bridge every chasm that yawns between humankind and God.

Now God does not intend to do this by homogenizing everything and everybody into one drab, oblong, religious blur. God will do it rather by penetrating all the nooks and crannies of our unique humanity and of our world with the glad, good news: "Jesus Christ has come and declared peace on all your wars." Jesus is Lord!

There were many wars and many walls in Paul's troubled world. Behind the wall of culture, the Greeks thought everyone else was a barbarian. Behind the wall of government, the Romans thought everyone else was a slave. Behind the wall of religion, the Jews thought everyone else was a pagan. There were social walls, class walls, color walls, gender walls everywhere.

Paul's point was that every one of these walls has crumpled before the relentless reconciling power of Jesus Christ. Now a bridge occupies every spot where there once was a wall.

For Paul, the tragedy of tragedies is that not everyone knows this open secret: They do not know that the hostilities have ceased. The war is over!

Thus the multitudes go right on living as if they have to be enemies—enemies to God and enemies to each other. It is tragic for peace to come and a person never know it. Consider a true incident:

One bitter cold morning in February 1958 a hunter stumbled into a police station in northern Japan mumbling, "I've seen it." He looked like he had seen a ghost. The police commissioner could not get much sense out of the frightened man, but he was convinced that the hunter had seen something. So a search party was sent out to comb the frozen woods and fields covered with snow. They were at the point of giving up when one of them poked what looked like a pile of leaves under an overhanging bank.

The mass of leaves exploded before his eyes as an apparition arose. A pair of dark eyes stared out from a dirt-encrusted face. "It" tried to speak, but could not. "It" finally put its fingertips to its lips and bowed three times—in typical Japanese fashion. Whatever "it" was, "it" was human and turned out to be as frightened as the searchers. Finally, the story came out: "it" was Liu-Liang-I.

He was 46 years old. He had been captured by the Japanese 15 years earlier in China and brought to a POW camp in Japan. Somehow he had escaped his captors and for 15 years had been hiding out. He had not communicated with another human being in all that time. He knew nothing of what had gone on around him. He did not know that the war had ended 13 years before. He thought the Japanese were still his enemies and would kill him if they caught him. He had a hard time of it—just surviving. Just staying alive though 15 bitter-cold winters was a challenge. To survive, he dug a deep hole into the earth with his knife.

The hole was just two feet wide at the top entrance and widened out below. This he lined with leaves and straw. Here, like an animal, he curled up and lived during the long winter months. He foraged the countryside during winter while the families were in their houses—bound by ice and snow. The sheer loneliness he endured was terrible.

One day he stole a rope from a farmer and would have hanged himself from a tree, but the rope broke. Liu was amazed, and took it as a sign that somehow he would not be permitted to die. So he struggled on—not living, but existing. He continued to live as if the war were still on. His rescuers gladly told him that peace had come 13 years before.

It is a parable of us and our 1996 world as Paul saw it. Must this world go on with all its walls and curtains and schisms and chasms, even though the Lord Christ has penetrated them every one to build bridges, to end all the hostilities? Paul's word to the Ephesians and to us is a resounding "No!"

We are not dealing with some visionary's pipe dream, concocted with a lick, a promise, and a rushed-up prayer. God has been working on this from the foundation of the world. That is God's whole purpose in Christ: to smash walls and to build bridges.

Listen: "For Christ is our living peace. He has made a unity of the conflicting elements of Jew and Gentile by breaking down the barrier which lay between us. By his sacrifice He removed the hostility of the law . . . and made in himself out of the two, Jew and Gentile, one new person, thus producing peace. For he reconciled both to God . . . Then he came and told both you who were far from God and us who were near that the war was over" (2:14-18).

Now we know what the purpose of God in history really is. That purpose must now become our purpose if we belong to Christ and if we intend to join him in his work in the world.

To see Jesus Christ is to know what the work of God really is. It is to know what will ultimately succeed and what will ultimately fail.

One thing a visitor, even for 10 days, to Palestine gets is a sense of his story. It convinces one that history is hardy; time is pretty steady stuff. It will smash everything finally that deserves to die.

The fate of the pure materialist—whether of Israel, Egypt, Assyria, Babylon, Persia, Greece, or Rome—is written in the ruins of a thousand splendid cities where now only lizards bask in the sun. No wonder so many of our materialistic young border so close to despair. Having lost their sense of history, they are also about to lose their sense of a future.

It is the fate of a moment: to lose the sense of history and future at the same time. Despair comes easy and often!

So, let the word go forth from this place: God has a dream for this world, and that is to unite all persons and all things under the Lordship of Jesus Christ. And if we belong to Christ, then his work of reconciliation becomes our own.

Remember that moving scene in *Madame Curie*? After the 487th experiment to isolate radium fails, Pierre cries out in despair, "It cannot be done. Maybe in a hundred years, but not in our lifetime. It is too much." To which Marie, his wife, responds: "If it takes a hundred years, then let it. It will be a pity. I dare not do less than work for it so long as I have life."

That's the spirit! That is the attitude of Paul—of Jesus—of anyone else who would join God in the work of redemption.

So in Christ, let us get on with the work—smashing walls, building bridges, shouting welcome to everyone. If God gives us a job to do, God will not withhold from us the resources to do it. The task and the resources are all in Christ.

The war is over. God has declared peace in Christ. Amen.

June 16, 1996

PHILIPPIANS

Count it all joy

Philippians 1:1-2, 12-14, 21; 2:5-11; 3:4-14

Who can analyze a love letter? That is precisely what the Philippian letter is. When Paul wrote these four chapters to the Christians at Philippi, he was addressing his very closest friends. Here, then, is a letter brimming over with love. It is one of Paul's most "personal" letters. Therefore, it is largely without system or outline, and extremely hard to analyze.

A man does not pour out his soul to his closest friends in painstaking logical fashion. Nor does a grateful heart overflow its banks in a precise, predictable sequence.

Paul had come to Philippi in the course of his second missionary journey and in response to his vision of the call from the man of Macedonia.

Philippi was a proud, sprawling, Greek city, 10 miles inland off the northern coast of the Aegean Sea.

Much of its former glory was gone by the time Paul got there. For almost 200 years Philippi had remained virtually voiceless under Rome's vast shadow.

But before that, Philippi had her days of glory. The city got her name from Philip of Macedon, father of Alexander the Great. The nearby gold mines helped Philip buy almost as much of Greece as his armies conquered.

Between Philip's capture of the city in 356 B.C. and Paul's arrival there about A.D. 50, one claim to fame fell to Philippi.

After the assassination of Julius Caesar, armies led by the assassins, Brutus and Cassius, faced other armies led by Mark Antony and Octavian. The battle they fought on the plain near Philippi in 42 B.C. was one of the most crucial in Roman history. It was there that Cassius committed suicide and that Antony and Octavian won a clear victory.

After the Battle of Philippi, Antony and Octavian were able to divide the vast Roman realm between themselves. And a dozen years later Octavian defeated Mark Antony, took over sole reign, and became the emperor Caesar Augustus. It was he who was destined to be on the throne at Rome when Jesus Christ was born in Bethlehem.

So, Philippi was a proud city when Paul arrived about A.D. 50 to found his first church in Europe.

Remember from the account in Acts 16 that he began his work down by the riverside where Lydia, a successful business woman from Thyatira, became his first convert. Strangely, both Jewish thought and Pauline theology militated against equality for women. Yet, here was Europe's first church planter—a female.

Almost immediately Paul and Silas were arrested, beaten, and thrown into the Philippian jail. At midnight, while they sang praises to God, an earthquake made shambles of their prison, and before morning they had stormed out of the debris with a jail door under one arm and a convert under the other. The Philippian jailor and his entire household were saved.

Now it was 12 or 14 years later. Paul was in prison again, this time at Rome awaiting Nero's verdict whether he would live or die.

Here in the Roman jail his mind went back to the Philippian jail and all the lifelong soul brothers and sisters he had known at Philippi. So he wrote them these four chapters and dispatched them to Philippi by Epaphroditus, the messenger from Philippi who had come earlier to Rome to check on Paul.

It is a surpassingly beautiful letter. It expresses Paul's deep and genuine gratitude for their partnership in the gospel since the first day they went to work together.

Some of the most penetrating and profound things Paul ever said are to be found in this letter to the Philippians. Here he provides that crisp autobiographical glimpse in chapter 3. And here in chapter 2 he summarizes in a single sweeping paragraph the entire mission of Jesus Christ. Philippians is Paul's ringing, lilting, shout of joy.

Recall the haunting but beautiful words of George Matheson?

O Joy that seekest me through pain,
I cannot close my heart to thee;
I trace the rainbow through the rain,
And feel the promise is not vain,
That morn shall tearless be.

The joy that seeks through pain: that is the subject of this letter from Paul in his prison to the Philippians. He traces the rainbow through the rain.

It reminds me of Martin Niemoller, a U-boat captain during World War I and a great German pastor during World War II. He was converted after World War I and became pastor of a German church. When Hitler came to power, Niemoller was thrown into prison because he refused to endorse and embrace the Nazi regime.

From prison, Niemoller wrote to a friend: "In the old days I used to be a bearer of the gospel. Now the gospel is bearing me."

The words sound strikingly like Paul's, now borne by the very gospel he had borne for so long. Hear him speak of "the joy that seeks through pain." It is the note throughout the four chapters. Listen:

- "Making my prayer in joy . . ." (1:4)
- "To the joyful glory and praise of God . . ." (1:11)
- "I rejoice . . . complete my joy." (1:25)
- "I am glad and rejoice . . ." (2: 17)
- "Rejoice at seeing him . . ." (2:28)
- "Receive him with joy in the Lord." (2:29)
- "Rejoice in the Lord . . ." (3: 1)
- "My joy and my crown . . ." (4:1)
- "Rejoice in the Lord always, again I will say it, rejoice." (4:4)
- "I rejoice in the Lord greatly . . ." (4: 10)

These Philippians formed a partnership with Paul for the furtherance of the gospel. They held the ropes while he went down into the well. They strengthened the stakes while Paul lengthened the cords.

The secret of this beautiful partnership was that from the very first it was a partnership forged "in Christ." Paul would say it was a fellowship created by grace. And right here we have our thought for the day. It is a tough thought and a tender one.

What in the world or who in the world is grace?

Lofton Hudson tells of a conversation with a friend of his who was not an especially committed Christian. His friend confessed how religious talk often confused and puzzled him. Dr. Hudson asked him, "What do you think of when I say the word "grace?" His immediate reply was "why, grace is a blue-eyed blond." And he was dead serious!

I have had something of the same experience. Right across the street from my boyhood home in Samson, Alabama, the Willie Smith family lived. They had a daughter just about my age. Her name was Grace. How well I remember as a youngster going to church, hearing the preacher say something about grace, and thinking he meant Willie Smith's girl.

Now I know that grace, like Paul means, is neither a blonde nor a brunette nor a redhead. But what exactly is it?

Well, frankly, that is where we all get out in the weather together. We use the word many different ways.

We read a newspaper review describing the free-flowing movement of a ballet dancer and find the word *grace*. A sportscaster describes an All-American basketball player's finesse and *grace*. The society page indicates the social charm and skill of a young woman as one of *grace*. We pause before we eat and someone suggests that we say *grace*. Judy Collins sang her way to stardom with a song titled, "Amazing *Grace*."

What has happened to Paul's mighty word "grace"? It has so many meanings nowadays that everyone knows what it means—and yet no one knows what it means.

So it complicates our situation when we try to find out what Paul meant when he used this heavy biblical word. But for him there was something caught up in the word "grace" that was worth getting excited about.

Yet, strangely, neither Paul nor any other biblical writer ever undertakes to define grace. They recognize that it is not possible to define grace primarily because it is an experience, a happening, an energy beyond definition.

So what we have in Philippians is not a definition, but an illustration of grace.

It is as if Paul hands us over a 16mm video cassette and says: "Look at this, and get a moving picture of grace." Philippians is a verbal video of *grace*. And what do we see?

Paul: man of Tarsus, tribe of Benjamin, rabbinic student, Pharisee by conviction, persecutor of the church, small of statue, slightly humped back, epileptic or something worse, failing eyesight, met Jesus Christ on the way to Damascus to torture Christians. Converted! Turned inside out, upside down! That is grace!

This Paul wanted desperately to preach the gospel at Rome—the hub of the whole world.

This was a natural desire. From Rome, soldiers and senators went out to rule at all the outposts on the rims of the earth. Speaking in Rome was like standing before a giant TV camera with world coverage. Whisper a message one day in Rome, and the next morning it was on its way to the four corners of the world.

But how is Paul, a poor missionary from Palestine, going to get there? And how is he going to get the microphone—to bend the ears of the movers and shakers?

Here is how: Let God give the devil a little more rope. Let violent hands be laid on the preacher Paul. Let enough lies be circulated about him to endanger his life and make it unsafe for his case to be disposed of in Caesarea. Then let the preacher, a Roman citizen, appeal to Caesar for a final verdict.

Now to Rome the apostle must go—and at government expense. That is grace!

But he still does not have the microphone. So let the prisoner have a guard—be chained to soldiers day and night. Let the guard change every six hours. That means every 24 hours Paul was chained to eight of them, but they also were chained to him. He could not get away from them, nor could they get away from him. So the preacher/prisoner bore his witness and won his guards to Christ. That is grace!

But what about the rulers and statesmen? They have to deal with the preacher too. His case demanded it; Roman justice required it. Governor Felix, Governor Festus, King Agrippa, and finally, as required by Roman law, Emperor Nero himself. And never has a prisoner borne a more effective witness to his judges and his jury than did Paul. That is grace!

What's more, other Christians throughout the empire, hear what is happening with Paul at Rome: how the prisoner gets his place and his microphone at the heart of the world, and it has an electrifying effect on them. It makes them bold to stand firm in their witness for Jesus Christ. If Paul can do it, then they can too! That is grace!

Think what Paul's imprisonment, along with his letters from prison, has meant to the world ever since, including what it has meant to us! That is grace!

There is a story out of the memoirs of the famed artist, Edwards Burne-Jones. One day his little granddaughter was not so nice. Her mother made her take time out and sit in a corner for a while. This disturbed the grandfather more than it did the child. That night when his granddaughter had gone to bed, the famous artist took his paint and brushes and went to work. Next morning the "punishment corner" was the most exciting and beautiful spot in the house. The grandfather had repainted it. He had put in a bit of sky, a flight of birds, some grass, and a soft kitten playing with its mother's tail.

So often, the "punishment corners" of our lives turn out like that for the children of God. And the process by which that happens is grace—sheer unmerited favor.

Now we know why grace is beyond definition and can only be illustrated.

Grace is God—giving God's love in redemptive relationships to us. And grace is Christians giving ourselves in redeeming relationships to others.

In grace, God's life and God's work come to be one and the same.

Thus grace is what happens between two persons in Christ accepting, forgiving, loving one another in freedom and responsibility. Grace comes totally unexpectedly, unearned, unmerited—it is the gift of God.

Now I know that sounds terribly complex. Sometimes it is. Sometimes it is not. But every time it occurs, grace is a distinctive saving kind of happening.

In a world full of persons turning their backs on one another, exploiting one another, trying to possess and dominate one another, killing one another, gossiping about one another, grace is one person in Christ confronting another freely and responsibly—just like that person has been confronted by God.

Primarily, then, grace is a face—the face of Christ and of Christians accepting one another—warts and all.

Dr. Karl Menninger tells a beautiful story in his book, *The Vital Balance*: President Thomas Jefferson and a group of companions were riding horseback across country. They came to a creek out of its banks and were obliged to ford it. Some travelers by foot had reached the swollen stream and were waiting forlornly for a chance to cross. One of the wayfarers waited until several members of the party had crossed. Then he hailed President Jefferson and asked to be ferried across. The president took him up on his horse and let him down gently on the other side.

"Tell me," inquired one of his companions, "why did you pick the president of the United States as the one you asked to carry you across?"

The man replied: "I did not know he was the president. All I know is that on some of the faces was written an answer 'no.' And on one of the faces was written the answer 'yes.' His was a 'yes' face."

That is what Paul is trying to tell the Philippians and us: God has a "yes face!"

Christ has accepted us and expects us to continue his accepting countenance and present his face to the world.

Grace is a face, the face of Jesus Christ and of Christians who are Christ-possessed in this world.

That is the grand final ground for Paul's joy—and of ours! It is the joy of a Savior who came in the form of a man of Nazareth to redeem all who would trust him.

That is what Paul means in that gigantic paragraph in his second chapter:

Let this mind be in you, which was also in Christ Jesus; Who, being in the form of God thought it not robbery to be equal with God: but made himself of no reputation, and took upon himself the form of a servant, and was made in the likeness of man: And being found in fashion as a man he humbled himself, and became obedient unto death, even the death of a cross. Wherefore God has highly exalted him, and given him a name which is above every name: that at the name of Jesus every knee should bow . . . and that every tongue should confess that Jesus Christ is Lord to the glory of God the Father.

That is grace. And it can happen here, now, in you, in me, in us.

In 1748 John Newton, a reputable seaman and renowned slave trader, pulled into the London port—sick with a fever and sick at heart. He had wearied in trafficking with trade of human beings. Recovering from his fever, he recovered from his shame. He was converted. He became a priest, and in time one of the most ardent opponents of slave trading. He wrote "Amazing Grace." Listen:

Amazing grace, how sweet the sound.
That saved a wretch like me.
I once was lost, but now am found.
Was blind, but now I see.

That is our story, too! Amen.

June 23, 1996

COLOSSIANS

A crown and a head for it

Colossians 1:1-2, 15-20, 24, 27; 2:6-10; 3:11

About 100 miles east of Ephesus in the Lycus River Valley there was a first-century "golden triangle." Here, three important Asian cities stood: Laodicea, Hieropolis, and Colossae. They reposed almost within sight of each other—one on either side of the valley, with the Lycus River flowing between. Colossae straddled the river, a few miles upstream from the two sister cities.

This region was notorious for earthquakes. Also, the waters of the Lycus and its tributaries were impregnated with chalk. This chalk collected and encrusted the whole countryside with amazing, bizarre, natural rock formations.

This Lycus Valley was a proud, wealthy region. Fine pasturelands made it a center for the woolen industry.

In addition, throughout this volcanic region there were many chasms in the ground from which there came hot vapors and springs that were famous for their medicinal powers. Thousands came every year to bathe in these springs and to drink the unusually warm water.

Strangely enough, Colossae was the smallest and most unimportant of the three cities. In fact, it was the most inconspicuous and out-of-the-way place to which Paul ever wrote a letter.

Besides, Paul had never visited Colossae personally. But while he was working those three years at Ephesus, a hundred miles away, one of his assistants, Ephaphras, had carried out a successful mission in the three cities of the Lycus Valley. From this mission the church at Colossae got its start.

In time there arose in this congregation a heresy that if it had gone unchecked, might well have meant the ruination of the Christian faith in Asia.

It was to confront that heresy head-on that Paul wrote these four chapters to the Colossians.

Get the picture: It was the year 62 A.D. Paul was in prison at Rome awaiting Nero's verdict whether he would live or die. Epaphras, faithful minister in the Colossian church, brought him news of the situation that was developing in the Lycus Valley.

There was trouble in River City. Colossae was in ferment. Paul believed that an ounce of prevention was worth a pound of cure. So he set out to check the heresy before it had time to spread.

In these four chapters he grabs the Colossian heresy by the throat and tries to shake the life right out of it.

But what exactly was this poison seeping in through all the cracks at Colossae? What was slowly but surely enveloping the church?

It was a set of false beliefs. Paul's letter itself indicates some of the elements within the heresy.

For example, the heresy attacked the total adequacy and supremacy of Jesus Christ. It questioned his role in creation. It questioned his real humanity. The heresy had an astrological element in it. It made much of the powers of demons. It insisted on the observance of special days and rituals. It laid down laws about food and drink.

The heresy gave some place to the worship of angels and other intermediaries between God and man.

In short, the Colossian heresy had all the markings that later came to be associated with that system of beliefs known as Gnosticism. So, in Colossians we see the first Christian skirmish with the Gnostics. John and others, 40 years later, would have to deal with this same set of false beliefs after they had become systematized.

But here Paul is firing the first volley at the advance guard of the Gnostic troops.

Here is the way the heresy worked. It began with two basic assumptions: Spirit alone is good. Matter is essentially evil.

So if God is Spirit and altogether good, then God cannot possibly have anything to do with this flawed and evil material world.

God, who is totally good, cannot have possibly created this world and certainly could never become enfleshed in a man of Nazareth.

So, what the Gnostics did was explain creation through a series of emanations, each one a little more remote from God until at the end of the series there was an emanation so distant from God that it could actually touch and handle matter. This was the God-force emanation that created the world.

But the Gnostics went further. Since each emanation was more distant from God, so each one was more ignorant of God. Gradually, as the series progressed, the ignorance turned to hostility.

So that by the time the God-force who created the earth was formed, that "God" was both completely ignorant of and utterly hostile toward the one true God. Thus the created world and everything in it was essentially bad. And Jesus Christ could not have possibly been a real man, or else he would have been hopelessly evil.

So the Gnostics perceived Jesus as a sort of phantom who would not even leave footprints in the sand when he walked.

Against the false teachers of this false teaching Paul raised his vigorous Colossian protest. They were trying to turn Christianity into a theosophy that was totally a fabrication. It was untrue!

If they had succeeded, then Christianity in Asia and perhaps throughout the world would have been in deep trouble. But they did not succeed. And a good part of the reason is Paul's letter to the Colossians.

Paul flew right into the teeth of the Gnostic heresy to meet it on its own theoretical and practical grounds.

Look what Paul did: he told the Colossians—and he tells us—that the God who created this earth and everything in it is the one and only God of the universe. Jesus Christ is the fullness of that Creator God. God made the world through Christ. God established humankind in Christ. God gave a complete self-revelation through Christ. Christ is the head of the church. Christ through his death and resurrection has reconciled humankind with God.

It is no secret what God has done, is doing, will do through Jesus Christ.

Moreover, Paul told the Colossians that there were no angelic or other intermediaries about whom they had to gain special knowledge. They did not have to observe senseless ascetic rituals or keep special days and observances along with their "touch not, taste not" superstitions.

All these were designed only to lead them back into slavery from which Jesus Christ had set them free!

In short, Paul pointed the Colossians to a crown and to a head for it. The crown was the crown of life and the only head fit for it was Jesus Christ's—the creator, sustainer, redeemer, and judge of us and this universe.

Listen as Paul declares his position in a breathtaking paragraph of his first chapter. He introduces us to the cosmic Christ:

> Now Christ is the visible expression of the invisible God. He existed before creation began, for it was through him that everything was made, whether spiritual or material, seen or unseen. Through him, and for him, also, were created power and dominion, ownership and authority. In fact, every single thing was created through, and for him. He is both the first principle and the upholding principle of the whole scheme of creation. And now he is the head of the body which is composed of all Christian people. Life from nothing began through him, and life from the dead began through him, and he is, therefore, justly called the Lord of all. It was in him that the full nature of God chose to live, and through him God planned to reconcile in his own person, as it were, everything on earth and everything in Heaven by virtue of the sacrifice of the cross. (Col. 1:15-20, Phillips)

Now that is a bold declaration, both for the Colossians and for us. In it Paul nails down three things that took care of the problem at Colossae. And they should take care of our problem in our city. This is where Colossians comes home to us.

First, he begins with Christ's relationship to God. Paul says that Jesus Christ is more than an image, more than a representative, more than a manifestation of God. Jesus Christ is God! Period. Exclamation! See Jesus and you see the only God there is walking this earth like a man, precisely to show us what humankind was meant to be.

Second, Paul emphasizes Christ's relation to creation. He says Jesus Christ is the instrument of creation, through him, in him, and by him—everything was made.

Without him, even now, nothing holds together. In Christ the whole creation coheres. He is the cosmic glue.

Finally, Paul stresses Christ as the head of the church. Without a head the body dies. That head now indwells the church—i.e. the body: "Christ in you—the hope of glory."

Look at the wild wonderful working of God: A Jew brings the gospel to Rome. A Roman takes the gospel to France. A Frenchman proclaims it in Scandinavia. A Scandinavian bears the good news to Scotland. A Scotchman evangelizes Ireland. In turn, an Irishman wins Scotland to Christ. And in time, the gospel gets to my foreparents and eventually to me.

That is the way it is: from the hands and hearts of strangers the church has spread. Yet through it all Christ has been the head of the body, the movement, the churches. That is the miracle of God's wild, wonderful grace through Christ Jesus.

Out of the legends of the Roman Empire comes this story: Julian, the emperor of Rome, was a friend of Agathon. They had grown up together as boys. Agathon became emperor and an apostate. One day they met and Julian began to taunt his old friend.

"Tell me, Agathon," he jibed, "what has become of your carpenter of Nazareth? Is he still around? Does he still do any little jobs? I've not seen any great things he has built lately!"

To which, Agathon quietly replied: "Yes, Julian, the carpenter of Nazareth is quite busy these days . . . Even now he is nailing together a coffin for you and your proud empire."

Just a few months later Julian was toppled from his throne. His empire gets a page or so in the history books of the Western world. But the carpenter—he works on sustaining and holding everything together.

J. B. Phillips has written a fine little book with an arresting title: *Your God Is Too Small.* His point is that we moderns do not serve a God big enough for our times. That was precisely their problem at old Colossae.

They watched the grain ripen in the fields and said the goddess Ceres was smiling on them.

They heard the sea rolling, moaning, and roaring and said Neptune was angry.

They watched the rosy fingers of dawn stretch across the eastern sky, and they said that lovely Aurora was drawing back the curtains of the night.

They saw the sun climb high into the heavens and concluded that Apollos was on his daily drive through the heavens.

When their passion ran hot and their sex impulses ran wild, they gave the credit to Venus, goddess of love.

When they fell into drunkenness and carousing, they said that Bacchus was the cause of it.

When slick, crafty diplomacy was pulled off, they said that Hermes was up to his old tricks.

When their armies began to march and "the dogs of war" strained at their leashes, they gave the credit to their war god, Mars.

Such was the pantheon of the ancients. They had an abundant supply of gods. But every one of them was too small! They left persons hungry, broken, fragmented, forsaken—lost. So Paul offered them—as he offers us—the one God big enough to help us become everything we were meant to be. And that God has a name and address: Jesus Christ of Nazareth. He is the God with sweat on his brow, sand in his beard, and blood on his clothing from walking this dusty earth setting all things right between all persons and himself.

Even now, whosoever will may trust him and find for the very first time a God not too small. You have in your hand the crown. It is the crown of life—your life.

Jesus Christ has the head for it. Hand it over, right here, right now. Affirm with Paul and with F. B. Meyer:

Christ! I am Christ's, and the name suffice you,
Ay, for me too He greatly hath sufficed:
Christ is the end, for Christ was the beginning,
Christ the beginning, for the end is Christ.

Amen!

June 30, 1996

1 AND 2 THESSALONIANS

When gratitude shows

1 Thessalonians 1:1-3; 2:17-3:8; 4:13-17; 5:2; 2 Thessalonians 2:1-5; 3:6, 10b, 11

The story of Paul's coming to Europe is one of the most dramatic in the Bible. He was on his second mission journey. He had passed through Phrygia and Galatia, and ahead of him lay the Hellespont. To his left was the teeming province of Asia. To his right there stretched the great land of Bithynia.

But he could not get clearance to go either way. Something kept driving him straight ahead—relentlessly on toward the shores of the Aegean Sea. So he came to Troas, still uncertain where he ought to go next.

And then there came to him the night vision of the man from Macedonia crying, "Come over here and help us."

So Paul set sail. And for the first time ever the gospel got to Europe. The whole territory of Macedonia—modern Greece—was saturated with memories and influences of Alexander the Great.

Just as Alexander had thought of "one world for Greece," now Paul must have thought not just of a country or a continent but of a whole world for Christ. Here in Europe the gospel would have both a great chance and a great test.

The story of Paul's stay at Thessalonica is told in Acts 17:1-10. His stay was almost as brief as Luke's account of it. He could not have been there much more than three weeks at most. But what happened in Thessalonica kicked off a chain of events that flavored his work forever.

When Paul got there about 50 A.D., Thessalonica was a teeming prosperous Greek city. Its harbor on the Thermaic Gulf was one of the largest and best in the world.

It was a proud and pompous city. In 315 B.C. Cassander had rebuilt Thessalonica and named it for his wife—who was a daughter of Philip of Macedon and a half-sister of Alexander the Great.

It was a free city. No Roman troops had ever been stationed there. Its major claim to fame, however, resided in the fact that Thessalonica lay astride the great Egnatian Road. This trade route ran from the Adriatic to the Bosphorus and then eastward on into Asia Minor. The city's main street really did connect the East with the West.

Through Thessalonica, traffic and trade flowed from Rome to the Orient. Let the gospel take root here, and it would soon spread over the whole world. Thus it is no wonder that Paul went right to work when he arrived at Thessalonica.

Jesus Christ's earthly career had ended just 20 years earlier. So Paul's preaching centered upon the basic and foundational truths of the "good news" about him. As was so often the case, Paul's preaching had little effect upon Thessalonica's Jewish colony. So he turned to the Gentiles, some of whom had become proselytes to Judaism. Here he had tremendous success!

The Jews became enraged. After a brief three weeks' stay they drove Paul and Silas out of the city in peril of their lives. Paul went on to Berea and to Athens.

Later he came to Corinth. And what exercised his mind was this: Could the gospel make such an impact on a city like Thessalonica in three short weeks that Christianity would take firm root within it?

If so, there was hope for winning his world to Christ. If not, it was an idle dream to suppose that the entire Roman Empire might ever become Christian.

So, Thessalonica was a test case! Paul sent Timothy back there to find out how the little cluster of Christians was doing. He waited anxiously at Corinth for some word from Thessalonica.

Timothy finally brought good news. The Thessalonian Christians were as strong as ever—standing firm and fast in their faith. But they desperately needed instructions that only Paul could give.

So, from Corinth in 50 A.D. Paul wrote the five chapters that we call 1 Thessalonians. What a letter it is! And remember when you read it that here in all probability is the earliest of Paul's writings to survive in the New Testament.

Students of scripture generally agree that the Thessalonian correspondence is the first thing ever written in our Christian scriptures, before a Gospel or any other letter. Therefore, it is extremely significant that the New Testament begins with a grateful heart. Here is the overflow of a proud pastor's soul.

The gospel had only a three-week chance at Thessalonica—but it stuck! So, read this letter. Feel the surge of gratitude and joy. Hear Paul's defense of his work. Listen as he encourages his friends to withstand persecution. Heed him as he gives wise and thoughtful advice about marriage and home, love and sharing, death and immortality.

But we have two letters in our New Testament addressed to the Thessalonians. Why? They are very much alike, and they must have been written within weeks of each other.

The second letter was written to clear up some misunderstanding and misconceptions about the first one. Especially was this true over the matter of Christ's second coming. In his first letter Paul said the return of Jesus Christ would come like a thief in the night. So he encouraged a readiness. He urged a vigilance.

But what he said had been misunderstood and misinterpreted. His words got twisted all out of context, and what he meant was hopelessly distorted. So he quickly wrote a second time to clear up some matters.

The first letter had created the unhappy and unhealthy situation whereby the Thessalonians did nothing but watch and wait for Christ's second coming. They needed someone to calm their hysteria and to tell them to go back to their daily work. That is precisely what Paul did in his second letter.

Its main aim was to calm their nerves and to counsel them to wait for the return of the Lord, not in excited idleness, but in the patient and diligent duties of their daily work. So Paul urged them back to their jobs and sought to balance their thoughts about Christ's second coming.

Some significant lessons are to be learned for our lives now when we review the letters to the Thessalonians. First, consider the gratitude. It shows on every page. Paul opens up his heart to these people whom he has led to Christ and established in the faith.

Remember something Charles Lindbergh said when he sighted the tip of Ireland as he neared the end of that first solo flight across the Atlantic?

> One senses only through change, appreciates only after absence. I haven't been far enough away to know the earth before. For 25 years I have lived on it, and yet, not seen it until this moment. For nearly 2,000 hours I have flown over it without realizing what wonders lay below, what crystal clarity—snow-white foam on the black-rock shores—curving hills above its valleys—the hospitality of little houses—the welcome of waving arms. During my entire life I have accepted these gifts of God to man, without knowing what was mine until this moment. It's like rain after drought, spring after a northern winter . . . I know how the dead must feel to live again.

Paul must have felt like that! So do we when our hearts overflow and our gratitude shows for something that God has wrought.

Out there on the rim of the world, in the midst of a hostile society, in a sea of idolatry was a small band of people manning an outpost in Jesus' name. Paul belonged to them! They belonged to him!

To be sure they had their problems. Those Thessalonians were a long way from perfection. But they were the most redemptive cluster of persons in Thessalonica, and Paul was grateful for that. He had helped them, but they had also helped him. Theirs had been a partnership in the gospel.

It reminds me of something that happened to Robert Newell: One day he gave out of gas on a lonely road. A friendly traveler came by, took a chain from the trunk of his car and towed the stalled car 30 miles to a service station. Newell insisted that the man take money. He refused. Newell offered to fill his tank with gas. Again he refused. When Newell insisted that he must be allowed to do something to return the kindness, the stranger simply said: "Well, if you really want to show your gratitude, buy a chain, and always carry it in your car."

That says it! The Christians at Thessalonica were carrying their chains. The church at Thessalonica was a tender community—young and fragile—but Paul was grateful for their toughness too.

Right here, I suppose, is as good a place as any to say a word that in my opinion ought to be said. Some people—inside and outside the church—are questioning whether the Christian church can survive the 21ˢᵗ century. They point to the seeds of decay that have taken root during the last decade that have slain a dozen great human societies in the past. So they ask, "Can the church survive?"

This is not the right question. The right question is whether the culture can survive the 21ˢᵗ century. So let us not be too hasty to call the coroner for an autopsy to declare the death of Christ's church. To be sure, the bride of Christ is wounded in this country and around the world, but the sickness is not fatal.

We mourn the wrong corpse! The church of Jesus Christ has served as pallbearer when nation after nation and society after society have gone down to death.

So let us share the gratitude of Paul. Christian faith is sturdy stuff. Observe China. Observe Russia and other totalitarian states. The gospel at Thessalonica was no faintly flickering fire with a few saints huddled around it to keep paganism from blowing it out.

The gospel at Thessalonica was a consuming flame—and all the city got sparks from it. So has gone the church's story for 2,000 years.

Let the word go forth: The gates of hell have been flung wide open against Christ's church, but they have not prevailed against it. The Herods have tried to kill it in its infancy. The Pilots have tried to crucify it in its days of trial. The Constantines have tried to compromise it by joining it with secular, military, and political forces in this world. The monks have tried to isolate it by taking it into caves and deserts. The priests have tried to smother it under the pale light of the altar and the sweet smell of incense. The reformers have tried to pervert it into an ally of some prejudicial cause.

Yet, "O where are kings and empires now, of old that went and came? But, Lord thy church is praying yet, A thousand years the same."

Maybe we aren't moving down Friendly Avenue at the rate of more than an inch in a hundred years, but we are moving!

And the church of Jesus Christ is the toughest, most persistent, and enduring force in this city. That made Paul grateful, and it ought to make us grateful too.

Now let us consider the confusion. Paul was partly to blame for it. In his first letter he had spoken of the second coming of Christ. He had done this especially to give comfort to those at Thessalonica who had lost loved ones.

His teaching had been misunderstood—as so much of the teaching on that subject is misunderstood today. Some of the Thessalonians had taken Paul to mean that Jesus was about to return right then and there during their lifetimes. So they had quit work and were living like parasites off other Christians. This doctrine had become the "one and only" truth for them.

How did Paul handle the situation? Very carefully and very skillfully!

He did two things: First, he insisted that the doctrine had been misinterpreted but not invalidated. The fault was not what the doctrine was doing to the people, but what the people were doing to the doctrine.

So Paul did not retract or revise his teaching. In fact, he reaffirmed his confidence in the second coming of Christ.

He simply told them that it was not the one and only truth in Christendom. Hard on the heels of that warning he did his second thing: he told the idle Thessalonians to go back to work. The very reason he had shared this great truth with them was so that the Thessalonians might better live their lives right where they were. Instead, they were using this doctrine to shirk life and to avoid it.

It is interesting to note that Paul's problem at Thessalonica was just the opposite of the one he faced at Corinth. In Corinth the Christians were giving all their time, thought, and energy to things of this world and making no room for the life to come. In Thessalonica, too much thought was being given to the other world with the unhappy result that this world was growing up in weeds.

In both cases Paul sought to correct the abuses not by denying the legitimacy of either world, but by trying to help the people see that a person lives effectively in one of these worlds only by giving proper attention to both.

We are citizens of two worlds! Ours is the task of keeping one foot firmly planted on earth and the other anchored faithfully in heaven. This has never been an easy thing. But it has always been an essential thing.

Paul's gospel has a double thrust: Jesus Christ has come! He will come again! But this fact ought to equip us *for* life rather than exempt us *from* life. The fact is, Jesus comes daily.

Remember Edwin Markham's beautiful epic poem, "The Great Guest Comes"? It is the story of Conrad, a cobbler who had a vision that Jesus Christ was coming to his little shop. He cleaned and swept and decorated his shop. He got food and milk ready.

As he waited for Christ to arrive, a beggar passed his shop. Conrad called him in and gave him shoes.

He waited longer, and there passed his door an old woman. He called her in and gave her bread that he was saving for the master.

A small, homeless child came and he gave her milk he had been saving for the divine guest. Then Markham writes:

> The day went down in the crimson west
> And with it the hope of the blessed Guest,
> And Conrad sighed as the world turned gray:
> "Why is it, Lord, that your feet delay?
> Did You forget that this was the day?"
> Then soft in the silence a Voice he heard:
> "Lift up your heart, for I kept my word.
> Three times I came to your friendly door;
> Three times my shadow was on your floor.
> I was the beggar with bruised feet;
> I was the woman you gave to eat;
> I was the child on the homeless street!"

So does Jesus Christ come daily to Greensboro. So one day, too, will he come in triumph and judgment to his world.

But this glorious truth does not exempt us from life every day. Rather, it equips us for it—fuller, richer, freer. We are stewards of this meantime.

Even so, Maranatha! Come Lord Jesus! Amen.

July 21, 1996

1 AND 2 TIMOTHY

Hooray for the homesteader
1 Timothy 1:1-2, 15-16; 3:1; 4:7b-9, 12; 2 Timothy 2:11-13; 4:6-8

First Thessalonians appears to be Paul's first letter. Second Timothy appears to be his last letter. Between these two correspondences almost 20 brilliant and busy years elapsed. The letters to Timothy, Titus, and Philemon in our New Testament have long been regarded as different from the others. The reason is that they were written to individuals, whereas all the other Pauline letters were written to churches. They are private rather than public correspondences.

Yet, these letters deal with the care and organization of the churches. In fact, in them—as nowhere else—we get a picture of the infant church growing, flexing its muscles, shaping its life and work. For this reason these three are often called the Pastoral Epistles.

Some students of Scripture doubt the direct Pauline authorship of the letters to Timothy and Titus. Their reasons range all the way from thought form to literary style.

Perhaps the key reason for doubting Paul's direct authorship is that these letters show the Apostle engaged in activities about which we are told nothing in the book of Acts. Since Acts is the essential book of history in our New Testament, we like to think there ought to be place or room for all the subsequent activities of Paul somewhere in it. But that cannot be said about the Pastoral Epistles.

Therefore, a whole new chapter has been traditionally tacked onto Paul's life in order to make room for the travels and experiences mentioned in the letters to Timothy and Titus.

Here is the way that chapter takes shape. The record of Acts ends in the year 64 A.D. It ends telling us that Paul lived at Rome for two years in a kind of semi-captivity—house arrest—amazingly free to continue preaching the gospel.

But Acts does not tell us how that captivity ended—whether Paul was released or executed.

Tradition has it that he was released by Nero not long before the spectacular fire at Rome in 64 A.D. that ignited Nero's awful persecution of Christians whom he blamed for the fire. Paul was therefore out of the city by the time Nero began to seize Christians, torture them, make sport of them, and make living torches of them.

He labored and traveled extensively for more than two years, perhaps even getting to make his long-awaited trip to Spain.

Then Paul was imprisoned a second time. This time he was condemned and executed—beheaded—by Emperor Nero toward the end of his reign in 67 or 68 A.D.

Thus it follows that the letters to Timothy are some of the last he ever wrote. He wrote them from Rome during his second imprisonment.

So much for the tradition . . . Suffice it to say we may never know precisely the facts in the case; therefore we accept the message of the letters as authentic quite apart from absolute certainty as to how Paul fits into their present form. The thoughts are surely Pauline, whether the style is or not.

Timothy received two of these "pastoral letters." Paul could never speak of Timothy without a trill in his voice and a lump in his throat. So, meet this man so central to Paul's life and work.

Timothy was a native of Lystra, a city in the Roman province of Galatia. It was a Roman colony, where troops were garrisoned to keep control of the wild Isaurian mountain tribes that roamed the regions to the north. In reality, Lystra was a little place out on the rim of Rome's vast empire.

Paul and Barnabas visited Lystra on their first mission tour (Acts 14:8ff). There is no mention of Timothy at this time. But it has been suggested that while he was at Lystra the first time, Paul lodged at Timothy's house. This could explain Paul's knowledge of the faith of Timothy's mother, Eunice, and of his grandmother, Lois (2 Tim. 1:5).

Timothy must have been very young—preteen age—but something about Paul and Barnabas' faith laid hold on him. The Apostle became his hero.

And when Paul returned to Lystra on his second missionary journey, life really began to change for young Timothy (Acts 16:1-3). Paul perceived that this eager, winsome, responsible young man might be just the person to become his traveling assistant.

So the two forged a friendship, and Paul began to train Timothy to take up his work when he was gone.

Timothy was the child of a mixed marriage. His mother was Jewish, and his father was Greek (Acts 16:1). Paul even encouraged Timothy to be circumcised so as not to offend the Jews and thereby to increase his effectiveness as an associate.

Throughout the book of Acts, Timothy is the one person whom Paul trusts implicitly: He stayed at Berea when Paul escaped for his life to Athens. He was sent as Paul's emissary to Thessalonica and to Macedonia. He was with Paul at Corinth when he wrote to the Romans. He was sent to Corinth when there was trouble in that unruly church. He was with Paul when he wrote to the Corinthians. He was with Paul at Rome when from prison, the first time, he wrote to the Philippians and Colossians and to Philemon.

Constantly then, Timothy was by Paul's side. When the apostle had a tough job to be done, he called on Timothy to do it.

So it is no wonder that Paul closed out his career thinking of Timothy and writing to him. It is only fitting that his "beloved son" in ministry should get his final letter of farewell before Paul was executed.

Now there are lots of ways to look at these letters to Timothy. I like the way J. Winston Pearce has pointed out that four times in these two letters Paul uses the phrase "This is a faithful, true, and certain saying."

The word he stresses to Timothy with that phrase is undoubtedly the very essence of his conviction about the Christ life.

It reminds me of something Alfred Noyes has one of his characters, an old astronomer, say to a young astronomer: "Listen to me now, for I have things to say that I can only tell the world through you."

So here we have it. In these letters an old man writes to a young man about matters that really do matter to him. Here an aging pastor takes a final look at his life and work, and stakes down some "faithful, true, and certain" things. Note that in these letters Paul writes as a pastor—not as an itinerant preacher, missionary, or evangelist.

You see, the pastor is not a pioneer like the itinerant preacher, teacher, missionary, or evangelist. The pastor is a homesteader. The pioneer opens up the frontier. He hacks back the forest, cuts away the underbrush. The homesteader establishes the community—building the houses, churches, schools, and trading posts.

The pastor is a guardian, a conserver of community. Pastors pass on torches. Their work is not as glamorous or as spectacular as the pioneer. But their work is crucial to the Kingdom of God. Without the pastors, the outposts are never established into frontier towns.

So, we read the letters to Timothy and feel like shouting "Hooray for the homesteader." Hooray for the people who settle in and stay by the stuff long enough to help an outpost become a frontier town.

What really mattered to Paul, then, ought really to matter to us now. So let's review his "faithful, true, and certain" sayings to Timothy—and to us.

The first is in chapter 1, verse 15: "This is a faithful saying, and worthy of full acceptance, that Christ Jesus came into the world to save sinners. And I am the foremost of sinners, but I received mercy."

It is nice to believe that Jesus Christ came into the world to save sinners, but it is not redemptive simply to believe that. My redemption comes by my accepting that he came to save *me*! Your redemption comes by your believing that he came to save *you*!

So this is the sure, certain, crucial saying: "Jesus Christ came to save you and me."

Paul was a master at translating the great truths of the gospel into down-to-earth terms. He never did that better than here: "Jesus Christ came to save sinners"—that is universal, general, inclusive. "And I am the foremost of sinners"—that is particular, individual, personal. Here is the gospel with my name and address on it—and yours also!

The J. L. Hudson Company is a giant chain of department stores. Its advertising/sales management teams have had trouble keeping the individual customer in mind. So the president put on each desk a little wooden carving. It is a typical shopper, with her feet firmly fixed and her hands on her hips. The carving is named "Mrs. Murphy." And underneath is the caption "Oh yeah, prove it to me!"

Hudson employees must never forget Mrs. Murphy. Nor can ministers and churches! The gospel remembers Mrs. Murphy, and it remembers you and me.

Paul tells Timothy never to forget that. In Jesus Christ, individuals encounter truth for themselves—right on the street where they live. That is a faithful saying!

A second one is in chapter 3, verse 1: "This is a true saying: if anyone aspires to the office of a bishop (minister), he desires a noble task."

In other words, Paul wants it clearly understood that an earnest desire to serve God through the churches as a minister is a worthy calling. We often fog up the entire situation surrounding the matter of a man or a woman deciding to serve God vocationally through the churches. We speak softly, mysteriously, even ominously of "a call."

Well, I would like the word to go forth as to how my "call" came. God got hold of my wanter! The reason I am serving you as a pastor is because I want to! I have not been trapped, driven, tricked, or pushed into this work. I did not come kicking and screaming into it.

Paul, as an old man, writes to a young man and tells him he has experienced some of the very best and some of the very worst that life can afford in service to God through the churches. He wants Timothy to want this kind of vocation.

Serving as a pastor is indeed a good work. Where else in a week's time can a human being participate in more spectacular variety?

In the seven days from Sunday to Sunday regularly for 45 years, I have had the unspeakable joy of joining families at the birth of their children. This joy has been tempered by trips with other families to the cemetery to bury father, mother, sister, brother, husband, wife, friend.

I have talked with couples about their plans for marriage, and with others about their plans for divorce. Dozens and dozens of persons have trusted me with counseling, where we have discussed the most intimate matters in their lives.

I have had hundreds of committee meetings, and have wrestled with thousands of administrative matters. I have visited hospitals almost every day, and nursing homes, and members' houses where we have shared the agonies of dwindling health and the excitement of returning strength.

I have stood with couples saying their wedding vows and talked with hundreds who are considering a church family like ours as their spiritual home. I have read and wrestled with and written weekly two sermons and a midweek worship, and have prepared for journeys out of town and out of the country for denominational meetings, mission meetings, and tours.

Where else, I ask you, can such endless and infinite variety be afforded one human being? And I would do it again if I had life to live over because I want to! It reminds me of something Dr. George W. Truett said on his 43rd anniversary as pastor:

> If Christ would multiply my life into a thousand lives this day, and if he should say to me, "You wanted during your first life to be a lawyer, but I wanted you to be a plain gospel preacher; now you may do what you want with the

thousand extra lives which I give you." I would not hesitate for as long as one second to say, "Master, if you please, let everyone of these added lives preach Christ and pastor his people to the end of them all."

That says it. It is a faithful saying. Another one is in chapter 4, verses 8-9: "Take time and trouble to keep yourself spiritually fit. Bodily fitness has a certain value, but spiritual fitness is essential both for this present life and for the life to come. This is a faithful saying."

Perhaps no more timely word has ever been written for a weight-conscious, cholesterol-conscious, diet-conscious, exercise-conscious, calorie-conscious generation. We are perilously close to focusing on bodily fitness so much that we are choking our spirits to death. Woe to the person who keeps physically fit and forgets that the spirit struggles, too, for food and nourishment peculiar to itself.

Paul's final faithful saying is in 2:11-13: "The saying is sure—If we have died with him, we shall also live with him; if we suffer, we shall also reign with him; if we deny him, he will also deny us; if we are faithless, he remains faithful."

So, Paul sets the record straight on matters of life and death, of time and eternity.

Who can ever forget Paul's incredible confidence in 2 Tim. 4:6-8? "For I am now ready to be offered; and the time of my departure is at hand. I have fought a good fight. I have finished the course. I have kept the faith. Henceforth there is laid up for me a crown of righteousness."

Woe to us if we have no strong assurance on such matters planted deep down in our souls.

Joseph Fort Newton has a surpassingly tender passage in his autobiography, *River of Years*:

A hush fell over our house. Father was very ill. Once, slyly, I got a glimpse of him—his head turning to and fro in agony. The next time I saw him he was white and still and untroubled; he was among the silent people we call the dead. On a snowy day, when a keen wind was blowing, my father was buried. Clinging to the hand of my mother, I looked for the first time into an open grave—to a sensitive child, a strange, terrifying experience.

The old country preacher adjusted his glasses and read the words of Jesus: "I am the resurrection and the life, let not your heart be troubled." Never shall I forget the power of those words. It was as if a great gentle hand, stronger than the hand of any man and more tender than the hand of my mother had been put forth from the unseen to caress and heal my spirit. From that day to this I have loved Jesus for who he is and trusted him with my very life.

God help all of us to plant these true, certain, and faithful sayings in our souls; sayings about salvation, vocation, spiritual exercises, eternal life. Amen!

July 28, 1996

TITUS

Out in the weather together
Titus 1:1-5, 15; 2:1, 7-8; 3:1-8

Titus is one of the Pastoral Epistles in our New Testament. Along with the letters to Timothy and Philemon, it is one of four personal—almost private—correspondences. It was written to an individual rather than to a church. In a way, when we read it, we are reading Titus' mail.

Titus, like 1 and 2 Timothy, appears to have been written in the interval between Paul's first and second imprisonments at Rome—65-68 A.D., along toward the end of Emperor Nero's reign.

Actually, we do not know much about Titus, the man to whom these three chapters are directed. It is most likely that Paul led Titus to accept Jesus Christ, perhaps at Iconium, on his first or second mission tour.

Interestingly enough, Titus is never mentioned in the book of Acts, thus indicating just how sketchy is our record of these years.

Moreover, twice in 2 Corinthians it is said that when Titus was sent to Corinth another brother was sent along also. This other brother is described in 2 Cor. 8:18 as "the brother whose praise is in all the churches."

This has given rise to the suggestion that Titus was actually Luke's brother, since Luke was described as the brother whose "praise was in all the churches." Thus the "we" passages in Acts are thought by some to include Titus as well as Luke journeying with Paul.

We cannot tell for sure whether that suggestion is true. Suffice it to say that from the sacred references to Titus in the New Testament there emerges the picture of one who was a trusted and valued associate with Paul. Titus was Paul's companion during an awkward and a difficult time.

Let us piece together the portrait of Titus—faithful, fellow laborer.

Paul has certain significant titles by which he calls him. In Titus 1:4 he calls him "my true child." This must mean that Titus was one of Paul's converts to Christianity.

They therefore enjoyed a common faith. Paul was Titus' father in the family and in the ministry of Jesus Christ.

In 2 Cor. 2:13 Paul calls Titus his "brother." Thus he was more than a son; he was a brother also. The child in the faith became a man in the faith. The one Paul taught and trained and nurtured took his place and went to work, no longer as a junior but as an equal alongside Paul.

In 2 Cor. 8:23 Paul designates him a "sharer in work and toil." And a bit later in that same context he says, "Titus walked in the same spirit" (2 Cor. 12:18).

Paul knew that Titus would deal with situations much as he would deal with them himself. So he frequently dispatched his young lieutenant into some hot spots.

For example, Paul sent Titus to Corinth when the pot was boiling over there (2 Cor. 8:16). He carried with him one of the most severe letters Paul ever wrote. But the Corinthians perceived Titus as one who obviously had the strength of spirit and toughness of mind to handle their difficult situations.

Moreover, Titus went along with Paul for that awkward and difficult journey to Jerusalem that Paul described in Gal. 2:1 and Luke described in Acts 15. Here the church leaders mistrusted and disliked Paul. They thought he was a heretic opening the floodgates to a heathen Gentile invasion of the church. But Titus and Barnabas stood their ground along with the apostle Paul during that tough Jerusalem conference.

And while the Christian world held its breath, the brethren decided that the gospel was for the Gentiles as well as for the Jews. From that moment on the die was cast to go into Europe with the good news of Jesus.

Titus had a gift for practical administration. He was the New Testament's first conflict manager. It was he whom Paul chose to organize the offering/collection for the floundering poor members of the Jerusalem church. And in 2 Cor. 8:6, 10 we see him developing the logistics for getting the young churches in Asia and Europe to help with the finances for the old mother church at Jerusalem.

Again in 2 Tim. 4:10 we read of Paul sending Titus to Dalmatia. Dalmatia is mentioned only here in the New Testament. It was what is now the Yugoslavian coast, on the Adriatic shore, opposite Italy. It had been for years the haunt of troublesome pirates whom Rome had constant problems subduing.

All these duties assigned to Titus remind me of something said about Dundas, the famed Scotsman: "Dundas is no orator, but Dundas will go out with you in any kind of weather."

Titus was like that. When Paul was out in the weather, Titus seemed always right there with him. They went out into the weather together!

That is always the pattern of participation made prominent by the people of God. Our partnership, our comradeship always thrusts us out in all kinds of weather together.

Thus we are not surprised to read in Titus 2:7 that Paul had sent him to the island of Crete to be a model for the Christians who were there.

Now, Crete was no easy place to model Jesus Christ. It was an island of many cities. Homer called it "Crete of the hundred cities."

The Christian church on Crete needed a tough mind and a tender heart. They needed an expert in managing church conflict.

So Paul sent Titus to encourage and train the tiny cluster of Christians there to stand together on their feet while increasing their belief in Jesus.

But look at Paul's charge to Titus: "This is why I left you in Crete, that you might amend what was defective . . . show yourself in all respects a model of good deeds."

Here was Paul's greatest compliment to his trusted young associate. He sent him to a wild and wooly Mediterranean island not just to talk to them about what a Christian should be and do, but to show them what a Christian should be and do.

My friends, that is precisely the task awaiting us in our city and in our world right now. Our task is to be a model of what it means to be a Christian right here, right now. We must *say* our word by *doing* our deed.

Remember Carnegie Simpson's fine volume, *Recollections*? At one place he tells of seeing the famed Passion Play at Oberammergau. Anna, the daughter of Anton Lang, was playing the part of Mary, the mother of Jesus. Afterward, Dr. Simpson was talking with the Lang family. He expressed his appreciation for "the play." Anna explained: "That is not a play, sir; it is an act of worship."

That says it! For a Christian, all of life is an act of worship. This does not make life heavy, somber, or drab. Rather, this makes life light, free, exciting—all of it lived "out in the weather" under the Lordship of Jesus Christ.

Someone said of the poet Emily Dickinson that she was star dust, lightning, and fragrance—all mixed together behind a smile. That is a good model of what it means to be a Christian here and now.

But how do we make all of life an act of worship? How do we model Christ in our world?

McLeod Bryan has said that there are three levels of the imitation of Christ:

One, the "Xerox copy" level: On this level, a person attempts to duplicate the Jesus model in the modern world. Frequently such a person inquires whether Jesus would smoke, drink, drive a sports car, play cards, attend a segregated school, sleep in a homeless shelter, serve in the military, etc. Then on the basis of a perception of what exactly Jesus would do, the person seeks to duplicate those self-same actions now.

Two, the creative imagination level: On this level, imagination is guided by the model of Jesus and the result applied to new and changing situations. Here the emphasis is not on duplicating precisely Jesus' first-century actions in the 20th century. The emphasis is on trying to imagine what behavior Jesus Christ would embrace under similar conditions. For example, would Jesus run for political office? Would he take a public stand on abortion, AIDS therapy, prayer in public schools? Would Jesus work in a plant manufacturing lethal weapons? Charles Sheldon's all-time best-seller, *In His Steps*, espouses this view.

Three, the lifestyle of grace level: On this level, the Christian tries to live a lifestyle of being "saved by grace." Here the imitation is based on a profound awareness of what God has done for us in Jesus Christ and our response in kind to this act of redeeming grace. Then the model becomes the saved person living a lifestyle in response to God's gracious example. Here, as Luther said, "Grace precedes example always."

We are redeemed in order to show what it means to be redeemed. We are liberated precisely in order to act responsibly in helping to liberate others.

Christians, therefore, may differ as to the minute details of their following Christ. Some can be Republicans, some Democrats. Some cheer the Wolf Pack, some the Tar Heels. Some may live in comfort, some in poverty. But all are under mandate to be a model of the Christ life in this world.

Thus the imitation of Christ means that the sin-enslaved person has been set free to live the lifestyle of one "saved by grace!"

So here we are out in the weather together. Our mandate is: be a model of Christ (*Imitato Jesu*).

We do it now just like Titus did it then: by remembering what God has done for us in Jesus Christ and living in response to that act of amazing grace.

William J. Reynolds has summed it all up in a fine 1990s song. He defines the "Christ model" for us:

How do you share the love of Jesus with a lonely man?
How do you tell a hungry man about the bread of life?
How do you tell a thirsty man about the living water of the Lord?
How do you tell him of His Word?

How do you tell a dying man about eternal life?
How do you tell an orphan child about the Father's love?
How do you tell a man who's poor about the wondrous riches of the Lord?
How do you tell him of His Word?

How do you tell a loveless world that God Himself is love?
How do you help a man who's down to lift His eyes above?
How do you tell a bleeding man about the healing power of the Lord?
How do you tell him of His Word?

People who know go to people who need to know Jesus
People who love go to people alone without Jesus
For there are people who need to see,
People who need to love
People who need to know God's redeeming love.
People who see go to those who are blind without Jesus
And this is people to people, yes,
People to people
All sharing together God's love.

You go and do likewise! Amen.

August 11, 1996

PHILEMON

Born bound—reborn free
Philemon 10-12, 15-18

He lived in the old city of Colossae. He was a young man who had his visions and dreamed his dreams. But he felt himself held out of life's big game because he wore a chain. His name was Onesimus, and he was a slave belonging to Philemon in a big house at Colossae. He stood on the sidelines just as long as he could. He decided to make a break for freedom.

So, one night he slipped out of the slave quarters into his master's great house. There he armed himself with food, clothing, and a considerable store of his master's gold. Thus equipped, he slipped out through a window, hugged the shadows, and hit the road for open country.

He was free at last. He had taken the bridle off. Now, could he ride the wild horses? Onesimus hurried to hide himself in nearby Ephesus. Strange isn't it, how quickly a free man will trade his liberty for safety?

Not quite sure he was safe at Ephesus, he made his way to that teeming game preserve of the first century—Rome. Here any man could trade off his liberty for the security of a place to sleep and a bite of bread. Here he could become nameless and faceless, homogenize into the masses. Here he could lose himself long enough to find himself, while remaining anonymous. Here at Rome, Onesimus was safe at last. Of course he made friends, such as they were—and fast friends too.

Not many days passed, I imagine, before a fellow occupant of Rome's back streets sought him out to say: "Have you heard, Onesimus, there is to be quite a spectacle in the arena today? Word is that Emperor Nero has a great sport planned. Wouldn't you like to go?"

"I would like to well enough," the young fugitive answered. "But you see, there is a price on my head and I had best stay out of sight."

"No one could possibly recognize you," urged his newfound friend. "You can hardly afford to miss this spectacular."

"Word is that the emperor has some Christians caught over there. And he has some lions that have not had a bite to eat for a week."

"It will be great sport when the two meet in Rome's arena. It will take a man's mind off his troubles."

"All right," Onesimus answered with mounting excitement. "Since my master, Philemon, was a Christian, I'll go and see a few of them mauled just out of respect for him."

So he went to the Circus Maximus that day. And some show it was! One after another, men and women from Nero's prison fell before the claws and fangs of the hungry beasts. Rich, red Christian blood flowed free.

But on the faces of those who were dying, Onesimus noticed a strange and unexplainable tranquility. What did it mean that these people could die with such signs of peace on their faces?

Now the bloody business was over. Almost nauseated, Onesimus walked silently through the crowds with his friend from the back street.

He scarcely noticed a third man who came alongside of them—a man in whose eyes showed the excitement of a great discovery. He watched Onesimus for a while as they walked. He knew something haunted him!

Then, as if to test him, he made in the dust with his stick the sign of a fish. It was the password among Christians. In their language the spelling of that word "fish"— *IXΘUS* (Iota, Chi, Theta, Upsilon, Sigma)—was a code word for their basic confession: "Jesus Christ, Son of God, Savior."

Young Onesimus recognized the sign at once. It half-frightened and half-angered him. Then he replied heatedly, "No! No! Not on your life am I one of them. I am no Christian!"

"Well," said the man with the stick, "I am sorry you are not. It has made all the difference in the world to me. I have a friend in town I would so like for you to meet. His feet have marked all of Rome's roads. He is much traveled. He is a fighting man. There is hardly a square inch of his body that does not bear a scar. He is a learned man. You could rub enough learning off his coat sleeve to make you a scholar. He is a prisoner now in Nero's prison right here in Rome. His name is Paul, from Tarsus. I do so wish that you could meet him. Methinks you could find something very much alive in conversation with him."

With that the third man was gone. The days and nights that immediately followed were filled with pondering. Paul! Paul! Somewhere Onesimus had heard that name.

Now, like a flash, he remembered. It was that day in Ephesus when his master, Philemon, had an audience with this touring preacher Paul. He had driven the chariot that day and had stood by half-listening as the two men talked.

And strange talk it had been too—talk about forgiveness, freedom, and fullness of life. Now young Onesimus recalled all this against the backdrop of those peaceful, dying faces he had seen in the arena. Not many days later, partly because he was homesick and partly because he was heartsick, Onesimus went to Nero's prison and sought out Paul, who was under "house arrest."

See the sight well at that prison: Paul, the bound man, was free. Onesimus, the "free" man, was bound.

There and then with sensitivity and love that bordered on genius, Paul introduced the runaway slave to Jesus Christ. In that encounter, "a good for nothing" was transformed into "a good for something" and eternal purpose was injected into the life of a drifter.

In the language of his countrymen, Onesimus' name meant "useful." Now, this young man was not only Onesimus by name; he was Onesimus by nature.

And the great lesson comes home to us. Here is a man born bound, but reborn free! This is the very same pilgrimage marked so vividly in every one of our fugitive lives!

You see, the tyranny of a man in the raw is that he is dissatisfied with both his slavery and his freedom. It is the genius of Jesus Christ to help a person blend these two together. For, you see, in Christ, freedom is bondage to the right things.

But note the strategy. Onesimus had run head-long into a mystery. He had hit the road, running away from Philemon's chains, and had run head-on into some other chains of his own choosing.

Here at Rome he had made such a sorry mess of his liberty. He was ready to trade it off for safety—just a place to sleep and a piece of bread. Someone had to help him loose those chains also. But who? And how?

The question is both proper and timely. Two things are staked down indelibly in this page snatched out of one man's spiritual autobiography.

In Christ, beginning again always begins with an individual under conviction.

Onesimus had shaken Philemon's chains, only to sulk around the alleys of Rome bound to his own feelings of guilt. It looked so automatic when he hit the road. He slipped away from his master's house, under the cover of darkness; his young blood surging; his young heart singing "Philemon, don't fence me in."

He would forever after live out his days in the exuberance of a man set free: no more chains with Onesimus' name on them!

No one would tell him what to do or when to do it: no rules to suppress his gaiety, no advice on how to spend his gold, no stuffy religion to hem him in. With a toss of the head, he left all these behind. Just a toss of the head, and he was free!

But Onesimus banged into some raw reality. It had been easier to live with Philemon at Colossae than it was to live with himself at Rome. He came to grapple with that hidden out-of-sight part of himself, that portion with which he thought he was finished.

In time he found that there are chains on the inside of a person. Until these are gone, that person is bound. In short, if Onesimus were ever really free, he would have to be freed from Onesimus just like he had been freed from Philemon.

Until persons take responsibility for their own lives—guilt, decisions, actions—then all others are helpless to help them.

Onesimus had banged up against a hard reality. The poet describes it like this:

I have to live with myself, and so,
I want to be fit for myself to know;

Always to look myself straight in the eye;
I don't want to stand with the setting sun
And hate myself for the things I have done.

I don't want to think as I come and go
That I'm for bluster and bluff and empty show.

I never can fool myself—and so,
Whatever happens, I want to be
Self-respecting and conscience free.

That is the basic heart hunger of every human. And that is the genius of Jesus Christ to prepare human beings "to look themselves straight in the eye, and fit them to live with themselves." Jesus Christ frees a man from himself. Jesus Christ frees a woman from herself—and the unsavory brew they always cook up when left alone in the kitchen.

Onesimus came to a teachable moment. He learned a hard lesson, and so must we. That freedom of his from Philemon did not pass out the way he had planned. The more he got what he wanted, the less he wanted what he got.

Freedom, you see, is not so much a matter of "rights" as it is of "the right." Dr. Buttrick speaks the truth: "Nero had all the rights in the world, but he used them every one to make himself a scoundrel."

That same paragraph could be written in the biography of us all. Freedom is of the Spirit. Freedom is within, as well as without.

Jesus Christ said it like this: "You shall know the right (truth) and the right shall make you free." There are chains that bind us on the inside. Until these are loosed, we can never really begin again. In Christ, beginning again always starts with an individual under that conviction. In Christ, beginning again also involves other persons who will help.

Not one of us lives on a private street or in a private room. Onesimus soon learned that his freedom in Rome was tied up with his unsettled business at Colossae. Before he could be finally free, he must go back to Philemon and set matters right with him.

That is where Paul's beautiful, one-page, personal letter comes in. In these 25 verses he contends with Philemon, the master (vv. 10-12), for Onesimus, the slave (vv. 15-18).

Before we can comprehend the intensity of this situation, we must understand the slave culture of the first century. In that world a slave was not even a person. He was rather a thing, a tool, a piece of property. He was totally and absolutely owned and possessed by the master. A master had absolute power of life and death over slaves—and that power was sanctioned by law.

To make bad matters worse, slaves were deliberately kept pushed down. Their existence posed a constant threat. The slightest move toward freedom or revolt was brutally crushed. A rebellious slave did not live past sundown. And if a slave ran away, like Onesimus, he was branded by a red-hot iron on the forehead with an "F," meaning *fugitive*—a runaway. He could also be tortured or even crucified as an example of his misconduct.

Paul well knew all this. He knew also that slavery was so ingrained in his world that even to send Onesimus back to Philemon, the Christian leader at Colossae, constituted a considerable risk.

Yet, Paul gave Onesimus the letter we have in our New Testament and sent him back to Philemon at Colossae.

Now we know that in Christ, personal liberty is empty apart from Christian community. There is no absolute individual freedom. In Christ, my freedom is always wrapped up in someone else. Every person is hemmed in by other persons who make up the solidarity of life. There was a time when we did not have to take our brother or our neighbor so seriously. But that time has passed!

The global community is here! There has never been anything like it before in the history of Planet Earth. The community of humankind has reached out and tied all of us up. Since Apollo we have known that all wars are civil wars.

Rugged individualism has run into something just as rugged as itself: a complicated, interrelated world community in which every person is linked up in life with other persons. The "me generation" has yielded the "we generation."

Most of us have not yet realized just how rugged this reality is. It has thrown all our notions of freedom into confusion. Little wonder we are all mixed up!

Mere freedom unto oneself and within oneself is not only immoral; it is also impossible. Like Onesimus of old, we are becoming painfully aware that our freedom in our house is all wrapped up with the liberty of others in someone else's house. Will we ever learn that we cannot really enjoy our freedom until all our neighbors enjoy theirs?

The liberty we have in Jesus Christ seeks not its own, but loves and serves the whole human family.

So, sad Onesimus, dissatisfied with both his slavery and his "freedom," found in Jesus Christ the solution for both.

So far as we know, Philemon received Onesimus home gladly; forgave and restored him!

Bob Bartlett, that irrepressible explorer, tells an arresting story: On a voyage one summer he and his associates were bringing back a large number of caged birds. In the mid-Atlantic one restless bird escaped from its cage. In utter freedom that bird flew away, and they watched as it became a tiny speck over the ocean. They all agreed: "that one is gone." But after several hours, to their surprise, they saw the bird flying back. This time, with heavy wing, it was heading for the ship. Panting and breathless, the feathered prodigal plopped onto the deck. Over the trackless ocean it had come to seek desperately that ship. It was for that bird no longer a prison, but a home—its only passage across the deep.

So with us all! We batter and bruise ourselves in vain attempts to get away from the presence of God. We find at long last that God is our only passage across the depths.

Pray God that all our excursions into the air of false freedom will bring us back alive to say: "Make me a captive, Lord, and then I shall be free." "For if the Son makes you free, you shall be free indeed" (John 8:36). Amen.

August 18, 1996

HEBREWS

This way to God

Hebrews 1:1-4; 2:1, 3-4; 4:14-16; 9:11-12; 11:1-3; 12:1-2; 13:8

Hebrews has never been an easy book to read. E. F. Scott has called these 13 chapters "the riddle of the New Testament." The knowledge that Hebrews demands of the Old Testament and of the Jewish sacrificial system never has been the possession of every person. Therefore, this scroll was difficult for the people to whom it was first addressed, and it is difficult for us.

These 13 chapters appear to be more a carefully written sermon or tract than they do a letter. They are intricately constructed and written in perhaps the most highly polished Greek in the New Testament.

It is obvious that the writer of Hebrews had a double background. He had a Greek heritage. And to the Greeks, somewhere there was a real world of which this world is only a poor, shadowy, imperfect copy.

Here we can only guess and grope about reality. Here we can work only with shadows and copies and imperfect patterns. But in the unseen world of pure forms, there are the real things, the perfect things as God conceived them.

Thus the great task in this life is to get away from the shadows and imperfections and to reach reality.

That is exactly what the writer to the Hebrews claims that Jesus Christ enables us to do. To the Greek he says: "All your lives you have been trying to get from the shadows to the truth. That is exactly what Jesus Christ enables you to do."

This writer also had a Hebrew background.

For the Jew it was always a dangerous thing to come too near to God. So there were developed intermediaries between the individual and Yahweh. These included: the covenant, the Torah (Law), the sacrificial system, the priesthood.

But at best, all these could do was to provide temporary access to God. All the rituals of the priest, all the bloody details of the sacrifice had to be repeated over and over again—week in, week out; year in, year out.

What the people needed was a perfect priest and a perfect sacrifice that did not need to be repeated each and every year.

The writer of Hebrews says that is exactly who Jesus Christ is. To the Jew he says: "All your lives you have been looking for the perfect priest who can bring the perfect sacrifice and give you perfect access to the perfect God forever. That is what you have in Jesus Christ."

So he has a word from both the Greek and the Hebrew streams of his heritage: Jesus Christ is the one person on earth who gives access to reality and access to God at the same time. That is the key thought of this book.

But who wrote it, when, and why? These are questions all shrouded in mystery. The information furnished by the letter itself indicates that it was most likely written to a relatively small cluster of Greek-speaking Jewish Christians at Rome between the reigns of Nero and Domitian—perhaps around 80 A.D.; certainly during the last quarter of the first century.

We honestly do not know who wrote these 13 chapters. The title in the earliest days was simply "to the Hebrews"—i.e. "to the Jews." No author is given.

In the earliest days no one directly related the letter to Paul. Neither the style, the thought, nor the theology is Pauline.

In fact, Origen, one of the early church fathers, said: "Only God knows for certain who wrote the letter to the Hebrews." Tertullian, Jerome, Augustine: all wondered about the authorship, agreeing that it was not a letter of Paul. Martin Luther and John Calvin both declared that the letter was not Paul's.

In fact, never in the history of the early church did students of scripture ever really think that Paul wrote Hebrews. Yet it became placed in the New Testament within the cluster of letters written by Paul. So in 1611 the editors of the King James Version followed a tradition common in the 17th century and titled it "The Epistle of Paul the Apostle to the Hebrews."

Now we know that was simply their editorial opinion, those translators' own comments, and was in no way a part of the early text.

Tertullian thought Barnabas wrote Hebrews. Martin Luther believed Apollos wrote it. But when all is said and done, Origen is nearer the truth: "only God knows who wrote Hebrews."

As always, the message lies beyond the messenger. The word is authentic and has been accepted as such by the worshiping Christian community for almost 2,000 years.

And what is the word from Hebrews? First, let's remember that religion has never been and can never be the same thing to everyone. Broadly speaking, there have been four great concepts of the Christian religion.

1. Christianity is inward fellowship with God. It is union with Christ so close that the Christian actually can be said to live "in Christ." That was Paul's concept of Christian faith.

2. Christianity is a standard for life and a power to reach that standard. It is the rule for a good life, and it is the power to keep that rule. This is what Christian faith was to Peter and to James.

3. Christianity is the highest satisfaction of the mind. For some people their intellects search and search until they find their rest in God. On the whole, that is what Christian faith was to John.

4. Christianity is access to God. It is that which brings persons into the very presence of reality and of God. It removes the barriers, takes away the estrangements, and opens the doors into fellowship with the Living God. That is what Christian faith was to the author of Hebrews.

The first word in his letter, as he originally wrote it, is "God." He begins where the first verse of Genesis begins. With that vaulted idea of God, his mind is haunted and dominated.

He found in Jesus Christ the one person who could provide access into the very presence of God. So he placarded one essential thought over the entire 13 chapters: "This way to God . . . Let us draw near."

If the writer of Hebrews had one text and one summons, it would be "Jesus Christ is the way to reality and he is the way to God."

But all this is objective! How could his readers—how can we—make this truth become subjective? How can we make it ours?

His answer is both swift and cryptic! *By faith!*

And right here is a word that permeates this book like no other. These pages virtually seethe with the meaning of faith. "Faith" covers Hebrews like the dew covers Dixie.

In Hebrews, faith is not only defined; it is demonstrated. In fact, the writer supposes that the only adequate definition of faith is a demonstration of it. For him—and for us—faith is not merely a belief but an intellectual activity.

Faith is energy that drives and propels the whole personality into a reliance upon God. He says it like this in his massive 11th chapter: "Faith means that we are certain of the things we hope for, convinced of the things we do not see" (11:1).

Then he illustrates what he means by a chapter-full of persons who did what they did because they believed. He hands over a video for our spiritual VCR; provides a documentary on what faith can do.

To all appearances, what these persons did was utter folly at the time. Faith is never a hope that takes refuge. It is hope founded on a conviction, on a reality.

So the writer of Hebrews causes us to redirect our thinking about faith. It is certainly not what the school boy said when he defined faith as "believing what you know ain't true."

Nor is it the procedure embraced by Alice in Wonderland when she banged up against something hard to believe. She was advised to "shut your eyes, draw a deep breath, and try again."

Suppose I did this believing that drinking cabbage juice would cause me to sprout another set of ears. That would not be faith. That is superstition.

Faith is entrusting the whole personality—mind, will, emotions—to another. Christian faith is trusting God in Christ with our entire life. And the best way to explain that is to do it! But how do we *do* faith?

We faith God in much the same way we faith a bridge. And how do we faith a bridge? We drive over it. We walk across it.

We faith God the same way we faith a chair or a pew. And how do we faith a chair or a pew? Sit on it!

We faith God the same way we faith an airliner and its crew or a surgeon and his scalpel. And how do we faith them? Fasten our seat belts and take off into a habitat entirely unnatural for humans. Go to sleep and let someone cut a gash in our bodies just to make us well.

To faith God is to trust our whole being into God's keeping. It is to believe that when the mind comes to its jumping-off place, there is God.

Corita Kent is a nun-turned-artist. She said it like this: "To faith God is to know that all the rules for my life will be fair, and that there will be wonderful surprises."

Lillian Smith in her fine book, *Killers of a Dream*, says that there are two journeys every human must make: one, into himself/herself, accepting what is found there; the other, into the world, accepting that he/she belongs there—making it home.

It is through this process of adventuring into ourselves and into our world that Jesus Christ, through faith, gives us access to reality and to God. This is the major thrust of the message of Hebrews.

But the writer has another thrust also. He touches on it in his famed 12th chapter, which opens with one of the best known passages in the New Testament:

> Therefore, since we have so great a cloud of witnesses enveloping us, let us strip off every weight, and let us rid ourselves of the sin which so persistently surrounds us, and let us run with steadfast endurance the race that is marked out for us, and as we do so, let us keep our gaze fixed on Jesus who, in order to win the joy that was set before Him, steadfastly endured the cross, thinking nothing of its shame and has now taken His seat at the right hand of the throne of God. (vv. 1-2)

In living the Christ life we have a goal. Christians are not unconcerned joggers trying to shed a few pounds. Christians are not tourists who return each night to the same hotel with their luggage. Christians are persons forever on a journey. They are going somewhere.

The goal of our journey is nothing less than Christ himself—his presence and his pattern for our lives.

That is where the Christian life is headed. And it would be well if at the end of each day's journey we asked: "Am I any farther along?"

Dr. Ralph Sockman relates an episode out of the 1948 Summer Olympics: He was seated right in front of the grandstand where the second and third runners exchanged batons in the four-man international relay. In one of the races the French team had built up an early lead. The first two runners had moved out a surprising distance in front. But in the exchange the third runner dropped the baton. His team was out of the race. He stumbled to the nearby turf, held his head in his hands, and wept uncontrollably. Teammates had to help him out of the stadium, he was so badly shaken.

Dr. Sockman says he knew what it meant. To take defeat so tearfully meant that he felt just how many people were affected by his failure: his watching countrymen, his teammates who had run so well before him, his teammates who never got to run behind him.

Life is actually like that. It really is a relay. We all pass the baton. Hebrews 12 puts up a placard: "Don't look now, but someone is following you."

So, we are reminded of the scores who have helped us on our journey. And that is so easy to forget—the continuity of our lives.

I am told that if any one of us could trace our complete family tree back a thousand years, we would find 20,000,000 relatives—lives directly surrounding our own. Moreover, no two persons alive today can be more than 60th cousins removed. We forget them only at our peril. There really is a circle of life.

This fact reminds me of something. Mark Hopkins, venerable president of Williams College, once told: The son of a wealthy alumnus/patron of the college had damaged some property. He had been brought to President Hopkins where he flippantly offered to pay for the damage he had done. To which President Hopkins replied: "No student can pay with a wallet for what he gets at Williams College. Who could pay for the sacrifices Colonel Williams made, and all the contributions of the benefactors of this school? No matter what his bank account, every student here is a charity case!"

Aren't we all? We are everyone counted on by a great cloud of witnesses who have journeyed before us. And we are counted on by those coming after us. We all run a relay!

On the 300th anniversary of Harvard University, a group of students took a banner and paraded down one of the streets at Cambridge. The banner read: "This university has waited 300 years for us."

It may sound a bit arrogant, but it is nonetheless true. "This church has waited 137 years for you." (First Baptist Church, Greensboro, was founded in March 1859.) It is the unavoidable sentiment of those who catch a gleam of what the writer of Hebrews is trying to say.

"Run, Christian, run toward God; and don't drop the baton." Amen.

August 25, 1996

JAMES

Let's be practical
James 1:1-3; 2:1-5, 8-9, 14-18

Seven short letters follow the book of Hebrews in our New Testament. One bears the name James. Two bear the name Peter. Three bear the name John. And one bears the name Jude. None of them are addressed to specific individuals or churches. Rather, their contents are thoroughly general. Thus, these seven letters are frequently called "General Epistles" or "Universal Letters."

The first of these letters consists of five chapters—108 verses—and is attributed to James. This book has had the hardest struggle of all to get into the New Testament and to stay in it. There have been persons through all the years who have tried to kick it out of the canon.

The most recent and perhaps the best known of these to us was Martin Luther. In the concluding paragraph of his *Preface to the New Testament* he passes his famous verdict on James:

> The gospel and the first epistle of St. John, St. Paul's epistles, especially those to the Romans, Galatians, and Ephesians; and St. Peter's first epistle are the books that show Christ to you. They teach everything you need to know for your salvation, even if you were never to see or hear any other book or hear any other teaching. In comparison with these the epistle of James is an epistle full of straw, because it contains nothing evangelical.

Luther took such a dim view of James because in his judgment it comes perilously close to teaching salvation by works. This he saw as a direct contradiction of Paul's great teaching of salvation by faith.

Besides, the book of James mentions Jesus Christ only twice—and then only incidentally in the first verses of chapters 1 and 2.

Not once does it give any reminder of Jesus' death and resurrection—the heart of the Christian gospel. The burden of this book is ethical rather than theological. The author was profoundly occupied with the practice of Christianity.

In fact, there appears to be a placard written big and bold and bright over these five chapters. The placard reads: "Let's be practical!"

This may be one of the lesser books in the New Testament, but it is also one of the boldest. This writer is unexcelled in telling Christians where the action is. He reminds all of us profoundly to make our faith work, or like a muscle we never use, it will dry up and dwindle away.

And who exactly is the author of James? To say that this question has been disputed is to deal in understatement. It has been rather hotly debated through the years.

One of the reasons is that there are no less than five Jameses named in the New Testament. Any one of them could be our author. Let's review the Jameses:

- James, the father of Jesus' disciple Judas, not Iscariot is mentioned in Luke 6:16. Nothing whatsoever is known about him.
- James, the son of Alphaeus, one of Jesus' 12 disciples is mentioned in Matt. 10:3, Mark 3:18, Luke 6:15, and Acts 1:13. He might well have been Matthew's brother.
- James, the son of Zebedee, one of Jesus' disciples was the brother of John. He is mentioned several times in the Gospels. He was beheaded in A.D. 44 on orders of Herod Agrippa, and was the first of the apostolic band to be killed.
- James, the Little (the Less is mentioned in Mark 15:40, Matt. 27:56, and John 19:25): we know nothing more of him.
- Finally, there is the James who is called the brother of Jesus.

Despite the efforts of some to make Mary a perpetual virgin even after Jesus' birth, it is clear from the New Testament that Jesus was her firstborn son. She and Joseph had other children as we see in Mark 6:3, Matt. 13:55, and John 7:5.

In 1 Corinthians 15, Paul provides a list of the post-resurrection appearances of Jesus. In that list we find these words: "After that, he was seen by James" (15:7).

There is good reason to believe that before his death and resurrection, Jesus was grossly misunderstood, perhaps even opposed, by the members of his own family. Remember: he had to place his mother in John's keeping. He had brothers, but none of them came to Golgotha. None requested his dead body from Pilate. But apparently after this encounter between James and the resurrected Christ, all that was changed.

There is unquestionable evidence in the book of Acts that James, the brother of Jesus, went on to become the leader of the church at Jerusalem. He was killed by Ananias, the Jewish high priest in Jerusalem, apparently to appease the Zealots in 62 A.D.

Tradition is sturdy and strong that it was this James—the brother of Jesus, a later son of Mary and Joseph—who wrote the book of James in our New Testament. For me, this is as good an explanation as any.

So much for the details behind the book. What of the message in it? It bristles with imperatives—60 of them in 108 verses.

James is intensely practical. It takes Christianity down out of the clouds, dresses it in working clothes, and sends it walking up and down earth's dusty roads.

Perhaps a poem circulated at a "poor people's rally" in Albuquerque, New Mexico, says it best:

I was hungry
And you formed a humanities club to discuss my hunger.

I was imprisoned
And you went to your chapel to pray for my release!

I was naked
And you debated the morality of my appearance.

I was sick
And you knelt and thanked God for your health.

I was homeless
And you delivered a sermon on the shelter of God's love.

I was lonely
And you left me alone to attend church.

You seem so close to God
But I am still very hungry, and lonely, and cold!

That is James' burden: Christians who seem so holy, so close to God while doing nothing to help the hungry, the lonely, and the cold ones close by and far away. Somehow that seems to James, and to us, such a screaming contradiction: orthodoxy without orthopraxy, belief without behavior, creed void of conduct, faith without works, theology without ethics.

Reading these five chapters is like sitting down with the author and viewing a series of slides. There are 22 separate paragraphs or topics in these five chapters—each one somewhat separate and distinct—yet all together comprising vivid pictures of what it means to put faith to work.

Let's put one slide in the projector and see one thing James says about Christian faith at work. It comes in his second chapter, verses 1-6:

My brethren, show no partiality as you hold the faith of our Lord Jesus Christ, the Lord of Glory. For, if a person with gold rings and in fine clothing comes into your assembly, and a poor person in shabby clothing also comes in, and you pay attention to the one who wears the fine clothing, and say, "Have a seat here, please" while you say to the poor person, "Stand there," or "Sit at my feet," have you not made a distinction among yourselves and become judges with evil thoughts? . . . You have dishonored the poor person.

Here is depicted the peril of partiality. It is not a pretty picture, is it?

A congregation is gathered in worship, exposing their lives to the God of Glory, the Creator and the Sovereign King of the universe. Two men enter the room; both are strangers. One is superbly dressed. Rings are on every finger except the middle one, exhibiting his wealth and status. The other is shabbily dressed. He has no jewelry—not even a Timex, much less a Rolex. The first man is ushered to a special seat of honor with great pomp and ceremony. The second man is asked to stand at the back or else to squat on the floor beside the footstool of one of the well-to-do.

We wish we could turn off the projector. It is not a pretty picture! But we cannot! James will not let us! For that is a picture that plays many a sad rerun far too often nowadays.

Snobbery does invade the church. And even Christians at worship show partiality. The literal meaning of that word partiality is "to receive the face"—that is, "face taking."

It means to make judgments about people superficially—to look no farther than mere outward appearances and no deeper than the obvious economic clues on the surface. But Christian faith demands that we embrace God's estimate of human worth.

God is not partial to the face. God does not see just skin deep. And God does not make junk.

So at worship, while all lives are equally exposed to the King of Glory, such distinctions disappear. They cannot count. Before this "Gospel According to James," distinctions of rank and face and place and title are all wiped out! Why? Because the ground is level at the foot of the cross. All kneel equally high/equally low there.

And that is where the Lord's table always takes us: to the foot of Golgotha. There are no pets of Providence on this hill. All are equally died for. There are no pets of Providence at the Lord's meal either. All are equally lived for and fed.

Bread and beverage, along with air, are the basic requirements for every human. Our Moravian friends speak of "the democracy of death"—and they dramatize it in God's Acre, their ever-expanding cemetery. The Lord's Supper speaks of "the democracy of worship"—and the table dramatizes that.

The *partiality peril* has many a rerun. For example, singles bang up against it all the time—even today!

There is a sort of "SAP arrangement" abroad in the land. By SAP I mean a kind of "Standard American Plan" for the ordering of lives. According to this plan, without quite realizing what we are doing, we are trying to outlaw single people. We are all but making marriage compulsory. We insist that everyone must enter into matrimony on cue. Consequently both our wedding rate and our divorce rate are the highest in the Western world.

By preaching and practicing compulsory matrimony, we make the benevolent and pathetically American assumption that what is good for some is good for all.

Just as we were the first society to aim at educating every child to the top of his ability, so we have become the first to insist that everyone marry on cue. It is, according to SAP, a duty—imposed upon every artist, writer, scientist, scholar, athlete, mystic, minister, student, and soldier.

Our ideal may be heroic, but it has its hazards. For one thing, we may be depriving ourselves of the very contributions that singles are best equipped to make.

This was at least one of Paul's reasons for saying, "I should like for you all to be as I am myself" (1 Cor. 7:7). He recognized that there are some things that the unmarried are uniquely equipped to be and to do. In the absence of this insight we just may be marrying ourselves into mediocrity. The unmarried have a vocation also, and we had better wake up again to that fact.

I say "again" for we have not always operated like this: 60 years ago about one-fifth of our women never married. Now all of us marry except 7.8 percent of the women and 8.5 percent of the men. We are on the way to matching India where less than 2 percent of either sex stay single.

One tragedy of the Standard American Plan of matrimony is that marriage becomes an end in itself. It is almost immoral to consider a marriage as a means to something beyond itself. Thus, feelings are regimented and talents are blighted. Therefore, we are marrying more and enjoying it less than any generation of Americans before us.

Some months ago I read an article by Dr. Leslie Koempel in *Saturday Evening Post*. She made me wonder what would have been the consequence if the Standard American Plan had been enforced throughout the past. Suppose we had demanded always that every man and every woman play the game of matrimony by the same rules? What would have become of the enormous share of history written by men and women who have chosen not to marry?

For instance, the medieval monks kept the dim light of the classics from being consumed by the Dark Ages. Single men staked out the New World and the American frontier. Every wave of immigration was spearheaded by a bachelor. Spinsters were some of our first and best school teachers, social workers, nurses, and writers. Florence Nightingale might never have founded nursing as a married woman. Clara Barton was an "old maid" when she established the American Red Cross.

The faculty at Princeton once named the 10 largest contributors to the advancement of human knowledge. The list included Plato, Isaac Newton, and Leonardo deVinci—all of whom never married—and Socrates—who tried and failed. It also included Aristotle and Darwin, who married long after embarking on their careers. In addition there were Galileo, Shakespeare, Pasteur, and Einstein—upon whom domesticity does not seem to have made inordinate demands.

Add to this the interesting facts that Michelangelo and Keats never married; and that Milton, Lincoln, Poe, and Shelley were all but failures in their marriages. At least the evidence is that there must be left room—even in the Standard American Plan—for some men and women who deliberately choose a career instead of marriage.

This is precisely the point in the apostle Paul's counsel: there is and there must ever be a choice to marry or not to marry. And for some, the energy that may be spent on marriage may be expressed much more productively in worthy vocations unto the Lord.

Now I am convinced that when he wrote to the Corinthians, Paul thought the time was short before our Lord's return. Therefore, he urged his readers to guard against "a divided mind," and with singleness of heart and unity of purpose, to pursue with haste their spiritual vocations.

In the mid 1990s the urgency and haste still exist, but they are oriented in quite opposite directions. Young ladies feel they have to be quick about snapping up a husband before all the husband material disappears. Young men must manage rapidly to acquire a bride before the springs of romance dry up and the dry thirst of a career sets in. We have been conditioned and we have a song that says it: "Love and marriage go together, like a horse and carriage." Our exhortation for everyone is that life begins with marriage. The never-never-land where they live "happily ever after" is the last frontier for adventure or personal identity, and everyone is expected to grab and grapple for it.

Paul raises a solemn protest against this compulsory, all-embracing Standard American Plan. In the process he establishes the unavoidable fact that the unmarried have a vocation also.

Take note of the features of that vocation, the "calling of singles" in a couple-centric culture: to establish diversity, to channel energy, to achieve chastity. No worthier vocation exists on this earth. Godspeed and God bless all single persons as they pursue it.

September 8, 1996

1 AND 2 PETER

A lamp in a dark place
1 Peter 1:1-2, 2:9-10, 4:12-14; 2 Peter 1:16-19

Of all the General Epistles, perhaps 1 Peter is the best known and most loved. Chances are it is the most frequently read. It is one of the New Testament's easiest letters to read. Edgar Goodspeed has called 1 Peter "the most moving piece of persecution literature ever written." "Suffering" appears 16 times in the five chapters.

Until recently it was practically universally agreed that the first letter that bears this name was written by the apostle Peter himself from Rome about 67 A.D., immediately following the first wave of persecution of Christians by Emperor Nero. But in recent times some have suggested that the letter was written much later than that, by someone unknown, and simply ascribed to Peter to lend it authority.

While this position may be plausible in regards to 2 Peter, I find no reason seriously to question the fact that Peter wrote the first letter that bears his name.

Or to put it more accurately, he wrote it through his amanuensis. Actually, in 1 Pet. 5:12 he says that he wrote it "by Silvanus." This Silvanus has been identified as the man named Silas in Acts. He was a colleague of Paul, a learned Roman citizen who accompanied Paul on his second mission tour.

If Peter's Silvanus is the same as Paul's Silas, then Peter wrote this letter with the help of someone well acquainted with Paul.

This may explain why Peter sounds so much like Paul. Silas' assistance in writing would also explain the excellence of the Greek, a matter that has troubled some students of scripture a long time.

The language and style of this letter are absolutely classic and scarcely seem possible as the work of an academically untrained Galilean fisherman like Simon Peter. Yet, the letter seems unmistakably the work of sand-rock Simon, Jesus' most outspoken disciple.

The immediate recipients of the letter are named. They are "the Christians of the dispersion in Pontus, Galatia, Cappodocia, Asia, and Bithynia" (1:1).

All these districts lay in the northeast corner of Asia Minor. They embraced a large land mass of the Roman Empire and contained a very large population.

It is clear from the letter that the immediate recipients were mainly Gentiles, not Jews. Peter says that they had previously been "no people," but now they are "God's people" (2:9-10). In the first letter also, Peter uses his Greek name rather than his Jewish name, Simeon.

The circumstances behind this letter are what make it come alive. It was written at a time when foreboding clouds of persecution were gathering. Behind it there are fiery trials; a campaign of slander, terror, and intense suffering for Christ's sake.

This letter makes me recall some vivid memories of my childhood. We lived in a southeast Alabama tornado belt. Almost every year a treacherous twister would devastate a field or a river bottom. One night a tornado struck one lone farmhouse in our community and killed four of my cousins in one fatal swoop.

The people in our community developed a way to combat this menace. They dug "storm pits"—holes in the ground, usually in banks of earth, resembling caves. Here in the heat of the day or the dead of the night our families would go to wait out a severe storm.

Many a night I recall the struggle to get out of bed, fight sleep, get on some clothes, and then race pell mell through the lightning flash and the thunder roll to reach the storm pit. Often as not, we took the brunt of the storm trying to reach safety.

But the thing I remember most was the kerosene lamp that stayed in the storm pit. I recall how warm and dry and safe that awful dark, damp hole in the ground became for me just as soon as someone lit the lamp.

That is the way it is with these letters. Peter lights a lamp in a dark place. But what made the place so dark?

To understand that, we have to go back aways. Remember, there was a time when Christians had nothing to fear from the Roman authorities. In fact, throughout the book of Acts it is repeatedly the Roman soldiers and officials who saved Paul, Peter, John, and others from the fury of angry mobs.

For some time the Romans simply regarded Christianity as a Jewish sect. And within the empire Judaism was a permitted religion, so Christians were not molested. But all that changed one hot summer day in Rome.

On July 19, A.D. 64, the great fire in Rome broke out—1,932 years ago. At that time Rome was a city of narrow streets and high flimsy wooden houses. The city was in real danger of being wiped out.

The fire raged for three days and nights. It was checked, and then broke out again with doubled fury.

The Roman citizenry had no doubt who was responsible for it. They placed the blame fairly and squarely upon their half-crazed Emperor Nero.

Nero had a passion for building, and they believed that he had deliberately taken steps to obliterate old Rome so he could rebuild it the way he wanted. Nero had his own sort of first-century urban renewal plan.

Whether this was actually the case we cannot know. But it is certain that Nero watched the raging inferno from the tower of Maecenas, and expressed delight over "the flower and loveliness of the flames."

Tradition may not have stretched the point that Nero actually fiddled while Rome burned. The fire fighters were hindered and harassed in every conceivable way, and representatives of the emperor were reported rekindling the fire in places where it was subsiding.

The people were overwhelmed! Their city was in ashes. Ancient landmarks and ancestral shrines were gone. The temple of Luna, the temple of Jupiter, the shrine of Vesta—the household gods of the people—were all burned.

Thousands were left homeless, and the condition of other thousands of the poor Romans was wretched. It is understandable just how bitter the Romans became.

Nero had to divert suspicion from himself. A scapegoat had to be found. And the Christians at Rome were it! Nero pinned the fire on them.

Now, he had some help because Christians had already become the victims of certain slander.

For example, the Lord's Supper to an onlooker was seen as a terribly secret thing. There were words associated with it about eating someone's body and drinking someone's blood. That was enough for a rumor to arise among the pagan Romans that Christians were indeed cannibals.

The rumor grew until at Rome it was gossiped that Christians at the Lord's Supper killed and ate either a Gentile or one of their own newborn children.

Besides this, it was true that the Christians spoke of a coming day when the world would dissolve in terrible flames at the return of the Lord. So it was not hard to label them as dangerous firebrands and incendiaries.

Nero had abundant material that could be twisted and distorted into false charges against Christians. And he made the most of it!

Thus the blame for the great Roman fire was tacked onto Christians. And a severe outbreak of persecution followed. Christians perished throughout the city, and they died in the most sadistic ways.

Nero rolled Christians in pitch and then set fire to them while they were still alive and used them as living torches to light the way to his garden parties. He sewed them up into skins of wild animals and set his hunting dogs loose upon them to tear them limb from limb while yet alive.

So Christians perished, not by legal means, but in a delirium of savagery. It was not the Roman law, but the Roman mob that threatened them.

Forever after, Christians were to live under threat in the empire. Mobs in all the Roman cities heard what had happened at Rome. At times the mobs craved blood and reveled in lynchings. Even the magistrants joined the populace in gratifying outbursts of blood-lust.

From then on, every Christian in the empire was in peril for their life. For years nothing might happen, then some spark would set off an explosion and the terror would break out fresh again.

This is the situation in the background of 1 and 2 Peter. This is written to and for Christians on the run—dispersed. In the face of the ever-present threat, Peter calls the people of God to hope, to courage, and to flawless Christian living. He knew that alone could give the lie to the slanders with which Christians were attacked.

Therefore this letter was written not to meet any theological heresy, but to strengthen men, women, and children in jeopardy of their lives. It is a lamp for a dark place! I see it as a light turned on in the storm pits all over the empire. So what does it say to us?

It is a strong and urgent word to all who are about to lose heart. Rome had decided that this upstart bunch of hot-heads and hot-hearts, who were out-living and out-dying the opposition, had best be stamped out. Christians were labeled outlaws. They lost their jobs, their freedom, their property.

Those who followed Christ were laying their lives on the line. It is no wonder that some of them were losing heart. They were justifiably frightened at what the future held for them.

It was to their situation that Peter wrote his lamp-lighter letter in the darkness. And he said to them—and to us—some things that are especially urgent whenever and wherever the darkness closes in.

In times that are tough, Christians have their best chance to live in this world for Jesus Christ.

We have more formulas for dealing with adversity than for dealing with prosperity. We must not whimper, "Look what the world is coming to." We shout, "Look what has come to the world!"

Tough times are not times for the people of God to want out. Tough times are when we have a chance to plunge in deeper toward life in Christ. Instead of shouting for the world to stop so we can get off, Peter reminds us to look for places we can get on. Listen: "Let us give thanks to the God and Father of our Lord Jesus Christ! Because of his great mercy, he gave us new life by raising Jesus Christ from the dead. This fills us with a living hope" (1:3).

That is the Easter truth! "A living hope"—that says it! This hope lives since it is fastened onto the fact of a living Christ. He has met death on its own turf and prevailed.

Christians in this world live in the power of that grave, the conquering Christ; we hope in him, not in our flimsy selves. Hope comes trickling, running, and finally surging back into a life as one serves Christ in this world.

But our problem today is like theirs in ancient Asia. We have anchored our lives to false hopes: partnerships that perish, rifles that rust, profits that plummet, dollars that devalue, contracts that collapse, economics that inflate/deflate.

We have not listened. Yet our Lord has told us: Moths will eat everything. Rust will reach everything. Thieves will steal everything.

We are like Sinbad the Sailor: he hitched his boat to a great fish, and thought it was a great rock.

When tensions tighten and faith comes hard, we are ready to throw in the towel, call the fight, turn off the lights, and walk home in the darkness. That is when Peter's strong word comes home to us.

Hope happens when persons put their hands to the tasks to be done in Christ's name in their own time.

Hopelessness is the result of two things happening at once: a fading vision of God and a failing duty of man. When the people of God quit or shirk their unique work in this world, they lose hope. We can act our way into a new way of thinking far better than we can think our way into a new way of acting. We must "trust and obey."

Peter says another timely thing: When times are toughest. the people of God stand to learn their greatest lessons. Listen: "Beloved, be not surprised at the fiery ordeal that comes upon you to test you, as though something strange were happening to you. But rejoice in so far as you share Christ's sufferings, that you may also rejoice and be glad when his glory is revealed" (4:12-13).

That line from the screenplay *The Last Convertible* is right: "Life is completely fair; sooner or later, it breaks everyone's heart."

We can learn some lessons taught only by tough times. Deep in the heart of this moral universe there is "a cross principle." We see it in Seed, Salt, Leaven, Light.

Suffering can be redemptive. It often is. Golgotha revealed that.

This is a visited planet. God has a word for a broken heart. God uses broken things to fashion miracles: Broken clouds produce rain. Broken soil produces crops. Broken seed produces grain. Broken grain produces bread. Broken bread produces strength.

God can use a broken life to shape a miracle, but God must have all the pieces. Max Cleland has said, "We are always stronger at the broken places."

Famed historian Charles L. Beard was asked what lessons his study of history had taught him. His reply: "Whom the gods would destroy, they first make mad with power. The mills of God grind slowly, but they grind exceedingly small. The bee fertilizes the flower it robs. When it is dark enough, you can see the stars." Peter would agree with that last lesson.

Legend has woven a lovely tale. The word is that some friends persuaded Peter to flee Nero's madness and leave Rome. He was retreating down the Appian Way when he encountered in a vision the risen Christ on his way to Rome.

Falling before him, Peter inquired: "*Quo Vadis, Domine?*"—"Where are you going, Master?" Jesus replied: "To Rome, to be crucified."

Whereupon, Peter returned to the city and was condemned to death by crucifixion. The word further is that he requested to be crucified head down because he was not worthy to die as his Lord had died. It may be legend, but there is truth in it as large as life.

"Suffering can be redemptive." Simon's, yours, mine . . . our suffering can be redemptive. Amen.

September 1, 1996

1, 2, 3 JOHN

Love that will not let us go

1 John 1:1-4; 3:1-3; 4:7-12, 16-21; 5:3-5; 2 John 6; 3 John 11

Clement of Alexandria, one of the early church fathers, told this story: In a city near Ephesus the apostle John, now an old man, found a young man—strong of body, handsome, warmhearted, tender. He led him to faith in Jesus Christ. When John left the city he commended the young convert into the care and keeping of the local bishop.

Later the apostle returned and inquired about the youthful convert. In great embarrassment the bishop had to report, "He is dead." "How did he die?" the aged apostle asked. "He has died to God in Christ," the bishop said. "For right now he is in the mountains, a member of a robber band."

The apostle sighed. "Let there be a horse furnished for me," he said, "and let someone show me the way." And he started out to look for the young man.

In time, guards posted by the bandits brought John to the youth he sought. When he caught sight of the aged apostle, he fled in shame. But John called out: "Why do you flee from me, your own father in Christ, unarmed and old? . . . Pity you, child, have no fear. You still have hope of life. I shall give an account for you to Christ. If need be, I will willingly endure your death. Believe! Christ has sent me."

The youthful robber wept bitter tears, ran back, fell into the arms of the old man, and went down the mountain restored to Christ and to the fellowship of the saints.

Small wonder that John became known throughout the early church as the "apostle of love." The "son of thunder" in his youth became the "son of Christ" in his maturity.

Therefore it is no wonder either that in these three short letters that bear his name at the back side of the New Testament, the word "love" appears more than 50 times. These seven chapters virtually seethe with a love that will not let us be and will not let us go.

These letters of John are intensely personal and pastoral. They are obviously written to deal with an actual situation in the early church. If we wish to understand these letters, then we must try to reconstruct the situation that produced them and that moved John to write them.

There is good reason to suppose that the letters were written sometime around 100 A.D. somewhere in Asia Minor, perhaps in Ephesus. Now let us see what had happened in Christendom by the turn of the first century.

By 100 A.D. almost all the eyewitnesses to Jesus Christ were gone. It had been 70 years since he died that Friday and rose that Easter morning in Jerusalem. Paul had been dead nearly 50 years. All the 12 apostles were gone now except John. And he knew that most of them had died violent deaths.

Nero and Domitian had bathed Christendom in the blood of awful persecution. Many of the Christians were now second- or third-generation believers. The thrill of the first days, their vast, new discovery, had to some extent faded. Fifty years before, among believers, there was a glory, a splendor, a radiance to life and work. But now all that had dimmed.

Christianity had become "a thing of habit"—traditional, halfhearted, nominal. Too many had grown too accustomed to it, and something in Christendom had died.

Especially at a place like the great Asian city of Ephesus, the first thrill was gone. The original flame had died down into faint embers. The route of following the resurrected Christ had settled down into a comfortable, religious rut. "The way" had run right into a swamp.

One result of all this was that believers were finding the standards that Christian faith demanded a burden rather than a joy. They did not give a hoot about being saints—that is, being ethically different from their neighbors.

The peril at the time of John's writing was seduction rather than persecution, dry rot instead of wet threat. There was little apparent danger of violence from outside the church. The peril rather came from inside.

The trouble these letters of John seeks to treat did not come from persons who were out to destroy the Christian faith. It came from persons who thought they were defending the Christian faith. They sought to improve it.

It came from persons whose aim was to make Christianity a little more intellectually respectable and palatable to the "spirit of the age." They, too, had their "new age" thought.

By this time, throughout the Greco-Roman world there had emerged a scheme of thought and belief known as Gnosticism. The basic belief in this scheme was that matter is essentially evil; only spirit is good.

This being so, the Gnostics naturally despised the world; since it was matter, it was evil by nature. This led them particularly to despise their bodies. The body, after all, was just a prison for the soul.

The only aim in life, therefore, was to liberate the human spirit from its vile prison-house of the body. This was accomplished, in the Gnostic view, through an elaborate mechanism of secret knowledge, ritual, and initiation supplied only by fellow Gnostics.

This scheme of thinking literally saturated the society in and around Ephesus at the turn of the first century. John, who had been no more than 20 years old when he became a disciple with Jesus, was now past 90. He had seen firsthand the treacherous and paralyzing effect of the contemporary Gnostic thought upon Christian faith.

It undercut the fact of any real incarnation of God in human flesh and knocked the pins out from under Jesus' claim of messiahship. So John wrote these three letters to knock the pins out from under Gnosticism.

Thus it was to combat a seductive heresy, creeping in through all the cracks at Ephesus, that John wrote his letters. He was not afraid to ascribe to Jesus Christ full and true humanity, nor did he hesitate to do it (1:1ff). He insisted that the Lord Christ became what we are in order to make us what he was.

John had two great things to say about God in these letters: God is light, and in God there is no darkness at all. God is love, and the one who knows us best loves us most. God loves us and equips us to love one another.

His clear command is that anyone who loves God will love his/her brother also. This means that our love for God is actually expressed by our love for one another. And by this John does not mean some syrupy, sentimental emotion.

He means a deep-moving and dynamic care that propels the whole life outward in search of ways to be helpful.

The heresies that John attacked are by no means just echoes of "old, unhappy, far-off things and battles long ago." They are just beneath the surface of all our lives right now. And frequently they erupt through the surface to show us just how ugly and destructive they can still be.

One of the worst heresies of all is lovelessness. It is a treacherous heresy of mind, will, and emotion. It dwarfs, distorts, and destroys a life like absolutely nothing else. Lovelessness just may be the most lethal force loose in our modern world. John has a strange and timely word for our situation:

> Beloved, let us love one another, because love has its source in God, and everyone who loves has God as the source of his life, and knows God. He who does not love has not come to know God. . . . In this is love, not that we love God, but that God loved us, and sent His Son to be an atoning sacrifice for our sins.

> Brothers, if God so loved us, we ought to love one another. . . . God is love and he who dwells in love dwells in God, and God dwells in him. . . . We love because God first loved us. . . . It is this command we have from God, that he who loves God loves his brother also. (1 John 4)

This amazing paragraph signals some of life's most powerful things. For one thing, John says we are creatures capable of loving because we are creatures designed and created by God who is love. We are enough like God to love like God. For another thing, he says that it is by love that God is known.

We can never see God. All we can ever see is the effect of God. We cannot see the wind, but we can see what the wind can do. We cannot see electricity, but we can see the effects of electricity—or the lack of it.

Now, the effect of God is love. God is known by a love-effect upon persons. And God's effect is that God equips persons to love one another.

This means that the best demonstration of God comes not from an argument or a debate, but from a life filled with love. In such a life, God is seen as nowhere else. We are living illustrations of the living Word.

"For God is love" . . . In that powerful and revolutionary statement John says more than most of us can ever fathom.

"God is love!" That is probably the greatest three words ever said about God in all the Bible. It is amazing how many doors that single sentence unlocks and how many questions it helps to answer. Let me illustrate.

"God is love." That explains creation.

Love does not happen in isolation. Love must have a subject—a beloved. Sometimes we are bound to wonder why God created this world. For God it is bound to be a heartbreak. The rebellion, the cold-heartedness, the hard-headedness, the rejection must be a continual grief to God.

This world has brought God plenty of trouble. Why put up with it?

The answer: "God is love." God creates, and keeps on creating this world because creation itself is a product of God's love. If God is love, then God cannot live in lonely isolation.

Love, to be love, must have someone to love, and someone to respond to love. So, God creates. And God goes on creating out of the divine nature as love. Thus there is a solidarity in life: those created in love are to love each other.

"God is love." That explains freedom.

Unless love is an unfettered, free response, it is not love. There can be no love that is not spontaneous. It cannot be coerced, pressured, forced.

Suppose God had been less than love. Then God might have created a world populated by automata—puppets on a string, obeying God completely because they had no choice or chance to do otherwise.

But if God had made persons like that, there would have been no possibility of loving. A person is more than a machine. Never will a computer love.

Love thrives on free choice and the free response of the beloved. Therefore, before persons could love God or each other in any real sense, their wills had to be free. This is why freedom is so impossible to stamp out of creation. We really are reborn free!

God is love." That explains redemption.

If God were less than love, God might leave persons to the consequences of their evil. After all, we are not so much punished *for* our sins, as *by* our sins.

This moral universe takes up arms against evil and eventually dissipates the soul that sins. Justice has an inexorable way of getting done. What we sow, we reap. Chickens do come home to roost. The very fact that God is love means that God will seek and save those who are lost to life.

Golgotha's cross and Joseph's empty tomb are God's ultimate remedies for evil. They are seals on the very nature of God as love. God went all the way to death to save sinners. Only love could make God do that!

"God is love." That explains hope.

If God were simply creator, then God just might create persons to live their tiny little life spans and then to disappear forever. The lives that ended too soon (at 8, 18, or 80) would all be the same—nothing more than a flower on which the death-frost settled.

But the fact that God is love makes it certain that the chances and changes of life are never the last word. There is something steady over all the wreckage! God goes on loving persons through death and after it—just like we do. And divine love never loses its own.

There is a love of God that speaks its strong word and tames death—that marauding king of terrors. God is love: that is terribly important both to John and to us. It is his ultimate weapon against the ultimate heresy: lovelessness.

In the mid-1800s a young Scottish minister rose to renown throughout his native land. His name: George Matheson. He was blind. He fell in love with a young lady whom he desperately wanted to marry. She pondered his proposal and decided that his blindness was too great a burden for the two of them to bear, so she refused to marry him. He was devastated, and in his despair wrote an immortal hymn.

Matheson says of his song: "It was composed with extreme haste . . . I was suffering from deep mental distress, and the hymn was the fruit of my pain. . . . All the other verses I have ever written are manufactured articles; this one came like a dayspring from on high." Listen to Matheson's love-song:

O Love that wilt not let me go,
I rest my weary soul in thee;
I give thee back the life I owe,
That in thine ocean depths its flow
May richer, fuller be.

O Joy that seekest me through pain,
I cannot close my heart to thee;
I trace the rainbow through the rain,
And feel the promise is not vain,
That morn shall tearless be.

That hymn aptly summarizes John's thought in his three letters. So take heart. Whosoever will, you are loved divinely by a love that will never, never, never, never, never let you go! Amen.

September 15, 1996

JUDE

Clouds without water
Jude 12-13

Jude is the last of the General Letters in our New Testament. These 25 verses comprise a brief, difficult, and often neglected page of the Bible. Many readers find Jude a bewildering rather than a profitable reading. But there are two verses of Jude known by just about everyone: "Now to him who is able to keep you from falling and to present you without blemish before the presence of his glory with rejoicing, to the only God, our Savior, through Jesus Christ our Lord, be glory, majesty, dominion, and authority, before all time and now and forever. Amen" (24-25).

This is the resounding and magnificent doxology with which the letter ends. But apart from these two majestic verses Jude is largely unknown and unread. Part of the reason is that it is written in the idiom of its own time—and not our time. We have to adapt to it rather than requiring it to adapt to us.

We also have trouble reconstructing the situation that prompted it. Besides, the quotations and word pictures are all strange to us. But this little letter hit like a hammer blow and was heard like a trumpet blast by those who first received it.

The fact is, here is a letter that almost did not get written. In verse 3 the author says that he wanted to write a message expounding the faith that all Christians share. But in verse 4 he says that task had to be laid aside due to the rise of persons whose thought and conduct were becoming a threat and a menace to the Christian churches.

These persons were heretical in belief and immoral in behavior. So he wrote to defend the faith rather than to expound it.

Now you might think that such an undertaking would guarantee a niche for Jude in the early days of the developing New Testament, but not so! In fact, it was the fourth century A.D. before this little book had a secure place as part of the Christian canon.

One of the main resources for its late acceptance was that Jerome, who translated the Latin Vulgate, had his doubts about Jude. He thought it strange that Jude quotes at least two apocryphal books just as if they were accepted parts of the Old Testament scriptures.

For example, in verse 9 Jude refers to the Assumption of Moses, an apocryphal book written sometime between the Old and New Testament periods—and never generally regarded as canonical.

In verses 14-15 he confirms and cements his argument with a quotation from the apocryphal Book of Enoch. He appears to regard that book also as a valid prophecy and valid scripture.

This habit of Jude to use noncanonical books as authorities has made some people regard him with suspicion. Besides this, in verses 17-18, he makes use of a saying of the apostles that is nowhere to be found in the four Gospels of our New Testament.

So, Jude has had tough sledding just to get into the New Testament. But by the fourth century it made its way as an accepted and respected part of Christian scriptures.

The date of Jude is debated by students of scripture. There are definite indications that it was not an early book. The whole atmosphere of it is the atmosphere of a man looking back on persons and events long since passed.

Interestingly, the book of 2 Peter makes great use of the book of Jude. It is simple to see that chapter 2 of 2 Peter and certain verses in Jude have a close affinity.

So, a date around 80 or 90 A.D. perhaps best suits these 25 verses. But who was Jude or Judah or Judas? Who wrote this book?

In verse 1 he calls himself "a servant of Jesus Christ and brother of James." In the New Testament there are at least five persons named Judas or Jude.

- There was Judas of Demascus, to whose house Paul went to pray after his conversion on the Damascus Road (Acts 9:11).
- There was Judas Barsabas, a leader of the church, who went with Silas to bear word to Antioch about the decision of the Jerusalem Council to open the gospel to the Gentiles (Acts 15:22, 27, 32).
- There was Judas Iscariot, Jesus' disciple who betrayed him.
- There was a second Judas among the 12 disciples of Jesus. John calls him "Judas, not Iscariot" (14:22). Luke notes that he was the son of James (6:16).
- There was Judas, the brother of Jesus. Remember in Matt. 13:55 how the natives of Nazareth were pondering the matter of who this Jesus really was. They asked: "Is not this (Jesus) the carpenter's son? . . . and, his brothers, James, and Joses, and Simon, and Judas?"

If one of these New Testament Judases or Judes wrote this letter, then it must have been this one who was the brother of James and also the brother of Jesus. If so, it is interesting to note that he had rather describe himself as a "servant" of Jesus Christ than as a "brother" of Jesus (v. 1).

Some students of scripture conjecture that this book was written by someone completely unknown to us, and attached to the name of Jude to give it prominence.

Being that as it will, the message endures, despite our difficulty in settling on the messenger who wrote it.

And what exactly is the message of Jude? He writes to give Christians some check-points against the perils of apostasy. His language is simple and rugged, vivid and picturesque. His message is hard hitting and straight to the bullseye. He has all of us in his sight.

Jude marshals his warnings against persons who had infiltrated the Christian churches and yet remained immoral in behavior and heretical in belief.

For some time, at home in his Nazareth family, Jude's own relations with Jesus were affected by his belief. He, too, doubted for a time that his "brother" was the Messiah.

He warns his readers against the worst possible form of pollution: faith pollution. Among other things the heretics he attacked were antinomians.

Antinomians are people who say the law is dead; only grace is alive. They insist that the injunctions of the law are no longer valid; grace alone is supreme. Grace can forgive any sin. In fact, the more the sin, the more the grace to forgive it.

So they can do precisely and absolutely what they want to do with their lives. Antinomians say that the body does not matter; what matters is spirit. Therefore, for them, everything goes! Nothing is forbidden even in Christ.

Animal instincts are to be freely satisfied. Lusts are to direct our lives. So the antinomians take off the bridle and try to ride all the wild horses.

They argue that since they are under the grace of Christ, the laws of God are irrelevant for them. They insist that they are so spiritual that nothing they do could possibly be conceived as sin.

In short, all antinomians say that if they love God with their hearts, then they can do anything they like with their bodies.

Does this sound like modern-day newsstand and bedroom stuff to you? You know, it is!

Hollywood has learned that antinomianism will sell. So they spin their celluloid tales of love gods and sex goddesses. And in every church and every community this familiar plot plays a dramatic and devastating rerun.

Enter: the antinomian who loves God with his heart and loves the devil with his body.

Enter: the church member who makes it to the Sunday school room on Sunday and makes it in the neighbor's bedroom on Monday.

So you think antinomianism is dead? You think Jude and his warnings are old fogey? Then you ought to work with me for a season.

Look at and listen to the tragic wreckage of lives who are trying to embrace God with one arm and to embrace the devil with the other. Our world is strewn with sad, modern smash-ups caused by this ancient heresy. There are still many people who try to traffic upon God's forgiveness and who make the grace of God an excuse to sin.

And Jude would say this very morning what he said so long ago: "Stop it! Life like that is like a cloud that promises rain but blows past and drops no water."

So, hear this ancient voice from the backside of our New Testament: "Antinomians, quit fooling yourselves; promise without performance is an empty thing." Belief without behavior is heresy. No amount of outward show, no number of fine professions will take the place of integrity, discipline, and usefulness. Integrity in discipleship and usefulness in service go together in Christian faith. An inward goodness that is not outwardly useful is an illusion.

As Jude would say, "If you are not good for *something*, then you are good for *nothing*."

See the sight well (v. 12): At times in Palestine the land is parched for lack of rain. The people are desperate for water. They pray. A cloud appears. The people are heartened. The clouds promise long-sought rain. But they soon blow over and the rains never come. It is a sad sight to people in a drought: clouds without water—but not one bit sadder than the episodes right out of real life.

Here and there are the sad spectres of men, women, youth who make great claims, offer fine promises from their Christian faith; but then turn out to be completely useless to the Christian community.

Clouds without water! It is a spiritual peril among the people of God.

In every generation we would do well to close the gap between what we profess and what we practice, what we promise and what we produce, what we say and what we do, belief and behavior, orthodoxy and orthopraxy.

Antinomianism dies hard. Jude knows that. So should we.

Jack Griffin has shaped the situation vividly in a bit of writing he has titled "It's Okay, Son, Everybody's Doing It." Listen:

When Stevie was 6 years old, he was with his father. They were caught speeding. His father handed the officer a $50 bill when he handed him his license. "It's okay, son," his father said as they drove off. "Everybody does it."

When Stevie was 8, he was present at a family council presided over by Uncle George, on the surest way to shave dollars off their income tax return. "It's okay, son," his uncle said. "Everybody does it."

When he was 9, Stevie's mother took him to a crowded theater. The man in the box office could not find any seats inside until his mother discovered an extra $10 in her purse. "It's okay, son," she said. "Everybody does it."

When he was 12, Stevie broke his glasses on the way to school. His Aunt Francine persuaded the insurance company that they had been stolen, and they collected $127. "It's okay, son," she said. "Everybody does it."

When Stevie was 15, he was right guard on the high school football team. His coach showed him how to block and at the same time how to grab the opposing end in an illegal hold so the officials could not see. "It's okay, son," the coach said. "Everybody does it."

When Stevie was 16, he took his first summer job at the market. His assignment was to put the over-ripe tomatoes in the bottom of the boxes and the good ones on top where they would show. "It's okay, son," his manager told him. "Everybody does it."

When he was 18, Stevie and a neighbor both wanted a college scholarship. Stevie was a marginal student. His neighbor was in the upper 3 percent of his class, but he couldn't play right guard. Stevie got the scholarship. "It's okay, son, they told him. "Everybody does it."

When he was 19, Stevie was approached by an upper classman who offered him the answers for a big test—only $20. "It's okay, friend." he said. "Everybody does it."

Stevie was caught cheating, so was disciplined and sent home in disgrace—kicked off the team and expelled from college.

"How could you do this to your mother and me?" his father howled in his rage. "You never learned anything like this at home." His aunt, uncle, football coach, and produce manager were also shocked. If there is one thing this grown-up world cannot stand, it is a youngster who cheats.

So goes the sad spectre of the laws of good and bad applying to everyone but me. That attitude is more contagious than measles.

Jude would have nothing of the sort. Neither can we. The Lordship of Jesus Christ delivers us from it. Amen!

September 22, 1996

REVELATION

Alpha and omega

Revelation 1:1-2, 8, 19; 4:1-2; 5:1-2; 8:1-2, 6; 11:15; 12:1; 13:1; 14:1; 15:1; 20:1-3; 21:1-2

While our daughters were still in high school my family and I undertook camping in each of the 50 states. We did it. We saw, heard, tasted, smelled, and touched many things during those six summers. One sight is particularly etched in my mind from our visit on the far eastern side of Nova Scotia.

We saw a particularly interesting hiker on the Cabot Trail. He was young, bearded, unbathed. His bedroll was on the road beside him. His shirt was off and tucked into the rope-belt around his waist. His body was bronze from the sun. He faced the infrequent cars with both hands raised and a thumb that pointed in each direction along the road. Propped against his bedroll on the ground was a cardboard square on which he had scribbled his destination. It read: ANYWHERE!

There is a certain sadness in an adventure like that—a young man on a summer road, alone, and going just anywhere. For you see, to be going *anywhere* is the same as to be going *nowhere*. Such futility and purposeless are the ultimate threats to life as it was meant to be.

That is precisely what the final book in our Bible is all about. It is written to affirm that we are not captive creatures on a spinning speck in the sky doomed to do nothing and to go nowhere.

The Revelation affirms that we are creatures of purpose. Human experience has a direction and a goal. History is headed *somewhere*!

But when we approach this last book of our Bible, we find ourselves catapulted into a new and different bit of biblical terrain.

Here is something quite unlike the rest of the New Testament. Not only is the Revelation different; it is difficult—notoriously difficult—for a contemporary mind to comprehend.

The result is that this last book is at once the most neglected and the most overused book in the Bible. It is neglected by those who think its mystery is too massive to unravel. It is overused by those who make it a happy hunting ground for all kinds of religious voodoo.

It has become for well-intentioned students of scripture like John Darby, James Brooks, Cyrus Schofield, Lewis Chafer, and Hal Lindsey an elaborate theological system for the end time. So if we find this final book both difficult and intriguing, then we are in good company.

We must remember one basic fact when we read and study the Revelation: it is apocalyptic literature. In fact, this book is sometime called "The Apocalypse."

The title of our final book in Greek is *Apokalupsis*. Literally this means "unveiling, uncovering, disclosing." Actually it means "to take the lid off, so one can see what is inside."

Now this type of apocalyptic literature became most common during the period between the Old and New Testaments. During that 400 or 500 years a great mass of it developed among the Jews. Actually, we have some apocalyptic literature in the Old Testament. Portions of Isaiah and much of Daniel and Ezekiel and Zechariah are written in typical apocalyptic style.

We would do well to remember that apocalyptic literature among the Jews was a result of their unquenchable hope coupled with their intolerable political helplessness. They were almost always the vassals of someone stronger. Let's see how this developed.

The Jews could never forget that they were the chosen people of God. To them, that meant that some day they must arrive at a special, favored place in God's scheme of things.

But the whole history of Israel dashed their hopes. In turn they had been ravaged and conquered by Egypt, Assyria, Babylon, Persia, Greece, and Rome.

The time of writing seems to fall somewhere between 90 and 100 A.D. The place of writing was the Island of Patmos—in the Aegean Sea, about half the size of Manhattan and located about 70 miles southwest of Ephesus.

Most of the book details a vision of John—typically apocalyptic and typically "taking the lid off" for a look at the present time, the in-between time, and the time to come. So, as we read, we must constantly remember the three threads that course through this book. Some of the events are *past*, some are *present*, and some are *yet to come*.

Here are history, commentary on current events, and prophecy all wrapped in one package of code.

It follows, therefore, that the more we know about the historical background and the contemporary situation surrounding Christians in 90-95 A.D., then the better we can grasp the meaning of this Revelation and apply its enduring truths to our lives in our times. So, let us take note of at least one crucial factor in the background.

By the time of this Revelation, Caesar worship was rampant throughout the entire Roman Empire. Because they refused to conform to its demands, Christians were being persecuted—even killed.

Now, Caesar worship makes sense when you look on the surface of things. The Roman Empire was vast and heterogeneous. It stretched from Europe to Asia—from one end of the known world to the other. It embraced rigorous nationalism, many lands, many cultures, many tongues, many races. Modern Bosnia is ancient Rome in miniature.

Rome's problem was how to weld those varied masses into one self-conscious, national entity. Everyone knows that there is no unifying force like the force of a common faith.

None of the other national religions and none of the local gods could possibly become universal for the empire. But Caesar worship could!

The essence of Caesar worship was that the reigning Roman emperor, embodying the spirit of Rome, was divine—much like the emperor of Japan before World War II.

This concept arose with the worship of Julius Caesar after his death. Caesar worship, at first, was not imposed on the people by the government. Rather, it arose from the people. In fact, it arose in spite of efforts by some of the early emperors to stop it or at least to curb it.

But with the ascent of Domitian as emperor of Rome from 81-96 A.D., all this changed. He was the first emperor to take his "divinity" seriously and to demand Caesar worship.

During Domitian's 15-year reign, once a year everyone in the empire had to appear before a local magistrate and burn a pinch of incense to the "divine emperor of Rome." As they burned it, they had to say, "Caesar is Lord."

Now, after they had done that, they might go away and worship any other god or goddess they wished. In the polytheism of the first century, Caesar was another god in the pantheon of idols. Nationalism required homage to him as a political, if not a religious, act. It was politically correct.

To refuse to burn the pinch of incense and to refuse to say, "Caesar is Lord," was not simply an act of heresy. It was an act of treason. Any person who refused to undergo the annual ritual was regarded by Rome to be a traitor—an outlaw. That is why Romans dealt so severely with persons who would not say, "Caesar is Lord."

But no Christian could possibly, in conscience, say this. The title of Lord—*Kurios*—could by given to only one person: Jesus Christ of Nazareth.

For Christians, therefore, Caesar worship threatened the center and the circumference of their belief that Jesus Christ exclusively was their Lord.

So during the reign of Domitian, Christians were confronted with an absolute choice: Caesar or Christ? All over the empire they had to call Domitian God—or die. To refuse was to become an outlaw and to be hunted and hounded every day they lived.

This is the background for Revelation. Christians had not many wealthy and powerful people among them. Against them stood all the might of Rome and the daily threat of death. They could not and they would not pay the expected bribe to escape the need to burn the pinch of incense. So they perished! Savagely, they died!

It was to encourage persons in times like these that the Revelation was inspired and written. In a time of mounting terror, John did not shut his eyes on the horror. He sensed dreadful things on the scene, and he saw still more dreadful things on the horizon.

But beyond them all he saw blazing hope and faith of a people who defied Caesar because they loved Christ.

So here is the testimony of one who believed that beyond the present terror there was the eventual glory. He affirms that every day, while life is an agony, there is something steady over all the wreckage. Above the reigns of mere men there is God always, whose process and purpose are going somewhere in history.

Domitian was assassinated in 96 A.D. His successor, Emperor Nerva, repealed the savage laws punishing Christians to death for refusing to worship Caesar. But by this time the "lid was off" and Christendom had forever the undauntable Revelation of John. It speaks to all of history, to every present time, and to the future hope of all persons in Jesus Christ.

Now, we have said that apocalyptic literature always has a key that unlocks the code and makes its message intelligible. Well, John's key to his Revelation comes in chapter 11, verse 15.

The seventh angel blows a trumpet, and all heaven shouts: "The kingdom of the world has become the kingdom of our Lord and his Christ, and he shall reign forever and ever." (That is both John's and Handel's "Hallelujah!")

All the other amazing figures and symbols of these 22 chapters are simply vehicles for conveying this conviction. The angels, thrones, horsemen, seals, trumpets, beasts; the bowls, the wars, the new cities of earth and heaven—all these are commentary.

The truth is all in the key verse 11:15. That is why John repeatedly, at three crucial junctures in his Revelation, unveils Jesus Christ as "the Alpha and the Omega" (1:18, 21:6, 22:13).

John's Greek alphabet had 24 letters. The first was "alpha" (our A). The last was "omega" (our Z). To say that Jesus Christ is "Alpha" and "Omega" is the same as to say that Jesus is everything from A to Z—the first, and the last, all in all!

Whether 2000 A.D. or 5000 A.D. or 10,000 A.D. turns out to be "the end of the age," Jesus is winner!

Whether it's Julius Caesar, Adolf Hitler, Saddam Hussein, or some anti-Christ that history has not yet seen—Jesus is winner!

Whether history ends soon or late—in our lifetime or a million years from now—Jesus is winner!

That is the screaming declaration of John's Revelation!

We began with a young hitchhiker on the side of a Nova Scotia road—going just *anywhere*. Let us conclude by offering him, and whosoever else will journey with us, the heart of John's word from Revelation.

Here is the heart: Jesus Christ is Lord. He is boss. He is Alpha and Omega, the one from whom all came, to whom all proceeds, and through whom the end is clear from the beginning. This Christ is the mystic, mighty, very God of God. This Christ exempts no one from the terrors of life; yet he gives everyone meaning and purpose in their struggles. With him, we are going *somewhere*. With him, we are winners!"

This Christ word changes the signs beside every road we are traveling. In Jesus there is direction into the very purposes of God for time and for eternity.

Maranatha—Come Lord Jesus!

September 29, 1996

CPSIA information can be obtained at www.ICGtesting.com
Printed in the USA
BVOW02s0624111215

429952BV00003B/10/P

9 781938 514869